Digital
Design

Digital Design

M. MORRIS MANO

Professor of Engineering
California State University, Los Angeles

Prentice-Hall, Inc., Englewood Cliffs, New Jersey 07632

Library of Congress Cataloging in Publication Data

Mano, M. Morris, (date)
   Digital design.

   Chapters 1-7 and 10 originally published as part of the
author's Digital logic and computer design, c1979.
   Includes index.
   1. Electronic digital computers—Circuits. 2. Logic
circuits. 3. Logic design. 4. Digital integrated
circuits. I. Mano, M. Morris, 1927-   . Digital logic
and computer design. II. Title.
TK7888.3.M343 1984   621.3815′37   83-24734
ISBN 0-13-212333-9

Editorial/production supervision: *Lynn S. Frankel*
Cover design: *Diane Saxe*
Manufacturing buyer: *Gordon Osbourne*

Printed in the United States of America

10   9   8   7   6   5

ISBN 0-13-212333-9

Prentice-Hall International, Inc., *London*
Prentice-Hall of Australia Pty. Limited, *Sydney*
Editora Prentice-Hall do Brasil, Ltda., *Rio de Janeiro*
Prentice-Hall Canada Inc., *Toronto*
Prentice-Hall of India Private Limited, *New Delhi*
Prentice-Hall of Japan, Inc., *Tokyo*
Prentice-Hall of Southeast Asia Pte. Ltd., *Singapore*
Whitehall Books Limited, *Wellington, New Zealand*

Contents

Preface

Digital design is concerned with the design of digital electronic circuits. The subject is also known by other names such as *logic design*, *switching circuits*, *digital logic*, and *digital systems*. Digital circuits are employed in the design of systems such as digital computers, electronic calculators, digital control devices, digital communication equipment, and many other applications that require electronic digital hardware. This book presents the basic tools used in the design of digital circuits and provides a number of methods and procedures suitable for a variety of digital design applications.

The components used to construct digital systems are enclosed within integrated circuit packages. Small scale integration (SSI) circuits contain several gates or flip-flops in a single package. Medium scale integration (MSI) devices provide specific digital functions, and large scale integration (LSI) devices provide complete computer modules. It is important that the digital designer be familiar with the various digital components encountered in integrated circuit form. For this reason, the most often used MSI and LSI components are introduced in the book together with explanations of their logic properties. The use of integrated circuits in the design of digital circuits is illustrated by means of examples in the text, in the problems at the end of chapters, and in a set of 15 recommended laboratory experiments.

The book consists of 11 chapters. Chapters 1 through 5 deal with combinational circuits. Chapters 6 and 7 cover synchronous sequential circuits. These seven chapters and Chapter 10, which covers digital integrated circuits, are taken from the author's book *Digital Logic and Computer Design* (Prentice-Hall, 1979). Chapters 8, 9, and 11 contain material on algorithmic state machines, asynchronous sequential circuits, and laboratory experiments with integrated circuits. Together, the 11 chapters provide a coherent set of subjects suitable for a first course in digital design.

Chapter 1 presents the various binary systems suitable for representing information in digital systems. **Chapter 2** introduces Boolean algebra together with the various logic gates employed in the construction of digital circuits. **Chapter 3** covers the map and tabulation methods of simplifying digital circuits and a systematic procedure for NAND and NOR logic implementation. The first three chapters provide the basic background needed for understanding the rest of the book.

Chapter 4 outlines a formal procedure for the analysis and design of combinational circuits. **Chapter 5** deals with combinational MSI and LSI circuit components. Often used functions such as adders, comparators, decoders, and multiplexers, are explained and their use in the design of digital circuits is illustrated with examples. The read only memory (ROM) and programmable logic array (PLA) are introduced, and their usefulness in the design of complex combinational circuits is demonstrated. **Chapter 6** outlines various formal procedures for the analysis and design of clocked synchronous sequential circuits. **Chapter 7** presents various sequential MSI components such as registers, counters, shift registers, and the random access memory (RAM).

Chapter 8 presents the algorithmic state machine (ASM) method of digital design. The ASM chart is a special flowchart suitable for describing both sequential and parallel operations in digital hardware. A number of design examples demonstrate the application of the ASM chart in the design of the control logic of digital systems. **Chapter 9** presents formal procedures for the analysis and design of asynchronous sequential circuits. Methods are outlined to show how an asynchronous sequential circuit can be implemented as a combinational circuit with feedback or as a circuit with SR latches. **Chapter 10** deals with the electronics of digital circuits and presents the most common integrated circuit digital logic families. It assumes some knowledge of basic electronics but there is no specific prerequisite for the rest of the book.

Chapter 11 outlines 15 experiments that can be performed in the laboratory with hardware that is readily and cheaply available commercially. These experiments use standard integrated circuits of the TTL type. The operation of the integrated circuits is explained by referring to diagrams in previous chapters where similar components are originally introduced. Each experiment is presented informally rather than in a step-by-step fashion so that the student is expected to produce the details of the circuit diagram and formulate a procedure for checking the operation of the circuit in the laboratory.

Each chapter includes a set of problems and a list of references. Answers to selected problems appear in the Appendix to aid the student and to help the independent reader. A *Solutions Manual* is available for the instructor from the publisher.

M. MORRIS MANO

Digital
Design

Binary Systems

1

1-1 DIGITAL COMPUTERS AND DIGITAL SYSTEMS

Digital computers have made possible many scientific, industrial, and commercial advances that would have been unattainable otherwise. Our space program would have been impossible without real-time, continuous computer monitoring, and many business enterprises function efficiently only with the aid of automatic data processing. Computers are used in scientific calculations, commercial and business data processing, air traffic control, space guidance, the educational field, and many other areas. The most striking property of a digital computer is its generality. It can follow a sequence of instructions, called a *program*, that operates on given data. The user can specify and change programs and/or data according to the specific need. As a result of this flexibility, general-purpose digital computers can perform a wide variety of information-processing tasks.

The general-purpose digital computer is the best-known example of a digital system. Other examples include telephone switching exchanges, digital voltmeters, frequency counters, calculating machines, and teletype machines. Characteristic of a digital system is its manipulation of *discrete elements* of information. Such discrete elements may be electric impulses, the decimal digits, the letters of an alphabet, arithmetic operations, punctuation marks, or any other set of meaningful symbols. The juxtaposition of discrete elements of information represents a quantity of information. For example, the letters *d*, *o*, and *g* form the word *dog*. The digits 237 form a number. Thus, a sequence of discrete elements forms a language, that is, a discipline that conveys information. Early digital computers were used mostly for numerical computations. In this case the discrete elements used are the digits. From this application, the term *digital computer* has emerged. A more appropriate name for a digital computer would be a "discrete information processing system."

Discrete elements of information are represented in a digital system by physical quantities called *signals*. Electrical signals such as voltages and currents are the most common. The signals in all present-day electronic digital systems have only two discrete values and are said to be *binary*. The digital-system designer is restricted to the use of binary signals because of the lower reliability of many-valued electronic circuits. In other words, a circuit with ten states, using one discrete voltage value for each state, can be designed, but it would possess a very low reliability of operation. In contrast, a transistor circuit that is either on or off has two possible signal values and can be constructed to be extremely reliable. Because of this physical restriction of components, and because human logic tends to be binary, digital systems that are constrained to take discrete values are further constrained to take binary values.

Discrete quantities of information emerge either from the nature of the process or may be purposely quantized from a continuous process. For example, a payroll schedule is an inherently discrete process that contains employee names, social security numbers, weekly salaries, income taxes, etc. An employee's paycheck is processed using discrete data values such as letters of the alphabet (names), digits (salary), and special symbols such as $. On the other hand, a research scientist may observe a continous process but record only specific quantities in tabular form. The scientist is thus quantizing his continuous data. Each number in his table is a discrete element of information.

Many physical systems can be described mathematically by differential equations whose solutions as a function of time give the complete mathematical behavior of the process. An *analog computer* performs a direct *simulation* of a physical system. Each section of the computer is the analog of some particular portion of the process under study. The variables in the analog computer are represented by continous signals, usually electric voltages that vary with time. The signal variables are considered analogous to those of the process and behave in the same manner. Thus measurements of the analog voltage can be substituted for variables of the process. The term *analog signal* is sometimes substituted for *continuous signal* because "analog computer" has come to mean a computer that manipulates continuous variables.

To simulate a physical process in a digital computer, the quantities must be quantized. When the variables of the process are presented by real-time continuous signals, the latter are quantized by an analog-to-digital conversion device. A physical system whose behavior is described by mathematical equations is simulated in a digital computer by means of numerical methods. When the problem to be processed is inherently discrete, as in commercial applications, the digital computer manipulates the variables in their natural form.

A block diagram of the digital computer is shown in Fig. 1-1. The memory unit stores programs as well as input, output, and intermediate data. The processor unit performs arithmetic and other data-processing tasks as specified by a program. The control unit supervises the flow of information between the various units. The control unit retrieves the instructions, one by one, from the program which is stored in memory. For each instruction, the control unit informs the processor to execute the operation specified by the instruction. Both program and data are

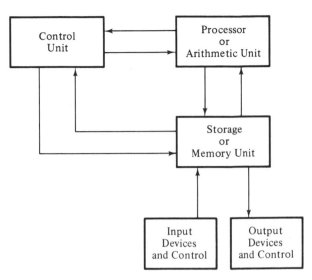

Figure 1-1 Block diagram of a digital computer

stored in memory. The control unit supervises the program instructions, and the processor manipulates the data as specified by the program.

The program and data prepared by the user are transferred into the memory unit by means of an input device such as punch-card reader or a teletypewriter. An output device, such as a printer, receives the result of the computations and the printed results are presented to the user. The input and output devices are special digital systems driven by electromechanical parts and controlled by electronic digital circuits.

An electronic calculator is a digital system similar to a digital computer, with the input device being a keyboard and the output device a numerical display. Instructions are entered in the calculator by means of the function keys, such as plus and minus. Data are entered through the numeric keys. Results are displayed directly in numeric form. Some calculators come close to resembling a digital computer by having printing capabilities and programmable facilities. A digital computer, however, is a more powerful device than a calculator. A digital computer can accommodate many other input and output devices; it can perform not only arithmetic computations but logical operations as well and can be programmed to make decisions based on internal and external conditions.

A digital computer is an interconnection of digital modules. To understand the operation of each digital module, it is necessary to have a basic knowledge of digital systems and their general behavior. The first four chapters of the book introduce the basic tools of digital design such as binary numbers and codes, Boolean algebra, and the basic building blocks from which electronic digital circuits are constructed. Chapters 5 and 7 present the basic components found in the processor unit of a digital computer. The operational characteristics of the memory unit are explained at the end of Chapter 7. The design of the control unit is discussed in Chapter 8 using the basic principles of sequential circuits from Chapter 6.

A processor, when combined with the control unit, forms a component referred to as a *central processor unit* or CPU. A CPU enclosed in small integrated-circuit package is called a *microprocessor*. The memory unit, as well as the part that controls the interface between the microprocessor and the input and output devices, may be enclosed within the microprocessor package or may be available in other small integrated-circuit packages. A CPU combined with memory and interface control to form a small-size computer is called a *microcomputer*. The availability of microcomputer components has revolutionized the digital system design technology, giving the designer the freedom to create structures that were previously uneconomical. The various components of a microcomputer system are constructed internally with digital circuits.

It has already been mentioned that a digital computer manipulates discrete elements of information and that these elements are represented in the binary form. Operands used for calculations may be expressed in the binary number system. Other discrete elements, including the decimal digits, are represented in binary codes. Data processing is carried out by means of binary logic elements using binary signals. Quantities are stored in binary storage elements. The purpose of this chapter is to introduce the various binary concepts as a frame of reference for further detailed study in the suceeding chapters.

1-2   BINARY NUMBERS

A decimal number such as 7392 represents a quantity equal to 7 thousands plus 3 hundreds, plus 9 tens, plus 2 units. The thousands, hundreds, etc., are powers of 10 implied by the position of the coefficients. To be more exact, 7392 should be written as:

$$7 \times 10^3 + 3 \times 10^2 + 9 \times 10^1 + 2 \times 10^0$$

However, the convention is to write only the coefficients and from their position deduce the necessary powers of 10. In general, a number with a decimal point is represented by a series of coefficients as follows:

$$a_5 a_4 a_3 a_2 a_1 a_0 . a_{-1} a_{-2} a_{-3}$$

The a_j coefficients are one of the ten digits (0, 1, 2, . . . , 9), and the subscript value j gives the place value and, hence, the power of 10 by which the coefficient must be multiplied.

$$10^5 a_5 + 10^4 a_4 + 10^3 a_3 + 10^2 a_2 + 10^1 a_1 + 10^0 a_0 + 10^{-1} a_{-1}$$
$$+ 10^{-2} a_{-2} + 10^{-3} a_{-3}$$

The decimal number system is said to be of *base*, or *radix*, 10 because it uses ten digits and the coefficients are multiplied by powers of 10. The *binary* system is a different number system. The coefficients of the binary numbers system have two possible values: 0 and 1. Each coefficient a_j is multiplied by 2^j. For example, the decimal equivalent of the binary number 11010.11 is 26.75, as shown from the multiplication of the coefficients by powers of 2:

$$1 \times 2^4 + 1 \times 2^3 + 0 \times 2^2 + 1 \times 2^1 + 0 \times 2^0 + 1 \times 2^{-1}$$
$$+ 1 \times 2^{-2} = 26.75$$

In general, a number expressed in base-r system has coefficients multiplied by powers of r:

$$a_n \cdot r^n + a_{n-1} \cdot r^{n-1} + \cdots + a_2 \cdot r^2 + a_1 \cdot r + a_0$$
$$+ a_{-1} \cdot r^{-1} + a_{-2} \cdot r^{-2} + \cdots + a_{-m} \cdot r^{-m}$$

The coefficients a_j range in value from 0 to $r - 1$. To distinguish between numbers of different bases, we enclose the coefficients in parentheses and write a subscript equal to the base used (except sometimes for decimal numbers, where the content makes it obvious that it is decimal). An example of a base-5 number is:

$$(4021.2)_5 = 4 \times 5^3 + 0 \times 5^2 + 2 \times 5^1 + 1 \times 5^0 + 2 \times 5^{-1} = (511.4)_{10}$$

Note that coefficient values for base 5 can be only 0, 1, 2, 3, and 4.

It is customary to borrow the needed r digits for the coefficients from the decimal system when the base of the number is less than 10. The letters of the alphabet are used to supplement the ten decimal digits when the base of the number is greater than 10. For example, in the *hexadecimal* (base 16) number system, the first ten digits are borrowed from the decimal system. The letters A, B, C, D, E, and F are used for digits 10, 11, 12, 13, 14, and 15, respectively. An example of a hexadecimal number is:

$$(B65F)_{16} = 11 \times 16^3 + 6 \times 16^2 + 5 \times 16 + 15 = (46687)_{10}$$

The first 16 numbers in the decimal, binary, octal, and hexadecimal systems are listed in Table 1-1.

Arithmetic operations with numbers in base r follow the same rules as for decimal numbers. When other than the familiar base 10 is used, one must be careful to use only the r allowable digits. Examples of addition, subtraction, and multiplication of two binary numbers are shown below:

augend:	101101	minuend:	101101	multiplicand:	1011
addend:	+100111	subtrahend:	−100111	multiplier:	× 101
sum:	1010100	difference:	000110		1011
					0000
					1011
				product:	110111

TABLE 1-1 Numbers with different bases

Decimal (base 10)	Binary (base 2)	Octal (base 8)	Hexadecimal (base 16)
00	0000	00	0
01	0001	01	1
02	0010	02	2
03	0011	03	3
04	0100	04	4
05	0101	05	5
06	0110	06	6
07	0111	07	7
08	1000	10	8
09	1001	11	9
10	1010	12	A
11	1011	13	B
12	1100	14	C
13	1101	15	D
14	1110	16	E
15	1111	17	F

The sum of two binary numbers is calculated by the same rules as in decimal, except that the digits of the sum in any significant position can be only 0 or 1. Any "carry" obtained in a given significant position is used by the pair of digits one significant position higher. The subtraction is slightly more complicated. The rules are still the same as in decimal, except that the "borrow" in a given significant position adds 2 to a minuend digit. (A borrow in the decimal system adds 10 to a minuend digit.) Multiplication is very simple. The multiplier digits are always 1 or 0. Therefore, the partial products are equal either to the multiplicand or to 0.

1-3 NUMBER BASE CONVERSIONS

A binary number can be converted to decimal by forming the sum of the powers of 2 of those coefficients whose value is 1. For example:

$$(1010.011)_2 = 2^3 + 2^1 + 2^{-2} + 2^{-3} = (10.375)_{10}$$

The binary number has four 1's and the decimal equivalent is found from the sum of four powers of 2. Similarly, a number expressed in base r can be converted to its decimal equivalent by multiplying each coefficient with the corresponding power of r and adding. The following is an example of octal-to-decimal conversion:

$$(630.4)_8 = 6 \times 8^2 + 3 \times 8 + 4 \times 8^{-1} = (408.5)_{10}$$

6

The conversion from decimal to binary or to any other base-r system is more convenient if the number is separated into an *integer part* and a *fraction part* and the conversion of each part done separately. The conversion of an *integer* from decimal to binary is best explained by example.

EXAMPLE 1-1: Convert decimal 41 to binary. First, 41 is divided by 2 to give an integer quotient of 20 and a remainder of $\frac{1}{2}$. The quotient is again divided by 2 to give a new quotient and remainder. This process is continued until the integer quotient becomes 0. The *coefficients* of the desired binary number are obtained from the *remainders* as follows:

integer quotient		remainder	coefficient
$\frac{41}{2} = 20$	$+$	$\frac{1}{2}$	$a_0 = 1$
$\frac{20}{2} = 10$	$+$	0	$a_1 = 0$
$\frac{10}{2} = 5$	$+$	0	$a_2 = 0$
$\frac{5}{2} = 2$	$+$	$\frac{1}{2}$	$a_3 = 1$
$\frac{2}{2} = 1$	$+$	0	$a_4 = 0$
$\frac{1}{2} = 0$	$+$	$\frac{1}{2}$	$a_5 = 1$

answer: $(41)_{10} = (a_5 a_4 a_3 a_2 a_1 a_0)_2 = (101001)_2$

The arithmetic process can be manipulated more conveniently as follows:

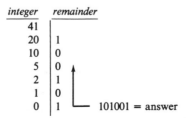

integer	remainder
41	
20	1
10	0
5	0
2	1
1	0
0	1

101001 = answer

The conversion from decimal integers to any base-r system is similar to the above example, except that division is done by r instead of 2.

EXAMPLE 1-2: Convert decimal 153 to octal. The required base r is 8. First, 153 is divided by 8 to give an integer quotient of 19 and a remainder of 1. Then 19 is divided by 8 to give an integer quotient of 2 and a remainder of 3. Finally, 2 is divided by 8 to give a quotient of 0 and a remainder of 2. This process can be conveniently manipulated as follows:

$$
\begin{array}{c|l}
153 & \\
19 & 1 \\
2 & 3 \\
0 & 2 \end{array} \quad = (231)_8
$$

The conversion of a decimal *fraction* to binary is accomplished by a method similar to that used for integers. However, multiplication is used instead of division, and integers are accumulated instead of remainders. Again, the method is best explained by example.

EXAMPLE 1-3: Convert $(0.6875)_{10}$ to binary. First, 0.6875 is multiplied by 2 to give an integer and a fraction. The new fraction is multiplied by 2 to give a new integer and a new fraction. This process is continued until the fraction becomes 0 or until the number of digits have sufficient accuracy. The coefficients of the binary number are obtained from the integers as follows:

	integer		fraction	coefficient
$0.6875 \times 2 =$	1	+	0.3750	$a_{-1} = 1$
$0.3750 \times 2 =$	0	+	0.7500	$a_{-2} = 0$
$0.7500 \times 2 =$	1	+	0.5000	$a_{-3} = 1$
$0.5000 \times 2 =$	1	+	0.0000	$a_{-4} = 1$

answer: $(0.6875)_{10} = (0.a_{-1}a_{-2}a_{-3}a_{-4})_2 = (0.1011)_2$

To convert a decimal fraction to a number expressed in base r, a similar procedure is used. Multiplication is by r instead of 2, and the coefficients found from the integers may range in value from 0 to $r - 1$ instead of 0 and 1.

EXAMPLE 1-4: Convert $(0.513)_{10}$ to octal.

$$
0.513 \times 8 = 4.104
$$
$$
0.104 \times 8 = 0.832
$$
$$
0.832 \times 8 = 6.656
$$
$$
0.656 \times 8 = 5.248
$$
$$
0.248 \times 8 = 1.984
$$
$$
0.984 \times 8 = 7.872
$$

The answer, to seven significant figures, is obtained from the integer part of the products:

$$(0.513)_{10} = (0.406517 \ldots)_8$$

The conversion of decimal numbers with both integer and fraction parts is done by converting the integer and fraction separately and then combining the two answers together. Using the results of Examples 1-1 and 1-3, we obtain:

$$(41.6875)_{10} = (101001.1011)_2$$

From Examples 1-2 and 1-4, we have:

$$(153.513)_{10} = (231.406517)_8$$

1-4 OCTAL AND HEXADECIMAL NUMBERS

The conversion from and to binary, octal, and hexadecimal plays an important part in digital computers. Since $2^3 = 8$ and $2^4 = 16$, each octal digit corresponds to three binary digits and each hexadecimal digit corresponds to four binary digits. The conversion from binary to octal is easily accomplished by partitioning the binary number into groups of three digits each, starting from the binary point and proceeding to the left and to the right. The corresponding octal digit is then assigned to each group. The following example illustrates the procedure:

$$(\underbrace{10}_{2} \; \underbrace{110}_{6} \; \underbrace{001}_{1} \; \underbrace{101}_{5} \; \underbrace{011}_{3} \cdot \underbrace{111}_{7} \; \underbrace{100}_{4} \; \underbrace{000}_{0} \; \underbrace{110}_{6})_2 = (26153.7406)_8$$

Conversion from binary to hexadecimal is similar, except that the binary number is divided into groups of four digits:

$$(\underbrace{10}_{2} \; \underbrace{1100}_{C} \; \underbrace{0110}_{6} \; \underbrace{1011}_{B} \cdot \underbrace{1111}_{F} \; \underbrace{0010}_{2})_2 = (2C6B.F2)_{16}$$

The corresponding hexadecimal (or octal) digit for each group of binary digits is easily remembered after studying the values listed in Table 1-1.

Conversion from octal or hexadecimal to binary is done by a procedure reverse to the above. Each octal digit is converted to its three-digit binary equivalent. Similarly, each hexadecimal digit is converted to its four-digit binary equivalent. This is illustrated in the following examples:

$$(673.124)_8 = (\underbrace{110}_{6} \; \underbrace{111}_{7} \; \underbrace{011}_{3} \cdot \underbrace{001}_{1} \; \underbrace{010}_{2} \; \underbrace{100}_{4})_2$$

$$(306.\,D)_{16} = (\underbrace{0011}_{3} \; \underbrace{0000}_{0} \; \underbrace{0110}_{6} \cdot \underbrace{1101}_{D})_2$$

Binary numbers are difficult to work with because they require three or four times as many digits as their decimal equivalent. For example, the binary number 111111111111 is equivalent to decimal 4095. However, digital computers use binary numbers and it is sometimes necessary for the human operator or user to communicate directly with the machine by means of binary numbers. One scheme that retains the binary system in the computer but reduces the number of digits the human must consider utilizes the relationship between the binary number system and the octal or hexadecimal system. By this method, the human thinks in terms of octal or hexadecimal numbers and performs the required conversion by inspection when direct communication with the machine is necessary. Thus the binary number 111111111111 has 12 digits and is expressed in octal as 7777 (four digits) or in hexadecimal as FFF (three digits). During communication between people (about binary numbers in the computer), the octal or hexadecimal representation is more desirable because it can be expressed more compactly with a third or a quarter of the number of digits required for the equivalent binary number. When the human communicates with the machine (through console switches or indicator lights or by means of programs written in *machine language*), the conversion from octal or hexadecimal to binary and vice versa is done by inspection by the human user.

1-5 COMPLEMENTS

Complements are used in digital computers for simplifying the subtraction operation and for logical manipulations. There are two types of complements for each base-r system: (1) the r's complement and (2) the $(r - 1)$'s complement. When the value of the base is substituted, the two types receive the names 2's and 1's complement for binary numbers, or 10's and 9's complement for decimal numbers.

The r's Complement

Given a positive number N in base r with an integer part of n digits, the r's complement of N is defined as $r^n - N$ for $N \neq 0$ and 0 for $N = 0$. The following numerical example will help clarify the definition.

The 10's complement of $(52520)_{10}$ is $10^5 - 52520 = 47480$.

The number of digits in the number is $n = 5$.

The 10's complement of $(0.3267)_{10}$ is $1 - 0.3267 = 0.6733$.

No integer part, so $10^n = 10^0 = 1$.

The 10's complement of $(25.639)_{10}$ is $10^2 - 25.639 = 74.361$.

The 2's complement of $(101100)_2$ is $(2^6)_{10} - (101100)_2 = (1000000 - 101100)_2$
    $= 010100$.

The 2's complement of $(0.0110)_2$ is $(1 - 0.0110)_2 = 0.1010$.

From the definition and the examples, it is clear that the 10's complement of a decimal number can be formed by leaving all least significant zeros unchanged, subtracting the first nonzero least significant digit from 10, and then subtracting all other higher significant digits from 9. The 2's complement can be formed by leaving all least significant zeros and the first nonzero digit unchanged, and then replacing 1's by 0's and 0's by 1's in all other higher significant digits. A third, simpler method for obtaining the r's complement is given after the definition of the $(r - 1)$'s complement.

The r's complement of a number exists for any base r (r greater than but not equal to 1) and may be obtained from the definition given above. The examples listed here use numbers with $r = 10$ (decimal) and $r = 2$ (binary) because these are the two bases of most interest to us. The name of the complement is related to the base of the number used. For example, the $(r - 1)$'s complement of a number in base 11 is named the 10's complement, since $r - 1 = 10$ for $r = 11$.

The $(r - 1)$'s Complement

Given a positive number N in base r with an integer part of n digits and a fraction part of m digits, the $(r - 1)$'s complement of N is defined as $r^n - r^{-m} - N$. Some numerical examples follow:

The 9's complement of $(52520)_{10}$ is $(10^5 - 1 - 52520) = 99999 - 52520 = 47479$.

No fraction part, so $10^{-m} = 10^0 = 1$.

The 9's complement of $(0.3267)_{10}$ is $(1 - 10^{-4} - 0.3267) = 0.9999 - 0.3267 = 0.6732$.

No integer part, so $10^n = 10^0 = 1$.

The 9's complement of $(25.639)_{10}$ is $(10^2 - 10^{-3} - 25.639) = 99.999 - 25.639 = 74.360$.

The 1's complement of $(101100)_2$ is $(2^6 - 1) - (101100) = (111111 - 101100)_2 = 010011$.

The 1's complement of $(0.0110)_2$ is $(1 - 2^{-4})_{10} - (0.0110)_2 = (0.1111 - 0.0110)_2 = 0.1001$.

From the examples, we see that the 9's complement of a decimal number is formed simply by subtracting every digit from 9. The 1's complement of a binary number is even simpler to form: the 1's are changed to 0's and the 0's to 1's. Since the $(r - 1)$'s complement is very easily obtained, it is sometimes convenient to use it when the r's complement is desired. From the definitions and from a comparison of the results obtained in the examples, it follows that the r's complement can be obtained from the $(r - 1)$'s complement after the addition of r^{-m} to the least significant digit. For example, the 2's complement of 10110100 is obtained from the 1's complement 01001011 by adding 1 to give 01001100.

It is worth mentioning that the complement of the complement restores the number to its original value. The r's complement of N is $r^n - N$ and the complement of $(r^n - N)$ is $r^n - (r^n - N) = N$; and similarly for the 1's complement.

Subtraction with r's Complements

The direct method of subtraction taught in elementary schools uses the borrow concept. In this method, we borrow a 1 from a higher significant position when the minuend digit is smaller than the corresponding subtrahend digit. This seems to be easiest when people perform subtraction with paper and pencil. When subtraction is implemented by means of digital components, this method is found to be less efficient than the method that uses complements and addition as stated below.

The subtraction of two positive numbers $(M - N)$, both of base r, may be done as follows:

1. Add the minuend M to the r's complement of the subtrahend N.

2. Inspect the result obtained in step 1 for an end carry:
   (a) If an end carry occurs, discard it.
   (b) If an end carry does not occur, take the r's complement of the number obtained in step 1 and place a negative sign in front.

The following examples illustrate the procedure:

> **EXAMPLE 1-5:** Using 10's complement, subtract $72532 - 3250$.

$$M = 72532 \qquad\qquad 72532$$
$$N = 03250$$

$$\text{10's complement of } N = 96750 \qquad\qquad \begin{array}{r} + \\ 96750 \end{array}$$

$$\text{end carry} \rightarrow 1 \quad \diagup \quad 69282$$

answer: 69282

> **EXAMPLE 1-6:** Subtract: $(3250 - 72532)_{10}$.

$$M = 03250 \qquad\qquad 03250$$
$$N = 72532$$

$$\text{10's complement of } N = 27468 \qquad\qquad \begin{array}{r} + \\ 27468 \end{array}$$

$$\text{no carry} \quad \diagup \quad 30718$$

answer: $-69282 = -$ (10's complement of 30718)

EXAMPLE 1-7: Use 2's complement to perform $M - N$ with the given binary numbers.

(a) $M = 1010100$ 1010100

                   $N = 1000100$

2's complement of $N = 0111100$

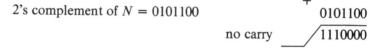

end carry → 1   0010000

answer: 10000

(b) $M = 1000100$ 1000100

                   $N = 1010100$

2's complement of $N = 0101100$ +

                                     0101100

no carry   1110000

answer: $-10000 = -$ (2's complement of 1110000)

The proof of the procedure is: The addition of M to the r's complement of N gives $(M + r^n - N)$. For numbers having an integer part of n digits, r^n is equal to a 1 in the $(n + 1)$th position (what has been called the "end carry"). Since both M and N are assumed to be positive, then:

(a) $(M + r^n - N) \geqslant r^n$ if $M \geqslant N$,   or
(b) $(M + r^n - N) < r^n$ if $M < N$

In case (a) the answer is positive and equal to $M - N$, which is directly obtained by discarding the end carry r^n. In case (b) the answer is negative and equal to $-(N - M)$. This case is detected from the absence of an end carry. The answer is obtained by taking a second complement and adding a negative sign:

$$-[r^n - (M + r^n - N)] = -(N - M).$$

Subtraction with $(r - 1)$'s Complement

The procedure for subtraction with the $(r - 1)$'s complement is exactly the same as the one used with the r's complement except for one variation, called "end-around carry," as shown below. The subtraction of $M' - N$, both positive numbers in base r, may be calculated in the following manner:

1. Add the minuend M to the $(r - 1)$'s complement of the subtrahend N.

2. Inspect the result obtained in step 1 for an end carry.
   (a) If an end carry occurs, add 1 to the least significant digit (end-around carry).

(b) If an end carry does not occur, take the $(r - 1)$'s complement of the number obtained in step 1 and place a negative sign in front.

The proof of this procedure is very similar to the one given for the r's complement case and is left as an exercise. The following examples illustrate the procedure.

EXAMPLE 1-8: Repeat Examples 1-5 and 1-6 using 9's complements.

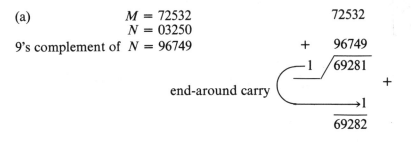

(a) $M = 72532$
                    $N = 03250$
9's complement of $N = 96749$

answer: 69282

(b) $M = 03250$
                    $N = \overline{72532}$
9's complement of $N = 27467$

answer: $-69282 = -$ (9's complement of 30717)

EXAMPLE 1-9: Repeat Example 1-7 using 1's complement.

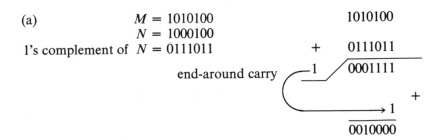

(a) $M = 1010100$
                    $N = 1000100$
1's complement of $N = 0111011$

answer: 10000

(b)

$$M = 1000100$$
$$N = 1010100$$
1's complement of $N = 0101011$

no carry

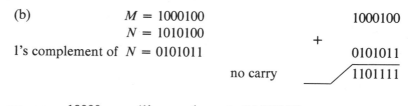

answer: $-10000 = -$ (1's complement of 1101111)

Comparison between 1's and 2's Complements

A comparison between 1's and 2's complements reveals the advantages and disadvantages of each. The 1's complement has the advantage of being easier to implement by digital components since the only thing that must be done is to change 0's into 1's and 1's into 0's. The implementation of the 2's complement may be obtained in two ways: (1) by adding 1 to the least significant digit of the 1's complement, and (2) by leaving all leading 0's in the least significant positions and the first 1 unchanged, and only then changing all 1's into 0's and all 0's into 1's. During subtraction of two numbers by complements, the 2's complement is advantageous in that only one arithmetic addition operation is required. The 1's complement requires two arithmetic additions when an end-around carry occurs. The 1's complement has the additional disadvantage of possessing two arithmetic zeros: one with all 0's and one with all 1's. To illustrate this fact, consider the subtraction of the two equal binary numbers $1100 - 1100 = 0$.

Using 1's complement:

$$+ \frac{\begin{aligned} 1100 \\ 0011 \end{aligned}}{+ \ \ 1111}$$

Complement again to obtain -0000.

Using 2's complement:

$$+ \frac{\begin{aligned} 1100 \\ 0100 \end{aligned}}{+ \ \ 0000}$$

While the 2's complement has only one arithmetic zero, the 1's complement zero can be positive or negative, which may complicate matters.

Complements, very useful for arithmetic manipulations in digital computers, are discussed more in Chapters 8 and 9. However, the 1's complement is also useful in logical manipulations (as will be shown later), since the change of 1's to

0's and vice versa is equivalent to a logical inversion operation. The 2's complement is used only in conjunction with arithmetic applications. Consequently, it is convenient to adopt the following convention: When the word *complement*, without mention of the type, is used in conjunction with a nonarithmetic application, the type is assumed to be the 1's complement.

1-6   BINARY CODES

Electronic digital systems use signals that have two distinct values and circuit elements that have two stable states. There is a direct analogy among binary signals, binary circuit elements, and binary digits. A binary number of n digits, for example, may be represented by n binary circuit elements, each having an output signal equivalent to a 0 or a 1. Digital systems represent and manipulate not only binary numbers, but also many other discrete elements of information. Any discrete element of information distinct among a group of quantities can be represented by a binary code. For example, *red* is one distinct color of the spectrum. The letter A is one distinct letter of the alphabet.

A *bit*, by definition, is a binary digit. When used in conjunction with a binary code, it is better to think of it as denoting a binary quantity equal to 0 or 1. To represent a group of 2^n distinct elements in a binary code requires a minimum of n bits. This is because it is possible to arrange n bits in 2^n distinct ways. For example, a group of four distinct quantities can be represented by a two-bit code, with each quantity assigned one of the following bit combinations: 00, 01, 10, 11. A group of eight elements requires a three-bit code, with each element assigned to one and only one of the following: 000, 001, 010, 011, 100, 101, 110, 111. The examples show that the distinct bit combinations of an n-bit code can be found by counting in binary from 0 to $(2^n - 1)$. Some bit combinations are unassigned when the number of elements of the group to be coded is not a multiple of the power of 2. The ten decimal digits 0, 1, 2, . . . , 9 are an example of such a group. A binary code that distinguishes among ten elements must contain at least four bits; three bits can distinguish a maximum of eight elements. Four bits can form 16 distinct combinations, but since only ten digits are coded, the remaining six combinations are unassigned and not used.

Although the *minimum* number of bits required to code 2^n distinct quantities is n, there is no *maximum* number of bits that may be used for a binary code. For example, the ten decimal digits can be coded with ten bits, and each decimal digit assigned a bit combination of nine 0's and a 1. In this particular binary code, the digit 6 is assigned the bit combination 0001000000.

Decimal Codes

Binary codes for decimal digits require a minimum of four bits. Numerous different codes can be obtained by arranging four or more bits in ten distinct possible combinations. A few possibilities are shown in Table 1-2.

TABLE 1-2 Binary codes for the decimal digits

Decimal digit	(BCD) 8421	Excess-3	84-2-1	2421	(Biquinary) 5043210
0	0000	0011	0000	0000	0100001
1	0001	0100	0111	0001	0100010
2	0010	0101	0110	0010	0100100
3	0011	0110	0101	0011	0101000
4	0100	0111	0100	0100	0110000
5	0101	1000	1011	1011	1000001
6	0110	1001	1010	1100	1000010
7	0111	1010	1001	1101	1000100
8	1000	1011	1000	1110	1001000
9	1001	1100	1111	1111	1010000

The BCD (binary-coded decimal) is a straight assignment of the binary equivalent. It is possible to assign weights to the binary bits according to their positions. The weights in the BCD code are 8, 4, 2, 1. The bit assignment 0110, for example, can be interpreted by the weights to represent the decimal digit 6 because $0 \times 8 + 1 \times 4 + 1 \times 2 + 0 \times 1 = 6$. It is also possible to assign negative weights to a decimal code, as shown by the 8, 4, -2, -1 code. In this case the bit combination 0110 is interpreted as the decimal digit 2, as obtained from $0 \times 8 + 1 \times 4 + 1 \times (-2) + 0 \times (-1) = 2$. Two other weighted codes shown in the table are the 2421 and the 5043210. A decimal code that has been used in some old computers is the excess-3 code. This is an unweighted code; its code assignment is obtained from the corresponding value of BCD after the addition of 3.

Numbers are represented in digital computers either in binary or in decimal through a binary code. When specifying data, the user likes to give the data in decimal form. The input decimal numbers are stored internally in the computer by means of a decimal code. Each decimal digit requires at least four binary storage elements. The decimal numbers are converted to binary when arithmetic operations are done internally with numbers represented in binary. It is also possible to perform the arithmetic operations directly in decimal with all numbers left in a coded form throughout. For example, the decimal number 395, when converted to binary, is equal to 110001011 and consists of nine binary digits. The same number, when represented internally in the BCD code, occupies four bits for each decimal digit, for a total of 12 bits: 001110010101. The first four bits represent a 3, the next four a 9, and the last four a 5.

It is very important to understand the difference between *conversion* of a decimal number to binary and the binary *coding* of a decimal number. In each case the final result is a series of bits. The bits obtained from conversion are binary digits. Bits obtained from coding are combinations of 1's and 0's arranged according to the rules of the code used. Therefore, it is extremely important to realize that a series of 1's and 0's in a digital system may sometimes represent a binary number and at other times represent some other discrete quantity of information as specified by a given binary code. The BCD code, for example, has been chosen to be both a code and a direct binary conversion, as long as the decimal numbers are integers from 0 to 9. For numbers greater than 9, the conversion and the coding are completely different. This concept is so important that it is worth repeating with another example. The binary conversion of decimal 13 is 1101; the coding of decimal 13 with BCD is 00010011.

From the five binary codes listed in Table 1-2, the BCD seems the most natural to use and is indeed the one most commonly encountered. The other four-bit codes listed have one characteristic in common that is not found in BCD. The excess-3, the 2, 4, 2, 1, and the 8, 4, -2, -1 are self-complementary codes, that is, the 9's complement of the decimal number is easily obtained by changing 1's to 0's and 0's to 1's. For example, the decimal 395 is represented in the 2, 4, 2, 1 code by 001111111011. Its 9's complement 604 is represented by 110000000100, which is easily obtained from the replacement of 1's by 0's and 0's by 1's. This property is useful when arithmetic operations are internally done with decimal numbers (in a binary code) and subtraction is calculated by means of 9's complement.

The biquinary code shown in Table 1-2 is an example of a seven-bit code with error-detection properties. Each decimal digit consists of five 0's and two 1's placed in the corresponding weighted columns. The error-detection property of this code may be understood if one realizes that digital systems represent binary 1 by one distinct signal and binary 0 by a second distinct signal. During transmission of signals from one location to another, an error may occur. One or more bits may change value. A circuit in the receiving side can detect the presence of more (or less) than two 1's and, if the received combination of bits does not agree with the allowable combination, an error is detected.

Error-Detection Codes

Binary information, be it pulse-modulated signals or digital computer input or output, may be transmitted through some form of communication medium such as wires or radio waves. Any external noise introduced into a physical communication medium changes bit values from 0 to 1 or vice versa. An error-detection code can be used to detect errors during transmission. The detected error cannot be corrected, but its presence is indicated. The usual procedure is to observe the frequency of errors. If errors occur only once in a while, at random, and without a pronounced effect on the overall information transmitted, then either nothing is done or the particular erroneous message is transmitted again. If errors occur so often as to distort the meaning of the received information, the system is checked for malfunction.

A *parity* bit is an extra bit included with a message to make the total number of 1's either odd or even. A message of four bits and a parity bit, P, are shown in Table 1-3. In (a), P is chosen so that the sum of all 1's is odd (in all five bits). In (b), P is chosen so that the sum of all 1's is even. During transfer of information

TABLE 1-3 Parity-bit generation

(a) Message	P (odd)	(b) Message	P (even)
0000	1	0000	0
0001	0	0001	1
0010	0	0010	1
0011	1	0011	0
0100	0	0100	1
0101	1	0101	0
0110	1	0110	0
0111	0	0111	1
1000	0	1000	1
1001	1	1001	0
1010	1	1010	0
1011	0	1011	1
1100	1	1100	0
1101	0	1101	1
1110	0	1110	1
1111	1	1111	0

from one location to another, the parity bit is handled as follows. In the sending end, the message (in this case the first four bits) is applied to a "parity-generation" network where the required P bit is generated. The message, including the parity bit, is transferred to its destination. In the receiving end, all the incoming bits (in this case five) are applied to a "parity-check" network to check the proper parity adopted. An error is detected if the checked parity does not correspond to the adopted one. The parity method detects the presence of one, three, or any odd combination of errors. An even combination of errors is undetectable. Further discussion of parity generation and checking can be found in Sec. 4-9.

The Reflected Code

Digital systems can be designed to process data in discrete form only. Many physical systems supply continous output data. These data must be converted into digital or discrete form before they are applied to a digital system. Continuous or analog information is converted into digital form by means of an analog-to-digital converter. It is sometimes convenient to use the reflected code shown in Table 1-4 to represent the digital data converted from the analog data. The advantage of the reflected code over pure binary numbers is that a number in the reflected code changes by only one bit as it proceeds from one number to the next. A typical application of the reflected code occurs when the analog data are represented by a continouous change of a shaft position. The shaft is partitioned into segments, and each segment is assigned a number. If adjacent segments are made to correspond to adjacent reflected-code numbers, ambiguity is reduced when detection is sensed

TABLE 1-4 Four-bit reflected code

Reflected code	Decimal equivalent
0000	0
0001	1
0011	2
0010	3
0110	4
0111	5
0101	6
0100	7
1100	8
1101	9
1111	10
1110	11
1010	12
1011	13
1001	14
1000	15

in the line that separates any two segments. The reflected code shown in Table 1-4 is only one of many possible such codes. To obtain a different reflected code, one can start with any bit combination and proceed to obtain the next bit combination by changing only one bit from 0 to 1 or 1 to 0 in any desired random fashion, as long as two numbers do not have identical code assignments. The reflected code is also known as the *Gray* code.

Alphanumeric Codes

Many applications of digital computers require the handling of data that consist not only of numbers, but also of letters. For instance, an insurance company with millions of policy holders may use a digital computer to process its files. To represent the policy holder's name in binary form, it is necessary to have a binary code for the alphabet. In addition, the same binary code must represent decimal numbers and some other special characters. An alphanumeric (sometimes abbreviated *alphameric*) code is a binary code of a group of elements consisting of the ten decimal digits, the 26 letters of the alphabet, and a certain number of special symbols such as $. The total number of elements in an alphanumeric group is greater than 36. Therefore, it must be coded with a minimum of six bits ($2^6 = 64$, but $2^5 = 32$ is insufficient).

One possible arrangement of a six-bit alphanumeric code is shown in Table 1-5 under the name "internal code." With a few variations, it is used in many computers to represent alphanumeric characters internally. The need to represent more than 64 characters (the lowercase letters and special control characters for the

TABLE 1-5 Alphanumeric character codes

Character	6-Bit internal code		7-Bit ASCII code		8-Bit EBCDIC code		12-Bit card code
A	010	001	100	0001	1100	0001	12,1
B	010	010	100	0010	1100	0010	12,2
C	010	011	100	0011	1100	0011	12,3
D	010	100	100	0100	1100	0100	12,4
E	010	101	100	0101	1100	0101	12,5
F	010	110	100	0110	1100	0110	12,6
G	010	111	100	0111	1100	0111	12,7
H	011	000	100	1000	1100	1000	12,8
I	011	001	100	1001	1100	1001	12,9
J	100	001	100	1010	1101	0001	11,1
K	100	010	100	1011	1101	0010	11,2
L	100	011	100	1100	1101	0011	11,3
M	100	100	100	1101	1101	0100	11,4
N	100	101	100	1110	1101	0101	11,5
O	100	110	100	1111	1101	0110	11,6
P	100	111	101	0000	1101	0111	11,7
Q	101	000	101	0001	1101	1000	11,8
R	101	001	101	0010	1101	1001	11,9
S	110	010	101	0011	1110	0010	0,2
T	110	011	101	0100	1110	0011	0,3
U	110	100	101	0101	1110	0100	0,4
V	110	101	101	0110	1110	0101	0,5
W	110	110	101	0111	1110	0110	0,6
X	110	111	101	1000	1110	0111	0,7
Y	111	000	101	1001	1110	1000	0,8
Z	111	001	101	1010	1110	1001	0,9
0	000	000	011	0000	1111	0000	0
1	000	001	011	0001	1111	0001	1
2	000	010	011	0010	1111	0010	2
3	000	011	011	0011	1111	0011	3
4	000	100	011	0100	1111	0100	4
5	000	101	011	0101	1111	0101	5
6	000	110	011	0110	1111	0110	6
7	000	111	011	0111	1111	0111	7
8	001	000	011	1000	1111	1000	8
9	001	001	011	1001	1111	1001	9
blank	110	000	010	0000	0100	0000	no punch
.	011	011	010	1110	0100	1011	12,8,3
(	111	100	010	1000	0100	1101	12,8,5
+	010	000	010	1011	0100	1110	12,8,6
$	101	011	010	0100	0101	1011	11,8,3
*	101	100	010	1010	0101	1100	11,8,4
)	011	100	010	1001	0101	1101	11,8,5
−	100	000	010	1101	0110	0000	11
/	110	001	010	1111	0110	0001	0,1
,	111	011	010	1100	0110	1011	0,8,3
=	001	011	011	1101	0111	1110	8,6

transmission of digital information) gave rise to seven- and eight-bit alphanumeric codes. One such code is known as ASCII (American Standard Code for Information Interchange); another is known as EBCDIC (Extended BCD Interchange Code). The ASCII code listed in Table 1-5 consists of seven bits but is, for all practical purposes, an eight-bit code because an eighth bit is invariably added for parity. When discrete information is transferred through punch cards, the alphanumeric characters use a 12-bit binary code. A punch card consists of 80 columns and 12 rows. In each column, an alphanumeric character is represented by holes punched in the appropriate rows. A hole is sensed as a 1 and the absence of a hole is sensed as a 0. The 12 rows are marked, starting from the top, as the 12, 11, 0, 1, 2,..., 9 punch. The first three are called the *zone* punch and the last nine are called the *numeric* punch. The 12-bit card code shown in Table 1-5 lists the rows where a hole is punched (giving the 1's). The remaining unlisted rows are assumed to be 0's. The 12-bit card code is inefficient with respect to the number of bits used. Most computers translate the input code into an internal six-bit code. As an example, the internal code representation of the name "John Doe" is:

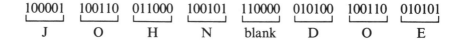

1-7 BINARY STORAGE AND REGISTERS

The discrete elements of information in a digital computer must have a physical existence in some information storage medium. Furthermore, when discrete elements of information are represented in binary form, the information storage medium must contain binary storage elements for storing individual bits. A *binary cell* is a device that possesses two stable states and is capable of storing one bit of information. The input to the cell receives excitation signals that set it to one of the two states. The output of the cell is a physical quantity that distinguishes between the two states. The information stored in a cell is a 1 when it is in one stable state and a 0 when in the other stable state. Examples of binary cells are electronic flip-flop circuits, ferrite cores used in memories, and positions punched with a hole or not punched in a card.

Registers

A *register* is a group of binary cells. Since a cell stores one bit of information, it follows that a register with n cells can store any discrete quantity of information that contains n bits. The *state* of a register is an n-tuple number of 1's and 0's, with each bit designating the state of one cell in the register. The *content* of a register is a function of the interpretation given to the information stored in it. Consider, for example, the following 16-cell register:

1	1	0	0	0	0	1	1	1	1	0	0	1	0	0	1
1	2	3	4	5	6	7	8	9	10	11	12	13	14	15	16

Physically, one may think of the register as composed of 16 binary cells, with each cell storing either a 1 or a 0. Suppose that the bit configuration stored in the register is as shown. The state of the register is the 16-tuple number 1100001111001001. Clearly, a register with n cells can be in one of 2^n possible states. Now, if one assumes that the content of the register represents a binary integer, then obviously the register can store any binary number from 0 to $2^{16} - 1$. For the particular example shown, the content of the register is the binary equivalent of the decimal number 50121. If it is assumed that the register stores alphanumeric characters of an eight-bit code, the content of the register is any two meaningful characters (unassigned bit combinations do not represent meaningful information). In the EBCDIC code, the above example represents the two characters C (left eight bits) and I (right eight bits). On the other hand, if one interprets the content of the register to be four decimal digits represented by a four-bit code, the content of the register is a four-digit decimal number. In the excess-3 code, the above example is the decimal number 9096. The content of the register is meaningless in BCD since the bit combination 1100 is not assigned to any decimal digit. From this example, it is clear that a register can store one or more discrete elements of information and that the same bit configuration may be interpreted differently for different types of elements of information. It is important that the user store meaningful information in registers and that the computer be programmed to process this information according to the *type* of information stored.

Register Transfer

A digital computer is characterized by its registers. The memory unit (Fig. 1-1) is merely a collection of thousands of registers for storing digital information. The processor unit is composed of various registers that store operands upon which operations are performed. The control unit uses registers to keep track of various computer sequences, and every input or output device must have at least one register to store the information transferred to or from the device. An *inter-register transfer* operation, a basic operation in digital systems, consists of a transfer of the information stored in one register into another. Figure 1-2 illustrates the transfer of information among registers and demonstrates pictorially the transfer of binary information from a teletype keyboard into a register in the memory unit. The input teletype unit is assumed to have a keyboard, a control circuit, and an input register. Each time a key is struck, the control enters into the input register an equivalent eight-bit alphanumeric character code. We shall assume that the code used is the ASCII code with an odd-parity eighth bit. The information from the input register

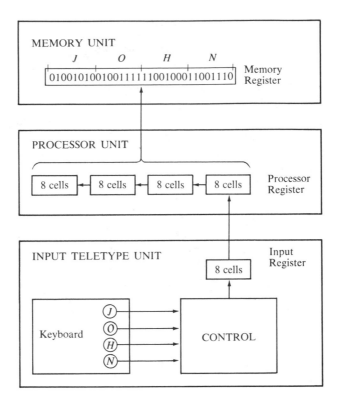

MEMORY UNIT

J   O   H   N

| 01001010 01001111 11001000 11001110 | Memory Register

PROCESSOR UNIT

| 8 cells | ← | 8 cells | ← | 8 cells | ← | 8 cells | Processor Register

INPUT TELETYPE UNIT   Input Register

| 8 cells |

Keyboard   Ⓙ Ⓞ Ⓗ Ⓝ   CONTROL

Figure 1-2 Transfer of information with registers

is transferred into the eight least significant cells of a processor register. After every transfer, the input register is cleared to enable the control to insert a new eight-bit code when the keyboard is struck again. Each eight-bit character transferred to the processor register is preceded by a shift of the previous character to the next eight cells on its left. When a transfer of four characters is completed, the processor register is full, and its contents are transferred into a memory register. The content stored in the memory register shown in Fig. 1-2 came from the transfer of the characters JOHN after the four appropirate keys were struck.

To process discrete quantities of information in binary form, a computer must be provided with (1) devices that hold the data to be processed and (2) circuit elements that manipulate individual bits of information. The device most commonly used for holding data is a register. Manipulation of binary variables is done by means of digital logic circuits. Figure 1-3 illustrates the process of adding two 10-bit binary numbers. The memory unit, which normally consists of thousands of registers, is shown in the diagram with only three of its registers. The part of the processor unit shown consists of three registers, R1, R2, and R3, together with digital logic circuits that manipulate the bits of R1 and R2 and transfer into R3 a binary number equal to their arithmetic sum. Memory registers store information and are incapable of processing the two operands. However, the information stored in memory can be transferred to processor registers. Results obtained in

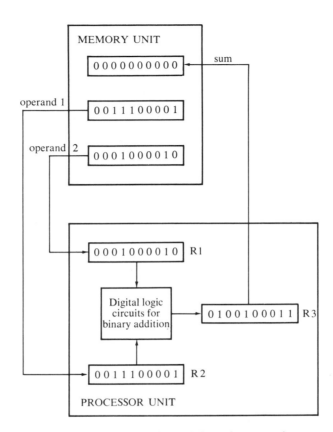

Figure 1-3 Example of binary information processing

processor registers can be transferred back into a memory register for storage until needed again. The diagram shows the contents of two operands transferred from two memory registers into R1 and R2. The digital logic circuits produce the sum, which is transferred to register R3. The contents of R3 can now be transferred back to one of the memory registers.

The last two examples demonstrated the information flow capabilities of a digital system in a very simple manner. The registers of the system are the basic elements for storing and holding the binary information. The digital logic circuits process the information. Digital logic circuits and their manipulative capabilities are introduced in the next section. Registers and memory are presented in Chapter 7.

1-8 BINARY LOGIC

Binary logic deals with variables that take on two discrete values and with operations that assume logical meaning. The two values the variables take may be called by different names (e.g., *true* and *false, yes* and *no*, etc.), but for our purpose it is convenient to think in terms of bits and assign the values of 1 and 0. Binary logic is used to describe, in a mathematical way, the manipulation and processing of binary information. It is particularly suited for the analysis and design of digital systems. For example, the digital logic circuits of Fig. 1-3 that perform the binary arithmetic are circuits whose behavior is most conveniently expressed by means of binary variables and logical operations. The binary logic to be introduced in this section is equivalent to an algebra called Boolean algebra. The formal presentation of a two-valued Boolean algebra is covered in more detail in Chapter 2. The purpose of this section is to introduce Boolean algebra in a heuristic manner and relate it to digital logic circuits and binary signals.

Definition of Binary Logic

Binary logic consists of binary variables and logical operations. The variables are designated by letters of the alphabet such as A, B, C, x, y, z, etc., with each variable having two and only two distinct possible values: 1 and 0. There are three basic logical operations: AND, OR, and NOT.

1. AND: This operation is represented by a dot or by the absence of an operator. For example, $x \cdot y = z$ or $xy = z$ is read "x AND y is equal to z." The logical operation AND is interpreted to mean that $z = 1$ if and only if $x = 1$ *and* $y = 1$; otherwise $z = 0$. (Remember that x, y, and z are binary variables and can be equal either to 1 or 0, and nothing else.)

2. OR: This operation is represented by a plus sign. For example, $x + y = z$ is read "x OR y is equal to z," meaning that $z = 1$ if $x = 1$ *or* if $y = 1$ *or* if both $x = 1$ and $y = 1$. If both $x = 0$ and $y = 0$, then $z = 0$.

3. NOT: This operation is represented by a prime (sometimes by a bar). For example, $x' = z$ (or $\bar{x} = z$) is read "x not is equal to z," meaning that z is what x is not. In other words, if $x = 1$, then $z = 0$; but if $x = 0$, then $z = 1$.

Binary logic resembles binary arithmetic, and the operations AND and OR have some similarities to multiplication and addition, respectively. In fact, the symbols used for AND and OR are the same as those used for multiplication and addition. However, binary logic should not be confused with binary arithmetic. One should realize that an arithmetic variable designates a number that may consist of many digits. A logic variable is always either a 1 or a 0. For example, in binary arithmetic we have $1 + 1 = 10$ (read: "one plus one is equal to 2"), while in binary logic we have $1 + 1 = 1$ (read: "one OR one is equal to one").

For each combination of the values of x and y, there is a value of z specified by the definition of the logical operation. These definitions may be listed in a compact form using *truth tables*. A truth table is a table of all possible combinations of the variables showing the relation between the values that the variables may take and the result of the operation. For example, the truth tables for the

TABLE 1-6 Truth tables of logical operations

AND		OR		NOT	
x y	$x \cdot y$	x y	$x + y$	x	x'
0 0	0	0 0	0	0	1
0 1	0	0 1	1	1	0
1 0	0	1 0	1		
1 1	1	1 1	1		

operations AND and OR with variables x and y are obtained by listing all possible values that the variables may have when combined in pairs. The result of the operation for each combination is then listed in a separate row. The truth tables for AND, OR, and NOT are listed in Table 1-6. These tables clearly demonstrate the definitions of the operations.

Switching Circuits and Binary Signals

The use of binary variables and the application of binary logic are demonstrated by the simple switching circuits of Fig. 1-4. Let the manual switches A and B represent two binary variables with values equal to 0 when the switch is open and 1 when the switch is closed. Similarly, let the lamp L represent a third binary variable equal to 1 when the light is on and 0 when off. For the switches in series, the light turns on if A *and* B are closed. For the switches in parallel, the light turns on if A *or* B is closed. It is obvious that the two circuits can be expressed by means of binary logic with the AND and OR operations, respectively:

$$L = A \cdot B \qquad \text{for the circuit of Fig. 1-4(a)}$$
$$L = A + B \qquad \text{for the circuit of Fig. 1-4(b)}$$

Electronic digital circuits are sometimes called *switching circuits* because they behave like a switch, with the active element such as a transistor either conducting (switch closed) or not conducting (switch open). Instead of changing the switch manually, an electronic switching circuit uses binary signals to control the conduction or nonconduction state of the active element. Electrical signals such as

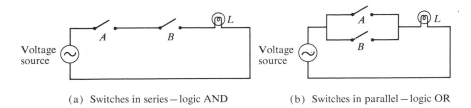

(a) Switches in series — logic AND   (b) Switches in parallel — logic OR

Figure 1-4 Switching circuits that demonstrate binary logic

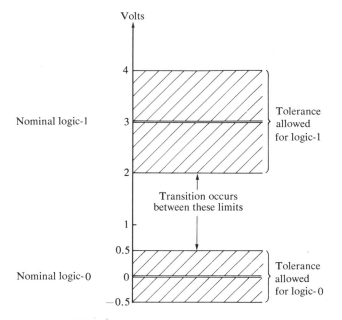

Volts

Nominal logic-1 3

Tolerance
allowed
for logic-1

Transition occurs
between these limits

Nominal logic-0 0

Tolerance
allowed
for logic-0

Figure 1-5 Example of binary signals

voltages or currents exist throughout a digital system in either one of two recogniz-
able values (except during transition). Voltage-operated circuits, for example,
respond to two separate voltage levels which represent a binary variable equal to
logic-1 or logic-0. For example, a particular digital system may define logic-1 as a
signal with a nominal value of 3 volts, and logic-0 as a signal with a nominal value
of 0 volt. As shown in Fig. 1-5, each voltage level has an acceptable deviation from
the nominal. The intermediate region between the allowed regions is crossed only
during state transitions. The input terminals of digital circuits accept binary signals
within the allowable tolerances and respond at the output terminal with binary
signals that fall within the specified tolerances.

 Logic Gates

Electronic digital circuits are also called *logic circuits* because, with the proper
input, they establish logical manipulation paths. Any desired information for
computing or control can be operated upon by passing binary signals through
various combinations of logic circuits, each signal representing a variable and
carrying one bit of information. Logic circuits that perform the logical operations
of AND, OR, and NOT are shown with their symbols in Fig. 1-6. These circuits,
called *gates*, are blocks of hardware that produce a logic-1 or logic-0 output signal
if input logic requirements are satisfied. Note that four different names have been
used for the same type of circuits: digital circuits, switching circuits, logic circuits,
and gates. All four names are widely used, but we shall refer to the circuits as

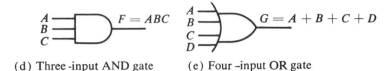

(a) Two-input AND gate   (b) Two-input OR gate   (c) NOT gate or inverter

(d) Three-input AND gate   (e) Four-input OR gate

Figure 1-6 Symbols for digital logic circuits

AND, OR, and NOT gates. The NOT gate is sometimes called an *inverter circuit* since it inverts a binary signal.

The input signals x and y in the two-input gates of Fig. 1-6 may exist in one of four possible states: 00, 10, 11, or 01. These input signals are shown in Fig. 1-7, together with the output signals for the AND and OR gates. The timing diagrams in Fig. 1-7 illustrate the response of each circuit to each of the four possible input binary combinations. The reason for the name "inverter" for the NOT gate is apparent from a comparison of the signal x (input of inverter) and that of x' (output of inverter).

AND and OR gates may have more than two inputs. An AND gate with three inputs and an OR gate with four inputs are shown in Fig. 1-6. The three-input AND gate responds with a logic-1 output if all three input signals are logic-1. The output produces a logic-0 signal if any input is logic 0. The four input OR gate responds with a logic-1 when any input is a logic-1. Its output becomes logic-0 if all input signals are logic-0.

The mathematical system of binary logic is better known as Boolean, or switching, algebra. This algebra is conveniently used to describe the operation of complex networks of digital circuits. Designers of digital systems use Boolean algebra to transform circuit diagrams to algebraic expressions and vice versa. Chapters 2 and 3 are devoted to the study of Boolean algebra, its properties, and manipulative capabilities. Chapter 4 shows how Boolean algebra may be used to express mathematically the interconnections among networks of gates.

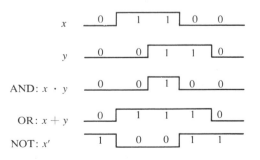

Figure 1-7 Input-output signals for gates (a), (b), and (c) of Fig. 1-6

1-9 INTEGRATED CIRCUITS

Digital circuits are invariably constructed with integrated circuits. An integrated circuit (abbreviated IC) is a small silicon semiconductor crystal, called a *chip*, containing electrical components such as transistors, diodes, resistors, and capacitors. The various components are interconnected inside the chip to form an electronic circuit. The chip is mounted on a metal or plastic package, and connections are welded to external pins to form the IC. Integrated circuits differ from other electronic circuits composed of detachable components in that individual components in the IC cannot be separated or disconnected and the circuit inside the package is accessible only through the external pins.

Integrated circuits come in two types of packages, the *flat* package and the *dual-in-line* (DIP) package, as shown in Fig. 1-8. The dual-in-line package is the most widely used type because of the low price and easy installation on circuit boards. The envelope of the IC package is made of plastic or ceramic. Most packages have standard sizes, and the number of pins ranges from 8 to 64. Each IC has a numeric designation printed on the surface of the package for identification. Each vendor publishes a data book or catalog that provides the necessary information concerning the various products.

The size of IC packages is very small. For example, four AND gates are enclosed inside a 14-pin dual-in-line package with dimensions of $20 \times 8 \times 3$ millimeters. An entire microprocessor is enclosed within a 40-pin dual-in-line package with dimensions of $50 \times 15 \times 4$ millimeters.

Besides a substantial reduction in size, ICs offer other advantages and benefits compared to electronic circuits with discrete components. The cost of ICs is very low, which makes them economical to use. Their reduced power consumption makes the digital system more economical to operate. They have a high reliability against failure, so the digital system needs less repairs. The operating speed is higher, which makes them suitable for high-speed operations. The use of ICs reduces the number of external wiring connections because many of the connections are internal to the package. Because of all these advantages, digital systems are always constructed with integrated circuits.

Integrated circuits are classified in two general categories, *linear* and *digital*. Linear ICs operate with continuous signals to provide electronic functions such as

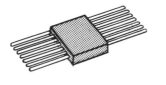

Flat package

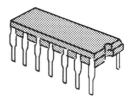

Dual-in-line package

Figure 1-8   Integrated-circuit packages

amplifiers and voltage comparators. Digital integrated circuits operate with binary signals and are made up of interconnected digital gates. Here we are concerned only with digital integrated circuits.

As the technology of ICs has improved, the number of gates that can be put on a single silicon chip has increased considerably. The differentiation between those ICs that have a few internal gates and those having tens or hundreds of gates is made by a customary reference to a package as being either a small-, medium-, or large-scale integration device. Several logic gates in a single package make it a small-scale integration (SSI) device. To qualify as a medium-scale integration (MSI) device, the IC must perform a complete logic function and have a complexity of 10 to 100 gates. A large-scale integration (LSI) device performs a logic function with more than 100 gates. There are also very-large-scale integration (VLSI) devices that contain thousands of gates in a single chip.

Many diagrams of digital circuits considered throughout this book are shown in detail up to the individual gates and their interconnections. Such diagrams are useful for demonstrating the logical construction of a particular function. However, it must be realized that, in practice, the function may be obtained from an MSI or LSI device, and the user has access only to external inputs and outputs but not to inputs and outputs of intermediate gates. For example, a designer who wants to incorporate a register in his system is more likely to choose such a function from an available MSI circuit instead of designing it with individual digital circuits as may be shown in a diagram.

REFERENCES

1. Richard, R. K., *Arithmetic Operations in Digital Computers*. New York: Van Nostrand Co., 1955.

2. Flores, I., *The Logic of Computer Arithmetic*. Englewood Cliffs, N. J.: Prentice-Hall, Inc., 1963.

3. Chu, Y., *Digital Computer Design Fundamentals*. New York: McGraw-Hill Book Co., 1962, Chaps. 1 and 2.

4. Kostopoulos, G. K., *Digital Engineering*. New York: John Wiley & Sons, Inc., 1975, Chap. 1.

5. Rhyne, V. T., *Fundamentals of Digital Systems Design*. Englewood Cliffs, N. J.: Prentice-Hall, Inc., 1973, Chap. 1.

PROBLEMS

1-1.   Write the first 20 decimal digits in base 3.

1-2.   Add and multiply the following numbers in the given base without converting to decimal.

(a) $(1230)_4$ and $(23)_4$

(b) $(135.4)_6$ and $(43.2)_6$

(c) $(367)_8$ and $(715)_8$

(d) $(296)_{12}$ and $(57)_{12}$

1-3. Convert the decimal number 250.5 to base 3, base 4, base 7, base 8, and base 16.

1-4. Convert the following decimal numbers to binary: 12.0625, 10^4, 673.23, and 1998.

1-5. Convert the following binary numbers to decimal: 10.10001, 101110.0101, 1110101.110, 1101101.111.

1-6. Convert the following numbers from the given base to the bases indicated:

(a) decimal 225.225 to binary, octal, and hexadecimal

(b) binary 11010111.110 to decimal, octal, and hexadecimal

(c) octal 623.77 to decimal, binary, and hexadecimal

(d) hexadecimal 2AC5.D to decimal, octal, and binary

1-7. Convert the following numbers to decimal:

(a) $(1001001.011)_2$ (e) $(0.342)_6$

(b) $(12121)_3$ (f) $(50)_7$

(c) $(1032.2)_4$ (g) $(8.3)_9$

(d) $(4310)_5$ (h) $(198)_{12}$

1-8. Obtain the 1's and 2's complement of the following binary numbers: 1010101, 0111000, 0000001, 10000, 00000.

1-9. Obtain the 9's and 10's complement of the following decimal numbers: 13579, 09900, 90090, 10000, 00000.

1-10. Find the 10's complement of $(935)_{11}$.

1-11. Perform the subtraction with the following decimal numbers using (1) 10's complement and (2) 9's complement. Check the answer by straight subtraction.

(a) $5250 - 321$ (c) $753 - 864$

(b) $3570 - 2100$ (d) $20 - 1000$

1-12. Perform the subtraction with the following binary numbers using (1) 2's complement and (2) 1's complement. Check the answer by straight subtraction.

(a) $11010 - 1101$ (c) $10010 - 10011$

(b) $11010 - 10000$ (d) $100 - 110000$

1-13. Prove the procedure stated in Sec. 1-5 for the subtraction of two numbers with $(r - 1)$'s complement.

1-14. For the weighted codes (a) 3, 3, 2, 1 and (b) 4, 4, 3, -2 for the decimal digits, determine all possible tables so that the 9's complement of each decimal digit is obtained by changing 1's to 0's and 0's to 1's.

1-15. Represent the decimal number 8620 (a) in BCD, (b) in excess-3 code, (c) in 2, 4, 2, 1 code, and (d) as a binary number.

1-16. A binary code uses ten bits to represent each of the ten decimal digits. Each digit is assigned a code of nine 0's and a 1. The code for digit 6, for example, is 0001000000. Determine the binary code for the remaining decimal digits.

1-17. Obtain the weighted binary code for the base-12 digits using weights of 5421.

1-18. Determine the odd-parity bit generated when the message consists of the ten decimal digits in the 8, 4, $-$ 2, $-$ 1 code.

1-19. Determine two other combinations for a reflected code other than the one shown in Table 1-4.

1-20. Obtain a binary code to represent all base-6 digits so that the 5's complement is obtained by replacing 1's by 0's and 0's by 1's in the bits of the code.

1-21. Assign a binary code in some orderly manner to the 52 playing cards. Use the minimum number of bits.

1-22. Write your first name, middle initial, and last name in an eight-bit code made up of the seven ASCII bits of Table 1-5 and an even parity bit in the most significant position. Include blanks between names and a period after the middle initial.

1-23. Show the bit configuration of a 24-cell register when its content represents (a) the number $(295)_{10}$ in binary, (b) the decimal number 295 in BCD, and (c) the characters XY5 in EBCDIC.

1-24. The state of a 12-cell register is 010110010111. What is its content if it represents (a) three decimal digits in BCD, (b) three decimal digits in excess-3 code, (c) three decimal digits in 2, 4, 2, 1 code, and (d) two characters in the internal code of Table 1-5?

1-25. Show the contents of all registers in Fig. 1-3 if the two binary numbers added have the decimal equivalent of 257 and 1050. (Assume registers with 11 cells.)

1-26. Express the following switching circuit in binary logic notation.

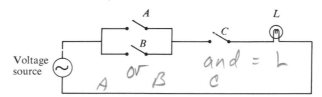

1-27. Show the signals (by means of a diagram similar to Fig. 1-7) of the outputs F and G in Fig. 1-6. Use arbitrary binary signals for the inputs A, B, C, and D.

Boolean Algebra and Logic Gates

2

2-1 BASIC DEFINITIONS

Boolean algebra, like any other deductive mathematical system, may be defined with a set of elements, a set of operators, and a number of unproved axioms or postulates. A *set* of elements is any collection of objects having a common property. If S is a set, and x and y are certain objects, then $x \in S$ denotes that x is a member of the set S, and $y \notin S$ denotes that y is not an element of S. A set with a denumerable number of elements is specified by braces: $A = \{1, 2, 3, 4\}$, i.e., the elements of set A are the numbers 1, 2, 3, and 4. A *binary operator* defined on a set S of elements is a rule that assigns to each pair of elements from S a unique element from S. As an example, consider the relation $a*b = c$. We say that $*$ is a binary operator if it specifies a rule for finding c from the pair (a, b) and also if a, b, $c \in S$. However, $*$ is not a binary operator if a, $b \in S$, while the rule finds $c \notin S$.

The postulates of a mathematical system form the basic assumptions from which it is possible to deduce the rules, theorems, and properties of the system. The most common postulates used to formulate various algebraic structures are:

1. *Closure*. A set S is closed with respect to a binary operator if, for every pair of elements of S, the binary operator specifies a rule for obtaining a unique element of S. For example, the set of natural numbers $N = \{1, 2, 3, 4, \ldots\}$ is closed with respect to the binary operator plus $(+)$ by the rules of arithmetic addition, since for any a, $b \in N$ we obtain a unique $c \in N$ by the operation $a + b = c$. The set of natural numbers is not closed with respect to the binary operator minus $(-)$ by the rules of arithmetic subtraction because $2 - 3 = -1$ and $2, 3 \in N$, while $(-1) \notin N$.

2. *Associative law*. A binary operator $*$ on a set S is said to be associative whenever:

$$(x*y)*z = x*(y*z) \qquad \text{for all } x, y, z \in S$$

3. *Commutative law*. A binary operator * on a set S is said to be commutative whenever:

$$x*y = y*x \qquad \text{for all } x, y \in S$$

4. *Identity element*. A set S is said to have an identity element with respect to a binary operation * on S if there exists an element $e \in S$ with the property:

$$e*x = x*e = x \qquad \text{for every } x \in S$$

Example: The element 0 is an identity element with respect to operation + on the set of integers I = { ...,$-3, -2, -1, 0, 1, 2, 3, ...$ } since:

$$x + 0 = 0 + x = x \qquad \text{for any } x \in I$$

The set of natural numbers N has no identity element since 0 is excluded from the set.

5. *Inverse*. A set S having the identity element e with respect to a binary operator * is said to have an inverse whenever, for every $x \in S$, there exists an element $y \in S$ such that:

$$x*y = e$$

Example: In the set of integers I with $e = 0$, the inverse of an element a is $(-a)$ since $a + (-a) = 0$.

6. *Distributive law*. If * and · are two binary operators on a set S, * is said to be distributive over · whenever:

$$x*(y \cdot z) = (x*y) \cdot (x*z)$$

An example of an algebraic structure is a *field*. A field is a set of elements, together with two binary operators, each having properties 1 to 5 and both operators combined to give property 6. The set of real numbers together with the binary operators + and · form the field of real numbers. The field of real numbers is the basis for arithmetic and ordinary algebra. The operators and postulates have the following meanings:

The binary operator + defines addition.

The additive identity is 0.

The additive inverse defines subtraction.

The binary operator · defines multiplication.

The multiplicative identity is 1.

The multiplicative inverse of $a = 1/a$ defines division, i.e., $a \cdot 1/a = 1$.

The only distributive law applicable is that of $\cdot$ over $+$:

$$a \cdot (b + c) = (a \cdot b) + (a \cdot c)$$

2-2 AXIOMATIC DEFINITION OF BOOLEAN ALGEBRA

In 1854 George Boole (1) introduced a systematic treatment of logic and developed for this purpose an algebraic system now called *Boolean algebra*. In 1938 C. E. Shannon (2) introduced a two-valued Boolean algebra called *switching algebra*, in which he demonstrated that the properties of bistable electrical switching circuits can be represented by this algebra. For the formal definition of Boolean algebra, we shall employ the postulates formulated by E. V. Huntington (3) in 1904. These postulates or axioms are not unique for defining Boolean algebra. Other sets of postulates have been used.* Boolean algebra is an algebraic structure defined on a set of elements B together with two binary operators $+$ and $\cdot$ provided the following (Huntington) postulates are satisfied:

1. (a) Closure with respect to the operator $+$.
   (b) Closure with respect to the operator $\cdot$.

2. (a) An identity element with respect to $+$, designated by 0: $x + 0 = 0 + x = x$.
   (b) An identity element with respect to $\cdot$, designated by 1: $x \cdot 1 = 1 \cdot x = x$.

3. (a) Commutative with respect to $+$: $x + y = y + x$.
   (b) Commutative with respect to $\cdot$: $x \cdot y = y \cdot x$.

4. (a) $\cdot$ is distributive over $+$: $x \cdot (y + z) = (x \cdot y) + (x \cdot z)$.
   (b) $+$ is distributive over $\cdot$: $x + (y \cdot z) = (x + y) \cdot (x + z)$.

5. For every element $x \in B$, there exists an element $x' \in B$ (called the complement of x) such that: (a) $x + x' = 1$ and (b) $x \cdot x' = 0$.

6. There exists at least two elements $x, y \in B$ such that $x \neq y$.

Comparing Boolean algebra with arithmetic and ordinary algebra (the field of real numbers), we note the following differences:

1. Huntington postulates do not include the associative law. However, this law holds for Boolean algebra and can be derived (for both operators) from the other postulates.

*See, for example, Birkoff and Bartee (4), Chapter 5.

2. The distributive law of $+$ over $\cdot$, i.e., $x + (y \cdot z) = (x + y) \cdot (x + z)$, is valid for Boolean algebra, but not for ordinary algebra.

3. Boolean algebra does not have additive or multiplicative inverses; therefore, there are no subtraction or division operations.

4. Postulate 5 defines an operator called *complement* which is not available in ordinary algebra.

5. Ordinary algebra deals with the real numbers, which constitute an infinite set of elements. Boolean algebra deals with the as yet undefined set of elements B, but in the two-valued Boolean algebra defined below (and of interest in our subsequent use of this algebra), B is defined as a set with only two elements, 0 and 1.

Boolean algebra resembles ordinary algebra in some respects. The choice of symbols $+$ and $\cdot$ is intentional to facilitate Boolean algebraic manipulations by persons already familiar with ordinary algebra. Although one can use some knowledge from ordinary algebra to deal with Boolean algebra, the beginner must be careful not to substitute the rules of ordinary algebra where they are not applicable.

It is important to distinguish between the elements of the set of an algebraic structure and the variables of an algebraic system. For example, the elements of the field of real numbers are numbers, whereas variables such as a, b, c, etc., used in ordinary algebra, are symbols that stand for real numbers. Similarly in Boolean algebra, one defines the elements of the set B, and variables such as x, y, z are merely symbols that represent the elements. At this point, it is important to realize that in order to have a Boolean algebra, one must show:

1. the elements of the set B,

2. the rules of operation for the two binary operators, and

3. that the set of elements B, together with the two operators, satisfies the six Huntington postulates.

One can formulate many Boolean algebras, depending on the choice of elements of B and the rules of operation.* In our subsequent work, we deal only with a two-valued Boolean algebra, i.e., one with only two elements. Two-valued Boolean algebra has applications in set theory (the algebra of classes) and in propositional logic. Our interest here is with the application of Boolean algebra to gate-type circuits.

Two-Valued Boolean Algebra

A two-valued Boolean algebra is defined on a set of two elements, $B = \{0, 1\}$, with rules for the two binary operators $+$ and $\cdot$ as shown in the following operator tables (the rule for the complement operator is for verification of postulate 5):

*See, for example, Hohn (6), Whitesitt (7), or Birkhoff and Bartee (4).

x y	$x \cdot y$
0 0	0
0 1	0
1 0	0
1 1	1

x y	$x + y$
0 0	0
0 1	1
1 0	1
1 1	1

x	x'
0	1
1	0

These rules are exactly the same as the AND, OR, and NOT operations, respectively, defined in Table 1-6. We must now show that the Huntington postulates are valid for the set $B = \{0, 1\}$ and the two binary operators defined above.

1. *Closure* is obvious from the tables since the result of each operation is either 1 or 0 and 1, $0 \in B$.

2. From the tables we see that:

    (a) $0 + 0 = 0$ $0 + 1 = 1 + 0 = 1$
    (b) $1 \cdot 1 = 1$ $1 \cdot 0 = 0 \cdot 1 = 0$

    which establishes the two *identity elements* 0 for + and 1 for · as defined by postulate 2.

3. The *commutative* laws are obvious from the symmetry of the binary operator tables.

4. (a) The *distributive* law $x \cdot (y + z) = (x \cdot y) + (x \cdot z)$ can be shown to hold true from the operator tables by forming a truth table of all possible values of x, y, and z. For each combination, we derive $x \cdot (y + z)$ and show that the value is the same as $(x \cdot y) + (x \cdot z)$.

x y z	$y + z$	$x \cdot (y + z)$	$x \cdot y$	$x \cdot z$	$(x \cdot y) + (x \cdot z)$
0 0 0	0	0	0	0	0
0 0 1	1	0	0	0	0
0 1 0	1	0	0	0	0
0 1 1	1	0	0	0	0
1 0 0	0	0	0	0	0
1 0 1	1	1	0	1	1
1 1 0	1	1	1	0	1
1 1 1	1	1	1	1	1

    (b) The *distributive* law of + over · can be shown to hold true by means of a truth table similar to the one above.

5. From the complement table it is easily shown that:

    (a) $x + x' = 1$, since $0 + 0' = 0 + 1 = 1$ and $1 + 1' = 1 + 0 = 1$
    (b) $x \cdot x' = 0$, since $0 \cdot 0' = 0 \cdot 1 = 0$ and $1 \cdot 1' = 1 \cdot 0 = 0$ which verifies postulate 5.

6. Postulate 6 is satisfied because the two-valued Boolean algebra has two distinct elements 1 and 0 with $1 \neq 0$.

We have just established a two-valued Boolean algebra having a set of two elements, 1 and 0, two binary operators with operation rules equivalent to the AND and OR operations, and a complement operator equivalent to the NOT operator. Thus, Boolean algebra has been defined in a formal mathematical manner and has been shown to be equivalent to the binary logic presented heuristically in Section 1-8. The heuristic presentation is helpful in understanding the application of Boolean algebra to gate-type circuits. The formal presentation is necessary for developing the theorems and properties of the algebraic system. The two-valued Boolean algebra defined in this section is also called "switching algebra" by engineers. To emphasize the similarities between two-valued Boolean algebra and other binary systems, this algebra was called "binary logic" in Section 1-8. From here on, we shall drop the adjective "two-valued" from Boolean algebra in subsequent discussions.

2-3   BASIC THEOREMS AND PROPERTIES OF BOOLEAN ALGEBRA

Duality

The Huntington postulates have been listed in pairs and designated by part (a) and part (b). One part may be obtained from the other if the binary operators and the identity elements are interchanged. This important property of Boolean algebra is called the *duality principle*. It states that every algebraic expression deducible from the postulates of Boolean algebra remains valid if the operators and identity elements are interchanged. In a two-valued Boolean algebra, the identity elements and the elements of the set B are the same: 1 and 0. The duality principle has many applications. If the *dual* of an algebraic expression is desired, we simply interchange OR and AND operators and replace 1's by 0's and 0's by 1's.

Basic Theorems

Table 2-1 lists six theorems of Boolean algebra and four of its postulates. The notation is simplified by omitting the · whenever this does not lead to confusion. The theorems and postulates listed are the most basic relationships in Boolean algebra. The reader is advised to become familiar with them as soon as possible. The theorems, like the postulates, are listed in pairs; each relation is the dual of the one paired with it. The postulates are basic axioms of the algebraic structure and need no proof. The theorems must be proven from the postulates. The proofs of the theorems with one variable are presented below. At the right is listed the number of the postulate which justifies each step of the proof.

TABLE 2-1 Postulates and theorems of Boolean algebra

Postulate 2	(a) $x + 0 = x$	(b) $x \cdot 1 = x$
Postulate 5	(a) $x + x' = 1$	(b) $x \cdot x' = 0$
Theorem 1	(a) $x + x = x$	(b) $x \cdot x = x$
Theorem 2	(a) $x + 1 = 1$	(b) $x \cdot 0 = 0$
Theorem 3, involution	$(x')' = x$	
Postulate 3, commutative	(a) $x + y = y + x$	(b) $xy = yx$
Theorem 4, associative	(a) $x + (y + z) = (x + y) + z$	(b) $x(yz) = (xy)z$
Postulate 4, distributive	(a) $x(y + z) = xy + xz$	(b) $x + yz = (x + y)(x + z)$
Theorem 5, DeMorgan	(a) $(x + y)' = x'y'$	(b) $(xy)' = x' + y'$
Theorem 6, absorption	(a) $x + xy = x$	(b) $x(x + y) = x$

THEOREM 1(a): $x + x = x$.

$$
\begin{aligned}
x + x &= (x + x) \cdot 1 && \text{by postulate: 2(b)} \\
&= (x + x)(x + x') && \text{5(a)} \\
&= x + xx' && \text{4(b)} \\
&= x + 0 && \text{5(b)} \\
&= x && \text{2(a)}
\end{aligned}
$$

THEOREM 1(b): $x \cdot x = x$.

$$
\begin{aligned}
x \cdot x &= xx + 0 && \text{by postulate: 2(a)} \\
&= xx + xx' && \text{5(b)} \\
&= x(x + x') && \text{4(a)} \\
&= x \cdot 1 && \text{5(a)} \\
&= x && \text{2(b)}
\end{aligned}
$$

Note that theorem 1(b) is the dual of theorem 1(a) and that each step of the proof in part (b) is the dual of part (a). Any dual theorem can be similarly derived from the proof of its corresponding pair.

THEOREM 2(a): $x + 1 = 1$.

$$
\begin{aligned}
x + 1 &= 1 \cdot (x + 1) && \text{by postulate: 2(b)} \\
&= (x + x')(x + 1) && \text{5(a)} \\
&= x + x' \cdot 1 && \text{4(b)} \\
&= x + x' && \text{2(b)} \\
&= 1 && \text{5(a)}
\end{aligned}
$$

THEOREM 2(b): $x \cdot 0 = 0$ by duality.

THEOREM 3: $(x')' = x$. From postulate 5, we have $x + x' = 1$ and $x \cdot x' = 0$, which defines the complement of x. The complement of x' is x and is also $(x')'$. Therefore, since the complement is unique, we have that $(x')' = x$.

The theorems involving two or three variables may be proven algebraically from the postulates and the theorems which have already been proven. Take, for example, the absorption theorem.

THEOREM 6(a): $x + xy = x$.

$$
\begin{aligned}
x + xy &= x \cdot 1 + xy && \text{by postulate 2(b)} \\
&= x(1 + y) && \text{by postulate 4(a)} \\
&= x(y + 1) && \text{by postulate 3(a)} \\
&= x \cdot 1 && \text{by theorem 2(a)} \\
&= x && \text{by postulate 2(b)}
\end{aligned}
$$

THEOREM 6(b): $x(x + y) = x$ by duality.

The theorems of Boolean algebra can be shown to hold true by means of truth tables. In truth tables, both sides of the relation are checked to yield identical results for all possible combinations of variables involved. The following truth table verifies the first absorption theorem.

x	y	xy	$x + xy$
0	0	0	0
0	1	0	0
1	0	0	1
1	1	1	1

The algebraic proofs of the associative law and De Morgan's theorem are long and will not be shown here. However, their validity is easily shown with truth tables. For example, the truth table for the first De Morgan's theorem $(x + y)' = x'y'$ is shown below.

x	y	$x + y$	$(x + y)'$	x'	y'	$x'y'$
0	0	0	1	1	1	1
0	1	1	0	1	0	0
1	0	1	0	0	1	0
1	1	1	0	0	0	0

Operator Precedence

The operator precedence for evaluating Boolean expressions is (1) parentheses, (2) NOT, (3) AND, and (4) OR. In other words, the expression inside the parentheses must be evaluated before all other operations. The next operation that holds precedence is the complement, then follows the AND, and finally the OR. As an example, consider the truth table for De Morgan's theorem. The left side of the expression is $(x + y)'$. Therefore, the expression inside the parentheses is evaluated first and the result then complemented. The right side of the expression is $x'y'$. Therefore, the complement of x and the complement of y are both evaluated first and the result is then ANDed. Note that in ordinary arithmetic the same precedence holds (except for the complement) when multiplication and addition are replaced by AND and OR, respectively.

Venn Diagram

A helpful illustration that may be used to visualize the relationships among the variables of a Boolean expression is the *Venn diagram*. This diagram consists of a rectangle such as shown in Fig. 2-1, inside of which are drawn overlapping circles, one for each variable. Each circle is labeled by a variable. We designate all points inside a circle as belonging to the named variable and all points outside a circle as not belonging to the variable. Take, for example, the circle labeled x. If we are inside the circle, we say that $x = 1$; when outside, we say $x = 0$. Now, with two overlapping circles, there are four distinct areas inside the rectangle: the area not belonging to either x or y ($x'y'$), the area inside circle y but outside x ($x'y$), the area inside circle x but outside y (xy'), and the area inside both circles (xy).

Venn diagrams may be used to illustrate the postulates of Boolean algebra or to show the validity of theorems. Figure 2-2, for example, illustrates that the area belonging to xy is inside the circle x and therefore $x + xy = x$. Figure 2-3 illustrates the distributive law $x(y + z) = xy + xz$. In this diagram we have three overlapping circles, one for each of the variables x, y, and z. It is possible to distinguish eight distinct areas in a three-variable Venn diagram. For this particular example, the distributive law is demonstrated by noting that the area intersecting the circle x with the area enclosing y or z is the same area belonging to xy or xz.

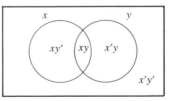

Figure 2-1   Venn diagram for two variables

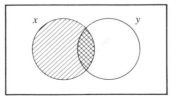

Figure 2-2   Venn diagram illustration $x = xy + x$

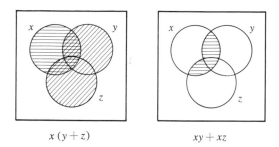

$$x(y+z)$$ $$xy+xz$$

Figure 2-3 Venn diagram illustration of the distributive law

2-4 BOOLEAN FUNCTIONS

A binary variable can take the value of 0 or 1. A Boolean function is an expression formed with binary variables, the two binary operators OR and AND, the unary operator NOT, parentheses, and equal sign. For a given value of the variables, the function can be either 0 or 1. Consider, for example, the Boolean function:

$$F_1 = xyz'$$

The function F_1 is equal to 1 if $x = 1$ *and* $y = 1$ *and* $z' = 1$; otherwise $F_1 = 0$. The above is an example of a Boolean function represented as an algebraic expression. A Boolean function may also be represented in a truth table. To represent a function in a truth table, we need a list of the 2^n combinations of 1's and 0's of the n binary variables, and a column showing the combinations for which the function is equal to 1 or 0. As shown in Table 2-2, there are eight possible distinct combinations for assigning bits to three variables. The column labeled F_1 contains either a 0 or a 1 for each of these combinations. The table shows that the function F_1 is equal to 1 only when $x = 1$, $y = 1$, and $z = 0$. It is equal to 0 otherwise. (Note that the statement $z' = 1$ is equivalent to saying that $z = 0$.) Consider now the function:

$$F_2 = x + y'z$$

$F_2 = 1$ if $x = 1$ or if $y = 0$, while $z = 1$. In Table 2-2, $x = 1$ in the last four rows and $yz = 01$ in rows 001 and 101. The latter combination applies also for $x = 1$. Therefore, there are five combinations that make $F_2 = 1$. As a third example, consider the function:

$$F_3 = x'y'z + x'yz + xy'$$

This is shown in Table 2-2 with four 1's and four 0's. F_4 is the same as F_3 and is considered below.

TABLE 2-2 Truth tables for $F_1 = xyz'$, $F_2 = x + y'z$,
$F_3 = x'y'z + x'yz + xy'$, and $F_4 = xy' + x'z$

x	y	z	F_1	F_2	F_3	F_4
0	0	0	0	0	0	0
0	0	1	0	1	1	1
0	1	0	0	0	0	0
0	1	1	0	0	1	1
1	0	0	0	1	1	1
1	0	1	0	1	1	1
1	1	0	1	1	0	0
1	1	1	0	1	0	0

Any Boolean function can be represented in a truth table. The number of rows in the table is 2^n, where n is the number of binary variables in the function. The 1's and 0's combinations for each row is easily obtained from the binary numbers by counting from 0 to $2^n - 1$. For each row of the table, there is a value for the function equal to either 1 or 0. The question now arises, Is an algebraic expression of a given Boolean function unique? In other words, Is it possible to find two algebraic expressions that specify the same function? The answer to this question is yes. As a matter of fact, the manipulation of Boolean algebra is applied mostly to the problem of finding simpler expressions for the same function. Consider, for example, the function:

$$F_4 = xy' + x'z$$

From Table 2-2, we find that F_4 is the same as F_3, since both have identical 1's and 0's for each combination of values of the three binary variables. In general, two functions of n binary variables are said to be equal if they have the same value for all possible 2^n combinations of the n variables.

A Boolean function may be transformed from an algebraic expression into a logic diagram composed of AND, OR, and NOT gates. The implementation of the four functions introduced in the previous discussion is shown in Fig. 2-4. The logic diagram includes an inverter circuit for every variable present in its complement form. (The inverter is unnecessary if the complement of the variable is available.) There is an AND gate for each term in the expression, and an OR gate is used to combine two or more terms. From the diagrams, it is obvious that the implementation of F_4 requires fewer gates and fewer inputs than F_3. Since F_4 and F_3 are equal Boolean functions, it is more economical to implement the F_4 form than the F_3 form. To find simpler circuits, one must know how to manipulate Boolean functions to obtain equal and simpler expressions. What constitutes the best form of a Boolean function depends on the particular application. In this section, consideration is given to the criterion of equipment minimization.

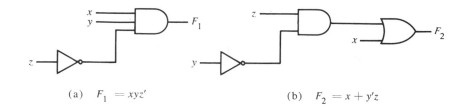

(a) $F_1 = xyz'$ (b) $F_2 = x + y'z$

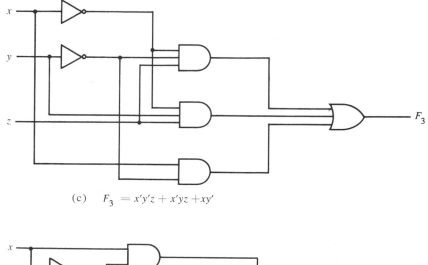

(c) $F_3 = x'y'z + x'yz + xy'$

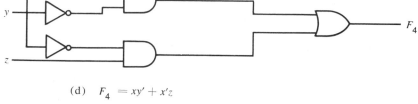
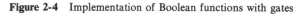

(d) $F_4 = xy' + x'z$

Figure 2-4 Implementation of Boolean functions with gates

Algebraic Manipulation

A *literal* is a primed or unprimed variable. When a Boolean function is implemented with logic gates, each literal in the function designates an input to a gate, and each term is implemented with a gate. The minimization of the number of literals and the number of terms results in a circuit with less equipment. It is not always possible to minimize both simultaneously; usually, further criteria must be available. At the moment, we shall narrow the minimization criterion to literal minimization. We shall discuss other criteria in Chapter 5. The number of literals in a Boolean function can be minimized by algebraic manipulations. Unfortunately, there are no specific rules to follow that will guarantee the final answer. The only method available is a cut-and-try procedure employing the postulates, the basic theorems, and any other manipulation method which becomes familiar with use. The following examples illustrate this procedure.

EXAMPLE 2-1: Simplify the following Boolean functions to a minimum number of literals.

1. $x + x'y = (x + x')(x + y) = 1 \cdot (x + y) = x + y$

2. $x(x' + y) = xx' + xy = 0 + xy = xy$

3. $x'y'z + x'yz + xy' = x'z(y' + y) + xy' = x'z + xy'$

4. $xy + x'z + yz = xy + x'z + yz(x + x')$
$$= xy + x'z + xyz + x'yz$$
$$= xy(1 + z) + x'z(1 + y)$$
$$= xy + x'z$$

5. $(x + y)(x' + z)(y + z) = (x + y)(x' + z)$ by duality from function 4.

Functions 1 and 2 are the duals of each other and use dual expressions in corresponding steps. Function 3 shows the equality of the functions F_3 and F_4 discussed previously. The fourth illustrates the fact that an increase in the number of literals sometimes leads to a final simpler expression. Function 5 is not minimized directly but can be derived from the dual of the steps used to derive function 4.

Complement of a Function

The complement of a function F is F' and is obtained from an interchange of 0's for 1's and 1's for 0's in the value of F. The complement of a function may be derived algebraically through De Morgan's theorem. This pair of theorems is listed in Table 2-1 for two variables. De Morgan's theorems can be extended to three or more variables. The three-variable form of the first De Morgan's theorem is derived below. The postulates and theorems are those listed in Table 2-1.

$$
\begin{aligned}
(A + B + C)' &= (A + X)' & &\text{let } B + C = X \\
&= A'X' & &\text{by theorem 5(a) (De Morgan)} \\
&= A' \cdot (B + C)' & &\text{substitute } B + C = X \\
&= A' \cdot (B'C') & &\text{by theorem 5(a) (De Morgan)} \\
&= A'B'C' & &\text{by theorem 4(b) (associative)}
\end{aligned}
$$

De Morgan's theorems for any number of variables resemble in form the two-variable case and can be derived by successive substitutions similar to the method used in the above derivation. These theorems can be generalized as follows:

$$(A + B + C + D + \cdots + F)' = A'B'C'D' \ldots F'$$
$$(ABCD \cdots F)' = A' + B' + C' + D' + \ldots + F'$$

The generalized form of De Morgan's theorem states that the complement of a function is obtained by interchanging AND and OR operators and complementing each literal.

> *EXAMPLE 2-2:* Find the complement of the functions $F_1 = x'yz' + x'y'z$ and $F_2 = x(y'z' + yz)$. Applying De Morgan's theorem as many times as necessary, the complements are obtained as follows:

$$F_1' = (x'yz' + x'y'z)' = (x'yz')'(x'y'z)' = (x + y' + z)(x + y + z')$$
$$F_2' = [x(y'z' + yz)]' = x' + (y'z' + yz)' = x' + (y'z')' \cdot (yz)'$$
$$= x' + (y + z)(y' + z')$$

A simpler procedure for deriving the complement of a function is to take the dual of the function and complement each literal. This method follows from the generalized De Morgan's theorem. Remember that the dual of a function is obtained from the interchange of AND and OR operators and 1's and 0's.

> *EXAMPLE 2-3:* Find the complement of the functions F_1 and F_2 of Example 2-2 by taking their duals and complementing each literal.

1. $F_1 = x'yz' + x'y'z$.
   The dual of F_1 is $(x' + y + z')(x' + y' + z)$.
   Complement each literal: $(x + y' + z)(x + y + z') = F_1'$.

2. $F_2 = x(y'z' + yz)$.
   The dual of F_2 is $x + (y' + z')(y + z)$.
   Complement each literal: $x' + (y + z)(y' + z') = F_2'$.

2-5 CANONICAL AND STANDARD FORMS

Minterms and Maxterms

A binary variable may appear either in its normal form (x) or in its complement form (x'). Now consider two binary variables x and y combined with an AND operation. Since each variable may appear in either form, there are four possible

$$F = xy'z + x'y'z$$
$$F = m_6 + m_0$$

TABLE 2-3 Minterms and maxterms for three binary variables

			Minterms		Maxterms	
x	y	z	Term	Designation	Term	Designation
0	0	0	$x'y'z'$	m_0	$x + y + z$	M_0
0	0	1	$x'y'z$	m_1	$x + y + z'$	M_1
0	1	0	$x'yz'$	m_2	$x + y' + z$	M_2
0	1	1	$x'yz$	m_3	$x + y' + z'$	M_3
1	0	0	$xy'z'$	m_4	$x' + y + z$	M_4
1	0	1	$xy'z$	m_5	$x' + y + z'$	M_5
1	1	0	xyz'	m_6	$x' + y' + z$	M_6
1	1	1	xyz	m_7	$x' + y' + z'$	M_7

combinations: $x'y'$, $x'y$, xy', and xy. Each of these four AND terms represents one of the distinct areas in the Venn diagram of Fig. 2-1 and is called a *minterm* or a *standard product*. In a similar manner, n variables can be combined to form 2^n minterms. The 2^n different minterms may be determined by a method similar to the one shown in Table 2-3 for three variables. The binary numbers from 0 to $2^n - 1$ are listed under the n variables. Each minterm is obtained from an AND term of the n variables, with each variable being primed if the corresponding bit of the binary number is a 0 and unprimed if a 1. A symbol for each minterm is also shown in the table and is of the form m_j, where j denotes the decimal equivalent of the binary number of the minterm designated.

In a similar fashion, n variables forming an OR term, with each variable being primed or unprimed, provide 2^n possible combinations, called *maxterms* or *standard sums*. The eight maxterms for three variables, together with their symbolic designation, are listed in Table 2-3. Any 2^n maxterms for n variables may be determined similarly. Each maxterm is obtained from an OR term of the n variables, with each variable being unprimed if the corresponding bit is a 0 and primed if a 1.* Note that each maxterm is the complement of its corresponding minterm, and vice versa.

A Boolean function may be expressed algebraically from a given truth table by forming a minterm for each combination of the variables which produces a 1 in the function, and then taking the OR of all those terms. For example, the function f_1 in Table 2-4 is determined by expressing the combinations 001, 100, and 111 as $x'y'z$, $xy'z'$, and xyz, respectively. Since each one of these minterms results in $f_1 = 1$, we should have:

$$f_1 = x'y'z + xy'z' + xyz = m_1 + m_4 + m_7$$

*Some books define a maxterm as an OR term of the n variables, with each variable being unprimed if the bit is a 1 and primed if a 0. The definition adopted in this book is preferable as it leads to simpler conversions between maxterm- and minterm-type functions.

TABLE 2-4 Functions of three variables

x y z	Function f_1	Function f_2
0 0 0	0	0
0 0 1	1	0
0 1 0	0	0
0 1 1	0	1
1 0 0	1	0
1 0 1	0	1
1 1 0	0	1
1 1 1	1	1

Similarly, it may be easily verified that:

$$f_2 = x'yz + xy'z + xyz' + xyz = m_3 + m_5 + m_6 + m_7$$

These examples demonstrate an important property of Boolean algebra: Any Boolean function can be expressed as a sum of minterms (by "sum" is meant the ORing of terms).

Now consider the complement of a Boolean function. It may be read from the truth table by forming a minterm for each combination that produces a 0 in the function and then ORing those terms. The complement of f_1 is read as:

$$f_1' = x'y'z' + x'yz' + x'yz + xy'z + xyz'$$

If we take the complement of f_1', we obtain the function f_1:

$$f_1 = (x + y + z)(x + y' + z)(x + y' + z')(x' + y + z')(x' + y' + z)$$
$$= M_0 \cdot M_2 \cdot M_3 \cdot M_5 \cdot M_6$$

Similarly, it is possible to read the expression for f_2 from the table:

$$f_2 = (x + y + z)(x + y + z')(x + y' + z)(x' + y + z)$$
$$= M_0 M_1 M_2 M_4$$

These examples demonstrate a second important property of Boolean algebra: Any Boolean function can be expressed as a product of maxterms (by "product" is meant the ANDing of terms). The procedure for obtaining the product of maxterms directly from the truth table is as follows. Form a maxterm for each combination of the variables which produces a 0 in the function, and then form the AND of all those maxterms. Boolean functions expressed as a sum of minterms or product of maxterms are said to be in *canonical form*.

Sum of Minterms

It was previously stated that for n binary variables, one can obtain 2^n distinct minterms, and that any Boolean function can be expressed as a sum of minterms. The minterms whose sum defines the Boolean function are those that give the 1's of the function in a truth table. Since the function can be either 1 or 0 for each minterm, and since there are 2^n minterms, one can calculate the possible functions that can be formed with n variables to be 2^{2^n}. It is sometimes convenient to express the Boolean function in its sum-of-minterms form. If not in this form, it can be made so by first expanding the expression into a sum of AND terms. Each term is then inspected to see if it contains all the variables. If it misses one or more variables, it is ANDed with an expression such as $x + x'$, where x is one of the missing variables. The following example clarifies this procedure.

>   **EXAMPLE 2-4:** Express the Boolean function $F = A + B'C$
>   in a sum of minterms. The function has three variables A, B, and C.
>   The first term A is missing two variables; therefore:

$$A = A(B + B') = AB + AB'$$

This is still missing one variable:

$$A = AB(C + C') + AB'(C + C')$$
$$= ABC + ABC' + AB'C + AB'C'$$

The second term $B'C$ is missing one variable:

$$B'C = B'C(A + A') = AB'C + A'B'C$$

Combining all terms, we have:

$$F = A + B'C$$
$$= ABC + ABC' + AB'C + AB'C' + AB'C + A'B'C$$

>   But $AB'C$ appears twice, and according to theorem 1 ($x + x = x$), it
>   is possible to remove one of them. Rearranging the minterms in
>   ascending order, we finally obtain:

$$F = A'B'C + AB'C' + AB'C + ABC' + ABC$$
$$= m_1 + m_4 + m_5 + m_6 + m_7$$

It is sometimes convenient to express the Boolean function, when in its sum of minterms, in the following short notation:

$$F(A, B, C) = \Sigma\,(1, 4, 5, 6, 7)$$

The summation symbol Σ stands for the ORing of terms; the numbers following it are the minterms of the function. The letters in parentheses following F form a list of the variables in the order taken when the minterm is converted to an AND term.

Product of Maxterms

Each of the 2^{2^n} functions of n binary variables can be also expressed as a product of maxterms. To express the Boolean function as a product of maxterms, it must first be brought into a form of OR terms. This may be done by using the distributive law $x + yz = (x + y)(x + z)$. Then any missing variable x in each OR term is ORed with xx'. This procedure is clarified by the following example.

> **EXAMPLE 2-5:** Express the Boolean function $F = xy + x'z$ in a product of maxterm form. First convert the function into OR terms using the distributive law:
>
> $$F = xy + x'z = (xy + x')(xy + z)$$
> $$= (x + x')(y + x')(x + z)(y + z)$$
> $$= (x' + y)(x + z)(y + z)$$
>
> The function has three variables: x, y, and z. Each OR term is missing one variable; therefore:
>
> $$x' + y = x' + y + zz' = (x' + y + z)(x' + y + z')$$
> $$x + z = x + z + yy' = (x + y + z)(x + y' + z)$$
> $$y + z = y + z + xx' = (x + y + z)(x' + y + z)$$
>
> Combining all the terms and removing those that appear more than once, we finally obtain:
>
> $$F = (x + y + z)(x + y' + z)(x' + y + z)(x' + y + z')$$
> $$= M_0 M_2 M_4 M_5$$
>
> A convenient way to express this function is as follows:
>
> $$F(x, y, z) = \Pi(0, 2, 4, 5)$$

The product symbol, Π, denotes the ANDing of maxterms; the numbers are the maxterms of the function.

Conversion between Canonical Forms

The complement of a function expressed as the sum of minterms equals the sum of minterms missing from the original function. This is because the original function is expressed by those minterms that make the function equal to 1, while its complement is a 1 for those minterms that the function is a 0. As an example, consider the function:

$$F(A, B, C) = \Sigma(1, 4, 5, 6, 7)$$

This has a complement that can be expressed as:

$$F'(A, B, C) = \Sigma(0, 2, 3) = m_0 + m_2 + m_3$$

Now, if we take the complement of F' by De Morgan's theorem, we obtain F in a different form:

$$F = (m_0 + m_2 + m_3)' = m_0' \cdot m_2' \cdot m_3' = M_0 M_2 M_3 = \Pi(0, 2, 3)$$

The last conversion follows from the definition of minterms and maxterms as shown in Table 2-3. From the table, it is clear that the following relation holds true:

$$m_j' = M_j$$

That is, the maxterm with subscript j is a complement of the minterm with the same subscript j, and vice versa.

The last example demonstrates the conversion between a function expressed in sum of minterms and its equivalent in product of maxterms. A similar argument will show that the conversion between the product of maxterms and the sum of minterms is similar. We now state a general conversion procedure. To convert from one canonical form to another, interchange the symbols Σ and Π and list those numbers missing from the original form. As another example, the function:

$$F(x, y, z) = \Pi(0, 2, 4, 5)$$

is expressed in the product of maxterm form. Its conversion to sum of minterms is:

$$F(x, y, z) = \Sigma(1, 3, 6, 7)$$

Note that, in order to find the missing terms, one must realize that the total number of minterms or maxterms is 2^n, where n is the number of binary variables in the function.

Standard Forms

The two canonical forms of Boolean algebra are basic forms that one obtains from reading a function from the truth table. These forms are very seldom the ones with the least number of literals, because each minterm or maxterm must contain, by definition, *all* the variables either complemented or uncomplemented.

Another way to express Boolean functions is in *standard* form. In this configuration, the terms that form the function may contain one, two or any number of literals. There are two types of standard forms: the sum of products and product of sums.

The *sum of products* is a Boolean expression containing AND terms, called *product terms*, of one or more literals each. The *sum* denotes the ORing of these terms. An example of a function expressed in sum of products is:

$$F_1 = y' + xy + x'yz'$$

The expression has three product terms of one, two, and three literals each, respectively. Their sum is in effect an OR operation.

A *product of sums* is a Boolean expression containing OR terms, called *sum terms*. Each term may have any number of literals. The *product* denotes the ANDing of these terms. An example of a function expressed in product of sums is:

$$F_2 = x(y' + z)(x' + y + z' + w)$$

This expression has three sum terms of one, two, and four literals each. The product is an AND operation. The use of the words *product* and *sum* stems from the similarity of the AND operation to the arithmetic product (multiplication) and the similarity of the OR operation to the arithmetic sum (addition).

A Boolean function may be expressed in a nonstandard form. For example, the function:

$$F_3 = (AB + CD)(A'B' + C'D')$$

is neither in sum of products nor in product of sums. It can be changed to a standard form by using the distributive law to remove the parentheses:

$$F_3 = A'B'CD + ABC'D'$$

2-6   OTHER LOGIC OPERATIONS

When the binary operators AND and OR are placed between two variables x and y, they form two Boolean functions $x \cdot y$ and $x + y$, respectively. It was stated previously that there are 2^{2^n} functions for n binary variables. For two variables, $n = 2$ and the number of possible Boolean functions is 16. Therefore, the AND and OR functions are only two of a total of 16 possible functions formed with two binary variables. It would be instructive to find the other 14 functions and investigate their properties.

The truth tables for the 16 functions formed with two binary variables x and y are listed in Table 2-5. In this table, each of the 16 columns F_0 to F_{15} represents a truth table of one possible function for the two given variables x and y. Note that the functions are determined from the 16 binary combinations that can be assigned to F. Some of the functions are shown with an operator symbol. For example, F_1

TABLE 2-5   Truth tables for the 16 functions of two binary variables

x	y	F_0	F_1	F_2	F_3	F_4	F_5	F_6	F_7	F_8	F_9	F_{10}	F_{11}	F_{12}	F_{13}	F_{14}	F_{15}
0	0	0	0	0	0	0	0	0	0	1	1	1	1	1	1	1	1
0	1	0	0	0	0	1	1	1	1	0	0	0	0	1	1	1	1
1	0	0	0	1	1	0	0	1	1	0	0	1	1	0	0	1	1
1	1	0	1	0	1	0	1	0	1	0	1	0	1	0	1	0	1
Operator Symbol			$\cdot$	/		/		$\oplus$	$+$	$\downarrow$	$\odot$	$'$	$\subset$	$'$	$\supset$	$\uparrow$	

represents the truth table for AND and F_7 represents the truth table for OR. The operator symbols for these functions are $(\cdot)$ and $(+)$, respectively.

The 16 functions listed in truth table form can be expressed algebraically by means of Boolean expressions. This is shown in the first column of Table 2-6. The Boolean expressions listed are simplified to their minimum number of literals.

Although each function can be expressed in terms of the Boolean operators AND, OR, and NOT, there is no reason one cannot assign special operator symbols for expressing the other functions. Such operator symbols are listed in the

TABLE 2-6   Boolean expressions for the 16 functions of two variables

Boolean functions	Operator symbol	Name	Comments
$F_0 = 0$		Null	Binary constant 0
$F_1 = xy$	$x \cdot y$	AND	x and y
$F_2 = xy'$	x/y	Inhibition	x but not y
$F_3 = x$		Transfer	x
$F_4 = x'y$	y/x	Inhibition	y but not x
$F_5 = y$		Transfer	y
$F_6 = xy' + x'y$	$x \oplus y$	Exclusive-OR	x or y but not both
$F_7 = x + y$	$x + y$	OR	x or y
$F_8 = (x + y)'$	$x \downarrow y$	NOR	Not-OR
$F_9 = xy + x'y'$	$x \odot y$	Equivalence*	x equals y
$F_{10} = y'$	y'	Complement	Not y
$F_{11} = x + y'$	$x \subset y$	Implication	If y then x
$F_{12} = x'$	x'	Complement	Not x
$F_{13} = x' + y$	$x \supset y$	Implication	If x then y
$F_{14} = (xy)'$	$x \uparrow y$	NAND	Not-AND
$F_{15} = 1$		Identity	Binary constant 1

*Equivalence is also known as equality, coincidence, and exclusive-NOR.

second column of Table 2-6. However, all the new symbols shown, except for the exclusive-OR symbol $\oplus$, are not in common use by digital designers.

Each of the functions in Table 2-6 is listed with an accompanying name and a comment that explains the function in some way. The 16 functions listed can be subdivided into three categories:

1. Two functions that produce a constant 0 or 1.

2. Four functions with unary operations complement and transfer.

3. Ten functions with binary operators that define eight different operations AND, OR, NAND, NOR, exclusive-OR, equivalence, inhibition, and implication.

Any function can be equal to a constant, but a binary function can be equal to only 1 or 0. The complement function produces the complement of each of the binary variables. A function which is equal to an input variable has been given the name *transfer*, because the variable x or y is transferred through the gate that forms the function without changing its value. Of the eight binary operators, two (inhibition and implication) are used by logicians but are seldom used in computer logic. The AND and OR operators have been mentioned in conjunction with Boolean algebra. The other four functions are extensively used in the design of digital systems.

The NOR function is the complement of the OR function and its name is an abbreviation of *not-OR*. Similarly, NAND is the complement of AND and is an abbreviation of *not-AND*. The exclusive-OR, abbreviated XOR or EOR, is similar to OR but excludes the combination of *both* x and y being equal to 1. The equivalence is a function that is 1 when the two binary variables are equal, i.e., when both are 0 or both are 1. The exclusive-OR and equivalence functions are the complements of each other. This can be easily verified by inspecting Table 2-5. The truth table for the exclusive-OR is F_6 and for the equivalence is F_9, and these two functions are the complements of each other. For this reason, the equivalence function is often called exclusive-NOR, i.e., exclusive-OR-NOT.

Boolean algebra, as defined in Sections 2-2, has two binary operators, which we have called AND and OR, and a unary operator, NOT (complement). From the definitions, we have deduced a number of properties of these operators and now have defined other binary operators in terms of them. There is nothing unique about this procedure. We could have just as well started with the operator NOR ($\downarrow$), for example, and later defined AND, OR, and NOT in terms of it. There are, nevertheless, good reasons for introducing Boolean algebra in the way it has been introduced. The concepts of "and," "or," and "not" are familiar and are used by people to express everyday logical ideas. Moreover, the Huntington postulates reflect the dual nature of the algebra, emphasizing the symmetry of $+$ and $\cdot$ with respect to each other.

2-7 DIGITAL LOGIC GATES

Since Boolean functions are expressed in terms of AND, OR, and NOT operations, it is easier to implement a Boolean function with these types of gates. The possibility of constructing gates for the other logic operations is of practical interest. Factors to be weighed when considering the construction of other types of logic gates are (1) the feasibility and economy of producing the gate with physical components, (2) the possibility of extending the gate to more than two inputs, (3) the basic properties of the binary operator such as commutativity and associativity, and (4) the ability of the gate to implement Boolean functions alone or in conjuction with other gates.

Of the 16 functions defined in Table 2-6, two are equal to a constant and four others are repeated twice. There are only ten functions left to be considered as candidates for logic gates. Two, inhibition and implication, are not commutative or associative and thus are impractical to use as standard logic gates. The other eight: complement, transfer, AND, OR, NAND, NOR, exclusive-OR, and equivalence, are used as standard gates in digital design.

The graphic symbols and truth tables of the eight gates are shown in Fig. 2-5. Each gate has one or two binary input variables designated by x and y and one binary output variable designated by F. The AND, OR, and inverter circuits were defined in Fig. 1-6. The inverter circuit inverts the logic sense of a binary variable. It produces the NOT, or complement, function. The small circle in the output of the graphic symbol of an inverter designates the logic complement. The triangle symbol by itself designates a buffer circuit. A buffer produces the *transfer* function but does not produce any particular logic operation, since the binary value of the output is equal to the binary value of the input. This circuit is used merely for power amplification of the signal and is equivalent to two inverters connected in cascade.

The NAND function is the complement of the AND function, as indicated by a graphic symbol which consists of an AND graphic symbol followed by a small circle. The NOR function is the complement of the OR function and uses an OR graphic symbol followed by a small circle. The NAND and NOR gates are extensively used as standard logic gates and are in fact far more popular than the AND and OR gates. This is because NAND and NOR gates are easily constructed with transistor circuits and because Boolean functions can be easily implemented with them.

The exclusive-OR gate has a graphic symbol similar to that of the OR gate, except for the additional curved line on the input side. The equivalence, or exclusive-NOR, gate is the complement of the exclusive-OR, as indicated by the small circle on the output side of the graphic symbol.

Extension to Multiple Inputs

The gates shown in Fig. 2-5, except for the inverter and buffer, can be extended to have more than two inputs. A gate can be extended to have multiple inputs if the

Name	Graphic symbol	Algebraic function	Truth table		

Name	Graphic symbol	Algebraic function			
AND	x ─┐ ┐─ F y ─┘	$F = xy$	x	y	F
			0	0	0
			0	1	0
			1	0	0
			1	1	1
OR	x ─ y ─ F	$F = x + y$	x	y	F
			0	0	0
			0	1	1
			1	0	1
			1	1	1
Inverter	x ──▷o── F	$F = x'$	x	F	
			0	1	
			1	0	
Buffer	x ──▷── F	$F = x$	x	F	
			0	0	
			1	1	
NAND	x ─ y ─ F	$F = (xy)'$	x	y	F
			0	0	1
			0	1	1
			1	0	1
			1	1	0
NOR	x ─ y ─ F	$F = (x + y)'$	x	y	F
			0	0	1
			0	1	0
			1	0	0
			1	1	0
Exclusive-OR (XOR)	x ─ y ─ F	$F = xy' + x'y$ $= x \oplus y$	x	y	F
			0	0	0
			0	1	1
			1	0	1
			1	1	0
Exclusive-NOR or equivalence	x ─ y ─ F	$F = xy + x'y'$ $= x \odot y$	x	y	F
			0	0	1
			0	1	0
			1	0	0
			1	1	1

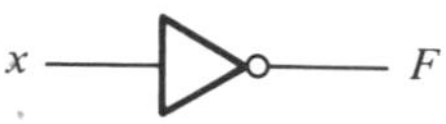

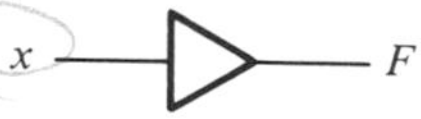

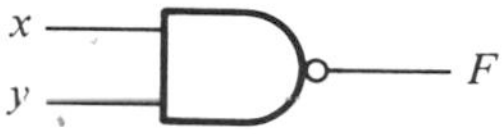

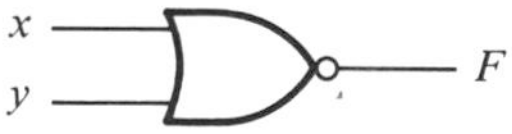

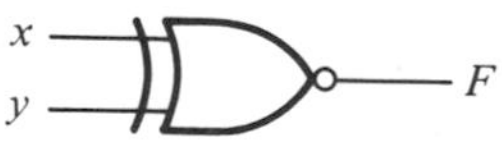

(handwritten annotations: "= S ½ adder" next to XOR truth table; "= ½ subtract" next to Exclusive-NOR truth table)

Figure 2-5 Digital logic gates

57

binary operation it represents is commutative and associative. The AND and OR operations, defined in Boolean algebra, possess these two properties. For the OR function we have:

$$x + y = y + x \qquad \text{commutative}$$

and

$$(x + y) + z = x + (y + z) = x + y + z \qquad \text{associative}$$

which indicates that the gate inputs can be interchanged and that the OR function can be extended to three or more variables.

The NAND and NOR functions are commutative and their gates can be extended to have more than two inputs, provided the definition of the operation is slightly modified. The difficulty is that the NAND and NOR operators are not associative, i.e., $(x \downarrow y) \downarrow z \neq x \downarrow (y \downarrow z)$, as shown in Fig. 2-6 and below:

$$(x \downarrow y) \downarrow z = [(x + y)' + z]' = (x + y)z' = xz' + yz'$$
$$x \downarrow (y \downarrow z) = [x + (y + z)']' = x'(y + z) = x'y + x'z$$

To overcome this difficulty, we define the multiple NOR (or NAND) gate as a complemented OR (or AND) gate. Thus, by definition, we have:

$$x \downarrow y \downarrow z = (x + y + z)'$$
$$x \uparrow y \uparrow z = (xyz)'$$

The graphic symbols for the three-input gates are shown in Fig. 2-7. In writing cascaded NOR and NAND operations, one must use the correct parentheses to signify the proper sequence of the gates. To demonstrate this, consider the circuit

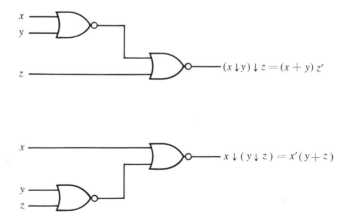

$$(x \downarrow y) \downarrow z = (x + y) z'$$

$$x \downarrow (y \downarrow z) = x'(y + z)$$

Figure 2-6   Demonstrating the nonassociativity of the NOR operator; $(x \downarrow y) \downarrow z \neq x(y \downarrow z)$

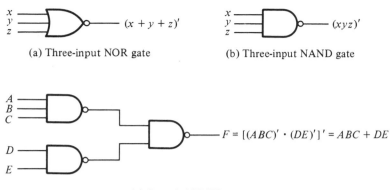

(a) Three-input NOR gate   (b) Three-input NAND gate

(c) Cascaded NAND gates

Figure 2-7 Multiple-input and cascaded NOR and NAND gates

of Fig. 2-7(c). The Boolean function for the circuit must be written as:

$$F = [(ABC)'(DE)']' = ABC + DE$$

The second expression is obtained from De Morgan's theorem. It also shows that an expression in sum of products can be implemented with NAND gates. Further discussion of NAND and NOR gates can be found in Sections 3-6, 4-7, and 4-8.

The exclusive-OR and equivalence gates are both commutative and associative and can be extended to more than two inputs. However, multiple-input exclusive-OR gates are uncommon from the hardware standpoint. In fact, even a two-input function is usually constructed with other types of gates. Moreover, the definition of these functions must be modified when extended to more than two variables. The exclusive-OR is an *odd* function, i.e., it is equal to 1 if the input variables have an odd number of 1's. The equivalence function is an *even* function, i.e., it is equal to 1 if the input variables have an even number of 0's. The construction of a three-input exclusive-OR function is shown in Fig. 2-8. It is

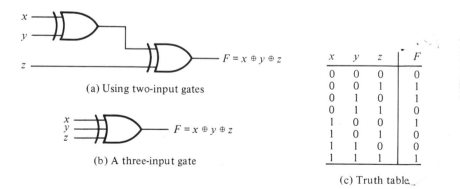

(a) Using two-input gates

(b) A three-input gate

x	y	z	F
0	0	0	0
0	0	1	1
0	1	0	1
0	1	1	0
1	0	0	1
1	0	1	0
1	1	0	0
1	1	1	1

(c) Truth table

Figure 2-8 Three-input exclusive-OR gate

normally implemented by cascading two-input gates as shown in (a). Graphically, it can be represented with a single three-input gate as shown in (b). The truth table in (c) clearly indicates that the output F is equal to 1 if only one input is equal to 1 or if all three inputs are equal to 1, i.e., when the total number of 1's in the input variables is *odd*. Further discussion of exclusive-OR and equivalence can be found in Section 4-9.

2-8   IC DIGITAL LOGIC FAMILIES

The IC was introduced in Section 1-9, where it was stated that digital circuits are invariably constructed with ICs. Having discussed various digital logic gates in the previous section, we are now in a position to present IC gates and discuss their general properties.

Digital IC gates are classified not only by their logic operation, but also by the specific logic-circuit family to which they belong. Each logic family has its own basic electronic circuit upon which more complex digital circuits and functions are developed. The basic circuit in each family is either a NAND or a NOR gate. The electronic components employed in the construction of the basic circuit are usually used to name the logic family. Many different logic families of digital ICs have been introduced commercially. The ones that have achieved widespread popularity are listed below.

TTL	Transistor-transistor logic
ECL	Emitter-coupled logic
MOS	Metal-oxide semiconductor
CMOS	Complementary metal-oxide semiconductor
I^2L	Integrated-injection logic

TTL has an extensive list of digital functions and is currently the most popular logic family. ECL is used in systems requiring high-speed operations. MOS and I^2L are used in circuits requiring high component density, and CMOS is used in systems requiring low power consumption.

The analysis of the basic electronic circuit in each logic family is presented in Chapter 10. The reader familiar with basic electronics can refer to Chapter 10 at this time to become acquainted with these electronic circuits. Here we restrict the discussion to the general properties of the various IC gates available commercially.

Because of the high density with which transistors can be fabricated in MOS and I^2L, these two families are mostly used for LSI functions. The other three families, TTL, ECL, and CMOS, have LSI devices and also a large number of MSI and SSI devices. SSI devices are those that come with a small number of gates or flip-flops (presented in Section 6-2) in one IC package. The limit on the number of circuits in SSI devices is the number of pins in the package. A 14-pin package, for example, can accommodate only four two-input gates, because each gate requires three external pins—two each for inputs and one each for output, for a total of 12 pins. The remaining two pins are needed for supplying power to the circuits.

Some typical SSI circuits are shown in Fig. 2-9. Each IC is enclosed within a 14- or 16-pin package. The pins are numbered along the two sides of the package and specify the connections that can be made. The gates drawn inside the ICs are for information only and cannot be seen because the actual IC package appears as shown in Fig. 1-8.

TTL ICs are usually distinguished by numerical designation as the 5400 and 7400 series. The former has a wide operating-temperature range, suitable for military use, and the latter has a narrower temperature range, suitable for industrial use. The numeric designation of the 7400 series means that IC packages are numbered as 7400, 7401, 7402, etc. Some vendors make available TTL ICs with different numerical designations, such as the 9000 or the 8000 series.

Figure 2-9(a) shows two TTL SSI circuits. The 7404 provides six (hex) inverters in a package. The 7400 provides four (quadruple) 2-input NAND gates. The terminals marked V_{CC} and GND are the power supply pins which require a voltage of 5 volts for proper operation.

The most common ECL type is designated as the 10,000 series. Figure 2-9(b) shows two ECL circuits. The 10102 provides four 2-input NOR gates. Note that an ECL gate may have two outputs, one for the NOR function and another for the OR function (pin 9 of the 10102 IC). The 10107 IC provides three exclusive-OR gates. Here again there are two outputs from each gate; the other output gives the exclusive-NOR function or equivalence. ECL gates have three terminals for power supply. V_{CC1} and V_{CC2} are usually connected to ground, and V_{EE} to a -5.2-volt supply.

CMOS circuits of the 4000 series are shown in Fig. 2-9(c). Only two 4-input NOR gates can be accommodated in the 4002 because of pin limitation. The 4050 type provides six buffer gates. Both ICs have two unused terminals marked NC (no connection). The terminal marked V_{DD} requires a power supply voltage from 3 to 15 volts, while V_{SS} is usually connected to ground.

Positive and Negative Logic

The binary signal at the inputs or output of any gate can have one of two values, except during transition. One signal value represents logic-1 and the other, logic-0. Since two signal values are assigned to two logic values, there exist two different assignments of signals to logic. Because of the principle of duality of Boolean algebra, an interchange of signal-value assignment results in a dual-function implementation.

Consider the two values of a binary signal as shown in Fig. 2-10. One value must be higher than the other since the two values must be different in order to distinguish between them. We designate the higher level by H and the lower level

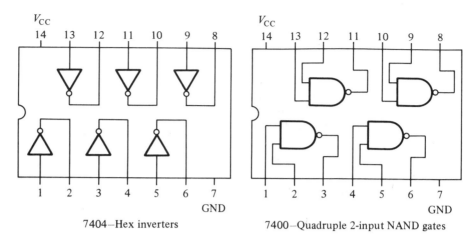

7404–Hex inverters

7400–Quadruple 2-input NAND gates

(a) TTL gates.

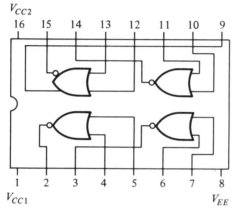

10102–Quadruple 2-input NOR gates

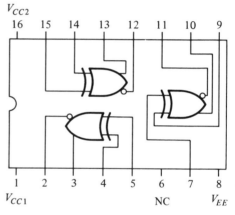

10107–Triple exclusive-OR/NOR gates

(b) ECL gates.

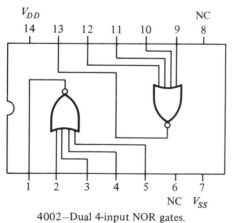

4002–Dual 4-input NOR gates.

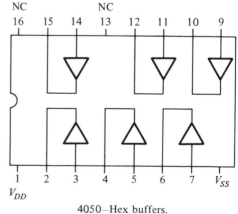

4050–Hex buffers.

(c) CMOS gates.

Figure 2-9   Some typical integrated-circuit gates

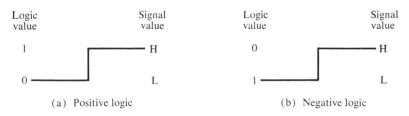

Logic value		Signal value	Logic value		Signal value
1		H	0		H
0		L	1		L

(a) Positive logic
(b) Negative logic

Figure 2-10 Signal-amplitude assignment and type of logic

by L. There are two choices for logic-value assignment. Choosing the high-level H to represent logic-1, as shown in Fig. 2-10(a), defines a *positive-logic* system. Choosing the low-level L to represent logic-1, as shown in Fig. 2-10(b), defines a *negative-logic* system. The terms *positive* and *negative* are somewhat misleading since both signal values may be positive or both may be negative. It is not signal polarity that determines the type of logic, but rather the assignment of logic values according to the relative amplitudes of the signals.

Integrated-circuit data sheets define digital functions not in terms of logic-1 or logic-0, but rather in terms of H and L levels. It is up to the user to decide on a positive or negative logic assignment. The high-level and low-level voltages for the three IC digital logic families are listed in Table 2-7. In each family, there is a range of voltage values that the circuit will recognize as a high or low level. The typical value is the most commonly encountered. The table also lists the voltage-supply requirements for each family as a reference.

TTL has typical values of $H = 3.5$ volts and $L = 0.2$ volt. ECL has two negative values, with $H = -0.8$ volt and $L = -1.8$ volt. Note that even though both levels are negative, the higher one is -0.8. CMOS gates can use a supply voltage V_{DD} anywhere from 3 to 15 volts; typically, either 5 or 10 volts is used. The signal values in CMOS are a function of the supply voltage with $H = V_{DD}$ and $L = 0$ volt. The polarity assignments for positive and negative logic are also indicated in the table.

In light of this discussion, it would be necessary to justify the logic symbols used for the ICs listed in Fig. 2-9. Take, for example, one of the gates of the 7400

TABLE 2-7 H and L levels in IC logic families

IC family type	Voltage supply (V)	High-level voltage (V)		Low-level voltage (V)	
		Range	Typical	Range	Typical
TTL	$V_{CC} = 5$	2.4–5	3.5	0–0.4	0.2
ECL	$V_{EE} = -5.2$	$-0.95 - -0.7$	-0.8	$-1.9 - -1.6$	-1.8
CMOS	$V_{DD} = 3 - 10$	V_{DD}	V_{DD}	0–0.5	0
Positive logic:			logic-1		logic-0
Negative logic:			logic-0		logic-1

IC. This gate is shown in block diagram form in Fig. 2-11(b). The manufacturer's truth table for this gate given in a data sheet is shown in Fig. 2-11(a). This specifies the physical behavior of the gate, with H being typically 3.5 volts and L being 0.2 volt. This physical gate can function as either a NAND or NOR gate, depending on the polarity assignment.

The truth table of Fig. 2-11(c) assumes positive-logic assignment with $H = 1$ and $L = 0$. Checking this truth table with the truth tables in Fig. 2-5, we recognize it as a NAND gate. The graphic symbol for a positive-logic NAND gate is shown in Fig. 2-11(d) and is similar to the one adopted previously.

Now consider the negative-logic assignment for this physical gate with $L = 1$ and $H = 0$. The result is the truth table shown in Fig. 2-11(e). This table can be recognized to represent the NOR function even though its entries are listed backwards. The graphic symbol for a negative-logic NOR gate is shown in Fig. 2-11(f). The small triangle in the input and output wires designates a *polarity indicator*. The presence of this polarity indicator along a terminal indicates that negative logic is assigned to the terminal. Thus, the same physical gate can function either as a positive-logic NAND or as a negative-logic NOR. The one

x	y	z
L	L	H
L	H	H
H	L	H
H	H	L

(a) Truth table in
    terms of H and L.

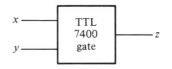

(b) Gate block diagram

x	y	z
0	0	1
0	1	1
1	0	1
1	1	0

(c) Truth table for
    positive logic:
    $H = 1, L = 0$.

(d) Graphic symbol for
    positive logic NAND gate.

x	y	z
1	1	0
1	0	0
0	1	0
0	0	1

(e) Truth table for
    negative logic;
    $L = 1, H = 0$.

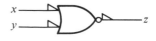

(f) Graphic symbol for
    negative logic NOR gate.

Figure 2-11 Demonstration of positive and negative logic

drawn in the diagram is completely dependent on the polarity assignment that the designer wishes to employ.

In a similar manner, it is possible to show that a positive-logic NOR is the same physical gate as a negative-logic NAND. The same relation holds between AND and OR gates or between exclusive-OR and equivalence gates. In any case, if negative logic is assumed in any input or output terminal, it is necessary to include the polarity indicator triangle symbol along the terminal. Some digital designers use this convention to facilitate the design of digital circuits when NAND or NOR gates are used exclusively. We will not use this symbology in this book but will resort to other methods for designing with NAND and NOR gates. Note that the ICs presented in Fig. 2-9 are shown with their positive-logic graphic symbols. They could have been shown with their negative-logic symbols if one wished to do so.

The conversion from positive logic to negative logic, and vice versa, is essentially an operation that changes 1's to 0's and 0's to 1's in both inputs and output of a gate. Since this operation produces the dual of a function, the change of all terminals from one polarity to the other results in taking the dual of the function. The result of this conversion is that all AND operations are converted to OR operations (or graphic symbols) and vice versa. In addition, one must not forget to include the polarity indicator in graphic symbols when negative logic is assumed.

The small triangle that represents a polarity indicator and the small circle that represents a complementation have similar effects but different meanings. Therefore, one can be replaced by the other, but the interpretation is different. A circle followed by a triangle, as in Fig. 2-11(f), represents a complementation followed by a negative-logic polarity indicator. The two cancel each other and both can be removed. But if both are removed, then the inputs and output of the gate will represent different polarities.

Special Characteristics

The characteristics of IC digital logic families are usually compared by analyzing the circuit of the basic gate in each family. The most important parameters that are evaluated and compared are fan-out, power dissipation, propagation delay, and noise margin. We first explain the properties of these parameters and then use them to compare the IC logic families.

Fan-out specifies the number of standard loads that the output of a gate can drive without impairing its normal operation. A standard load is usually defined as the amount of current needed by an input of another gate in the same IC family. Sometimes the term *loading* is used instead of fan-out. This term is derived from the fact that the output of a gate can supply a limited amount of current, above which it ceases to operate properly and is said to be overloaded. The output of a gate is usually connected to the inputs of other similar gates. Each input consumes a certain amount of power from the gate input, so that each additional connection adds to the load of the gate. "Loading rules" are usually listed for a family of standard digital circuits. These rules specify the maximum amount of loading allowed for each output of each circuit. Exceeding the specified maximum load may cause a malfunction because the circuit cannot supply the power demanded from it. The fan-out is the maximum number of inputs that can be connected to the output of a gate, and it is expressed by a number.

The fan-out capabilities of a gate must be considered when simplifying Boolean functions. Care must be taken not to develop expressions that result in an overloaded gate. Noninverting amplifiers or buffers are sometimes employed to provide additional driving capabilities for heavy loads.

Power dissipation is the supplied power required to operate the gate. This parameter is expressed in milliwatts (mW) and represents the actual power dissipated in the gate. The number that represents this parameter does not include the power delivered from another gate; rather, it represents the power delivered to the gate from the power supply. An IC with four gates will require, from its power supply, four times the power dissipated in each gate. In a given system, there may be many ICs, and the power required by each IC must be considered. The total power dissipation in a system is the sum total of the power dissipated in all ICs.

Propagation delay is the average transition delay time for a signal to propagate from input to output when the binary signals change in value. The signals through a gate take a certain amount of time to propagate from the inputs to the output. This interval of time is defined as the propagation delay of the gate. Propagation delay is expressed in nanoseconds (ns), and 1 ns is equal to 10^{-9} of a second.

The signals that travel from the inputs of a digital circuit to its outputs pass through a series of gates. The sum of the propagation delays through the gates is the total propagation delay of the circuit. When speed of operation is important, each gate must have a small propagation delay and the digital circuit must have a minimum number of series gates between inputs and outputs.

The input signals in most digital circuits are applied simultaneously to more than one gate. All those gates that receive their inputs exclusively from external inputs constitute the first logic level of the circuit. Gates that receive at least one input from an output of a first-logic-level gate are considered to be in the second logic level, and similarly for third and higher levels. The total propagation delay of the circuit is equal to the propagation delay of a gate times the number of logic levels in the circuit. Thus, a reduction in the number of logic levels results in a reduction of signal delay and faster circuits. The reduction of the propagation delay in circuits may be more important than the reduction in the total number of gates if speed of operation is a major factor.

Noise margin is the maximum noise voltage added to the input signal of a digital circuit that does not cause an undesirable change in the circuit output. There are two types of noise to be considered. DC noise is caused by a drift in the voltage levels of a signal. AC noise is a random pulse that may be created by other switching signals. Thus, noise is a term used to denote an undesirable signal that is superimposed upon the normal operating signal. The ability of circuits to operate reliably in a noise environment is important in many applications. Noise margin is expressed in volts (V) and represents the maximum noise signal that can be tolerated by the gate.

Characteristics of IC Logic Families

The basic circuit of the TTL logic family is the NAND gate. There are many versions of TTL, and three of them are listed in Table 2-8. This table gives the general characteristics of the IC logic families. Values listed are representative on a comparison basis. For any one family or version, the values may vary somewhat.

TABLE 2-8   Typical characteristics of IC logic families

IC logic family	Fan-out	Power dissipation (mW)	Propagation delay (ns)	Noise margin (V)
Standard TTL	10	10	10	0.4
Schottky TTL	10	22	3	0.4
Low-power Schottky TTL	20	2	10	0.4
ECL	25	25	2	0.2
CMOS	50	0.1	25	3

The standard TTL gate was the first version of the TTL family. Additional improvements were added as the technology progressed. The Schottky TTL is a later improvement that reduces the propagation delay but results in an increase in power dissipation. The low-power Schottky TTL version sacrifices some speed for reduced power dissipation. It has the same propagation delay as the standard TTL, but the power dissipation is reduced considerably. The fan-out of the standard TTL is 10 but the low-power Schottky version has a fan-out of 20. Under certain conditions the other versions may also have a fan-out of 20. The noise margin is better than 0.4 V, with a typical value of 1 V.

The basic circuit of the ECL family is the NOR gate. The special advantage of ECL gates is their low propagation delay. Some ECL versions may have a propagation delay as low as 0.5 ns. The power dissipation in ECL gates is comparatively high and the noise margin low. These two parameters impose a disadvantage when choosing ECL over other logic families. However, because of its low propagation delay, ECL offers the highest speed of any family and is the ultimate choice for very fast systems.

The basic circuit of CMOS is the inverter from which both NAND and NOR gates can be constructed. The special advantage of CMOS is its extremely low power dissipation. Under static conditions, the CMOS gate power dissipation is negligible and averages about 10 nW. When the gate signal changes state, there is a dynamic power dissipation which is proportional to the frequency at which the circuit is exercised. The number listed in the table is a typical value of dynamic power dissipation in CMOS gates.

The one major disadvantage of CMOS is its high propagation delay. This means that it is not practical for use in systems requiring high-speed operations. The characteristic parameters for the CMOS gate depend on the power supply voltage V_{DD} that is used. The power dissipation increases with increase in voltage supply. The propagation delay decreases with increase in voltage supply, and the noise margin is estimated to be about 40% of the voltage supply value.

REFERENCES

1. Boole, G., *An Investigation of the Laws of Thought*. New York: Dover Pub., 1954.

2. Shannon, C. E., "A Symbolic Analysis of Relay and Switching Circuits." *Trans. of the AIEE*, Vol. 57 (1938), 713-23.

3. Huntington, E. V., "Sets of Independent Postulates for the Algebra of Logic." *Trans. Am. Math. Soc.*, Vol. 5 (1904), 288-309.

4. Birkhoff, G., and T. C. Bartee, *Modern Applied Algebra*. New York: McGraw-Hill Book Co., 1970.

5. Birkhoff, G., and S. Maclane, *A Survey of Modern Algebra*, 3rd ed. New York: The Macmillan Co., 1965.

6. Hohn, F. E., *Applied Boolean Algebra*, 2nd ed. New York: The Macmillan Co., 1966.

7. Whitesitt, J. E., *Boolean Algebra and its Applications*. Reading, Mass.: Addison-Wesley Pub. Co., 1961.

8. *The TTL Data Book for Design Engineers*. Dallas, Texas: Texas Instruments Inc., 1976.

9. *MECL Integrated Circuits Data Book*. Phoenix, Ariz.: Motorola Semiconductor Products, Inc., 1972.

10. *RCA Solid State Data Book Series*: *COS/MOS Digital Integrated Circuits*. Somerville, N. J.: RCA Solid State Div., 1974.

PROBLEMS

2-1. Which of the six basic laws (closure, associative, commutative, identity, inverse, and distributive) are satisfied for the pair of binary operators listed below?

+	0	1	2
0	0	0	0
1	0	1	1
2	0	1	2

·	0	1	2
0	0	1	2
1	1	1	2
2	2	2	2

2-2. Show that the set of three elements {0, 1, 2} and the two binary operators + and · as defined by the above table is not a Boolean algebra. State which of the Huntington postulates is not satisfied.

2-3. Demonstrate by means of truth tables the validity of the following theorems of Boolean algebra.

(a) The associative laws.

(b) De Morgan's theorems for three variables.

(c) The distributive law of + over ·.

2-4. Repeat problem 2-3 using Venn diagrams.

2-5. Simplify the following Boolean functions to a minimum number of literals.

(a) $xy + xy'$

(b) $(x + y)(x + y')$

(c) $xyz + x'y + xyz'$

(d) $zx + zx'y$

(e) $(A + B)'(A' + B')'$

(f) $y(wz' + wz) + xy$

2-6. Reduce the following Boolean expressions to the required number of literals.

(a) $ABC + A'B'C + A'BC + ABC' + A'B'C'$ to five literals

(b) $BC + AC' + AB + BCD$ to four literals

(c) $[(CD)' + A]' + A + CD + AB$ to three literals

(d) $(A + C + D)(A + C + D')(A + C' + D)(A + B')$ to four literals

2-7. Find the complement of the following Boolean functions and reduce them to a minimum number of literals.

(a) $(BC' + A'D)(AB' + CD')$

(b) $B'D + A'BC' + ACD + A'BC$

(c) $[(AB)'A][(AB)'B]$

(d) $AB' + C'D'$

2-8. Given two Boolean functions F_1 and F_2:

(a) Show that the Boolean function $E = F_1 + F_2$, obtained by ORing the two functions, contains the sum of all the minterms in F_1 and F_2.

(b) Show that the Boolean function $G = F_1F_2$, obtained from ANDing the two functions, contains those minterms common to both F_1 and F_2.

2-9. Obtain the truth table of the function:

$$F = xy + xy' + y'z$$

2-10. Implement the simplified Boolean functions from problem 2-6 with logic gates.

2-11. Given the Boolean function:

$$F = xy + x'y' + y'z$$

(a) Implement it with AND, OR, and NOT gates.

(b) Implement it with *only* OR and NOT gates.

(c) Implement it with *only* AND and NOT gates.

2-12. Simplify the functions T_1 and T_2 to a minimum number of literals.

A	B	C	T_1	T_2
0	0	0	1	0
0	0	1	1	0
0	1	0	1	0
0	1	1	0	1
1	0	0	0	1
1	0	1	0	1
1	1	0	0	1
1	1	1	0	1

2-13. Express the following functions in a sum of minterms and a product of maxterms.
(a) $F(A, B, C, D) = D(A' + B) + B'D$
(b) $F(w, x, y, z) = y'z + wxy' + wxz' + w'x'z$
(c) $F(A, B, C, D) = (A + B' + C)(A + B')(A + C' + D')$
$(A' + B + C + D')(B + C' + D')$
(d) $F(A, B, C) = (A' + B)(B' + C)$
(e) $F(x, y, z) = 1$
(f) $F(x, y, z) = (xy + z)(y + xz)$

2-14. Convert the following to the other canonical form.
(a) $F(x, y, z) = \Sigma(1, 3, 7)$
(b) $F(A, B, C, D) = \Sigma(0, 2, 6, 11, 13, 14)$
(c) $F(x, y, z) = \Pi(0, 3, 6, 7)$
(d) $F(A, B, C, D) = \Pi(0, 1, 2, 3, 4, 6, 12)$

2-15. What is the difference between canonical form and standard form? Which form is preferable when implementing a Boolean function with gates? Which form is obtained when reading a function from a truth table?

2-16. The sum of all minterms of a Boolean function of n variables is 1.
(a) Prove the above statement for $n = 3$.
(b) Suggest a procedure for a general proof.

2-17. The product of all maxterms of a Boolean function of n variables is 0.
(a) Prove the above statement for $n = 3$.
(b) Suggest a procedure for a general proof. Can we use the duality principle after proving (b) of problem 2-16?

2-18. Show that the dual of the exclusive-OR is equal to its complement.

2-19. By substituting the Boolean function equivalent of the binary operations as defined in Table 2-6, show that:
(a) The inhibition and implication operators are neither commutative nor associative.
(b) The exclusive-OR and equivalence operators are commutative and associative.

(c) The NAND operator is not associative.

(d) The NOR and NAND operators are not distributive.

2-20. A *majority* gate is a digital circuit whose output is equal to 1 if the majority of the inputs are 1's. The output is 0 otherwise. By means of a truth table, find the Boolean function implemented by a 3-input majority gate. Simplify the function.

2-21. Verify the truth table for the 3-input exclusive-OR gate listed in Fig. 2-8(c). List all eight combinations of $x, y,$ and z; evaluate $A = x \oplus y$; then evaluate $F = A \oplus z = x \oplus y \oplus z$.

2-22. TTL SSI come mostly in 14-pin packages. Two pins are reserved for power supply and the other pins are used for input and output terminals. How many gates are enclosed in one such package if it contains the following types of gates:

(a) 2-input exclusive-OR gates.

(b) 3-input AND gates.

(c) 4-input NAND gates.

(d) 5-input NOR gates.

(e) 8-input NAND gates.

2-23. Show that a positive-logic AND gate is a negative-logic OR gate, and vice versa.

2-24. An IC logic family has NAND gates with fan-out of 5 and buffer gates with fan-out of 10. Show how the output signal of a single NAND gate can be applied to 50 other gate inputs.

Simplification of
Boolean Functions

3

3-1 THE MAP METHOD

The complexity of the digital logic gates that implement a Boolean function is directly related to the complexity of the algebraic expression from which the function is implemented. Although the truth table representation of a function is unique, expressed algebraically, it can appear in many different forms. Boolean functions may be simplified by algebraic means as discussed in Section 2-4. However, this procedure of minimization is awkward because it lacks specific rules to predict each succeeding step in the manipulative process. The map method provides a simple straightforward procedure for minimizing Boolean functions. This method may be regarded either as a pictorial form of a truth table or as an extension of the Venn diagram. The map method, first proposed by Veitch (1) and slightly modified by Karnaugh (2), is also known as the "Veitch diagram" or the "Karnaugh map."

The map is a diagram made up of squares. Each square represents one minterm. Since any Boolean function can be expressed as a sum of minterms, it follows that a Boolean function is recognized graphically in the map from the area enclosed by those squares whose minterms are included in the function. In fact, the map presents a visual diagram of all possible ways a function may be expressed in a standard form. By recognizing various patterns, the user can derive alternative algebraic expressions for the same function, from which he can select the simplest one. We shall assume that the simplest algebraic expression is any one in a sum of products or product of sums that has a minimum number of literals. (This expression is not necessarily unique.)

3-2 TWO- AND THREE-VARIABLE MAPS

A two-variable map is shown in Fig. 3-1. There are four minterms for two variables; hence the map consists of four squares, one for each minterm. The map is redrawn in (b) to show the relationship between the squares and the two

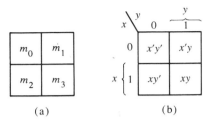

(a)

(b)

Figure 3-1 Two-variable map

variables. The 0's and 1's marked for each row and each column designate the values of variables x and y, respectively. Notice that x appears primed in row 0 and unprimed in row 1. Similarly, y appears primed in column 0 and unprimed in column 1.

If we mark the squares whose minterms belong to a given function, the two-variable map becomes another useful way to represent any one of the 16 Boolean functions of two variables. As an example, the function xy is shown in Fig. 3-2(a). Since xy is equal to m_3, a 1 is placed inside the square that belongs to m_3. Similarly, the function $x + y$ is represented in the map of Fig. 3-2(b) by three squares marked with 1's. These squares are found from the minterms of the function:

$$x + y = x'y + xy' + xy = m_1 + m_2 + m_3$$

The three squares could have also been determined from the intersection of variable x in the second row and variable y in the second column, which encloses the area belonging to x or y.

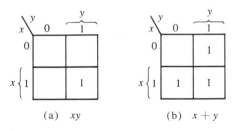

(a) xy

(b) $x + y$

Figure 3-2 Representation of functions in the map

A three-variable map is shown in Fig. 3-3. There are eight minterms for three binary variables. Therefore, a map consists of eight squares. Note that the minterms are arranged, not in a binary sequence, but in a sequence similar to the reflected code listed in Table 1-4. The characteristic of this sequence is that only one bit changes from 1 to 0 or from 0 to 1 in the listing sequence. The map drawn in part (b) is marked with numbers in each row and each column to show the relationship between the squares and the three variables. For example, the square assigned to m_5 corresponds to row 1 and column 01. When these two numbers are concatenated, they give the binary number 101, whose decimal equivalent is 5.

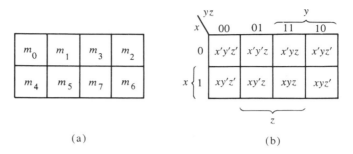

Figure 3-3 Three-variable map

Another way of looking at square $m_5 = xy'z$ is to consider it to be in the row marked x and the column belonging to $y'z$ (column 01). Note that there are four squares where each variable is equal to 1 and four where each is equal to 0. The variable appears unprimed in those four squares where it is equal to 1 and primed in those squares where it is equal to 0. For convenience, we write the variable with its letter symbol under the four squares where it is unprimed.

To understand the usefulness of the map for simplifying Boolean functions, we must recognize the basic property possessed by adjacent squares. Any two adjacent squares in the map differ by only one variable which is primed in one square and unprimed in the other. For example, m_5 and m_7 lie in two adjacent squares. Variable y is primed in m_5 and unprimed in m_7, while the other two variables are the same in both squares. From the postulates of Boolean algebra, it follows that the sum of two minterms in adjacent squares can be simplified to a single AND term consisting of only two literals. To clarify this, consider the sum of two adjacent squares such as m_5 and m_7:

$$m_5 + m_7 = xy'z + xyz = xz(y' + y) = xz$$

Here the two squares differ by the variable y, which can be removed when the sum of the two minterms is formed. Thus, any two minterms in adjacent squares that are ORed together will cause a removal of the different variable. The following example explains the procedure for minimizing a Boolean function with a map.

EXAMPLE 3-1: Simplify the Boolean function:

$$F = x'yz + x'yz' + xy'z' + xy'z$$

First, a 1 is marked in each square as needed to represent the function as shown in Fig. 3-4. This can be accomplished in two ways: either by converting each minterm to a binary number and then marking a 1 in the corresponding square, or by obtaining the coincidence of the variables in each term. For example, the term $x'yz$ has the corresponding binary number 011 and represents minterm m_3 in square 011. The second way to recognize the square is by the coincidence of variables x', y, and z, which is found in the map by

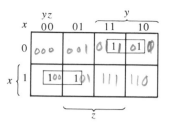

Figure 3-4 Map for Example 3-1; $x'yz + x'yz' + xy'z' + xy'z = x'y + xy'$

observing that x' belongs to the four squares in the first row, y belongs to the four squares in the two right columns, and z belongs to the four squares in the two middle columns. The area that belongs to all three literals is the single square in the first row and third column. In a similar manner, the other three squares belonging to the function F are marked by 1's in the map. The function is thus represented by an area containing four squares, each marked with a 1, as shown in Fig. 3-4. The next step is to subdivide the given area into adjacent squares. These are indicated in the map by two rectangles, each enclosing two 1's. The upper right rectangle represents the area enclosed by $x'y$; the lower left, the area enclosed by xy'. The sum of these two terms gives the answer:

$$F = x'y + xy'$$

Next consider the two squares labeled m_0 and m_2 in Fig. 3-3(a) or $x'y'z'$ and $x'yz'$ in Fig. 3-3(b). These two minterms also differ by one variable y, and their sum can be simplified to a two-literal expression:

$$x'y'z' + x'yz' = x'z'$$

Consequently, we must modify the definition of adjacent squares to include this and other similar cases. This is done by considering the map as being drawn on a surface where the right and left edges touch each other to form adjacent squares.

EXAMPLE 3-2: Simplify the Boolean function:

$$F = x'yz + xy'z' + xyz + xyz'$$

The map for this function is shown in Fig. 3-5. There are four squares marked with 1's, one for each minterm of the function. Two adjacent squares are combined in the third column to give a two-literal term yz. The remaining two squares with 1's are also adjacent by the new definition and are shown in the diagram enclosed by half rectangles. These two squares, when combined, give the two-literal term xz'. The simplified function becomes:

$$F = yz + xz'$$

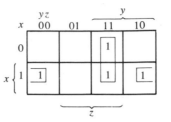

Figure 3-5 Map for Example 3-2; $x'yz + xy'z' + xyz + xyz' = yz + xz'$

Consider now any combination of four adjacent squares in the three-variable map. Any such combination represents the ORing of four adjacent minterms and results in an expression of only one literal. As an example, the sum of the four adjacent minterms m_0, m_2, m_4, and m_6 reduces to the single literal z' as shown:

$$x'y'z' + x'yz' + xy'z' + xyz' = x'z'(y' + y) + xz'(y' + y)$$
$$= x'z' + xz' = z'(x' + x) = z'$$

EXAMPLE 3-3: Simplify the Boolean function:

$$F = A'C + A'B + AB'C + BC$$

The map to simplify this function is shown in Fig. 3-6. Some of the terms in the function have less than three literals and are represented in the map by more than one square. For example, to find the squares corresponding to $A'C$, we form the coincidence of A' (first row) and C (two middle columns) and obtain squares 001 and 011. Note that when marking 1's in the squares, it is possible to find a 1 already placed there by a preceding term. In this example, the second term $A'B$ has 1's in squares 011 and 010, but square 011 is common to the first term $A'C$ and only one 1 is marked in it. The function in this example has five minterms, as indicated by the five squares marked with 1's. It is simplified by combining four squares in the center to give the literal C. The remaining single square marked with a 1 in 010 is combined with an adjacent square that has already been used once. This is permissible and even desirable since

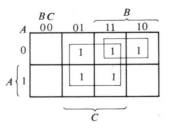

Figure 3-6 Map for Example 3-3; $A'C + A'B + AB'C + BC = C + A'B$

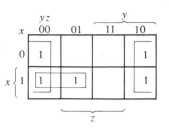

Figure 3-7 $f(x, y, z) = \Sigma(0, 2, 4, 5, 6) = z' + xy'$

the combination of the two squares gives the term $A'B$ while the single minterm represented by the square gives the three-variable term $A'BC'$. The simplified function is:

$$F = C + A'B$$

EXAMPLE 3-4: Simplify the Boolean function:

$$F(x, y, z) = \Sigma(0, 2, 4, 5, 6)$$

Here we are given the minterms by their decimal numbers. The corresponding squares are marked by 1's as shown in Fig. 3-7. From the map we obtain the simplified function:

$$F = z' + xy'$$

3-3 FOUR-VARIABLE MAP

The map for Boolean functions of four binary variables is shown in Fig. 3-8. In (a) are listed the 16 minterms and the squares assigned to each. In (b) the map is redrawn to show the relationship with the four variables. The rows and columns

m_0	m_1	m_3	m_2
m_4	m_5	m_7	m_6
m_{12}	m_{13}	m_{15}	m_{14}
m_8	m_9	m_{11}	m_{10}

(a)

wx \ yz	00	01	11	10
00	$w'x'y'z'$	$w'x'y'z$	$w'x'yz$	$w'x'yz'$
01	$w'xy'z'$	$w'xy'z$	$w'xyz$	$w'xyz'$
11	$wxy'z'$	$wxy'z$	$wxyz$	$wxyz'$
10	$wx'y'z'$	$wx'y'z$	$wx'yz$	$wx'yz'$

(b)

Figure 3-8 Four-variable map

are numbered in a reflected-code sequence, with only one digit changing value between two adjacent rows or columns. The minterm corresponding to each square can be obtained from the concatenation of the row number with the column number. For example, the numbers of the third row (11) and the second column (01), when concatenated, give the binary number 1101, the binary equivalent of decimal 13. Thus, the square in the third row and second column represents minterm m_{13}.

The map minimization of four-variable Boolean functions is similar to the method used to minimize three-variable functions. Adjacent squares are defined to be squares next to each other. In addition, the map is considered to lie on a surface with the top and bottom edges, as well as the right and left edges, touching each other to form adjacent squares. For example, m_0 and m_2 form adjacent squares, as do m_3 and m_{11}. The combination of adjacent squares that is useful during the simplification process is easily determined from inspection of the four-variable map:

One square represents one minterm, giving a term of four literals.

Two adjacent squares represent a term of three literals.

Four adjacent squares represent a term of two literals.

Eight adjacent squares represent a term of one literal.

Sixteen adjacent squares represent the function equal to 1.

No other combination of squares can simplify the function. The following two examples show the procedure used to simplify four-variable Boolean functions.

EXAMPLE 3-5: Simplify the Boolean function:

$$F(w, x, y, z) = \Sigma(0, 1, 2, 4, 5, 6, 8, 9, 12, 13, 14)$$

Since the function has four variables, a four-variable map must be used. The minterms listed in the sum are marked by 1's in the map of Fig. 3-9. Eight adjacent squares marked with 1's can be combined to form the one literal term y'. The remaining three 1's on the right cannot be combined together to give a simplified term. They must be combined as two or four adjacent squares. The larger the number of squares combined, the less the number of literals in the term. In this example, the top two 1's on the right are combined with the top two 1's on the left to give the term $w'z'$. Note that it is permissible to use the same square more than once. We are now left with a square marked by 1 in the third row and fourth column (square 1110). Instead of taking this square alone (which will give a term of four literals), we combine it with squares already used to form an area of

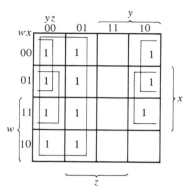

Figure 3-9 Map for Example 3-5; $F(w, x, y, z) =$
$\Sigma(0, 1, 2, 4, 5, 6, 8, 9, 12, 13, 14) = y' + w'z' + xz'$

four adjacent squares. These squares comprise the two middle rows and the two end columns, giving the term xz'. The simplified function is:

$$F = y' + w'z' + xz'$$

EXAMPLE 3-6: Simplify the Boolean function:

$$F = A'B'C' + B'CD' + A'BCD' + AB'C'$$

The area in the map covered by this function consists of the squares marked with 1's in Fig. 3-10. This function has four variables and, as expressed, consists of three terms, each with three literals, and one term of four literals. Each term of three literals is represented in the map by two squares. For example, $A'B'C'$ is represented in squares 0000 and 0001. The function can be simplified in the map by taking

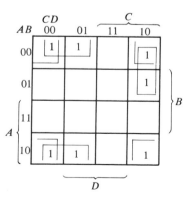

Figure 3-10 Map for Example 3-6; $A'B'C' + B'CD' + A'BCD' + AB'C'$
$= B'D' + B'C' + A'CD'$

79

the 1's in the four corners to give the term $B'D'$. This is possible because these four squares are adjacent when the map is drawn in a surface with top and bottom or left and right edges touching one another. The two left-hand 1's in the top row are combined with the two 1's in the bottom row to give the term $B'C'$. The remaining 1 may be combined in a two-square area to give the term $A'CD'$. The simplified function is:

$$F = B'D' + B'C' + A'CD'$$

3-4 FIVE- AND SIX-VARIABLE MAPS

Maps of more than four variables are not as simple to use. The number of squares becomes excessively large and the geometry for combining adjacent squares becomes more involved. The number of squares is always equal to the number of minterms. For five-variable maps, we need 32 squares; for six-variable maps, we need 64 squares. Maps with seven or more variables need too many squares. They are impractical to use. The five- and six-variable maps are shown in Figs. 3-11 and 3-12, respectively. The rows and columns are numbered in a reflected-code sequence; the minterm assigned to each square is read from these numbers. In this way, the square in the third row (11) and second column (001), in the five-variable map, is number 11001, the equivalent of decimal 25. Therefore, this square represents minterm m_{25}. The letter symbol of each variable is marked along those squares where the corresponding bit value of the reflected-code number is a 1. For example, in the five-variable map, the variable A is a 1 in the last two rows; B is a 1 in the middle two rows. The reflected numbers in the columns show variable C with a 1 in the rightmost four columns, variable D with a 1 in the middle four

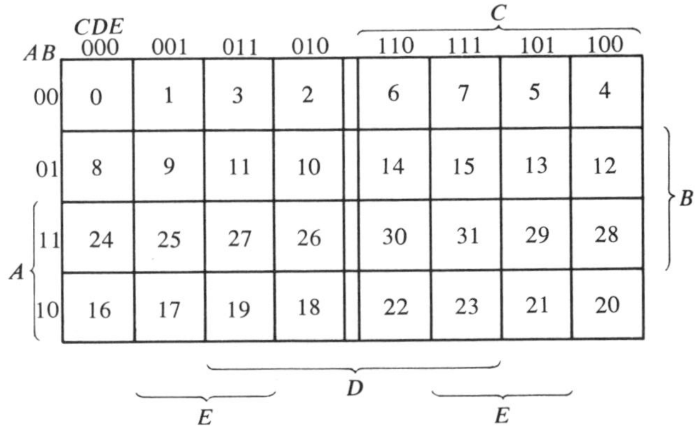

Figure 3-11 Five-variable map

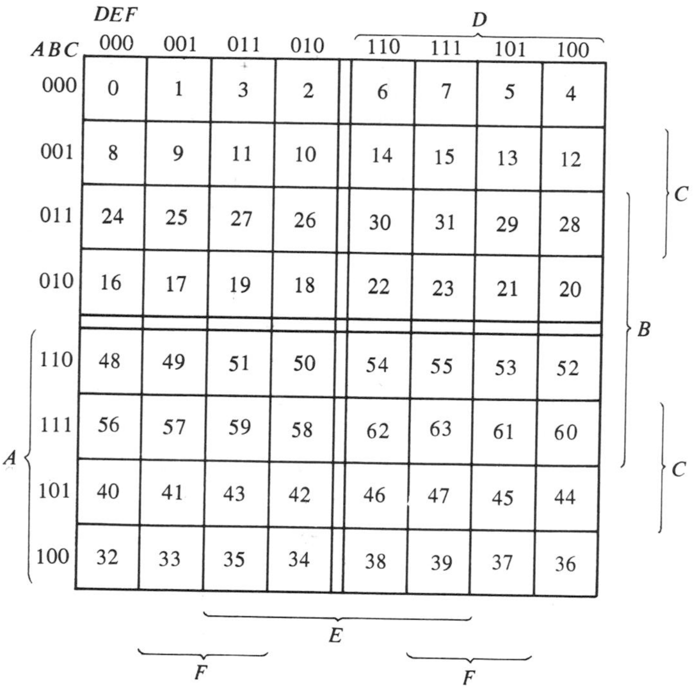

	DEF				D			
ABC	000	001	011	010	110	111	101	100
000	0	1	3	2	6	7	5	4
001	8	9	11	10	14	15	13	12
011	24	25	27	26	30	31	29	28
010	16	17	19	18	22	23	21	20
110	48	49	51	50	54	55	53	52
111	56	57	59	58	62	63	61	60
101	40	41	43	42	46	47	45	44
100	32	33	35	34	38	39	37	36

Figure 3-12 Six-variable map

columns, and the 1's for variable E not physically adjacent but split in two parts. The variable assignment in the six-variable map is determined similarly.

The definition of adjacent squares for the maps of Figs. 3-11 and 3-12 must be modified again to take into account the fact that some variables are split into two parts. The five-variable map must be thought to consist of two four-variable maps, and the six-variable map to consist of four four-variable maps. Each of these four-variable maps is recognized from the double lines in the center of the map; each retains the previously defined adjacency when taken individually. In addition, the center double line must be considered as the center of a book, with each half of the map being a page. When the book is closed, two adjacent squares will fall one on the other. In other words, the center double line is like a mirror with each square being adjacent, not only to its four neighboring squares, but also to its mirror image. For example, minterm 31 in the five-variable map is adjacent to minterms 30, 15, 29, 23, *and* 27. The same minterm in the six-variable map is adjacent to all these minterms plus minterm 63.

From inspection, and taking into account the new definition of adjacent squares, it is possible to show that any 2^k adjacent squares, for $k = 0, 1, 2, \ldots, n$, in an n-variable map, will represent an area that gives a term of $n - k$ literals. For the above statement to have any meaning, n must be larger than k. When $n = k$,

TABLE 3-1 The relationship between the number of adjacent squares and the number of literals in the term

k	2^k	Number of literals in a term in an n-variable map					
		$n = 2$	$n = 3$	$n = 4$	$n = 5$	$n = 6$	$n = 7$
0	1	2	3	4	5	6	7
1	2	1	2	3	4	5	6
2	4	0	1	2	3	4	5
3	8		0	1	2	3	4
4	16			0	1	2	3
5	32				0	1	2
6	64					0	1

the entire area of the map is combined to give the identity function. Table 3-1 shows the relationship between the number of adjacent squares and the number of literals in the term. For example, eight adjacent squares combine an area in the five-variable map to give a term of two literals.

EXAMPLE 3-7: Simplify the Boolean function:

$$F(A, B, C, D, E) = \Sigma(0, 2, 4, 6, 9, 11, 13, 15, 17, 21, 25, 27, 29, 31)$$

The five-variable map of this function is shown in Fig. 3-13. Each minterm is converted to its equivalent binary number and the

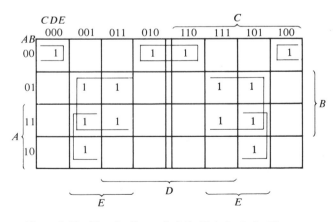

Figure 3-13 Map for Example 3-7; $F(A, B, C, D, E) =$
$\Sigma(0, 2, 4, 6, 9, 11, 13, 15, 17, 21, 25, 27, 29, 31)$
$= BE + AD'E + A'B'E'$

1's are marked in their corresponding squares. It is now necessary to find combinations of adjacent squares that will result in the largest possible area. The four squares in the center of the right-half map are reflected across the double line and are combined with the four squares in the center of the left-half map to give eight allowable adjacent squares equivalent to the term BE. The two 1's in the bottom row are the reflection of each other about the center double line. By combining them with the other two adjacent squares, we obtain the term $AD'E$. The four 1's in the top row are all adjacent and can be combined to give the term $A'B'E'$. All the 1's are now included. The simplified function is:

$$F = BE + AD'E + A'B'E'$$

3-5 PRODUCT OF SUMS SIMPLIFICATION

The minimized Boolean functions derived from the map in all previous examples were expressed in the sum of products form. With a minor modification, the product of sums form can be obtained.

The procedure for obtaining a minimized function in product of sums follows from the basic properties of Boolean functions. The 1's placed in the squares of the map represent the minterms of the function. The minterms not included in the function denote the complement of the function. From this we see that the complement of a function is represented in the map by the squares not marked by 1's. If we mark the empty squares by 0's and combine them into valid adjacent squares, we obtain a simplified expression of the complement of the function, i.e., of F'. The complement of F' gives us back the function F. Because of the generalized DeMorgan's theorem, the function so obtained is automatically in the product of sums form. The best way to show this is by example.

> **EXAMPLE 3-8:** Simplify the following Boolean function in (a) sum of products and (b) product of sums.

$$F(A, B, C, D) = \Sigma(0, 1, 2, 5, 8, 9, 10)$$

The 1's marked in the map of Fig. 3-14 represent all the minterms of the function. The squares marked with 0's represent the minterms not included in F and therefore denote the complement of F. Combining the squares with 1's gives the simplified function in sum of products:

(a) $F = B'D' + B'C' + A'C'D$

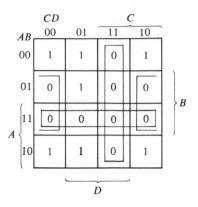

Figure 3-14 Map for Example 3-8; $F(A, B, C, D) =$
$\Sigma(0, 1, 2, 5, 8, 9, 10) = B'D' + B'C' + A'C'D$
$= (A' + B')(C' + D')(B' + D)$

If the squares marked with 0's are combined, as shown in the diagram, we obtain the simplified complemented function:

$$F' = AB + CD + BD'$$

Applying DeMorgan's theorem (by taking the dual and complementing each literal as described in Section 2-4), we obtain the simplified function in product of sums:

$$\text{(b)} \quad F = (A' + B')(C' + D')(B' + D)$$

The implementation of the simplified expressions obtained in Example 3-8 is shown in Fig. 3-15. The sum of products expression is implemented in (a) with a group of AND gates, one for each AND term. The outputs of the AND gates are connected to the inputs of a single OR gate. The same function is implemented in (b) in its product of sums form with a group of OR gates, one for each OR term. The outputs of the OR gates are connected to the inputs of a single AND gate. In each case, it is assumed that the input variables are directly available in their complement, so inverters are not needed. The configuration pattern established in Fig. 3-15 is the general form by which any Boolean function is implemented when expressed in one of the standard forms. AND gates are connected to a single OR gate when in sum of products; OR gates are connected to a single AND gate when in product of sums. Either configuration forms two levels of gates. Thus, the implementation of a function in a standard form is said to be a two-level implementation.

Example 3-8 showed the procedure for obtaining the product of sums simplification when the function is originally expressed in the sum of minterms canonical form. The procedure is also valid when the function is originally expressed in the product of maxterm canonical form. Consider, for example, the

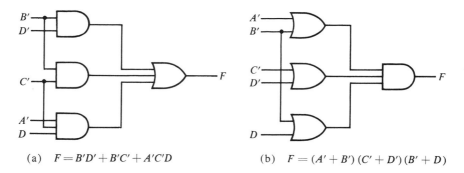

(a) $F = B'D' + B'C' + A'C'D$ (b) $F = (A' + B')(C' + D')(B' + D)$

Figure 3-15 Gate implementation of the function of Example 3-8

TABLE 3-2 Truth table of function F

x	y	z	F
0	0	0	0
0	0	1	1
0	1	0	0
0	1	1	1
1	0	0	1
1	0	1	0
1	1	0	1
1	1	1	0

truth table that defines the function F in Table 3-2. In sum of minterms, this function is expressed as:

$$F(x, y, z) = \Sigma(1, 3, 4, 6)$$

In product of maxterms, it is expressed as:

$$F(x, y, z) = \Pi(0, 2, 5, 7)$$

In other words, the 1's of the function represent the minterms, and the 0's represent the maxterms. The map for this function is drawn in Fig. 3-16. One can start

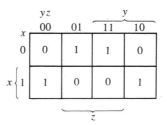

Figure 3-16 Map for the function of Table 3-2

simplifying this function by first marking the 1's for each minterm that the function is a 1. The remaining squares are marked by 0's. If, on the other hand, the product of maxterms is initially given, one can start marking 0's in those squares listed in the function; the remaining squares are then marked by 1's. Once the 1's and 0's are marked, the function can be simplified in either one of the standard forms. For the sum of products, we combine the 1's to obtain:

$$F = x'z + xz'$$

For the product of sums, we combine the 0's to obtain the simplified complemented function:

$$F' = xz + x'z'$$

which shows that the exclusive-OR function is the complement of the equivalence function (Section 2-6). Taking the complement of F', we obtain the simplified function in product of sums:

$$F = (x' + z')(x + z)$$

To enter a function expressed in product of sums in the map, take the complement of the function and from it find the squares to be marked by 0's. For example, the function:

$$F = (A' + B' + C)(B + D)$$

can be entered in the map by first taking its complement:

$$F' = ABC' + B'D'$$

and then marking 0's in the squares representing the minterms of F'. The remaining squares are marked with 1's.

3-6   NAND AND NOR IMPLEMENTATION

Digital circuits are more frequently constructed with NAND or NOR gates than with AND and OR gates. NAND and NOR gates are easier to fabricate with electronic components and are the basic gates used in all IC digital logic families. Because of the prominence of NAND and NOR gates in the design of digital circuits, rules and procedures have been developed for the conversion from Boolean functions given in terms of AND, OR, and NOT into equivalent NAND or NOR logic diagrams. The procedure for two-level implementation is presented in this section. Multilevel implementation is discussed in Section 4-7.

To facilitate the conversion to NAND and NOR logic, it is convenient to define two other graphic symbols for these gates. Two equivalent symbols for the NAND gate are shown in Fig. 3-17(a). The AND-invert symbol has been defined

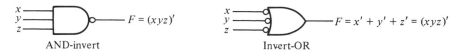

AND-invert   Invert-OR

(a) Two graphic symbols for NAND gate.

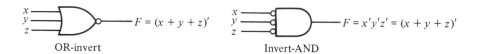

OR-invert   Invert-AND

(b) Two graphic symbols for NOR gate.

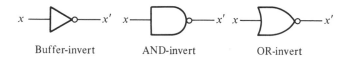

Buffer-invert   AND-invert   OR-invert

(c) Three graphic symbols for inverter.

Figure 3-17 Graphic symbols for NAND and NOR gates

previously and consists of an AND graphic symbol followed by a small circle. Instead, it is possible to represent a NAND gate by an OR graphic symbol preceded by small circles in all the inputs. The invert-OR symbol for the NAND gate follows from DeMorgan's theorem and from the convention that small circles denote complementation.

Similarly, there are two graphic symbols for the NOR gate as shown in Fig. 3-17(b). The OR-invert is the conventional symbol. The invert-AND is a convenient alternative that utilizes DeMorgan's theorem and the convention that small circles in the inputs denote complementation.

A one-input NAND or NOR gate behaves like an inverter. As a consequence, an inverter gate can be drawn in three different ways as shown in Fig. 3-17(c). The small circles in all inverter symbols can be transferred to the input terminal without changing the logic of the gate.

It should be pointed out that the alternate symbols for the NAND and NOR gates could be drawn with small triangles in all input terminals instead of the circles. A small triangle is a negative-logic polarity indicator (see Section 2-8 and Fig. 2-11). With small triangles in the input terminals, the graphic symbol denotes a negative-logic polarity for the inputs, but the output of the gate (not having a triangle) would have a positive-logic assignment. In this book, we prefer to stay with positive logic throughout and employ small circles when necessary to denote complementation.

NAND Implementation

The implementation of a Boolean function with NAND gates requires that the function be simplified in the sum of products form. To see the relationship between a sum of products expression and its equivalent NAND implementation,

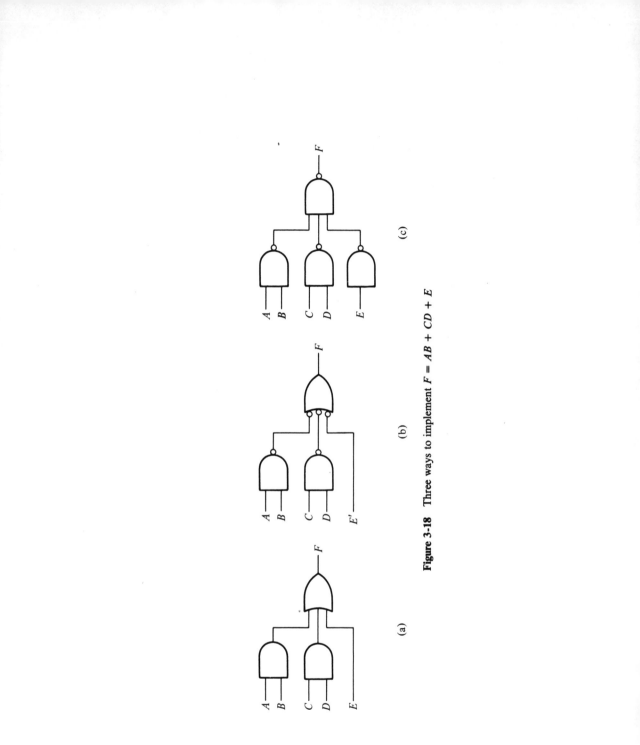

Figure 3-18 Three ways to implement $F = AB + CD + E$

(a)

(b)

(c)

consider the logic diagrams drawn in Fig. 3-18. All three diagrams are equivalent and implement the function:

$$F = AB + CD + E$$

The function is implemented in Fig. 3-18(a) in sum of products form with AND and OR gates. In (b) the AND gates are replaced by NAND gates and the OR gate is replaced by a NAND gate with an invert-OR symbol. The single variable E is complemented and applied to the second-level invert-OR gate. Remember that a small circle denotes complementation. Therefore, two circles on the same line represent double complementation and both can be removed. The complement of E goes through a small circle which complements the variable again to produce the normal value of E. Removing the small circles in the gates of Fig. 3-18(b) produces the circuit in (a). Therefore, the two diagrams implement the same function and are equivalent.

In Fig. 3-18(c), the output NAND gate is redrawn with the conventional symbol. The one-input NAND gate complements variable E. It is possible to remove this inverter and apply E' directly to the input of the second-level NAND gate. The diagram in (c) is equivalent to the one in (b), which in turn is equivalent to the diagram in (a). Note the similarity between the diagrams in (a) and (c). The AND and OR gates have been changed to NAND gates, but an additional NAND gate has been included with the single variable E. When drawing NAND logic diagrams, the circuit shown in either (b) or (c) is acceptable. The one in (b), however, represents a more direct relationship to the Boolean expression it implements.

The NAND implementation in Fig. 3-18(c) can be verified algebraically. The NAND function it implements can be easily converted to a sum of products form by using DeMorgan's theorem:

$$F = [(AB)' \cdot (CD)' \cdot E']' = AB + CD + E$$

From the transformation shown in Fig. 3-18, we conclude that a Boolean function can be implemented with two levels of NAND gates. The rule for obtaining the NAND logic diagram from a Boolean function is as follows:

1. Simplify the function and express it in sum of products.

2. Draw a NAND gate for each product term of the function that has at least two literals. The inputs to each NAND gate are the literals of the term. This constitutes a group of first-level gates.

3. Draw a single NAND gate (using the AND-invert or invert-OR graphic symbol) in the second level, with inputs coming from outputs of first-level gates.

4. A term with a single literal requires an inverter in the first level or may be complemented and applied as an input to the second-level NAND gate.

Before applying these rules to a specific example, it should be mentioned that there is a second way to implement a Boolean function with NAND gates. Remember that if we combine the 0's in a map, we obtain the simplified expression of the *complement* of the function in sum of products. The complement of the function can then be implemented with two levels of NAND gates using the rules stated above. If the normal output is desired, it would be necessary to insert a one-input NAND or inverter gate to generate the true value of the output variable. There are occasions where the designer may want to generate the complement of the function; so this second method may be preferable.

EXAMPLE 3-9: Implement the following function with NAND gates:

$$F(x, y, z) = \Sigma(0, 6)$$

The first step is to simplify the function in sum of products form. This is attempted with the map shown in Fig. 3-19(a). There are only two 1's in the map, and they cannot be combined. The simplified function in sum of products for this example is:

$$F = x'y'z' + xyz'$$

The two-level NAND implementation is shown in Fig. 3-19(b). Next we try to simplify the complement of the function in sum of products. This is done by combining the 0's in the map:

$$F' = x'y + xy' + z$$

The two-level NAND gate for generating F' is shown in Fig. 3-19(c). If output F is required, it is necessary to add a one-input NAND gate to invert the function. This gives a three-level implementation. In each case, it is assumed that the input variables are available in both the normal and complement forms. If they were available in only one form, it would be necessary to insert inverters in the inputs, which would add another level to the circuits. The one-input NAND gate associated with the single variable z can be removed provided the input is changed to z'.

NOR Implementation

The NOR function is the dual of the NAND function. For this reason, all procedures and rules for NOR logic are the dual of the corresponding procedures and rules developed for NAND logic.

The implementation of a Boolean function with NOR gates requires that the function be simplified in product of sums form. A product of sums expression

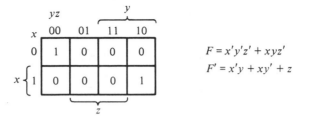

$$F = x'y'z' + xyz'$$
$$F' = x'y + xy' + z$$

(a) Map simplification in sum of products.

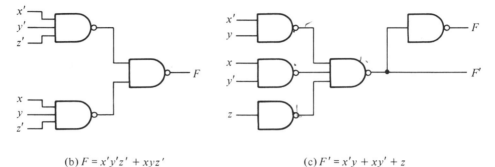

(b) $F = x'y'z' + xyz'$

(c) $F' = x'y + xy' + z$

Figure 3-19 Implementation of the function of Example 3-9 with NAND gates

specifies a group of OR gates for the sum terms, followed by an AND gate to produce the product. The transformation from the OR-AND to the NOR-NOR diagram is depicted in Fig. 3-20. It is similar to the NAND transformation discussed previously, except that now we use the product of sums expression:

$$F = (A + B)(C + D)E$$

The rule for obtaining the NOR logic diagram from a Boolean function can be derived from this transformation. It is similar to the three-step NAND rule, except that the simplified expression must be in the product of sums and the terms for the first-level NOR gates are the sum terms. A term with a single literal

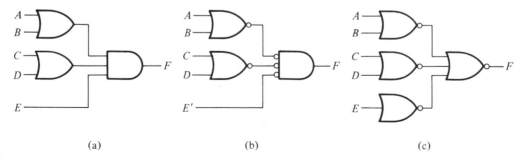

(a)   (b)   (c)

Figure 3-20 Three ways to implement $F = (A + B)(C + D)E$

requires a one-input NOR or inverter gate or may be complemented and applied directly to the second-level NOR gate.

A second way to implement a function with NOR gates would be to use the expression for the complement of the function in product of sums. This will give a two-level implementation for F' and a three-level implementation if the normal output F is required.

To obtain the simplified product of sums from a map, it is necessary to combine the 0's in the map and then complement the function. To obtain the simplified product of sums expression for the complement of the function, it is necessary to combine the 1's in the map and then complement the function. The following example demonstrates the procedure for NOR implementation.

EXAMPLE 3-10: Implement the function of Example 3-9 with NOR gates.

The map of this function is drawn in Fig. 3-19(a). First, combine the 0's in the map to obtain:

$$F' = x'y + xy' + z$$

This is the complement of the function in sum of products. Complement F' to obtain the simplified function in product of sums as required for NOR implementation:

$$F = (x + y')(x' + y)z'$$

The two-level implementation with NOR gates is shown in Fig. 3-21(a). The term with a single literal z' requires a one-input NOR or inverter gate. This gate can be removed and input z applied directly to the input of the second-level NOR gate.

A second implementation is possible from the complement of

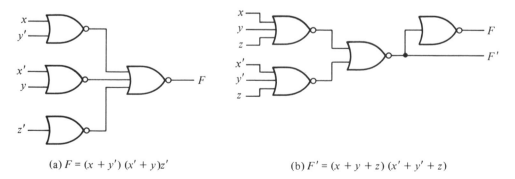

(a) $F = (x + y')(x' + y)z'$ (b) $F' = (x + y + z)(x' + y' + z)$

Figure 3-21 Implementation with NOR gates

TABLE 3-3   Rules for NAND and NOR implementation

Case	Function to simplify	Standard form to use	How to derive	Implement with	Number of levels to F
(a)	F	Sum of products	Combine 1's in map	NAND	2
(b)	F'	Sum of products	Combine 0's in map	NAND	3
(c)	F	Product of sums	Complement F' in (b)	NOR	2
(d)	F'	Product of sums	Complement F in (a)	NOR	3

the function in product of sums. For this case, first combine the 1's in the map to obtain:

$$F = x'y'z' + xyz'$$

This is the simplified expression in sum of products. Complement this function to obtain the complement of the function in product of sums as required for NOR implementation:

$$F' = (x + y + z)(x' + y' + z)$$

The two-level implementation for F' is shown in Fig. 3-21(b). If output F is desired, it can be generated with an inverter in the third level.

Table 3-3 summarizes the procedures for NAND or NOR implementation. One should not forget to always simplify the function in order to reduce the number of gates in the implementation. The standard forms obtained from the map simplification procedures apply directly and are very useful when dealing with NAND or NOR logic.

3-7 OTHER TWO-LEVEL IMPLEMENTATIONS

The types of gates most often found in integrated circuits are NAND and NOR. For this reason, NAND and NOR logic implementations are the most important from a practical point of view. Some NAND or NOR gates (but not all) allow the possibility of a wire connection between the outputs of two gates to provide a specific logic function. This type of logic is called *wired logic*. For example, open-collector TTL NAND gates, when tied together, perform the wired-AND logic. (The open-collector TTL gate is shown in Chapter 10, Fig. 10-11). The wired-AND logic performed with two NAND gates is depicted in Fig. 3-22(a). The

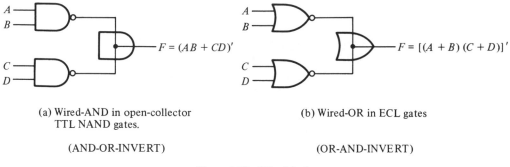

(a) Wired-AND in open-collector
TTL NAND gates.

(b) Wired-OR in ECL gates

(AND-OR-INVERT)

(OR-AND-INVERT)

Figure 3-22   Wired logic

AND gate is drawn with the lines going through the center of the gate to distinguish it from a conventional gate. The wired-AND gate is not a physical gate but only a symbol to designate the function obtained from the indicated wired connection. The logic function implemented by the circuit of Fig. 3-22(a) is:

$$F = (AB)' \cdot (CD)' = (AB + CD)'$$

and is called an AND-OR-INVERT function.

Similarly, the NOR output of ECL gates can be tied together to perform a wired-OR function. The logic function implemented by the circuit of Fig. 3-22(b) is:

$$F = (A + B)' + (C + D)' = [(A + B)(C + D)]'$$

and is called an OR-AND-INVERT function.

A wired-logic gate does not produce a physical second-level gate since it is just a wire connection. Nevertheless, for discussion purposes, we will consider the circuits of Fig. 3-22 as two-level implementations. The first level consists of NAND (or NOR) gates and the second level has a single AND (or OR) gate. The wired connection in the graphic symbol will be omitted in subsequent discussions.

Nondegenerate Forms

It will be instructive from a theoretical point of view to find out how many two-level combinations of gates are possible. We consider four types of gates: AND, OR, NAND, and NOR. If we assign one type of gate for the first level and one type for the second level, we find that there are 16 possible combinations of two-level forms. (The same type of gate can be in the first and second levels, as in NAND-NAND implementation.) Eight of these combinations are said to be *degenerate* forms because they degenerate to a single operation. This can be seen from a circuit with AND gates in the first level and an AND gate in the second level. The output of the circuit is merely the AND function of all input variables.

The other eight *nondegenerate* forms produce an implementation in sum of products or product of sums. The eight nondegenerate forms are:

AND-OR	OR-AND
NAND-NAND	NOR-NOR
NOR-OR	NAND-AND
OR-NAND	AND-NOR

The first gate listed in each of the forms constitutes a first level in the implementation. The second gate listed is a single gate placed in the second level. Note that any two forms listed in the same line are the duals of each other.

The AND-OR and OR-AND forms are the basic two-level forms discussed in Section 3-5. The NAND-NAND and NOR-NOR were introduced in Section 3-6. The remaining four forms are investigated in this section.

AND-OR-INVERT Implementation

The two forms NAND-AND and AND-NOR are equivalent forms and can be treated together. Both perform the AND-OR-INVERT function, as shown in Fig. 3-23. The AND-NOR form resembles the AND-OR form with an inversion done by the small circle in the output of the NOR gate. It implements the function:

$$F = (AB + CD + E)'$$

By using the alternate graphic symbol for the NOR gate, we obtain the diagram of Fig. 3-23(b). Note that the single variable E is *not* complemented because the only change made is in the graphic symbol of the NOR gate. Now we move the circles from the input terminal of the second-level gate to the output terminals of the first-level gates. An inverter is needed for the single variable to maintain the circle. Alternatively, the inverter can be removed provided input E is complemented. The circuit of Fig. 3-23(c) is a NAND-AND form and was shown in Fig. 3-22 to implement the AND-OR-INVERT function.

An AND-OR implementation requires an expression in sum of products. The AND-OR-INVERT implementation is similar except for the inversion. Therefore, if the *complement* of the function is simplified in sum of products (by combining the 0's in the map), it will be possible to implement F' with the AND-OR part of the function. When F' passes through the always present output inversion (the INVERT part), it will generate the output F of the function. An example for the AND-OR-INVERT implementation will be shown subsequently.

OR-AND-INVERT Implementation

The OR-NAND and NOR-OR forms perform the OR-AND-INVERT function. This is shown in Fig. 3-24. The OR-NAND form resembles the OR-AND form,

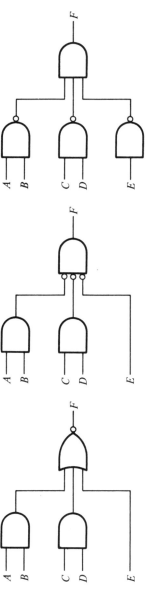

(a) AND-NOR

(b) AND-NOR

(c) NAND-AND

Figure 3-23 AND-OR-INVERT circuits; $F = (AB + CD + E)'$

$\overline{NOR} = and$

$\overline{and} = Nand$

$\overline{OR} = NOR$

$\overline{Nand} = OR$

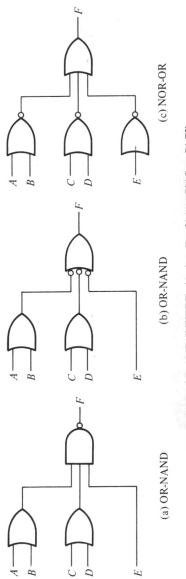

(a) OR-NAND

(b) OR-NAND

(c) NOR-OR

Figure 3-24 OR-AND-INVERT circuits; $F = [(A + B)(C + D)E]'$

except for the inversion done by the circle in the NAND gate. It implements the function:

$$F = [(A + B)(C + D)E]'$$

By using the alternate graphic symbol for the NAND gate, we obtain the diagram of Fig. 3-24(b). The circuit in (c) is obtained by moving the small circles from the inputs of the second-level gate to the outputs of the first-level gates. The circuit of Fig. 3-24(c) is a NOR-OR form and was shown in Fig. 3-22 to implement the OR-AND-INVERT function.

The OR-AND-INVERT implementation requires an expression in product of sums. If the complement of the function is simplified in product of sums, we can implement F' with the OR-AND part of the function. When F' passes through the INVERT part, we obtain the complement of F', or F, in the output.

Tabular Summary and Example

Table 3-4 summarizes the procedures for implementing a Boolean function in any one of the four two-level forms. Because of the INVERT part in each case, it is convenient to use the simplification of F' (the complement) of the function. When F' is implemented in one of these forms, we obtain the complement of the function in the AND-OR or OR-AND form. The four two-level forms invert this function, giving an output which is the complement of F'. This is the normal output F.

TABLE 3-4   Implementation with other two-level forms

Equivalent nondegenerate form		Implements the function	Simplify F' in	To get an output of
(a)	(b)*			
AND-NOR	NAND-AND	AND-OR-INVERT	Sum of products by combining 0's in the map	F
OR-NAND	NOR-OR	OR-AND-INVERT	Product of sums by combining 1's in the map and then complementing	F

*Form (b) requires a one-input NAND or NOR (inverter) gate for a single literal term.

EXAMPLE 3-11: Implement the function of Fig. 3-19(a) with the four two-level forms listed in Table 3-4. The complement of the function is simplified in sum of products by combining the 0's in the map:

$$F' = x'y + xy' + z$$

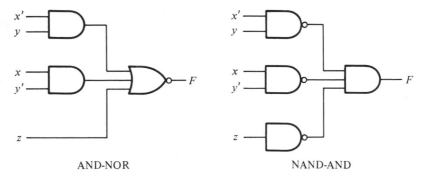

AND-NOR   NAND-AND

(a) $F = (x'y + xy' + z)'$

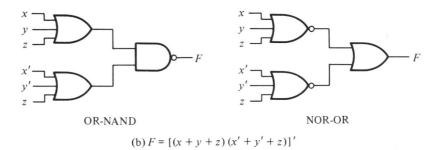

OR-NAND   NOR-OR

(b) $F = [(x + y + z)(x' + y' + z)]'$

Figure 3-25 Other two-level implementations

The normal output for this function can be expressed as

$$F = (x'y + xy' + z)'$$

which is in the AND-OR-INVERT form. The AND-NOR and NAND-AND implementations are shown in Fig. 3-25(a). Note that a one-input NAND or inverter gate is needed in the NAND-AND implementation, but not in the AND-NOR case. The inverter can be removed if we apply the input variable z' instead of z.

The OR-AND-INVERT forms require a simplified expression of the complement of the function in product of sums. To obtain this expression, we must first combine the 1's in the map:

$$F = x'y'z' + xyz'$$

Then we take the complement of the function:

$$F' = (x + y + z)(x' + y' + z)$$

The normal output F can now be expressed in the form:

$$F = [(x + y + z)(x' + y' + z)]'$$

which is in the OR-AND-INVERT form. From this expression we can implement the function in the OR-NAND and NOR-OR forms as shown in Fig. 3-25(b).

3-8   DON'T-CARE CONDITIONS

The 1's and 0's in the map signify the combination of variables that makes the function equal to 1 or 0, respectively. The combinations are usually obtained from a truth table that lists the conditions under which the function is a 1. The function is assumed equal to 0 under all other conditions. This assumption is not always true since there are applications where certain combinations of input variables never occur. A four-bit decimal code, for example, has six combinations which are not used. Any digital circuit using this code operates under the assumption that these unused combinations will never occur as long as the system is working properly. As a result, we don't care what the function output is to be for these combinations of the variables because they are guaranteed never to occur. These don't-care conditions can be used on a map to provide further simplification of the function.

It should be realized that a don't-care combination cannot be marked with a 1 on the map because it would require that the function always be a 1 for such input combination. Likewise, putting a 0 in the square requires the function to be 0. To distinguish the don't-care conditions from 1's and 0's, an X will be used.

When choosing adjacent squares to simplify the function in the map, the X's may be assumed to be either 0 or 1, whichever gives the simplest expression. In addition, an X need not be used at all if it does not contribute to covering a larger area. In each case, the choice depends only on the simplification that can be achieved.

EXAMPLE 3-12: Simplify the Boolean function:

$$F(w, x, y, z) = \Sigma(1, 3, 7, 11, 15)$$

and the don't-care conditions:

$$d(w, x, y, z) = \Sigma(0, 2, 5)$$

The minterms of F are the variable combinations that make the function equal to 1. The minterms of d are the don't-care combinations known never to occur. The minimization is shown in Fig. 3-26. The minterms of F are marked by 1's, those of d are marked by X's, and the remaining squares are filled with 0's. In (a), the 1's and X's are combined in any convenient manner so as to enclose the maximum number of adjacent squares. It is not necessary to include all or any of the X's, but only those useful for simplifying a term. One

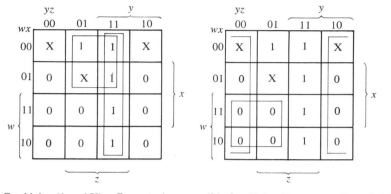

(a) Combining 1's and X's $F = w'z + yz$ (b) Combining 0's and X's $F = z(w' + y)$

Figure 3-26 Example with don't-care conditions

combination that gives a minimum function encloses one X and leaves two out. This results in a simplified sum-of-products function:

$$F = w'z + yz$$

In (b), the 0's are combined with any X's convenient to simplify the complement of the function. The best results are obtained if we enclose the two X's as shown. The complement function is simplified to:

$$F' = z' + wy'$$

Complementing again, we obtain a simplified product of sums function:

$$F = z(w' + y)$$

The two expressions obtained in Example 3-12 give two functions which can be shown to be algebraically equal. This is not always the case when don't-care conditions are involved. As a matter of fact, if an X is used as a 1 when combining the 1's and again as a 0 when combining the 0's, the two resulting functions will not yield algebraically equal answers. The selection of the don't-care condition as a 1 in the first case and as a 0 in the second results in different minterm expressions and thus different functions. This can be seen from Example 3-12. In the solution of this example, the X chosen to be a 1 was not chosen to be a 0. Now, if in Fig. 3-26(a) we choose the term $w'x'$ instead of $w'z$, we still obtain a minimized function:

$$F = w'x' + yz$$

But it is not algebraically equal to the one obtained in product of sums because the same X's are used as 1's in the first minimization and as 0's in the second.

This example also demonstrates that an expression with the minimum number of literals is not necessarily unique. Sometimes the designer is confronted with a choice between two terms with an equal number of literals, with either choice resulting in a minimized expression.

3-9   THE TABULATION METHOD

The map method of simplification is convenient as long as the number of variables does not exceed five or six. As the number of variables increases, the excessive number of squares prevents a reasonable selection of adjacent squares. The obvious disadvantage of the map is that it is essentially a trial-and-error procedure which relies on the ability of the human user to recognize certain patterns. For functions of six or more variables, it is difficult to be sure that the best selection has been made.

The tabulation method overcomes this difficulty. It is a specific step-by-step procedure that is guaranteed to produce a simplified standard-form expression for a function. It can be applied to problems with many variables and has the advantage of being suitable for machine computation. However, it is quite tedious for human use and is prone to mistakes because of its routine, monotonous process. The tabulation method was first formulated by Quine (3) and later improved by McCluskey (4). It is also known as the Quine-McCluskey method.

The tabular method of simplification consists of two parts. The first is to find by an exhaustive search all the terms that are candidates for inclusion in the simplified function. These terms are called *prime-implicants*. The second operation is to choose among the prime-implicants those that give an expression with the least number of literals.

3-10   DETERMINATION OF PRIME-IMPLICANTS*

The starting point of the tabulation method is the list of minterms that specify the function. The first tabular operation is to find the prime-implicants by using a matching process. This process compares each minterm with every other minterm. If two minterms differ in only one variable, that variable is removed and a term with one less literal is found. This process is repeated for every minterm until the exhaustive search is completed. The matching-process cycle is repeated for those new terms just found. Third and further cycles are continued until a single pass through a cycle yields no further elimination of literals. The remaining terms and all the terms that did not match during the process comprise the prime-implicants. This tabulation method is illustrated by the following example.

*This section and the next may be omitted without loss of continuity.

EXAMPLE 3-13: Simplify the following Boolean function by using the tabulation method:

$$F = \Sigma(0, 1, 2, 8, 10, 11, 14, 15)$$

Step 1: Group binary representation of the minterms according to the number of 1's contained, as shown in Table 3-5, column (a). This is done by grouping the minterms into five sections separated by horizontal lines. The first section contains the number with no 1's in it. The second section contains those numbers that have only one 1. The third, fourth, and fifth sections contain those binary numbers with two, three, and four 1's, respectively. The decimal equivalents of the minterms are also carried along for identification.

Step 2: Any two minterms which differ from each other by only one variable can be combined, and the unmatched variable removed. Two minterm numbers fit into this category if they both have the same bit value in all positions except one. The minterms in one section are compared with those of the next section down only, because two terms differing by more than one bit cannot match. The minterm in the first section is compared with each of the three minterms in the second section. If any two numbers are the same in every position but one, a check is placed to the right of both minterms to show that they have been used. The resulting term,

TABLE 3-5 Determination of prime-implicants for Example 3-13

(a)		(b)		(c)	
	w x y z		*w x y z*		*w x y z*
0	0 0 0 0 √	0, 1	0 0 0 −	0, 2, 8, 10	− 0 − 0
		0, 2	0 0 − 0 √	0, 8, 2, 10	− 0 − 0
1	0 0 0 1 √	0, 8	− 0 0 0 √	10, 11, 14, 15	1 − 1 −
2	0 0 1 0 √			10, 14, 11, 15	1 − 1 −
8	1 0 0 0 √	2, 10	− 0 1 0 √		
		8, 10	1 0 − 0 √		
10	1 0 1 0 √				
		10, 11	1 0 1 − √		
11	1 0 1 1 √	10, 14	1 − 1 0 √		
14	1 1 1 0 √				
		11, 15	1 − 1 1 √		
15	1 1 1 1 √	14, 15	1 1 1 − √		

together with the decimal equivalents, is listed in column (b) of the table. The variable eliminated during the matching is denoted by a dash in its original position. In this case m_0 (0000) combines with m_1 (0001) to form (000 −). This combination is equivalent to the algebraic operation:

$$m_0 + m_1 = w'x'y'z' + w'x'y'z = w'x'y'$$

Minterm m_0 also combines with m_2 to form (00-0) and with m_8 to form (-000). The result of this comparison is entered into the first section of column (b). The minterms of sections two and three of column (a) are next compared to produce the terms listed in the second section of column (b). All other sections of (a) are similarly compared and subsequent sections formed in (b). This exhaustive comparing process results in the four sections of (b).

Step 3: The terms of column (b) have only three variables. A 1 under the variable means it is unprimed, a 0 means it is primed, and a dash means the variable is not included in the term. The searching and comparing process is repeated for the terms in column (b) to form the two-variable terms of column (c). Again, terms in each section need to be compared only if they have dashes in the same position. Note that the term (000-) does not match with any other term. Therefore, it has no check mark at its right. The decimal equivalents are written on the left-hand side of each entry for identification purposes. The comparing process should be carried out again in column (c) and in subsequent columns as long as proper matching is encountered. In the present example, the operation stops at the third column.

Step 4: The unchecked terms in the table form the prime-implicants. In this example we have the term $w'x'y'$ (000-) in column (b), and the terms $x'z'$(-0-0) and wy (1-1-) in column (c). Note that each term in column (c) appears twice in the table, and as long as the term forms a prime-implicant, it is unnecessary to use the same term twice. The sum of the prime-implicants gives a simplified expression for the function. This is because each checked term in the table has been taken into account by an entry of a simpler term in a subsequent column. Therefore, the unchecked entries (prime-implicants) are the terms left to formulate the function. For the present example, the sum of prime-implicants gives the minimized function in sum of products:

$$F = w'x'y' + x'z' + wy$$

It is worth comparing this answer with that obtained by the map method. Figure 3-27 shows the map simplification of this function. The combinations of

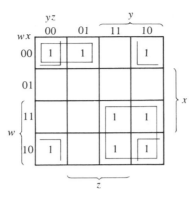

Figure 3-27 Map for the function of Example 3-13; $F = w'x'y' + x'z' + wy$

adjacent squares give the three prime-implicants of the function. The sum of these three terms is the simplified expression in sum of products.

It is important to point out that Example 3-13 was purposely chosen to give the simplified function from the sum of prime-implicants. In most other cases, the sum of prime-implicants does not necessarily form the expression with the minimum number of terms. This is demonstrated in Example 3-14.

The tedious manipulation that one must undergo when using the tabulation method is reduced if the comparing is done with decimal numbers instead of binary. A method will now be shown that uses subtraction of decimal numbers instead of the comparing and matching of binary numbers. We note that each 1 in a binary number represents the coefficient multiplied by a power of 2. When two minterms are the same in every position except one, the minterm with the extra 1 must be larger than the number of the other minterm by a power of 2. Therefore, two minterms can be combined if the number of the first minterm differs by a power of 2 from a second larger number in the next section down the table. We shall illustrate this procedure by repeating Example 3-13.

As shown in Table 3-6, column (a), the minterms are arranged in sections as before, except that now only the decimal equivalents of the minterms are listed. The process of comparing minterms is as follows: Inspect every two decimal numbers in adjacent sections of the table. If the number in the section below is *greater* than the number in the section above by a power of 2 (i.e., 1, 2, 4, 8, 16, etc.), check both numbers to show that they have been used, and write them down in column (b). The pair of numbers transferred to column (b) includes a third number in parentheses that designates the power of 2 by which the numbers differ. The number in parentheses tells us the position of the dash in the binary notation. The result of all comparisons of column (a) is shown in column (b).

The comparison between adjacent sections in column (b) is carried out in a similar fashion, except that only those terms with the same number in parentheses are compared. The pair of numbers in one section must differ by a power of 2 from the pair of numbers in the next section. And the numbers in the next section

TABLE 3-6 Determination of prime-implicants of Example 3-13 with decimal notation

(a)	(b)	(c)
0 √	0, 1 (1)	0, 2, 8, 10 (2, 8)
	0, 2 (2) √	0, 2, 8, 10 (2, 8)
1 √	0, 8 (8) √	
2 √		10, 11, 14, 15 (1, 4)
8 √	2, 10 (8) √	10, 11, 14, 15 (1, 4)
	8, 10 (2) √	
10 √		
	10, 11 (1) √	
11 √	10, 14 (4) √	
14 √		
	11, 15 (4) √	
15 √	14, 15 (1) √	

below must be *greater* for the combination to take place. In column (c), write all four decimal numbers with the two numbers in parentheses designating the positions of the dashes. A comparison of Tables 3-5 and 3-6 may be helpful in understanding the derivations in Table 3-6.

The prime-implicants are those terms not checked in the table. These are the same as before, except that they are given in decimal notation. To convert from decimal notation to binary, convert all decimal numbers in the term to binary and then insert a dash in those positions designated by the numbers in parentheses. Thus 0, 1 (1) is converted to binary as 0000, 0001; a dash in the first position of either number results in (000-). Similarly, 0, 2, 8, 10 (2, 8) is converted to the binary notation from 0000, 0010, 1000, and 1010, and a dash inserted in positions 2 and 8, to result in (-0-0)

> **EXAMPLE 3-14:** Determine the prime-implicants of the function:
>
> $$F(w, x, y, z) = \Sigma(1, 4, 6, 7, 8, 9, 10, 11, 15)$$

The minterm numbers are grouped in sections as shown in Table 3-7, column (a). The binary equivalent of the minterm is included for the purpose of counting the number of 1's. The binary numbers in the first section have only one 1; in the second section, two 1's; etc. The minterm numbers are compared by the decimal method and a match is found if the number in the section below is greater than that in the section above. If the number in the section below is smaller than the

TABLE 3-7   Determination of prime-implicants for Example 3-14

(a)			(b)			(c)
0001	1	√	1, 9	(8)		8, 9, 10, 11 (1, 2)
0100	4	√	4, 6	(2)		8, 9, 10, 11 (1, 2)
1000	8	√	8, 9	(1)	√	
			8, 10	(2)	√	
0110	6	√				
1001	9	√	6, 7	(1)		
1010	10	√	9, 11	(2)	√	
			10, 11	(1)	√	
0111	7	√				
1011	11	√	7, 15	(8)		
			11, 15	(4)		
1111	15	√				

Prime-implicants

Decimal	Binary w x y z	Term
1, 9 (8)	− 0 0 1	$x'y'z$
4, 6 (2)	0 1 − 0	$w'xz'$
6, 7 (1)	0 1 1 −	$w'xy$
7, 15 (8)	− 1 1 1	xyz
11, 15 (4)	1 − 1 1	wyz
8, 9, 10, 11 (1, 2)	1 0 − −	wx'

one above, a match is not recorded even if the two numbers differ by a power of 2. The exhaustive search in column (a) results in the terms of column (b), with all minterms in column (a) being checked. There are only two matches of terms in column (b). Each gives the same two-literal term recorded in column (c). The prime-implicants consist of all the unchecked terms in the table. The conversion from the decimal to the binary notation is shown at the bottom of the table. The prime-implicants are found to be $x'y'z$, $w'xz'$, $w'xy$, xyz, wyz, and wx'.

The sum of the prime-implicants gives a valid algebraic expression for the function. However, this expression is not necessarily the one with the minimum number of terms. This can be demonstrated from inspection of the map for the

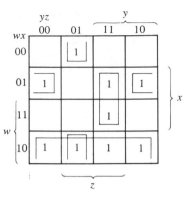

Figure 3-28   Map for the function of Example 3-14; $F = x'y'z + w'xz' + xyz + wx'$

function of Example 3-14. As shown in Fig. 3-28, the minimized function is recognized to be:

$$F = x'y'z + w'xz' + xyz + wx'$$

which consists of the sum of four of the six prime-implicants derived in Example 3-14. The tabular procedure for selecting the prime-implicants that give the minimized function is the subject of the next section.

3-11   SELECTION OF PRIME-IMPLICANTS

The selection of prime-implicants that form the minimized function is made from a prime-implicant table. In this table, each prime-implicant is represented in a row and each minterm in a column. Crosses are placed in each row to show the composition of minterms that make the prime-implicants. A minimum set of prime-implicants is then chosen that covers all the minterms in the function. This procedure is illustrated in Example 3-15.

>   *EXAMPLE 3-15:* Minimize the function of Example 3-14. The prime-implicant table for this example is shown in Table 3-8. There are six rows, one for each prime-implicant (derived in Example 3-14), and nine columns, each representing one minterm of the function. Crosses are placed in each row to indicate the minterms contained in the prime-implicant of that row. For example, the two crosses in the first row indicate that minterms 1 and 9 are contained in the prime-implicant $x'y'z$. It is advisable to include the decimal equivalent of the prime-implicant in each row, as it conveniently gives the minterms contained in it. After all the crosses have been marked, we proceed to select a minimum number of prime-implicants.
>   The completed prime-implicant table is inspected for columns

TABLE 3-8   Prime-implicant table for Example 3-15

		1	4	6	7	8	9	10	11	15
√ $x'y'z$	1, 9	X					X			
√ $w'xz'$	4, 6		X	X						
$w'xy$	6, 7			X	X					
xyz	7, 15				X					X
wyz	11, 15								X	X
√ wx'	8, 9, 10, 11					X	X	X	X	
		√	√	√		√	√	√	√	

containing only a single cross. In this example, there are four minterms whose columns have a single cross: 1, 4, 8, and 10. Minterm 1 is covered by prime-implicant $x'y'z$, i.e., the selection of prime-implicant $x'y'z$ guarantees that minterm 1 is included in the function. Similarly, minterm 4 is covered by prime-implicant $w'xz'$, and minterms 8 and 10, by prime-implicant wx'. Prime-implicants that cover minterms with a single cross in their column are called *essential prime-implicants*. To enable the final simplified expression to contain all the minterms, we have no alternative but to include essential prime-implicants. A check mark is placed in the table next to the essential prime-implicants to indicate that they have been selected.

Next we check each column whose minterm is covered by the selected essential prime-implicants. For example, the selected prime-implicant $x'y'z$ covers minterms 1 and 9. A check is inserted in the bottom of the columns. Similarly, prime-implicant $w'xz'$ covers minterms 4 and 6, and wx' covers minterms 8, 9, 10, and 11. Inspection of the prime-implicant table shows that the selection of the essential prime-implicants covers all the minterms of the function except 7 and 15. These two minterms must be included by the selection of one or more prime-implicants. In this example, it is clear that prime-implicant xyz covers both minterms and is therefore the one to be selected. We have thus found the minimum set of prime-implicants whose sum gives the required minimized function:

$$F = x'y'z + w'xz' + wx' + xyz$$

The simplified expressions derived in the preceding examples were all in the sum of products form. The tabulation method can be adapted to give a simplified expression in product of sums. As in the map method, we have to start with the complement of the function by taking the 0's as the initial list of minterms. This list contains those minterms not included in the original function which are numerically equal to the maxterms of the function. The tabulation process is carried out with the 0's of the function and terminates with a simplified expression in sum of products of the complement of the function. By taking the complement again, we obtain the simplified product of sums expression.

A function with don't-care conditions can be simplified by the tabulation method after a slight modification. The don't-care terms are included in the list of minterms when the prime-implicants are determined. This allows the derivation of prime-implicants with the least number of literals. The don't-care terms are not included in the list of minterms when the prime-implicant table is set up, because don't-care terms do not have to be covered by the selected prime-implicants.

3-12   CONCLUDING REMARKS

Two methods of Boolean function simplification were introduced in this chapter. The criterion for simplification was taken to be the minimization of the number of literals in sum of products or product of sums expressions. Both the map and the tabulation methods are restricted in their capabilities since they are useful for simplifying only Boolean functions expressed in the standard forms. Although this is a disadvantage of the methods, it is not very critical. Most applications prefer the standard forms over any other form. We have seen from Fig. 3-15 that the gate implementation of expressions in standard form consists of no more than two levels of gates. Expressions not in the standard form are implemented with more than two levels. Humphrey (5) shows an extension of the map method that produces simplified multilevel expressions.

One should recognize that the reflected-code sequence chosen for the maps is not unique. It is possible to draw a map and assign a binary reflected-code sequence to the rows and columns different from the sequence employed here. As long as the binary sequence chosen produces a change in only one bit between adjacent squares, it will produce a valid and useful map.

Two alternate versions of the three-variable maps which are often found in the digital logic literature are shown in Fig. 3-29. The minterm numbers are written

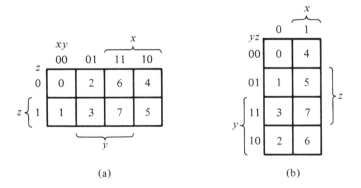

(a)   (b)

Figure 3-29   Variations of the three-variable map

in each square for reference. In (a), the assignment of the variables to the rows and columns is different from the one used in this book. In (b), the map has been rotated in a vertical position. The minterm number assignment in all maps remains in the order xyz. For example, the square for minterm 6 is found by assigning to the ordered variables the binary number $xyz = 110$. The square for this minterm is found in (a) from the column marked $xy = 11$ and the row with $z = 0$. The corresponding square in (b) belongs in the column marked with $x = 1$ and the row with $yz = 10$. The simplification procedure with these maps is exactly the same as described in this chapter except, of course, for the variations in minterm and variable assignment.

Two other versions of the four-variable map are shown in Fig. 3-30. The map in (a) is very popular and is used quite often in the literature. Here again, the difference is slight and is manifested by a mere interchange of variable assignment from rows to columns and vice versa. The map in (b) is the original Veitch diagram (1) which Karnaugh (2) modified to the one shown in (a). Again, the simplification procedures do not change when these maps are used instead of the one employed in this book. There are also variations of the five- and six-variable maps. In any case, any map that looks different from the one used in this book, or is called by a different name, should be recognized merely as a variation of minterm assignment to the squares in the map.

As is evident from Examples 3-13 and 3-14, the tabularion method has the drawback that errors inevitably occur in trying to compare numbers over long lists. The map method would seem to be preferable, but for more than five variables, we cannot be certain that the best simplified expression has been found. The real advantage of the tabulation method lies in the fact that it consists of specific step-by-step procedures that guarantee an answer. Moreover, this formal procedure is suitable for computer mechanization.

It was stated in Section 3-9 that the tabulation method always starts with the minterm list of the function. If the function is not in this form, it must be converted. In most applications, the function to be simplified comes from a truth

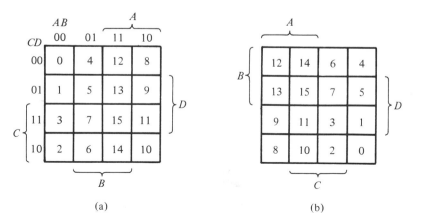

Figure 3-30   Variations of the four-variable map

the minterm list is readily available. Otherwise, the conversion to minterms adds considerable manipulative work to the problem. However, an extension of the tabulation method exists for finding prime-implicants from arbitrary sum of products expressions. See, for example, McCluskey (7).

In this chapter, we have considered the simplification of functions with many input variables and a single output variable. However, some digital circuits have more than one output. Such circuits are described by a set of Boolean functions, one for each output variable. A circuit with multiple outputs may sometimes have common terms among the various functions which can be utilized to form common gates during the implementation. This results in further simplification not taken into consideration when each function is simplified separately. There exists an extension of the tabulation method for multiple-output circuits (6, 7). However, this method is too specialized and very tedious for human manipulation. It is of practical importance only if a computer program based on this method is available to the user.

REFERENCES

1. Veitch, E. W., "A Chart Method for Simplifying Truth Functions." *Proc. of the ACM* (*May* 1952), 127–33.

2. Karnaugh, M., "A Map Method for Synthesis of Combinational Logic Circuits." *Trans. AIEE, Comm. and Electronics*, Vol. 72, Part I (November 1953), 593–99.

3. Quine, W. V., "The Problem of Simplifying Truth Functions." *Am. Math. Monthly*, Vol. 59, No. 8 (October 1952), 521–31.

4. McCluskey, E. J., Jr., "Minimization of Boolean Functions." *Bell System Tech. J.*, Vol. 35, No. 6 (November 1956), 1417–44.

5. Humphrey, W. S., Jr., *Switching Circuits with Computer Applications*. New York: McGraw-Hill Book Co., 1958, Chap. 4.

6. Hill, F. J., and G. R. Peterson, *Introduction to Switching Theory and Logical Design*, 3rd ed. New York: John Wiley & Sons, Inc., 1981.

7. McCluskey, E. J., Jr., *Introduction to the Theory of Switching Circuits*. New York: McGraw-Hill Book Co., 1965, Chap. 4.

8. Kohavi, Z., *Switching and Finite Automata Theory*. New York: McGraw-Hill Book Co., 1970.

9. Nagle, H. T. Jr., B. D. Carrol, and J. D. Irwin, *An Introduction to Computer Logic*. Englewood Cliffs, N.J.: Prentice-Hall, Inc., 1975.

PROBLEMS

3-1.   Obtain the simplified expressions in sum of products for the following Boolean functions:

(a) $F(x, y, z) = \Sigma(2, 3, 6, 7)$

(b) $F(A, B, C, D) = \Sigma(7, 13, 14, 15)$

(c) $F(A, B, C, D) = \Sigma(4, 6, 7, 15)$

(d) $F(w, x, y, z) = \Sigma(2, 3, 12, 13, 14, 15)$

3-2.   Obtain the simplified expressions in sum of products for the following Boolean functions:

(a) $xy + x'y'z' + x'yz'$

(b) $A'B + BC' + B'C'$

(c) $a'b' + bc + a'bc'$

(d) $xy'z + xyz' + x'yz + xyz$

3-3.   Obtain the simplified expressions in sum of products for the following Boolean functions:

(a) $D(A' + B) + B'(C + AD)$

(b) $ABD + A'C'D' + A'B + A'CD' + AB'D'$

(c) $k'lm' + k'm'n + klm'n' + lmn'$

(d) $A'B'C'D' + AC'D' + B'CD' + A'BCD + BC'D$

(e) $x'z + w'xy' + w(x'y + xy')$

3-4.   Obtain the simplified expressions in sum of products for the following Boolean functions:

(a) $F(A, B, C, D, E) = \Sigma(0, 1, 4, 5, 16, 17, 21, 25, 29)$

(b) $BDE + B'C'D + CDE + A'B'CE + A'B'C + B'C'D'E'$

(c) $A'B'CE' + A'B'C'D' + B'D'E' + B'CD' + CDE' + BDE'$

3-5.   Given the following truth table:

x	y	z	F_1	F_2
0	0	0	0	0
0	0	1	1	0
0	1	0	1	0
0	1	1	0	1
1	0	0	1	0
1	0	1	0	1
1	1	0	0	1
1	1	1	1	1

(a) Express F_1 and F_2 in product of maxterms.

(b) Obtain the simplified functions in sum of products.

(c) Obtain the simplified functions in product of sums.

3-6.   Obtain the simplified expressions in product of sums:

(a) $F(x, y, z) = \Pi(0, 1, 4, 5)$

(b) $F(A, B, C, D) = \Pi(0, 1, 2, 3, 4, 10, 11)$

(c) $F(w, x, y, z) = \Pi(1, 3, 5, 7, 13, 15)$

3-7.   Obtain the simplified expressions in (1) sum of products and (2) product of sums:

(a) $x'z' + y'z' + yz' + xyz$

(b) $(A + B' + D)(A' + B + D)(C + D)(C' + D')$

(c) $(A' + B' + D')(A + B' + C')(A' + B + D')(B + C' + D')$

(d) $(A' + B' + D)(A' + D')(A + B + D')(A + B' + C + D)$

(e) $w'yz' + vw'z' + vw'x + v'wz + v'w'y'z'$

3-8. Draw the gate implementation of the simplified Boolean functions obtained in problem 3-7 using AND and OR gates.

3-9. Simplify each of the following functions and implement them with NAND gates. Give two alternatives.

(a) $F_1 = AC' + ACE + ACE' + A'CD' + A'D'E'$

(b) $F_2 = (B' + D')(A' + C' + D)(A + B' + C' + D)(A' + B + C' + D')$

3-10. Repeat problem 3-9 for NOR implementations.

3-11. Implement the following functions with NAND gates. Assume that both the normal and complement inputs are available.

(a) $BD + BCD + AB'C'D' + A'B'CD'$ with no more than six gates, each having three inputs.

(b) $(AB + A'B')(CD' + C'D)$ with two-input gates.

3-12. Implement the following functions with NOR gates. Assume that both the normal and complement inputs are available.

(a) $AB' + C'D' + A'CD' + DC'(AB + A'B') + DB(AC' + A'C)$

(b) $AB'CD' + A'BCD' + AB'C'D + A'BC'D$

3-13. List the eight degenerate two-level forms and show that they reduce to a single operation. Explain how the degenerate two-level forms can be used to extend the fan-in of gates.

3-14. Implement the functions of problem 3-9 with the following two-level forms: NOR-OR, NAND-AND, OR-NAND, and AND-NOR.

3-15. Simplify the Boolean function F in sum of products using the don't-care conditions d:

(a) $F = y' + x'z'$

$d = yz + xy$

(b) $F = B'C'D' + BCD' + ABC'D$

$d = B'CD' + A'BC'D'$

3-16. Simplify the Boolean function F using the don't-care conditions d, in (1) sum of products and (2) product of sums:

map F & d
can use d as
0's or 1's which
ever is better

(a) $F = A'B'D' + A'CD + A'BC$

$d = A'BC'D + ACD + AB'D'$

(b) $F = w'(x'y + x'y' + xyz) + x'z'(y + w)$.

$d = w'x(y'z + yz') + wyz$

(c) $F = ACE + A'CD'E' + A'C'DE$

$d = DE' + A'D'E + AD'E'$

(d) $F = B'DE' + A'BE + B'C'E' + A'BC'D'$

$d = BDE' + CD'E'$

3-17. Implement the following functions using the don't-care conditions. Assume that both the normal and complement inputs are available.

(a) $F = A'B'C' + AB'D + A'B'CD'$ with no more than two NOR gates.
$d = ABC + AB'D'$

(b) $F = (A + D)(A' + B)(A' + C')$ with no more than three NAND gates.

(c) $F = B'D + B'C + ABCD$ with NAND gates.
$d = A'BD + AB'C'D'$

3-18. Implement the following function with either NAND or NOR gates. Use only four gates. Only the normal inputs are available.

$$F = w'xz + w'yz + x'yz' + wxy'z$$
$$d = wyz$$

3-19. The following Boolean expression:

$$BE + B'DE'$$

is a simplified version of the expression:

$$A'BE + BCDE + BC'D'E + A'B'DE' + B'C'DE'$$

Are there any don't-care conditions? If so, what are they?

3-20. Give three possible ways to express the function:

$$F = A'B'D' + AB'CD' + A'BD + ABC'D$$

with eight or less literals.

3-21. With the use of maps, find the simplest form in sum of products of the function $F = fg$, where f and g are given by:

$$f = wxy' + y'z + w'yz' + x'yz'$$
$$g = (w + x + y' + z')(x' + y' + z)(w' + y + z')$$

Hint: See problem 2-8(b).

3-22. Simplify the Boolean function of problem 3-2(a) using the map defined in Fig. 3-29(a). Repeat with the map of Fig. 3-29(b).

3-23. Simplify the Boolean function of problem 3-3(a) using the map defined in Fig. 3-30(a). Repeat with the map of Fig. 3-30(b).

3-24. Simplify the following Boolean functions by means of the tabulation method.

(a) $F(A, B, C, D, E, F, G) = \Sigma(20, 28, 52, 60)$
(b) $F(A, B, C, D, E, F, G) = \Sigma(20, 28, 38, 39, 52, 60, 102, 103, 127)$
(c) $F(A, B, C, D, E, F) = \Sigma(6, 9, 13, 18, 19, 25, 27, 29, 41, 45, 57, 61)$

3-25. Repeat problem 3-6 using the tabulation method.

3-26. Repeat problem 3-16(c) and (d) using the tabulation method.

Combinational Logic

4

4-1 INTRODUCTION

Logic circuits for digital systems may be combinational or sequential. A combinational circuit consists of logic gates whose outputs at any time are determined directly from the present combination of inputs without regard to previous inputs. A combinational circuit performs a specific information-processing operation fully specified logically by a set of Boolean functions. Sequential circuits employ memory elements (binary cells) in addition to logic gates. Their outputs are a function of the inputs and the state of the memory elements. The state of memory elements, in turn, is a function of previous inputs. As a consequence, the outputs of a sequential circuit depend not only on present inputs, but also on past inputs, and the circuit behavior must be specified by a time sequence of inputs and internal states. Sequential circuits are discussed in Chapter 6.

In Chapter 1 we learned to recognize binary numbers and binary codes that represent discrete quantities of information. These binary variables are represented by electric voltages or by some other signal. The signals can be manipulated in digital logic gates to perform required functions. In Chapter 2 we introduced Boolean algebra as a way to express logic functions algebraically. In Chapter 3 we learned how to simplify Boolean functions to achieve economical gate implementations. The purpose of this chapter is to use the knowledge acquired in previous chapters and formulate various systematic design and analysis procedures of combinational circuits. The solution of some typical examples will provide a useful catalog of elementary functions important for the understanding of digital computers and systems.

A combinational circuit consists of input variables, logic gates, and output variables. The logic gates accept signals from the inputs and generate signals to the outputs. This process transforms binary information from the given input data to the required output data. Obviously, both input and output data are represented by binary signals, i.e., they exist in two possible values, one representing logic-1

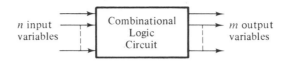

Figure 4-1 Block diagram of a combinational circuit

and the other logic-0. A block diagram of a combinational circuit is shown in Fig. 4-1. The n input binary variables come from an external source; the m output variables go to an external destination. In many applications, the source and/or destination are storage registers (Section 1-7) located either in the vicinity of the combinational circuit or in a remote external device. By definition, an external register does not influence the behavior of the combinational circuit because, if it does, the total system becomes a sequential circuit.

For n input variables, there are 2^n possible combinations of binary input values. For each possible input combination, there is one and only one possible output combination. A combinational circuit can be described by m Boolean functions, one for each output variable. Each output function is expressed in terms of the n input variables.

Each input variable to a combinational circuit may have one or two wires. When only one wire is available, it may represent the variable either in the normal form (unprimed) or in the complement form (primed). Since a variable in a Boolean expression may appear primed and/or unprimed, it is necessary to provide an inverter for each literal not available in the input wire. On the other hand, an input variable may appear in two wires, supplying both the normal and complement forms to the input of the circuit. If so, it is unnecessary to include inverters for the inputs. The type of binary cells used in most digital systems are flip-flop circuits (Chapter 6) that have outputs for both the normal and complement values of the stored binary variable. In our subsequent work, we shall assume that each input variable appears in two wires, supplying both the normal and complement values simultaneously. We must also realize that an inverter circuit can always supply the complement of the variable if only one wire is available.

4-2 DESIGN PROCEDURE

The design of combinational circuits starts from the verbal outline of the problem and ends in a logic circuit diagram, or a set of Boolean functions from which the logic diagram can be easily obtained. The procedure involves the following steps:

1. The problem is stated.

2. The number of available input variables and required output variables is determined.

3. The input and output variables are assigned letter symbols.

4. The truth table that defines the required relationships between inputs and outputs is derived.

5. The simplified Boolean function for each output is obtained.

6. The logic diagram is drawn.

A truth table for a combinational circuit consists of input columns and output columns. The 1's and 0's in the input columns are obtained from the 2^n binary combinations available for n input variables. The binary values for the outputs are determined from examination of the stated problem. An output can be equal to either 0 or 1 for every valid input combination. However, the specifications may indicate that some input combinations will not occur. These combinations become don't-care conditions.

The output functions specified in the truth table give the exact definition of the combinational circuit. It is important that the verbal specifications be interpreted correctly into a truth table. Sometimes the designer must use his intuition and experience to arrive at the correct interpretation. Word specifications are very seldom complete and exact. Any wrong interpretation which results in an incorrect truth table produces a combinational circuit that will not fulfill the stated requirements.

The output Boolean functions from the truth table are simplified by any available method, such as algebraic manipulation, the map method, or the tabulation procedure. Usually there will be a variety of simplified expressions from which to choose. However, in any particular application, certain restrictions, limitations, and criteria will serve as a guide in the process of choosing a particular algebraic expression. A practical design method would have to consider such constraints as (1) minimum number of gates, (2) minimum number of inputs to a gate, (3) minimum propagation time of the signal through the circuit, (4) minimum number of interconnections, and (5) limitations of the driving capabilities of each gate. Since all these criteria cannot be satisfied simultaneously, and since the importance of each constraint is dictated by the particular application, it is difficult to make a general statement as to what constitutes an acceptable simplification. In most cases the simplification begins by satisfying an elementary objective, such as producing a simplified Boolean function in a standard form, and from that proceeds to meet any other performance criteria.

In practice, designers tend to go from the Boolean functions to a wiring list that shows the interconnections among various standard logic gates. In that case the design need not go any further than the required simplified output Boolean functions. However, a logic diagram is helpful for visualizing the gate implementation of the expressions.

4-3 ADDERS

Digital computers perform a variety of information-processing tasks. Among the basic functions encountered are the various arithmetic operations. The most basic arithmetic operation, no doubt, is the addition of two binary digits. This simple addition consists of four possible elementary operations, namely, $0 + 0 = 0$, $0 + 1 = 1$, $1 + 0 = 1$, and $1 + 1 = 10$. The first three operations produce a sum whose length is one digit, but when both augend and addend bits are equal to 1, the binary sum consists of two digits. The higher significant bit of this result is called a *carry*. When the augend and addend numbers contain more significant digits, the carry obtained from the addition of two bits is added to the next higher-order pair of significant bits. A combinational circuit that performs the addition of two bits is called a *half-adder*. One that performs the addition of three bits (two significant bits and a previous carry) is a *full-adder*. The name of the former stems from the fact that two half-adders can be employed to implement a full-adder. The two adder circuits are the first combinational circuits we shall design.

Half-Adder

From the verbal explanation of a half-adder, we find that this circuit needs two binary inputs and two binary outputs. The input variables designate the augend and addend bits; the output variables produce the sum and carry. It is necessary to specify two output variables because the result may consist of two binary digits. We arbitrarily assign symbols x and y to the two inputs and S (for sum) and C (for carry) to the outputs.

Now that we have established the number and names of the input and output variables, we are ready to formulate a truth table to identify exactly the function of the half-adder. This truth table is shown below:

x	y	C	S
0	0	0	0
0	1	0	1
1	0	0	1
1	1	1	0

The carry output is 0 unless both inputs are 1. The S output represents the least significant bit of the sum.

The simplified Boolean functions for the two outputs can be obtained directly from the truth table. The simplified sum of products expressions are:

$$S = x'y + xy'$$
$$C = xy$$

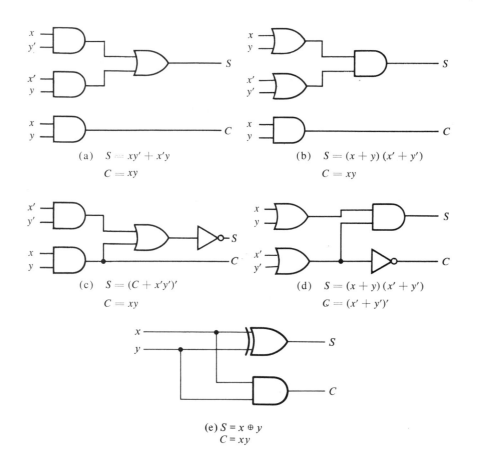

(a) $S = xy' + x'y$
    $C = xy$

(b) $S = (x + y)(x' + y')$
    $C = xy$

(c) $S = (C + x'y')'$
    $C = xy$

(d) $S = (x + y)(x' + y')$
    $C = (x' + y')'$

(e) $S = x \oplus y$
    $C = xy$

Figure 4-2 Various implementations of a half-adder

The logic diagram for this implementation is shown in Fig. 4-2(a), as are four other implementations for a half-adder. They all achieve the same result as far as the input-output behavior is concerned. They illustrate the flexibility available to the designer when implementing even a simple combinational logic function such as this.

Figure 4-2(a), as mentioned above, is the implementation of the half-adder in sum of products. Figure 4-2(b) shows the implementation in product of sums:

$$S = (x + y)(x' + y')$$
$$C = xy$$

To obtain the implementation of Fig. 4-2(c), we note that S is the exclusive-OR of x and y. The complement of S is the equivalence of x and y (Section 2-6):

$$S' = xy + x'y'$$

but $C = xy$, and therefore we have:

$$S = (C + x'y')'$$

In Fig. 4-2(d) we use the product of sums implementation with C derived as follows:

$$C = xy = (x' + y')'$$

The half-adder can be implemented with an exclusive-OR and an AND gate as shown in Fig. 4-2(e). This form is used later to show that two half-adder circuits are needed to construct a full-adder circuit.

Full-Adder

A full-adder is a combinational circuit that forms the arithmetic sum of three input bits. It consists of three inputs and two outputs. Two of the input variables, denoted by x and y, represent the two significant bits to be added. The third input, z, represents the carry from the previous lower significant position. Two outputs are necessary because the arithmetic sum of three binary digits ranges in value from 0 to 3, and binary 2 or 3 needs two digits. The two outputs are designated by the symbols S for sum and C for carry. The binary variable S gives the value of the least significant bit of the sum. The binary variable C gives the output carry. The truth table of the full-adder is as follows:

x	y	z	C	S
0	0	0	0	0
0	0	1	0	1
0	1	0	0	1
0	1	1	1	0
1	0	0	0	1
1	0	1	1	0
1	1	0	1	0
1	1	1	1	1

The eight rows under the input variables designate all possible combinations of 1's and 0's that these variables may have. The 1's and 0's for the output variables are determined from the arithmetic sum of the input bits. When all input bits are 0's, the output is 0. The S output is equal to 1 when only one input is equal to 1 or when all three inputs are equal to 1. The C output has a carry of 1 if two or three inputs are equal to 1.

The input and output bits of the combinational circuit have different interpretations at various stages of the problem. Physically, the binary signals of the input wires are considered binary digits added arithmetically to form a two-digit sum at

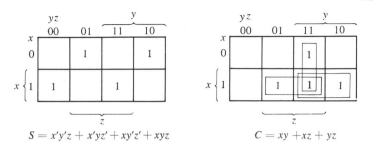

$$S = x'y'z + x'yz' + xy'z' + xyz$$

$$C = xy + xz + yz$$

Figure 4-3 Maps for full-adder

the output wires. On the other hand, the same binary values are considered variables of Boolean functions when expressed in the truth table or when the circuit is implemented with logic gates. It is important to realize that two different interpretations are given to the values of the bits encountered in this circuit.

The input-output logical relationship of the full-adder circuit may be expressed in two Boolean functions, one for each output variable. Each output Boolean function requires a unique map for its simplification. Each map must have eight squares, since each output is a function of three input variables. The maps of Fig. 4-3 are used for simplifying the two output functions. The 1's in the squares for the maps of S and C are determined directly from the truth table. The squares with 1's for the S output do not combine in adjacent squares to give a simplified expression in sum of products. The C output can be simplified to a six-literal expression. The logic diagram for the full-adder implemented in sum of products is shown in Fig. 4-4. This implementation uses the following Boolean expressions:

$$S = x'y'z + x'yz' + xy'z' + xyz$$
$$C = xy + xz + yz$$

Other configurations for a full-adder may be developed. The product-of-sums implementation requires the same number of gates as in Fig. 4-4, with the

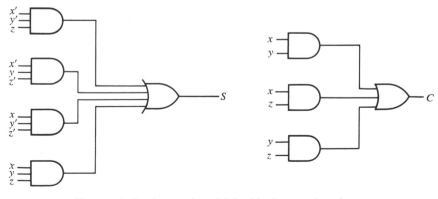

Figure 4-4 Implementation of full-adder in sum of products

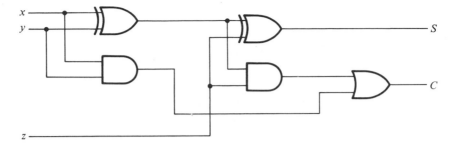

Figure 4-5 Implementation of a full-adder with two half-adders and an OR gate

number of AND and OR gates interchanged. A full-adder can be implemented with two half-adders and one OR gate, as shown in Fig. 4-5. The S output from the second half-adder is the exclusive-OR of z and the output of the first half-adder, giving:

$$
\begin{aligned}
S &= z \oplus (x \oplus y) \\
&= z'(xy' + x'y) + z(xy' + x'y)' \\
&= z'(xy' + x'y) + z(xy + x'y') \\
&= xy'z' + x'yz' + xyz + x'y'z
\end{aligned}
$$

and the carry output is:

$$
C = z(xy' + x'y) + xy = xy'z + x'yz + xy
$$

4-4 SUBTRACTORS

The subtraction of two binary numbers may be accomplished by taking the complement of the subtrahend and adding it to the minuend (Section 1-5). By this method, the subtraction operation becomes an addition operation requiring full-adders for its machine implementation. It is possible to implement subtraction with logic circuits in a direct manner, as done with paper and pencil. By this method, each subtrahend bit of the number is subtracted from its corresponding significant minuend bit to form a difference bit. If the minuend bit is smaller than the subtrahend bit, a 1 is borrowed from the next significant position. The fact that a 1 has been borrowed must be conveyed to the next higher pair of bits by means of a binary signal coming out (output) of a given stage and going into (input) the next higher stage. Just as there are half- and full-adders, there are half- and full-subtractors.

Half-Subtractor

A half-subtractor is a combinational circuit that subtracts two bits and produces their difference. It also has an output to specify if a 1 has been borrowed. Designate the minuend bit by x and the subtrahend bit by y. To perform $x - y$,

123

we have to check the relative magnitudes of x and y. If $x \geqslant y$, we have three possibilities: $0 - 0 = 0$, $1 - 0 = 1$, and $1 - 1 = 0$. The result is called the *difference bit*. If $x < y$, we have $0 - 1$, and it is necessary to borrow a 1 from the next higher stage. The 1 borrowed from the next higher stage adds 2 to the minuend bit, just as in the decimal system a borrow adds 10 to a minuend digit. With the minuend equal to 2, the difference becomes $2 - 1 = 1$. The half-subtractor needs two outputs. One output generates the difference and will be designated by the symbol D. The second output, designated B for borrow, generates the binary signal that informs the next stage that a 1 has been borrowed. The truth table for the input-output relationships of a half-subtractor can now be derived as follows:

x	y	B	D
0	0	0	0
0	1	1	1
1	0	0	1
1	1	0	0

The output borrow B is a 0 as long as $x \geqslant y$. It is a 1 for $x = 0$ and $y = 1$. The D output is the result of the arithmetic operation $2B + x - y$.

The Boolean functions for the two outputs of the half-subtractor are derived directly from the truth table:

$$D = x'y + xy'$$
$$B = x'y$$

It is interesting to note that the logic for D is exactly the same as the logic for output S in the half-adder.

Full-Subtractor

A full-subtractor is a combinational circuit that performs a subtraction between two bits, taking into account that a 1 may have been borrowed by a lower significant stage. This circuit has three inputs and two outputs. The three inputs, x, y, and z, denote the minuend, subtrahend, and previous borrow, respectively. The two outputs, D and B, represent the difference and output borrow, respectively. The truth table for the circuit is as follows:

x	y	z	B	D
0	0	0	0	0
0	0	1	1	1
0	1	0	1	1
0	1	1	1	0
1	0	0	0	1
1	0	1	0	0
1	1	0	0	0
1	1	1	1	1

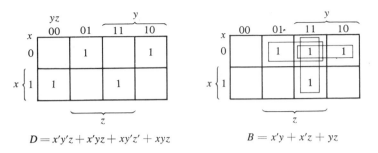

$$D = x'y'z + x'yz + xy'z' + xyz$$

$$B = x'y + x'z + yz$$

Figure 4-6 Maps for full-subtractor

The eight rows under the input variables designate all possible combinations of 1's and 0's that the binary variables may take. The 1's and 0's for the output variables are determined from the subtraction of $x - y - z$. The combinations having input borrow $z = 0$ reduce to the same four conditions of the half-adder. For $x = 0$, $y = 0$, and $z = 1$, we have to borrow a 1 from the next stage, which makes $B = 1$ and adds 2 to x. Since $2 - 0 - 1 = 1$, $D = 1$. For $x = 0$ and $yz = 11$, we need to borrow again, making $B = 1$ and $x = 2$. Since $2 - 1 - 1 = 0$, $D = 0$. For $x = 1$ and $yz = 01$, we have $x - y - z = 0$, which makes $B = 0$ and $D = 0$. Finally, for $x = 1, y = 1, z = 1$, we have to borrow 1, making $B = 1$ and $x = 3$, and $3 - 1 - 1 = 1$, making $D = 1$.

The simplified Boolean functions for the two outputs of the full-subtractor are derived in the maps of Fig. 4-6. The simplified sum of products output functions are:

$$D = x'y'z + x'yz' + xy'z' + xyz$$
$$B = x'y + x'z + yz$$

Again we note that the logic function for output D in the full-subtractor is exactly the same as output S in the full-adder. Moreover, the output B resembles the function for C in the full-adder, except that the input variable x is complemented. Because of these similarities, it is possible to convert a full-adder into a full-subtractor by merely complementing input x prior to its application to the gates that form the carry output.

4-5 CODE CONVERSION

The availability of a large variety of codes for the same discrete elements of information results in the use of different codes by different digital systems. It is sometimes necessary to use the output of one system as the input to another. A conversion circuit must be inserted between the two systems if each uses different codes for the same information. Thus, a code converter is a circuit that makes the two systems compatible even though each uses a different binary code.

To convert from binary code A to binary code B, the input lines must supply the bit combination of elements as specified by code A and the output lines must generate the corresponding bit combination of code B. A combinational circuit performs this transformation by means of logic gates. The design procedure of code converters will be illustrated by means of a specific example of conversion from the BCD to the excess-3 code.

The bit combinations for the BCD and excess-3 codes are listed in Table 1-2 (Section 1-6). Since each code uses four bits to represent a decimal digit, there must be four input variables and four output variables. Let us designate the four input binary variables by the symbols A, B, C, and D, and the four output variables by w, x, y, and z. The truth table relating the input and output variables is shown in Table 4-1. The bit combinations for the inputs and their corresponding outputs are obtained directly from Table 1-2. We note that four binary variables may have 16 bit combinations, only 10 of which are listed in the truth table. The six bit combinations not listed for the *input* variables are don't-care combinations. Since they will never occur, we are at liberty to assign to the output variables either a 1 or a 0, whichever gives a simpler circuit.

TABLE 4-1   Truth table for code-conversion example

Input BCD				Output Excess-3 code			
A	B	C	D	w	x	y	z
0	0	0	0	0	0	1	1
0	0	0	1	0	1	0	0
0	0	1	0	0	1	0	1
0	0	1	1	0	1	1	0
0	1	0	0	0	1	1	1
0	1	0	1	1	0	0	0
0	1	1	0	1	0	0	1
0	1	1	1	1	0	1	0
1	0	0	0	1	0	1	1
1	0	0	1	1	1	0	0

The maps in Fig. 4-7 are drawn to obtain a simplified Boolean function for each output. Each of the four maps of Fig. 4-7 represents one of the four outputs of this circuit as a function of the four input variables. The 1's marked inside the squares are obtained from the minterms that make the output equal to 1. The 1's are obtained from the truth table by going over the output columns one at a time. For example, the column under output z has five 1's; therefore, the map for z must have five 1's, each being in a square corresponding to the minterm that makes z equal to 1. The six don't-care combinations are marked by X's. One possible way to simplify the functions in sum of products is listed under the map of each variable.

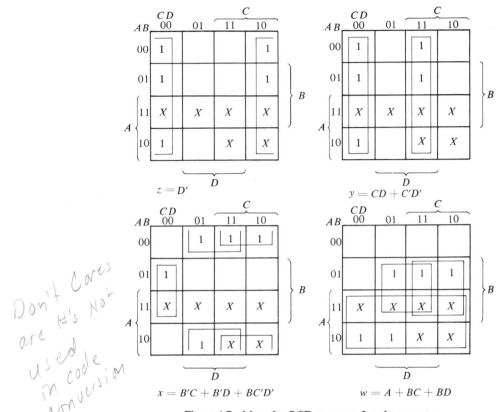

Figure 4-7 Maps for BCD-to-excess-3 code converter

A two-level logic diagram may be obtained directly from the Boolean expressions derived by the maps. There are various other possibilities for a logic diagram that implements this circuit. The expressions obtained in Fig. 4-7 may be manipulated algebraically for the purpose of using common gates for two or more outputs. This manipulation, shown below, illustrates the flexibility obtained with multiple-output systems when implemented with three or more levels of gates.

$$z = D'$$
$$y = CD + C'D' = CD + (C + D)'$$
$$x = B'C + B'D + BC'D' = B'(C + D) + BC'D'$$
$$= B'(C + D) + B(C + D)'$$
$$w = A + BC + BD = A + B(C + D)$$

The logic diagram that implements the above expressions is shown in Fig. 4-8. In it we see that the OR gate whose output is $C + D$ has been used to implement partially each of three outputs.

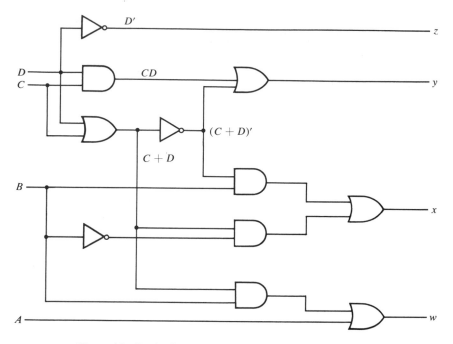

Figure 4-8 Logic diagram for BCD-to-excess-3 code converter

Not counting input inverters, the implementation in sum of products requires seven AND gates and three OR gates. The implementation of Fig. 4-8 requires four AND gates, four OR gates, and one inverter. If only the normal inputs are available, the first implementation will require inverters for variables B, C, and D, whereas the second implementation requires inverters for variables B and D.

4-6 ANALYSIS PROCEDURE

The design of a combinational circuit starts from the verbal specifications of a required function and culminates with a set of output Boolean functions or a logic diagram. The *analysis* of a combinational circuit is somewhat the reverse process. It starts with a given logic diagram and culminates with a set of Boolean functions, a truth table, or a verbal explanation of the circuit operation. If the logic diagram to be analyzed is accompanied by a function name or an explanation of what it is assumed to accomplish, then the analysis problem reduces to a verification of the stated function.

The first step in the analysis is to make sure that the given circuit is combinational and not sequential. The diagram of a combinational circuit has logic gates with no feedback paths or memory elements. A feedback path is a connection from the output of one gate to the input of a second gate that forms part of the input to the first gate. Feedback paths or memory elements in a digital circuit define a sequential circuit and must be analyzed according to procedures outlined in Chapter 6.

Once the logic diagram is verified as a combinational circuit, one can proceed to obtain the output Boolean functions and/or the truth table. If the circuit is accompanied by a verbal explanation of its function, then the Boolean functions or the truth table is sufficient for verification. If the function of the circuit is under investigation, then it is necessary to interpret the operation of the circuit from the derived truth table. The success of such investigation is enhanced if one has previous experience and familiarity with a wide variety of digital circuits. The ability to correlate a truth table with an information-processing task is an art one acquires with experience.

To obtain the output Boolean functions from a logic diagram, proceed as follows:

1. Label with arbitrary symbols all gate outputs that are a function of the input variables. Obtain the Boolean functions for each gate.

2. Label with other arbitrary symbols those gates which are a function of input variables and/or previously labeled gates. Find the Boolean functions for these gates.

3. Repeat the process outlined in step 2 until the outputs of the circuit are obtained.

4. By repeated substitution of previously defined functions, obtain the output Boolean functions in terms of input variables only.

Analysis of the combinational circuit in Fig. 4-9 illustrates the proposed procedure. We note that the circuit has three binary inputs, A, B, and C, and two binary outputs, F_1 and F_2. The outputs of various gates are labeled with intermediate symbols. The outputs of gates that are a function of input variables only are F_2, T_1, and T_2. The Boolean functions for these three outputs are:

$$F_2 = AB + AC + BC$$
$$T_1 = A + B + C$$
$$T_2 = ABC$$

Next we consider outputs of gates which are a function of already defined symbols:

$$T_3 = F_2'T_1$$
$$F_1 = T_3 + T_2$$

The output Boolean function F_2 expressed above is already given as a function of the inputs only. To obtain F_1 as a function of A, B, and C, form a series of

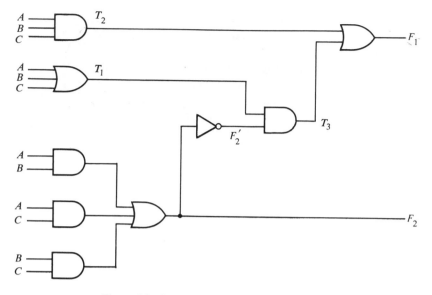

Figure 4-9 Logic diagram for analysis example

substitutions as follows:

$$F_1 = T_3 + T_2 = F_2'T_1 + ABC = (AB + AC + BC)'(A + B + C) + ABC$$
$$= (A' + B')(A' + C')(B' + C')(A + B + C) + ABC$$
$$= (A' + B'C')(AB' + AC' + BC' + B'C) + ABC$$
$$= A'BC' + A'B'C + AB'C' + ABC$$

If we want to pursue the investigation and determine the information-transformation task achieved by this circuit, we can derive the truth table directly from the Boolean functions and try to recognize a familiar operation. For this example, we note that the circuit is a full-adder, with F_1 being the sum output and F_2 the carry output. A, B, and C are the three inputs added arithmetically.

The derivation of the truth table for the circuit is a straightforward process once the output Boolean functions are known. To obtain the truth table directly from the logic diagram without going through the derivations of the Boolean functions, proceed as follows:

1. Determine the number of input variables to the circuit. For n inputs, form the 2^n possible input combinations of 1's and 0's by listing the binary numbers from 0 to $2^n - 1$.

2. Label the outputs of selected gates with arbitrary symbols.

3. Obtain the truth table for the outputs of those gates that are a function of the input variables only.

4. Proceed to obtain the truth table for the outputs of those gates that are a function of previously defined values until the columns for all outputs are determined.

This process can be illustrated using the circuit of Fig. 4-9. In Table 4-2, we form the eight possible combinations for the three input variables. The truth table for F_2 is determined directly from the values of A, B, and C, with F_2 equal to 1 for any combination that has two or three inputs equal to 1. The truth table for F_2' is the complement of F_2. The truth tables for T_1 and T_2 are the OR and AND functions of the input variables, respectively. The values for T_3 are derived from T_1 and F_2': T_3 is equal to 1 when both T_1 and F_2' are equal to 1, and to 0 otherwise. Finally, F_1 is equal to 1 for those combinations in which either T_2 or T_3 or both are equal to 1. Inspection of the truth table combinations for A, B, C, F_1, and F_2 of Table 4-2 shows that it is identical to the truth table of the full-adder given in Section 4-3 for x, y, z, S, and C, respectively.

TABLE 4-2   Truth table for logic diagram of Fig. 4-9

A	B	C	F_2	F_2'	T_1	T_2	T_3	F_1
0	0	0	0	1	0	0	0	0
0	0	1	0	1	1	0	1	1
0	1	0	0	1	1	0	1	1
0	1	1	1	0	1	0	0	0
1	0	0	0	1	1	0	1	1
1	0	1	1	0	1	0	0	0
1	1	0	1	0	1	0	0	0
1	1	1	1	0	1	1	0	1

Consider now a combinational circuit that has don't-care input combinations. When such a circuit is designed, the don't-care combinations are marked by X's in the map and assigned an output of either 1 or 0, whichever is more convenient for the simplification of the output Boolean function. When a circuit with don't-care combinations is being analyzed, the situation is entirely different. Even though we assume that the don't-care input combinations will never occur, the fact of the matter is that if any one of these combinations is applied to the inputs (intentionally or in error), a binary output will be present. The value of the output will depend on the choice for the X's taken during the design. Part of the analysis of such a circuit may involve the determination of the output values for the don't-care input combinations. As an example, consider the BCD-to-excess-3 code converter designed in Section 4-5. The outputs obtained when the six unused combinations of the BCD code are applied to the inputs are:

Unused BCD inputs				Outputs			
A	B	C	D	w	x	y	z
1	0	1	0	1	1	0	1
1	0	1	1	1	1	1	0
1	1	0	0	1	1	1	1
1	1	0	1	1	0	0	0
1	1	1	0	1	0	0	1
1	1	1	1	1	0	1	0

These outputs may be derived by means of the truth table analysis method as outlined in this section. In this particular case, the outputs may be obtained directly from the maps of Fig. 4-7. From inspection of the maps, we determine whether the X's in the corresponding minterm squares for each output have been included with the 1's or the 0's. For example, the square for minterm m_{10} (1010) has been included with the 1's for outputs w, x, and z, but not for y. Therefore, the outputs for m_{10} are $wxyz = 1101$, as listed in the above table. We also note that the first three outputs in the table have no meaning in the excess-3 code, and the last three outputs correspond to decimal 5, 6, and 7, respectively. This coincidence is entirely a function of the choice for the X's taken during the design.

4-7 MULTILEVEL NAND CIRCUITS

Combinational circuits are more frequently constructed with NAND or NOR gates rather than AND and OR gates. NAND and NOR gates are more common from the hardware point of view because they are readily available in integrated-circuit form. Because of the prominence of NAND and NOR gates in the design of combinational circuits, it is important to be able to recognize the relationships that exist between circuits constructed with AND-OR gates and their equivalent NAND or NOR diagrams.

The implementation of two-level NAND and NOR logic diagrams was presented in Section 3-6. Here we consider the more general case of multilevel circuits. The procedure for obtaining NAND circuits is presented in this section, and for NOR circuits in the next section.

Universal Gate

The NAND gate is said to be a universal gate because any digital system can be implemented with it. Combinational circuits and sequential circuits as well can be constructed with this gate because the flip-flop circuit (the memory element most frequently used in sequential circuits) can be constructed from two NAND gates connected back to back, as shown in Section 6-2.

To show that any Boolean function can be implemented with NAND gates, we need only show that the logical operations AND, OR, and NOT can be

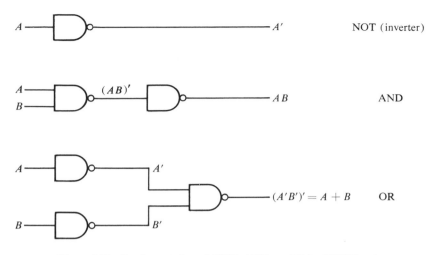

Figure 4-10   Implementation of NOT, AND, or OR by NAND gates

implemented with NAND gates. The implementation of the AND, OR, and NOT operations with NAND gates is shown in Fig. 4-10. The NOT operation is obtained from a one-input NAND gate, actually another symbol for an inverter circuit. The AND operation requires two NAND gates. The first produces the inverted AND and the second acts as an inverter to produce the normal output. The OR operation is achieved through a NAND gate with additional inverters in each input.

A convenient way to implement a combinational circuit with NAND gates is to obtain the simplified Boolean functions in terms of AND, OR, and NOT and convert the functions to NAND logic. The conversion of the algebraic expression from AND, OR, and NOT operations to NAND operations is usually quite complicated because it involves a large number of applications of De Morgan's theorem. This difficulty is avoided by the use of simple circuit manipulations and simple rules as outlined below.

Boolean Function Implementation— Block Diagram Method

The implementation of Boolean functions with NAND gates may be obtained by means of a simple block diagram manipulation technique. This method requires that two other logic diagrams be drawn prior to obtaining the NAND logic diagram. Nevertheless, the procedure is very simple and straightforward:

1. From the given algebraic expression, draw the logic diagram with AND, OR, and NOT gates. Assume that both the normal and complement inputs are available.

2. Draw a second logic diagram with the equivalent NAND logic, as given in Fig. 4-10, substituted for each AND, OR, and NOT gate.

3. Remove any two cascaded inverters from the diagram, since double inversion does not perform a logic function. Remove inverters connected to single external inputs and complement the corresponding input variable. The new logic diagram obtained is the required NAND gate implementation.

This procedure is illustrated in Fig. 4-11 for the function:

$$F = A(B + CD) + BC'$$

The AND-OR implementation of this function is shown in the logic diagram of Fig. 4-11(a). For each AND gate, we substitute a NAND gate followed by an inverter; for each OR gate, we substitute input inverters followed by a NAND gate. This substitution follows directly from the logic equivalences of Fig. 4-10 and is shown in the diagram of Fig. 4-11(b). This diagram has seven inverters and five two-input NAND gates listed with numbers inside the gate symbol. Pairs of inverters connected in cascade (from each AND box to each OR box) are removed since they form double inversion. The inverter connected to input B is removed and the input variable is designated by B'. The result is the NAND logic diagram shown in Fig. 4-11(c), with the number inside each symbol identifying the gate from Fig. 4-11(b).

This example demonstrates that the number of NAND gates required to implement the Boolean function is equal to the number of AND-OR gates, provided both the normal and the complement inputs are available. If only the normal inputs are available, inverters must be used to generate any required complemented inputs.

A second example of NAND implementation is shown in Fig. 4-12. The Boolean function to be implemented is:

$$F = (A + B')(CD + E)$$

The AND-OR implementation is shown in Fig. 4-12(a), and its NAND logic substitution, in Fig. 4-12(b). One pair of cascaded inverters may be removed. The three external inputs E, A, and B', which go directly to inverters, are complemented and the corresponding inverters removed. The final NAND gate implementation is in Fig. 4-12(c).

The number of NAND gates for the second example is equal to the number of AND-OR gates plus an additional inverter in the output (NAND gate 5). In general, the number of NAND gates required to implement a function equals the number of AND-OR gates, except for an occasional inverter. This is true provided both normal and complement inputs are available, because the conversion forces certain input variables to be complemented.

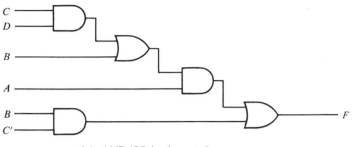

(a) AND/OR implementation

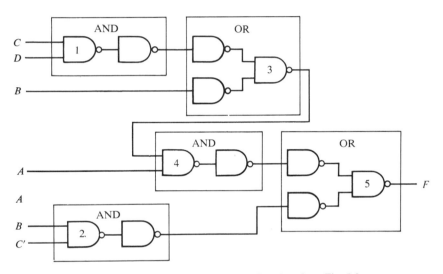

(b) Substituting equivalent NAND functions from Fig. 5-8

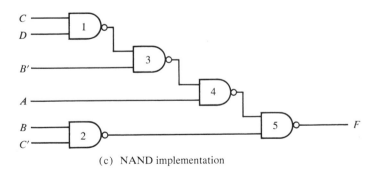

(c) NAND implementation

Figure 4-11 Implementation of $F = A(B + CD) + BC'$ with NAND gates

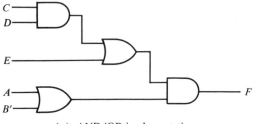

(a) AND/OR implementation

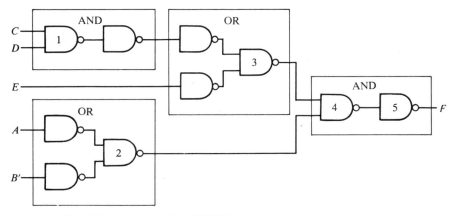

(b) Substituting equivalent NAND functions

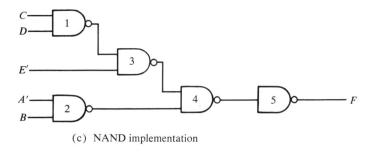

(c) NAND implementation

Figure 4-12 Implementation of $(A + B')(CD + E)$ with NAND gates

The block diagram method is somewhat tiresome to use because it requires the drawing of two logic diagrams to obtain the answer in a third. With some experience, it is possible to reduce the amount of labor by anticipating the pairs of cascaded inverters and the inverters in the inputs. Starting from the procedure just outlined, it is not too difficult to derive general rules for implementing Boolean functions with NAND gates directly from an algebraic expression.

Analysis Procedure

The foregoing procedure considered the problem of deriving a NAND logic diagram from a given Boolean function. The reverse process is the analysis problem which starts with a given NAND logic diagram and culminates with a Boolean expression or a truth table. The analysis of NAND logic diagrams follows the same procedures presented in Section 4-6 for the analysis of combinational circuits. The only difference is that NAND logic requires a repeated application of De Morgan's theorem. We shall now demonstrate the derivation of the Boolean function from a logic diagram. Then we will show the derivation of the truth table directly from the NAND logic diagram. Finally, a method will be presented for converting a NAND logic diagram to AND-OR logic diagram by means of block diagram manipulation.

Derivation of the Boolean Function by Algebraic Manipulation

The procedure for deriving the Boolean function from a logic diagram is outlined in Section 4-6. This procedure is demonstrated for the NAND logic diagram shown in Fig. 4-13, which is the same as that in Fig. 4-11(c). First, all gate outputs are labeled with arbitrary symbols. Second, the Boolean functions for the outputs of gates that receive only external inputs are derived:

$$T_1 = (CD)' = C' + D'$$
$$T_2 = (BC')' = B' + C$$

The second form follows directly from De Morgan's theorem and may, at times, be more convenient to use. Third, Boolean functions of gates which have inputs from

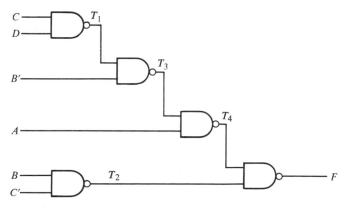

Figure 4-13 Analysis example

previously derived functions are determined in consecutive order until the output is expressed in terms of input variables:

$$T_3 = (B'T_1)' = (B'C' + B'D')'$$
$$= (B + C)(B + D) = B + CD$$
$$T_4 = (AT_3)' = [A(B + CD)]'$$
$$F = (T_2T_4)' = \{(BC')'[A(B + CD)]'\}'$$
$$= BC' + A(B + CD)$$

Derivation of the Truth Table

The procedure for obtaining the truth table directly from a logic diagram is also outlined in Section 4-6. This procedure is demonstrated for the NAND logic diagram of Fig. 4-13. First, the four input variables, together with their 16 combinations of 1's and 0's, are listed as in Table 4-3. Second, the outputs of all gates are labeled with arbitrary symbols as in Fig. 4-13. Third, we obtain the truth table for the outputs of those gates that are a function of the input variables only. These are T_1 and T_2. $T_1 = (CD)'$; so we mark 0's in those rows where both C and D are equal to 1 and fill the rest of the rows of T_1 with 1's. Also, $T_2 = (BC')'$; so we mark 0's in those rows where $B = 1$ and $C = 0$, and fill the rest of the rows of T_2 with 1's. We then proceed to obtain the truth table for the outputs of those gates that are a function of previously defined outputs until the column for the output F is determined. It is now possible to obtain an algebraic expression for the

TABLE 4-3 Truth table for the circuit of Figure 4-13

A	B	C	D	T_1	T_2	T_3	T_4	F
0	0	0	0	1	1	0	1	0
0	0	0	1	1	1	0	1	0
0	0	1	0	1	1	0	1	0
0	0	1	1	0	1	1	1	0
0	1	0	0	1	0	1	1	1
0	1	0	1	1	0	1	1	1
0	1	1	0	1	1	1	1	0
0	1	1	1	0	1	1	1	0
1	0	0	0	1	1	0	1	0
1	0	0	1	1	1	0	1	0
1	0	1	0	1	1	0	1	0
1	0	1	1	0	1	1	0	1
1	1	0	0	1	0	1	0	1
1	1	0	1	1	0	1	0	1
1	1	1	0	1	1	1	0	1
1	1	1	1	0	1	1	0	1

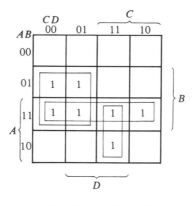

$$F = AB + BC' + ACD$$

Figure 4-14 Derivation of F from Table 4-3

output from the derived truth table. The map shown in Fig. 4-14 is obtained directly from Table 4-3 and has 1's in the squares of those minterms for which F is equal to 1. The simplified expression obtained from the map is:

$$F = AB + ACD + BC' = A(B + CD) + BC'$$

This is the same as the expression of Fig. 4-11, thus verifying the correct answer.

Block Diagram Transformation

It is sometimes convenient to convert a NAND logic diagram to its equivalent AND-OR logic diagram to facilitate the analysis procedure. By doing so, the Boolean function can be derived more easily without employing De Morgan's theorem. The conversion of logic diagrams is accomplished through a process reverse from that used for implementation. In Section 3-6, we showed two alternate graphic symbols for the NAND gate. These symbols are repeated in Fig. 4-15 for convenience. By judicious use of both symbols, it is possible to convert a NAND diagram to an equivalent AND-OR form.

The conversion of a NAND logic diagram to an AND-OR diagram is achieved through a change in symbols from AND-invert to invert-OR in *alternate* levels of gates. The first level to be changed to an invert-OR symbol should be the last level. These changes produce pairs of circles along the same line, and these can

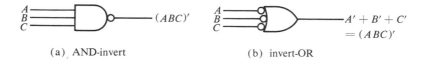

(a) AND-invert   (b) invert-OR

Figure 4-15 Two symbols for NAND gate

be removed since they represent double complementation. Moreover, a one-input AND or OR gate can be removed since it does not perform a logical function. A one-input AND or OR with a circle in the input or output is changed to an inverter circuit.

This procedure is demonstrated in Fig. 4-16. The NAND logic diagram of Fig. 4-16(a) is to be converted to an AND-OR diagram. The symbol of the gate in the last level is changed to an invert-OR. Looking for alternate levels, we find one more gate requiring a change of symbol as shown in Fig. 4-16(b). Any two circles along the same line are removed. Circles that go to external inputs are also removed, provided the corresponding input variable is complemented. The required AND-OR logic diagram is drawn in Fig. 4-16(c).

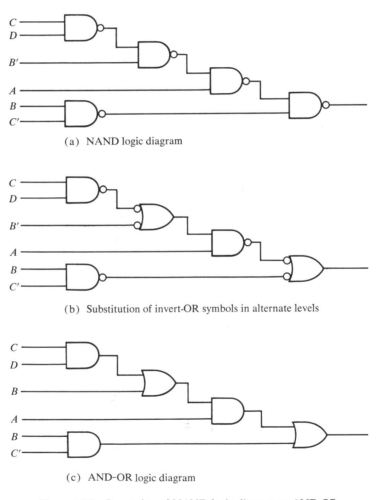

(a) NAND logic diagram

(b) Substitution of invert-OR symbols in alternate levels

(c) AND-OR logic diagram

Figure 4-16 Conversion of NAND logic diagram to AND-OR

4-8 MULTILEVEL NOR CIRCUITS

The NOR function is the dual of the NAND function. For this reason, all procedures and rules for NOR logic form a dual of the corresponding procedures and rules developed for NAND logic. This section enumerates various methods for NOR logic implementation and analysis by following the same list of topics used for NAND logic. However, less detailed explanation is included so as to avoid excessive repetition of the material in Section 4-7.

Universal Gate

The NOR gate is universal because any Boolean function can be implemented with it, including a flip-flop circuit as shown in Section 6-2. The conversion of AND, OR, and NOT to NOR is shown in Fig. 4-17. The NOT operation is obtained from a one-input NOR gate, yet another symbol for an inverter circuit. The OR operation requires two NOR gates. The first produces the inverted-OR and the second acts as an inverter to obtain the normal output. The AND operation is achieved through a NOR gate with additional inverters at each input.

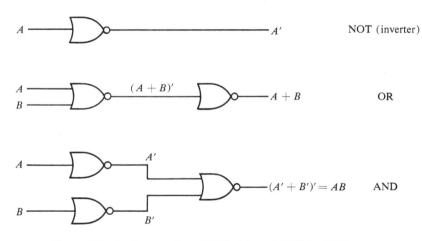

Figure 4-17 Implementation of NOT, OR, and AND by NOR gates

Boolean Function Implementation—
Block Diagram Method

The block diagram procedure for implementing Boolean functions with NOR gates is similar to the procedure outlined in the previous section for NAND gates.

1. Draw the AND-OR logic diagram from the given algebraic expression. Assume that both the normal and the complement inputs are available.

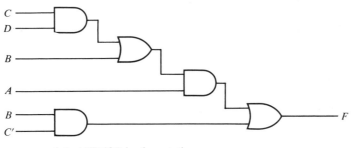

(a) AND/OR implementation

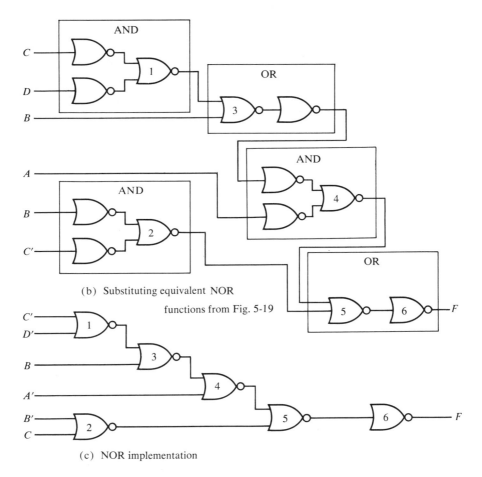

(b) Substituting equivalent NOR

functions from Fig. 5-19

(c) NOR implementation

Figure 4-18   Implementation of $F = A(B + CD) + BC'$ with NOR gates

2. Draw a second logic diagram with equivalent NOR logic, as given in Fig. 4-17, substituted for each AND, OR, and NOT gate.

3. Remove pairs of cascaded inverters from the diagram. Remove inverters connected to single external inputs and complement the corresponding input variable.

The procedure is illustrated in Fig. 4-18 for the function:

$$F = A(B + CD) + BC'$$

The AND-OR implementation of the function is shown in the logic diagram of Fig. 4-18(a). For each OR gate, we substitute a NOR gate followed by an inverter. For each AND gate, we substitute input inverters followed by a NOR gate. The pair of cascaded inverters from the OR box to the AND box is removed. The four inverters connected to external inputs are removed and the input variables complemented. The result is the NOR logic diagram shown in Fig. 4-18(c). The number of NOR gates in this example equals the number of AND-OR gates plus an additional inverter in the output (NOR gate 6). In general, the number of NOR gates required to implement a Boolean function equals the number of AND-OR gates, except for an occasional inverter. This is true provided both normal and complement inputs are available, because the conversion forces certain input variables to be complemented.

Analysis Procedure

The analysis of NOR logic diagrams follows the same procedures presented in Section 4-6 for the analysis of combinational circuits. To derive the Boolean function from a logic diagram, we mark the outputs of various gates with arbitrary symbols. By repetitive substitutions, we obtain the output variable as a function of the input variables. To obtain the truth table from a logic diagram without first deriving the Boolean function, we form a table listing the n input variables with 2^n rows of 1's and 0's. The truth table of various NOR gate outputs is derived in succession until the output truth table is obtained. The output function of a typical NOR gate is of the form $T = (A + B' + C)'$; so the truth table for T is marked with a 0 for those combinations where $A = 1$ or $B = 0$ or $C = 1$. The rest of the rows are filled with 1's.

Block Diagram Transformation

To convert a NOR logic diagram to its equivalent AND-OR logic diagram, we use the two symbols for NOR gates shown in Fig. 4-19. The OR-invert is the normal symbol for a NOR gate and the invert-AND is a convenient alternative that utilizes De Morgan's theorem and the convention that small circles at the inputs denote complementation.

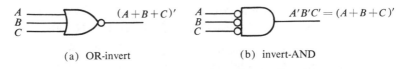

(a) OR-invert   (b) invert-AND

Figure 4-19 Two symbols for NOR gate

The conversion of a NOR logic diagram to an AND-OR diagram is achieved through a change in symbols from OR-invert to invert-AND starting from the last level and in alternate levels. Pairs of small circles along the same line are removed. A one-input AND or OR gate is removed, but if it has a small circle at the input or output, it is converted to an inverter.

This procedure is demonstrated in Fig. 4-20, where the NOR logic diagram in (a) is converted to an AND-OR diagram. The symbol of the gate in the last level

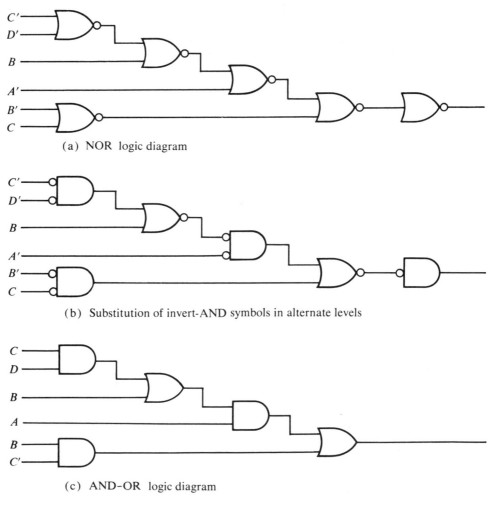

(a) NOR logic diagram

(b) Substitution of invert-AND symbols in alternate levels

(c) AND-OR logic diagram

Figure 4-20 Conversion of NOR logic diagram to AND-OR

144

(5) is changed to an invert-AND. Looking for alternate levels, we find one gate in level 3 and two in level 1. These three gates undergo a symbol change as shown in (b). Any two circles along the same line are removed. Circles that go to external inputs are also removed, provided the corresponding input variable is complemented. The gate in level 5 becomes a one-input AND gate and is removed. The required AND-OR logic diagram is drawn in Fig. 4-20(c).

4-9 EXCLUSIVE-OR AND EQUIVALENCE FUNCTIONS

Exclusive-OR and equivalence, denoted by $\oplus$ and $\odot$, respectively, are binary operations that perform the following Boolean functions:

$$x \oplus y = xy' + x'y$$
$$x \odot y = xy + x'y'$$

The two operations are the complements of each other. Each is commutative and associative. Because of these two properties, a function of three or more variables can be expressed without parentheses as follows:

$$(A \oplus B) \oplus C = A \oplus (B \oplus C) = A \oplus B \oplus C$$

This would imply the possibility of using exclusive-OR (or equivalence) gates with three or more inputs. However, multiple-input exclusive-OR gates are very uneconomical from a hardware standpoint. In fact, even a two-input function is usually constructed with other types of gates. For example, Fig. 4-21(a) shows the implementation of a two-input exclusive-OR function with AND, OR, and NOT gates. Figure 4-21(b) shows it with NAND gates.

Only a limited number of Boolean functions can be expressed exclusively in terms of exclusive-OR or equivalence operations. Nevertheless, these functions emerge quite often during the design of digital systems. The two functions are particularly useful in arithmetic operations and in error detection and correction.

An n-variable exclusive-OR expression is equal to the Boolean function with $2^n/2$ minterms whose equivalent binary numbers have an odd number of 1's. This is demonstrated in the map of Fig. 4-22(a) for the four-variable case. There are 16 minterms for four variables. Half the minterms have a numerical value with an odd number of 1's; the other half have a numerical value with an even number of 1's. The numerical value of a minterm is determined from the row and column numbers of the square that represents the minterm. The map of Fig. 4-22(a) has 1's in the squares whose minterm numbers have an odd number of 1's. The function can be expressed in terms of the exclusive-OR operations on the four variables. This is justified by the following algebraic manipulation:

$$A \oplus B \oplus C \oplus D = (AB' + A'B) \oplus (CD' + C'D)$$
$$= (AB' + A'B)(CD + C'D') + (AB + A'B')(CD' + C'D)$$
$$= \Sigma(1, 2, 4, 7, 8, 11, 13, 14)$$

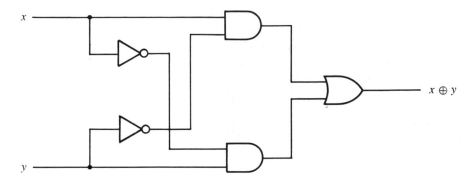

(a) with AND–OR–NOT gates

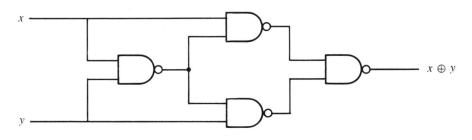

(b) with NAND gates

Figure 4-21 Exclusive-OR implementations

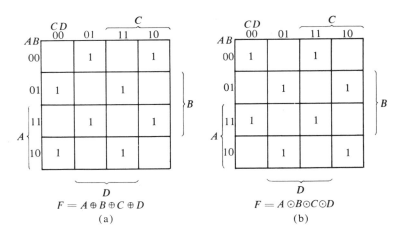

$F = A \oplus B \oplus C \oplus D$

(a)

$F = A \odot B \odot C \odot D$

(b)

Figure 4-22 Map for a four-variable (a) exclusive-OR function and (b) equivalence function

An n-variable equivalence expression is equal to the Boolean function with $2^n/2$ minterms, whose equivalent binary numbers have an even number of 0's. This is demonstrated in the map of Fig. 4-22(b) for the four-variable case. The squares with 1's represent the eight minterms with an even number of 0's, and the function can be expressed in terms of the equivalence operations on the four variables.

When the number of variables in a function is odd, the minterms with an even number of 0's are the same as the minterms with an odd number of 1's. This is demonstrated in the three-variable map of Fig. 4-23(a). Therefore, an exclusive-OR expression is equal to an equivalence expression when both have the same odd number of variables. However, they form the complements of each other when the number of variables is even, as demonstrated in the two maps of Fig. 4-22(a) and (b).

When the minterms of a function with an odd number of variables have an even number of 1's (or equivalently, an odd number of 0's), the function can be expressed as the complement of either an exclusive-OR or an equivalence expression. For example, the three-variable function shown in the map of Fig. 4-23(b) can be expressed as follows:

$$(A \oplus B \oplus C)' = A \oplus B \odot C$$

or

$$(A \odot B \odot C)' = A \odot B \oplus C$$

The S output of a full-adder and the D output of a full-subtractor (Section 4-3) can be implemented with exclusive-OR functions because each function consists of four minterms with numerical values having an odd number of 1's. The exclusive-OR function is extensively used in the implementation of digital arithmetic operations because the latter are usually implemented through procedures that require a repetitive addition or subtraction operation.

Exclusive-OR and equivalence functions are very useful in systems requiring error-detection and error-correction codes. As discussed in Section 1-6, a parity bit is a scheme for detecting errors during transmission of binary information. A

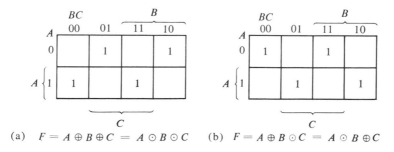

(a) $F = A \oplus B \oplus C = A \odot B \odot C$ (b) $F = A \oplus B \odot C = A \odot B \oplus C$

Figure 4-23   Map for three-variable functions

parity bit is an extra bit included with a binary message to make the number of 1's either odd or even. The message, including the parity bit, is transmitted and then checked at the receiving end for errors. An error is detected if the checked parity does not correspond to the one transmitted. The circuit that generates the parity bit in the transmitter is called a *parity generator*; the circuit that checks the parity in the receiver is called a *parity checker*.

As an example, consider a three-bit message to be transmitted with an odd-parity bit. Table 4-4 shows the truth table for the parity generator. The three bits x, y, and z constitute the message and are the inputs to the circuit. The parity bit P is the output. For odd parity, the bit P is generated so as to make the total number of 1's odd (including P). From the truth table, we see that $P = 1$ when the number of 1's in x, y, and z is even. This corresponds to the map of Fig. 4-23(b); so the function for P can be expressed as follows:

$$P = x \oplus y \odot z$$

The logic diagram for the parity generator is shown in Fig. 4-24(a). It consists of one two-input exclusive-OR gate and one two-input equivalence gate. The two gates can be interchanged and still produce the same function, since P is also equal to:

$$P = x \odot y \oplus z$$

The three-bit message and the parity bit are transmitted to their destination, where they are applied to a parity-checker circuit. An error occurs during transmission if the parity of the four bits received is even, since the binary information transmitted was originally odd. The output C of the parity checker should be a 1 when an error occurs, i.e., when the number of 1's in the four inputs is even. Table 4-5 is the truth table for the odd-parity checker circuit. From it we see that the function for C consists of the eight minterms with numerical values having an even number of 0's. This corresponds to the map of Fig. 4-22(b); so the function can be

TABLE 4-4   Odd-parity generation

| Three-bit message | | | Parity bit generated |
x	y	z	P
0	0	0	1
0	0	1	0
0	1	0	0
0	1	1	1
1	0	0	0
1	0	1	1
1	1	0	1
1	1	1	0

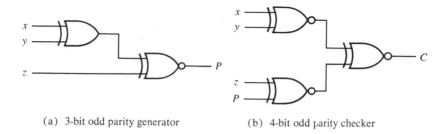

(a) 3-bit odd parity generator   (b) 4-bit odd parity checker

Figure 4-24 Logic diagrams for parity generation and checking

expressed with equivalence operators as follows:

$$C = x \odot y \odot z \odot P$$

The logic diagram for the parity checker is shown in Fig. 4-24(b) and consists of three two-input equivalence gates.

It is worth noting that the parity generator can be implemented with the circuit of Fig. 4-24(b) if the input P is permanently held at logic-0 and the output is marked P, the advantage being that the same circuit can be used for both parity generation and checking.

It is obvious from the foregoing example that parity generation and checking circuits always have an output function that includes half of the minterms whose numerical values have either an even or odd number of 1's. As a consequence, they can be implemented with equivalence and/or exclusive-OR gates.

TABLE 4-5 Odd-parity check

Four-bits received				Parity-error check
x	y	z	P	C
0	0	0	0	1
0	0	0	1	0
0	0	1	0	0
0	0	1	1	1
0	1	0	0	0
0	1	0	1	1
0	1	1	0	1
0	1	1	1	0
1	0	0	0	0
1	0	0	1	1
1	0	1	0	1
1	0	1	1	0
1	1	0	0	1
1	1	0	1	0
1	1	1	0	0
1	1	1	1	1

REFERENCES

1. Rhyne, V. T., *Fundamentals of Digital Systems Design*. Englewood Cliffs, N.J.: Prentice-Hall, Inc., 1973.

2. Peatman, J. P., *The Design of Digital Systems*. New York: McGraw-Hill Book Co., 1972.

3. Nagle, H. T. Jr., B. D. Carrol, and J. D. Irwin, *An Introduction to Computer Logic*. Englewood Cliffs, N. J.: Prentice-Hall, Inc., 1975.

4. Hill, F. J., and G. R. Peterson, *Introduction to Switching Theory and Logical Design*, 3rd ed. New York: John Wiley & Sons, Inc., 1981.

5. Maley, G. A., and J. Earle, *The Logic Design of Transistor Digital Computers*. Englewood Cliffs, N. J.: Prentice-Hall, Inc., 1963.

6. Friedman, A. D., and P. R. Menon, *Theory and Design of Switching Circuits*. Woodland Hills, Calif.: Computer Science Press, Inc., 1975.

PROBLEMS

4-1   A combinational circuit has four inputs and one output. The output is equal to 1 when (1) all the inputs are equal to 1 or (2) none of the inputs are equal to 1 or (3) an odd number of inputs are equal to 1.

(a) Obtain the truth table.

(b) Find the simplified output function in sum of products.

(c) Find the simplified output function in product of sums.

(d) Draw the two logic diagrams.

4-2   Design a combinational circuit that accepts a three-bit number and generates an output binary number equal to the square of the input number.

4-3.   It is necessary to multiply two binary numbers, each two bits long, in order to form their product in binary. Let the two numbers be represented by a_1, a_0 and b_1, b_0, where subscript 0 denotes the least significant bit.

(a) Determine the number of output lines required.

(b) Find the simplified Boolean expressions for each output.

4-4.   Repeat problem 4-3 to form the sum (instead of the product) of the two binary numbers.

4-5.   Design a combinational circuit with four input lines that represent a decimal digit in BCD and four output lines that generate the 9's complement of the input digit.

4-6.   Design a combinational circuit whose input is a four-bit number and whose output is the 2's complement of the input number.

4-7.   Design a combinational circuit that multiplies by 5 an input decimal digit represented in BCD. The output is also in BCD. Show that the outputs can be obtained from the input lines without using any logic gates.

4-8.   Design a combinational circuit that detects an error in the representation of a decimal digit in BCD. In other words, obtain a logic diagram whose output is logic-1 when the inputs contain an unused combination in the code.

4-9.   Implement a full-subtractor with two half-subtractors and an OR gate.

4-10. Show how a full-adder can be converted to a full-subtractor with the addition of one inverter circuit.

4-11. Design a combinational circuit that converts a decimal digit from the $8, 4, -2, -1$ code to BCD.

4-12. Design a combinational circuit that converts a decimal digit from the $2, 4, 2, 1$ code to the $8, 4, -2, -1$ code.

4-13. Obtain the logic diagram that converts a four-digit binary number to a decimal number in BCD. Note that two decimal digits are needed since the binary numbers range from 0 to 15.

4-14. A BCD-to-seven-segment decoder is a combinational circuit that accepts a decimal digit in BCD and generates the appropriate outputs for selection of segments in a display indicator used for displaying the decimal digit. The seven outputs of the decoder (a, b, c, d, e, f, g) select the corresponding segments in the display as shown in Fig. P4-14(a). The numeric designation chosen to represent the decimal digit is shown in Fig. P4-14(b). Design the BCD-to-seven-segment decoder circuit.

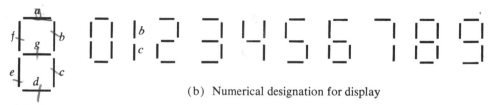

(b) Numerical designation for display

(a) Segment designation

Figure P4-14

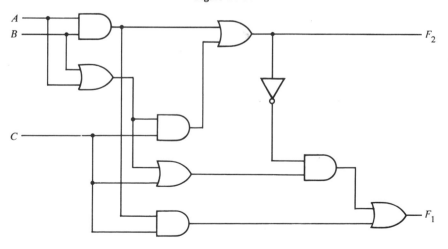

Figure P4-15

4-15. Analyze the two-output combinational circuits shown in Fig. P4-15. Obtain the Boolean functions for the two outputs and explain the circuit operation.

4-16. Derive the truth table of the circuit shown in Fig. P4-15.

4-17. Using the block diagram method, convert the logic diagram of Fig. 4-8 to a NAND implementation.

4-18. Repeat problem 4-17 for NOR implementation.

4-19. Obtain the NAND logic diagram of a full-adder from the Boolean functions:

$$C = xy + xz + yz$$
$$S = C'(x + y + z) + xyz$$

4-20. Determine the Boolean function for the output F of the circuit in Fig. P4-20. Obtain an equivalent circuit with fewer NOR gates.

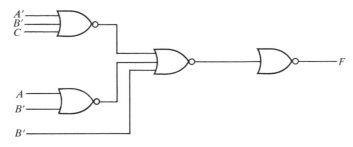

Figure P4-20

4-21. Determine the output Boolean functions of the circuits in Fig. P4-21.

4-22. Obtain the truth table for the circuits in Fig. P4-21.

4-23. Obtain the equivalent AND-OR logic diagram of Fig. P4-21(a).

4-24. Obtain the equivalent AND-OR logic diagram of Fig. P4-21(b).

4-25. Obtain the logic diagram of a two-input equivalence function using (a) AND, OR, and NOT gates; (b) NOR gates; and (c) NAND gates.

4-26. Show that the circuit in Fig. 4-21(b) is an exclusive-OR.

4-27. Show that $A \odot B \odot C \odot D = \Sigma(0, 3, 5, 6, 9, 10, 12, 15)$.

4-28. Design a combinational circuit that converts a four-bit reflected-code number (Table 1-4) to a four-bit binary number. Implement the circuit with exclusive-OR gates.

4-29. Design a combinational circuit to check for even parity of four bits. A logic-1 output is required when the four bits do not constitute an even parity.

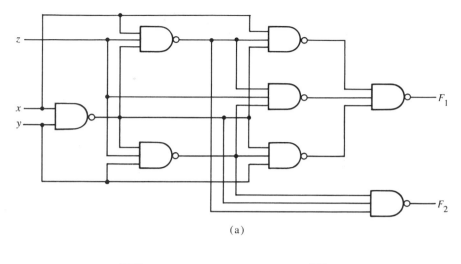

(a)

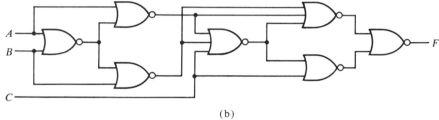

(b)

Figure P4-21

4-30. Implement the four Boolean functions listed using three half-adder circuits (Fig. 4-2e).

$$D = A \oplus B \oplus C$$
$$E = A'BC + AB'C$$
$$F = ABC' + (A' + B')C$$
$$G = ABC$$

4-31. Implement the Boolean function:

$$F = AB'CD' + A'BCD' + AB'C'D + A'BC'D$$

with exclusive-OR and AND gates.

Combinational Logic
with MSI and LSI

5

5-1 INTRODUCTION

The purpose of Boolean function simplification is to obtain an algebraic expression that, when implemented, results in a low-cost circuit. However, the criteria that determine a low-cost circuit or system must be defined if we are to evaluate the success of the achieved simplification. The design procedure for combinational circuits presented in Section 4-2 minimizes the number of gates required to implement a given function. This classical procedure assumes that, given two circuits that perform the same function, the one that requires fewer gates is preferable because it will cost less. This is not necessarily true when integrated circuits are used.

Since several logic gates are included in a single IC package, it becomes economical to use as many of the gates from an already used package even if, by doing so, we increase the total number of gates. Moreover, some of the interconnections among gates in many ICs are internal to the chip and it is more economical to use as many internal interconnections as possible in order to minimize the number of wires between external pins. With integrated circuits, it is not the count of gates that determines the cost but the number and type of ICs employed and the number of external interconnections needed to implement the given function.

There are numerous occasions where the classical method of Section 4-2 will not produce the best combinational circuit for implementing a given function. Moreover, the truth table and the simplification procedure in this method become too cumbersome if the number of input variables is excessively large. The final circuit obtained dictates that it be implemented with a random connection of SSI gates, which may require a relatively large number of ICs and interconnecting wires. In many cases the application of an alternate design procedure can produce a combinational circuit for a given function which is far better than the one obtained by following the classical design method. The possibility of an alternate design procedure depends on the particular problem and the ingenuity of the designer. The classical method constitutes a general procedure that, if followed, guarantees to produce a result. However, before applying the classical method, it is always wise to investigate the possibility of an alternate method which may be more efficient for the particular problem at hand.

The first question that must be answered before going through a detailed design of a combinational circuit is whether the function is already available in an IC package. Numerous MSI devices are available commercially. These devices perform specific digital functions commonly employed in the design of digital computer systems. If an MSI device cannot be found to produce exactly the function needed, a resourceful designer may be able to formulate a method so as to incorporate an MSI device in his circuit. The selection of MSI components in preference to SSI gates is extremely important, since it would invariably result in a considerable reduction of IC packages and interconnecting wires.

The first half of this chapter presents examples of combinational circuits designed by methods other than the classical procedure. All of the examples demonstrate the internal construction of existing MSI functions. Thus we present new design tools and at the same time acquaint the reader with existing MSI functions. Familiarity with available MSI functions is very important not only in the design of combinational circuits, but also in the design of more complicated digital computer systems.

Occasionally one finds MSI and LSI circuits that can be applied directly to the design and implementation of any combinational circuit. Four techniques of combinational logic design by means of MSI and LSI are introduced in the second half of the chapter. These techniques make use of the general properties of decoders, multiplexers, read-only memories (ROM), and programmable logic arrays (PLA). These four IC components have a large number of applications. Their use in implementing combinational circuits as described here is just one of many other applications.

5-2   BINARY PARALLEL ADDER

The full-adder introduced in Section 4-3 forms the sum of two bits and a previous carry. Two binary numbers of n bits each can be added by means of this circuit. To demonstrate with a specific example, consider two binary numbers, $A = 1011$ and $B = 0011$, whose sum is $S = 1110$. When a pair of bits are added through a full-adder, the circuit produces a carry to be used with the pair of bits one significant position higher. This is shown in the following table:

	4 3 2 1		*Full-adder of Fig. 4-5*
Subscript i			
Input carry	0 1 1 0	C_i	z
Augend	1 0 1 1	A_i	x
Addend	0 0 1 1	B_i	y
Sum	1 1 1 0	S_i	S
Output carry	0 0 1 1	C_{i+1}	C

The bits are added with full-adders, starting from the least significant position (subscript 1), to form the sum bit and carry bit. The inputs and outputs of the full-adder circuit of Fig. 4-5 are also indicated above. The input carry C_1 in the least significant position must be 0. The value of C_{i+1} in a given significant position is the output carry of the full-adder. This value is transferred into the input carry of the full-adder that adds the bits one higher significant position to the left. The sum bits are thus generated starting from the rightmost position and are available as soon as the corresponding previous carry bit is generated.

The sum of two n-bit binary numbers, A and B, can be generated in two ways: either in a serial fashion or in parallel. The serial addition method uses only one full-adder circuit and a storage device to hold the generated output carry. The pair of bits in A and B are transferred serially, one at a time, through the single full-adder to produce a string of output bits for the sum. The stored output carry from one pair of bits is used as an input carry for the next pair of bits. The parallel method uses n full-adder circuits, and all bits of A and B are applied simultaneously. The output carry from one full-adder is connected to the input carry of the full-adder one position to its left. As soon as the carries are generated, the correct sum bits emerge from the sum outputs of all full-adders.

A *binary parallel adder* is a digital function that produces the arithmetic sum of two binary numbers in parallel. It consists of full-adders connected in cascade, with the output carry from one full-adder connected to the input carry of the next full-adder.

Figure 5-1 shows the interconnection of four full-adder (FA) circuits to provide a 4-bit binary parallel adder. The augend bits of A and the addend bits of B are designated by subscript numbers from right to left, with subscript 1 denoting the low-order bit. The carries are connected in a chain through the full-adders. The input carry to the adder is C_1 and the output carry is C_5. The S outputs generate the required sum bits. When the 4-bit full-adder circuit is enclosed within an IC package, it has four terminals for the augend bits, four terminals for the addend bits, four terminals for the sum bits, and two terminals for the input and output carries.*

An n-bit parallel adder requires n full-adders. It can be constructed from 4-bit, 2-bit, and 1-bit full-adders ICs by cascading several packages. The output carry from one package must be connected to the input carry of the one with the next higher-order bits.

The 4-bit full-adders is a typical example of an MSI function. It can be used in many applications involving arithmetic operations. Observe that the design of this circuit by the classical method would require a truth table with $2^9 = 512$ entries, since there are nine inputs to the circuit. By using an iterative method of cascading an already known function, we were able to obtain a simple and well-organized implementation.

The application of this MSI function to the design of a combinational circuit is demonstrated in the following example.

*An example of a 4-bit full-adders is the TTL type 74283 IC.

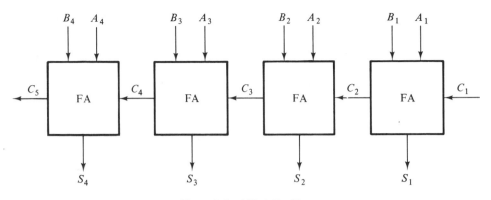

Figure 5-1 4-bit full-adders

EXAMPLE 5-1: Design a BCD-to-excess-3 code converter.

This circuit was designed in Section 4-5 by the classical method. The circuit obtained from this design is shown in Fig. 4-8 and requires 11 gates. When implemented with SSI gates, it requires 3 IC packages and 14 internal wire connections (not including input and output connections). Inspection of the truth table immediately reveals that the excess-3 equivalent code can be obtained from the BCD code by the addition of binary 0011. This addition can be easily implemented by means of a 4-bit full-adders MSI circuit, as shown in Fig. 5-2. The BCD digit is applied to inputs A. Inputs B are set to a constant 0011. This is done by applying logic-1 to B_1 and B_2 and logic-0 to B_3, B_4, and C_1. Logic-1 and logic-0 are physical

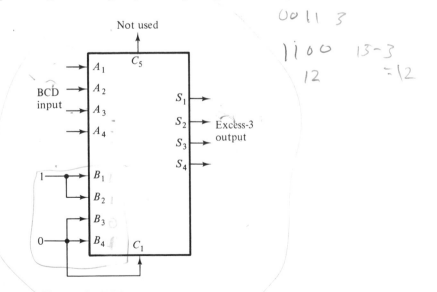

Figure 5-2 BCD-to-excess-3 code converter

157

signals whose values depend on the IC logic family used. For TTL circuits, logic-1 is equivalent to 3.5 volts and logic-0 is equivalent to ground. The S outputs from the circuit give the excess-3 equivalent code of the input BCD digit. This implementation requires one IC package and five wire connections, not including input and output wiring.

Carry Propagation

The addition of two binary numbers in parallel implies that all the bits of the augend and the addend are available for computation at the same time. As in any combinational circuit, the signal must propagate through the gates before the correct output sum is available in the output terminals. The total propagation time is equal to the propagation delay of a typical gate times the number of gate levels in the circuit. The longest propagation delay time in a parallel adder is the time it takes the carry to propagate through the full-adders. Since each bit of the sum output depends on the value of the input carry, the value of S_i in any given stage in the adder will be in its steady-state final value only after the input carry to that stage has been propagated. Consider output S_4 in Fig. 5-1. Inputs A_4 and B_4 reach a steady value as soon as input signals are applied to the adder. But input carry C_4 does not settle to its final steady-state value until C_3 is available in its steady-state value. Similarly, C_3 has to wait for C_2, and so on down to C_1. Thus only after the carry propagates through all stages will the last output S_4 and carry C_5 settle to their final steady-state value.

The number of gate levels for the carry propagation can be found from the circuit of the full-adder. This circuit was derived in Fig. 4-5 and is redrawn in Fig. 5-3 for convenience. The input and output variables use the subscript i to denote a typical stage in the parallel adder. The signals at P_i and G_i settle to their steady-state value after the propagation through their respective gates. These two signals are common to all full-adders and depend only on the input augend and addend bits. The signal from the input carry, C_i, to the output carry, C_{i+1}, propagates through an AND gate and an OR gate, which constitute two gate levels.

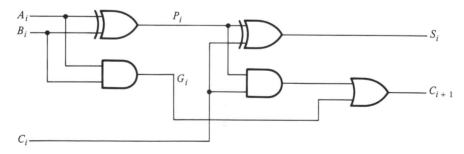

Figure 5-3 Full-adder circuit

If there are four full-adders in the parallel adder, the output carry C_5 would have $2 \times 4 = 8$ gate levels from C_1 to C_5. The total propagation time in the adder would be the propagation time in one half-adder plus eight gate levels. For an n-bit parallel adder, there are $2n$ gate levels for the carry to propagate through.

The carry propagation time is a limiting factor on the speed with which two numbers are added in parallel. Although a parallel adder, or any combinational circuit, will always have some value at its output terminals, the outputs will not be correct unless the signals are given enough time to propagate through the gates connected from the inputs to the outputs. Since all other arithmetic operations are implemented by successive additions, the time consumed during the addition process is very critical. An obvious solution for reducing the carry propagation delay time is to employ faster gates with reduced delays. But physical circuits have a limit to their capability. Another solution is to increase the equipment complexity in such a way that the carry delay time is reduced. There are several techniques for reducing the carry propagation time in a parallel adder. The most widely used technique employs the principle of *look-ahead* carry and is described below.

Consider the circuit of the full-adder shown in Fig. 5-3. If we define two new binary variables:

$$P_i = A_i \oplus B_i$$
$$G_i = A_i B_i$$

the output sum and carry can be expressed as:

$$S_i = P_i \oplus C_i$$
$$C_{i+1} = G_i + P_i C_i$$

G_i is called a *carry generate* and it produces an output carry when both A_i and B_i are one, regardless of the input carry. P_i is called a *carry propagate* because it is the term associated with the propagation of the carry from C_i to C_{i+1}.

We now write the Boolean function for the carry output of each stage and substitute for each C_i its value from the previous equations:

$$C_2 = G_1 + P_1 C_1$$
$$C_3 = G_2 + P_2 C_2 = G_2 + P_2(G_1 + P_1 C_1) = G_2 + P_2 G_1 + P_2 P_1 C_1$$
$$C_4 = G_3 + P_3 C_3 = G_3 + P_3 G_2 + P_3 P_2 G_1 + P_3 P_2 P_1 C_1$$

Since the Boolean function for each output carry is expressed in sum of products, each function can be implemented with one level of AND gates followed by an OR gate (or by a two-level NAND). The three Boolean functions for C_2, C_3, and C_4 are implemented in the look-ahead carry generator shown in Fig. 5-4. Note that C_4

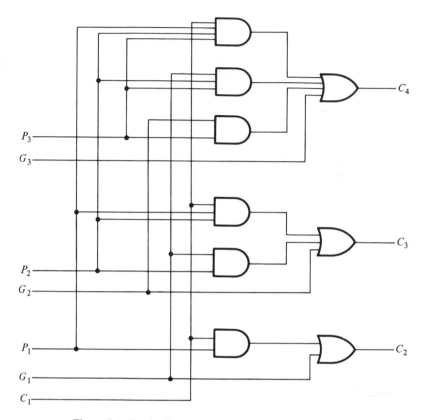

Figure 5-4 Logic diagram of a look-ahead carry generator

does not have to wait for C_3 and C_2 to propagate; in fact, C_4 is propagated at the same time as C_2 and C_3.*

The construction of a 4-bit parallel adder with a look-ahead carry scheme is shown in Fig. 5-5. Each sum output requires two exclusive-OR gates. The output of the first exclusive-OR gate generate the P_i variable, and the AND gate generates the G_i variable. All the P's and G's are generated in two gate levels. The carries are propagated through the look-ahead carry generator (similar to that in Fig. 5-4) and applied as inputs to the second exclusive-OR gate. After the P and G signals settle into their steady-state values, all output carries are generated after a delay of two levels of gates. Thus, outputs S_2 through S_4 have equal propagation delay times. The two-level circuit for the output carry C_5 is not shown in Fig. 5-4. This circuit can be easily derived by the equation-substitution method as done above (see Problem 5-4).

*A typical look-ahead carry generator is the IC type 74182. It is implemented with AND-OR-INVERT gates. It also has two outputs, G and P, to generate $C_5 = G + PC_1$.

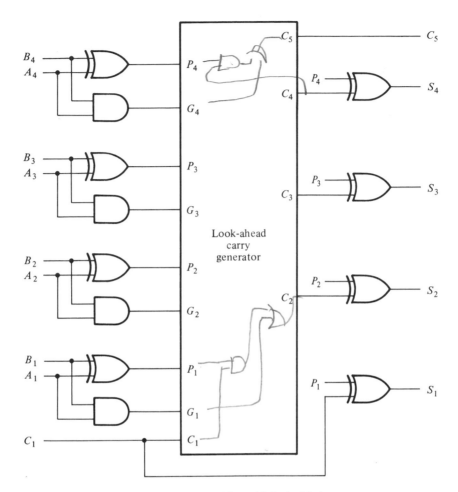

Figure 5-5 4-bit full-adders with look-ahead carry

5-3 DECIMAL ADDER

Computers or calculators that perform arithmetic operations directly in the decimal number system represent decimal numbers in binary-coded form. An adder for such a computer must employ arithmetic circuits that accept coded decimal numbers and present results in the accepted code. For binary addition, it was sufficient to consider a pair of significant bits at a time, together with a previous carry. A decimal adder requires a minimum of nine inputs and five outputs, since four bits are required to code each decimal digit and the circuit must have an input carry and output carry. Of course, there is a wide variety of possible decimal adder circuits, dependent upon the code used to represent the decimal digits.

The design of a nine-input, five-output combinational circuit by the classical method requires a truth table with $2^9 = 512$ entries. Many of the input combinations are don't-care conditions, since each binary code input has six combinations that are invalid. The simplified Boolean functions for the circuit may be obtained by a computer-generated tabular method, and the result would probably be a connection of gates forming an irregular pattern. An alternate procedure is to add the numbers with full-adder circuits, taking into consideration the fact that six combinations in each 4-bit input are not used. The output must be modified so that only those binary combinations which are valid combinations of the decimal code are generated.

BCD adder

Consider the arithmetic addition of two decimal digits in BCD, together with a possible carry from a previous stage. Since each input digit does not exceed 9, the output sum cannot be greater than $9 + 9 + 1 = 19$, the 1 in the sum being an input carry. Suppose we apply two BCD digits to a 4-bit binary adder. The adder will form the sum in *binary* and produce a result which may range from 0 to 19. These binary numbers are listed in Table 5-1 and are labeled by symbols K, Z_8, Z_4, Z_2, and Z_1. K is the carry, and the subscripts under the letter Z represent the weights 8, 4, 2, and 1 that can be assigned to the four bits in the BCD code. The first column in the table lists the binary sums as they appear in the outputs of a 4-bit *binary* adder. The output sum of two *decimal digits* must be represented in BCD and should appear in the form listed in the second column of the table. The problem is to find a simple rule by which the binary number in the first column can be converted to the correct BCD-digit representation of the number in the second column.

In examining the contents of the table, it is apparent that when the binary sum is equal to or less than 1001, the corresponding BCD number is identical, and therefore no conversion is needed. When the binary sum is greater than 1001, we obtain a nonvalid BCD representation. The addition of binary 6 (0110) to the binary sum converts it to the correct BCD representation and also produces an output carry as required.

The logic circuit that detects the necessary correction can be derived from the table entries. It is obvious that a correction is needed when the binary sum has an output carry $K = 1$. The other six combinations from 1010 to 1111 that need a correction have a 1 in position Z_8. To distinguish them from binary 1000 and 1001 which also have a 1 in position Z_8, we specify further that either Z_4 or Z_2 must have a 1. The condition for a correction and an output carry can be expressed by the Boolean function:

$$C = K + Z_8 Z_4 + Z_8 Z_2$$

when $C = 1$, it is necessary to add 0110 to the binary sum and provide an output carry for the next stage.

TABLE 5-1 Derivation of a BCD adder

Binary sum					BCD sum					Decimal
K	Z_8	Z_4	Z_2	Z_1	C	S_8	S_4	S_2	S_1	
0	0	0	0	0	0	0	0	0	0	0
0	0	0	0	1	0	0	0	0	1	1
0	0	0	1	0	0	0	0	1	0	2
0	0	0	1	1	0	0	0	1	1	3
0	0	1	0	0	0	0	1	0	0	4
0	0	1	0	1	0	0	1	0	1	5
0	0	1	1	0	0	0	1	1	0	6
0	0	1	1	1	0	0	1	1	1	7
0	1	0	0	0	0	1	0	0	0	8
0	1	0	0	1	0	1	0	0	1	9
0	1	0	1	0	1	0	0	0	0	10
0	1	0	1	1	1	0	0	0	1	11
0	1	1	0	0	1	0	0	1	0	12
0	1	1	0	1	1	0	0	1	1	13
0	1	1	1	0	1	0	1	0	0	14
0	1	1	1	1	1	0	1	0	1	15
1	0	0	0	0	1	0	1	1	0	16
1	0	0	0	1	1	0	1	1	1	17
1	0	0	1	0	1	1	0	0	0	18
1	0	0	1	1	1	1	0	0	1	19

A *BCD adder* is a circuit that adds two BCD digits in parallel and produces a sum digit also in BCD. A BCD adder must include the correction logic in its internal construction. To add 0110 to the binary sum, we use a second 4-bit binary adder as shown in Fig. 5-6. The two decimal digits, together with the input carry, are first added in the top 4-bit binary adder to produce the binary sum. When the output carry is equal to zero, nothing is added to the binary sum. When it is equal to one, binary 0110 is added to the binary sum through the bottom 4-bit binary adder. The output carry generated from the bottom binary adder can be ignored, since it supplies information already available at the output-carry terminal.

The BCD adder can be constructed with three IC packages. Each of the 4-bit adders is an MSI function and the three gates for the correction logic need one SSI package. However, the BCD adder is available in one MSI circuit.* To achieve shorter propagation delays, an MSI BCD adder includes the necessary circuits for look-ahead carries. The adder circuit for the correction does not need all four full-adders, and this circuit can be optimized within the IC package.

*TTL IC type 82S83 is a BCD adder.

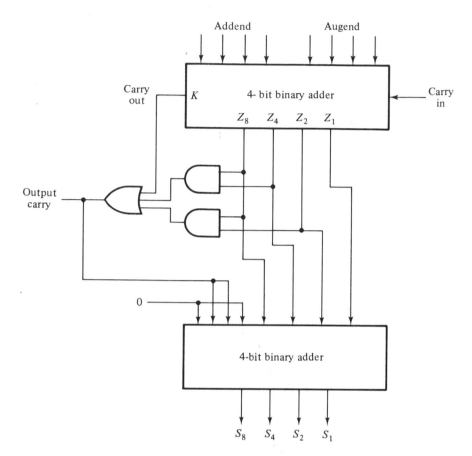

Figure 5-6 Block diagram of a BCD adder

A decimal parallel adder that adds n decimal digits needs n BCD adder stages. The output carry from one stage must be connected to the input carry of the next higher-order stage.

5-4 MAGNITUDE COMPARATOR

The comparison of two numbers is an operation that determines if one number is greater than, less than, or equal to the other number. A *magnitude comparator* is a combinational circuit that compares two numbers, A and B, and determines their relative magnitudes. The outcome of the comparison is specified by three binary variables that indicate whether $A > B$, $A = B$, or $A < B$.

The circuit for comparing two n-bit numbers has 2^{2n} entries in the truth table and becomes too cumbersome even with $n = 3$. On the other hand, as one may suspect, a comparator circuit possesses a certain amount of regularity. Digital functions which possess an inherent well-defined regularity can usually be designed by means of an algorithmic procedure if one is found to exist. An *algorithm* is a procedure that specifies a finite set of steps which, if followed, give the solution to a problem. We illustrate this method here by deriving an algorithm for the design of a 4-bit magnitude comparator.

The algorithm is a direct application of the procedure a person uses to compare the relative magnitudes of two numbers. Consider two numbers, A and B, with four digits each. Write the coefficients of the numbers with descending significance as follows:

$$A = A_3A_2A_1A_0$$
$$B = B_3B_2B_1B_0$$

where each subscripted letter represents one of the digits in the number. The two numbers are equal if all pairs of significant digits are equal i.e., if $A_3 = B_3$ and $A_2 = B_2$ and $A_1 = B_1$ and $A_0 = B_0$. When the numbers are binary, the digits are either 1 or 0 and the equality relation of each pair of bits can be expressed logically with an equivalence function:

$$x_i = A_iB_i + A'_iB'_i \qquad i = 0, 1, 2, 3$$

where $x_i = 1$ only if the pair of bits in position i are equal, i.e., if both are 1's or both are 0's.

The equality of the two numbers, A and B, is displayed in a combinational circuit by an output binary variable which we designate by the symbol $(A = B)$. This binary variable is equal to 1 if the input numbers, A and B, are equal, and it is equal to 0 otherwise. For the equality condition to exist, all x_i variables must be equal to 1. This dictates an AND operation of all variables:

$$(A = B) = x_3x_2x_1x_0$$

the *binary* variable $(A = B)$ is equal to 1 only if all pairs of digits of the two numbers are equal.

To determine if A is greater than or less than B, we inspect the relative magnitudes of pairs of significant digits starting from the most significant position. If the two digits are equal, we compare the next lower significant pair of digits. This comparison continues until a pair of unequal digits is reached. If the corresponding digit of A is 1 and that of B is 0, we conclude that $A > B$. If the corresponding digit of A is 0 and that of B is 1, we have that $A < B$. The sequential comparison can be expressed logically by the following two Boolean functions:

$$(A > B) = A_3B'_3 + x_3A_2B'_2 + x_3x_2A_1B'_1 + x_3x_2x_1A_0B'_0$$
$$(A < B) = A'_3B_3 + x_3A'_2B_2 + x_3x_2A'_1B_1 + x_3x_2x_1A'_0B_0$$

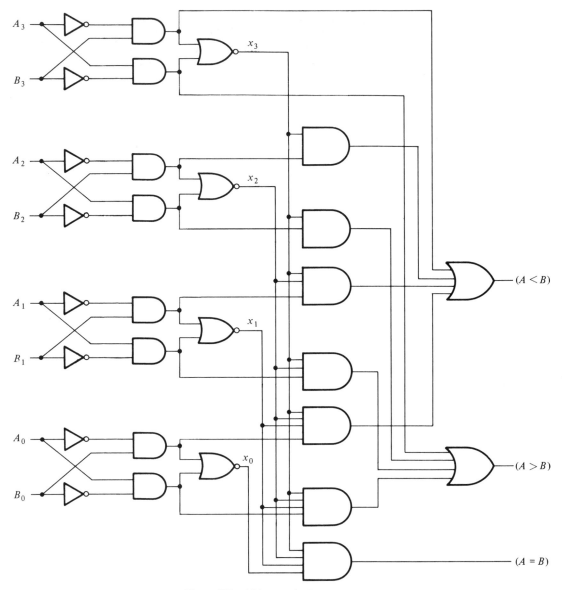

Figure 5-7 4-bit magnitude comparator

the symbols $(A > B)$ and $(A < B)$ are *binary* output variables which are equal to 1 when $A > B$ or $A < B$, respectively.

The gate implementation of the three output variables just derived is simpler than it seems because it involves a certain amount of repetition. The "unequal" outputs can use the same gates that are needed to generate the "equal" output. The logic diagram of the 4-bit magnitude comparator is shown in Fig. 5-7.* The four x

*TTL type 7485 is a 4-bit magnitude comparator. It has three more inputs for connecting comparators in cascade (see Problem 5-14).

outputs are generated with equivalence (exclusive-NOR) circuits and applied to an AND gate to give the output binary variable ($A = B$). The other two outputs use the x variables to generate the Boolean functions listed above. This is a multilevel implementation and, as clearly seen, it has a regular pattern. The procedure for obtaining magnitude comparator circuits for binary numbers with more than four bits should be obvious from this example. The same circuit can be used to compare the relative magnitudes of two BCD digits.

5-5 DECODERS

Discrete quantities of information are represented in digital systems with binary codes. A binary code of n bits is capable of representing up to 2^n distinct elements of the coded information. A *decoder* is a combinational circuit that converts binary information from n input lines to a maximum of 2^n unique output lines. If the n-bit decoded information has unused or don't-care combinations, the decoder output will have less than 2^n outputs.

    The decoders presented here are called *n-to-m* line decoders where $m \leqslant 2^n$. Their purpose is to generate the 2^n (or less) minterms of n input variables. The

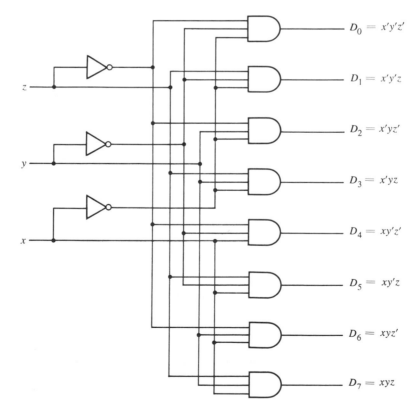

Figure 5-8   A 3-to-8 line decoder

name *decoder* is also used in conjunction with some code converters such as a BCD-to-seven-segment decoder (see Problem 4-14).

As an example, consider the 3-to-8 line decoder circuit of Fig. 5-8. The three inputs are decoded into eight outputs, each output representing one of the minterms of the 3-input variables. The three inverters provide the complement of the inputs, and each one of the eight AND gates generates one of the minterms. A particular application of this decoder would be a binary-to-octal conversion. The input variables may represent a binary number, and the outputs will then represent the eight digits in the octal number system. However, a 3-to-8 line decoder can be used for decoding any 3-bit code to provide eight outputs, one for each element of the code.

The operation of the decoder may be further clarified from its input-output relationships, listed in Table 5-2. Observe that the output variables are mutually exclusive because only one output can be equal to 1 at any one time. The output line whose value is equal to 1 represents the minterm equivalent of the binary number presently available in the input lines.*

TABLE 5-2   Truth table of a 3-to-8 line decoder

Inputs			Outputs							
x	y	z	D_0	D_1	D_2	D_3	D_4	D_5	D_6	D_7
0	0	0	1	0	0	0	0	0	0	0
0	0	1	0	1	0	0	0	0	0	0
0	1	0	0	0	1	0	0	0	0	0
0	1	1	0	0	0	1	0	0	0	0
1	0	0	0	0	0	0	1	0	0	0
1	0	1	0	0	0	0	0	1	0	0
1	1	0	0	0	0	0	0	0	1	0
1	1	1	0	0	0	0	0	0	0	1

EXAMPLE 5-2: Design a BCD-to-decimal decoder.

The elements of information in this case are the ten decimal digits represented by the BCD code. The code itself has four bits. Therefore, the decoder should have four inputs to accept the coded digit and ten outputs, one for each decimal digit. This will give a 4-line to 10-line BCD-to-decimal decoder.

There is really no need to design such a decoder because it can be found in IC form as an MSI function. We will design it anyway for two reasons. First, it gives insight on what to expect in such an MSI function. Second, this is a good example for demonstrating the practical consquences of don't-care conditions.

---

*IC type 74138 is a 3-to-8 line decoder. It is constructed with NAND gates. The outputs are the complements of the values shown in Table 5-2.

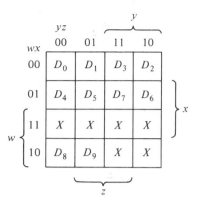

Figure 5-9 Map for simplifying a BCD-to-decimal decoder

Since the circuit has ten outputs, it would be necessary to draw ten maps to simplify each one of the output functions. There are six don't-care conditions here, and they must be taken into consideration when we simplify each of the output functions. Instead of drawing ten maps, we will draw only one map and write each of the output variables, D_0 to D_9, inside its corresponding minterm square as shown in Fig. 5-9. Six input combinations will never occur, so we mark their corresponding minterm squares with X's.

It is the designer's responsibility to decide on how to treat the don't-care conditions. Assume that it is decided to use them in such a way as to simplify the functions to the minimum number of literals. D_0 and D_1 cannot be combined with any don't-care minterms. D_2 can be combined with the don't care minterm m_{10} to give:

$$D_2 = x'yz'$$

The square with D_9 can be combined with three other don't-care squares to give:

$$D_9 = wz$$

Using the don't-care terms for the other outputs, we obtain the circuit shown in Fig. 5-10. Thus the don't-care terms cause a reduction in the number of inputs in most of the AND gates.

A careful designer should investigate the effect of the above minimization. Although it is true that under normal operating conditions the invalid six combinations will never occur, what if there is a malfunction and they do occur? An analysis of the circuit of Fig. 5-10 shows that the six invalid input combinations will produce outputs as listed in Table 5-3. The reader can look at the table and decide whether this is a good or bad design.

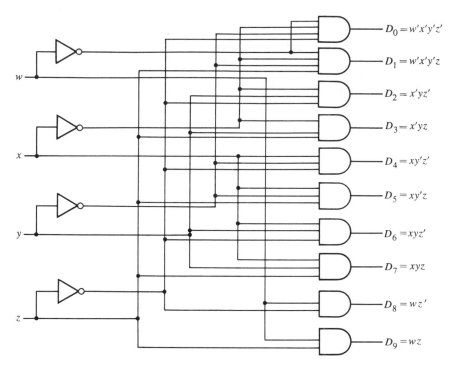

$D_0 = w'x'y'z'$

$D_1 = w'x'y'z$

$D_2 = x'yz'$

$D_3 = x'yz$

$D_4 = xy'z'$

$D_5 = xy'z$

$D_6 = xyz'$

$D_7 = xyz$

$D_8 = wz'$

$D_9 = wz$

Figure 5-10   BCD-to-decimal decoder

TABLE 5-3   Partial truth table for the circuit of Fig. 5-10

Inputs				Outputs									
w	x	y	z	D_0	D_1	D_2	D_3	D_4	D_5	D_6	D_7	D_8	D_9
1	0	1	0	0	0	1	0	0	0	0	0	1	0
1	0	1	1	0	0	0	1	0	0	0	0	0	1
1	1	0	0	0	0	0	0	1	0	0	0	1	0
1	1	0	1	0	0	0	0	0	1	0	0	0	1
1	1	1	0	0	0	0	0	0	0	1	0	1	0
1	1	1	1	0	0	0	0	0	0	0	1	0	1

Another reasonable design decision would be to make all outputs equal to 0 when an invalid input combination occurs.* This would require ten 4-input AND gates. Other possibilities may be considered. In any case, one should not treat don't-care conditions indiscriminately but should try to investigate their effect once the circuit is in operation.

*IC type 7442 is a BCD-to-decimal decoder. The selected outputs are in the 0 state, and all the invalid combinations give an output of all 1's.

Combinational Logic Implementation

A decoder provides the 2^n minterm of n input variables. Since any Boolean function can be expressed in sum of minterms canonical form, one can use a decoder to generate the minterms and an external OR gate to form the sum. In this way, any combinational circuit with n inputs and m outputs can be implemented with an n-to-2^n line decoder and m OR gates.

The procedure for implementing a combinational circuit by means of a decoder and OR gates requires that the Boolean functions for the circuit be expressed in sum of minterms. This form can be easily obtained from the truth table or by expanding the functions to their sum of minterms (see Section 2-5). A decoder is then chosen which generates all the minterms of the n input variables. The inputs to each OR gate are selected from the decoder outputs according to the minterm list in each function.

> ***EXAMPLE 5-3:*** Implement a full-adder circuit with a decoder and two OR gates.
>
> From the truth table of the full-adder (Section 4-3), we obtain the functions for this combinational circuit in sum of minterms:
>
> $$S(x, y, z) = \Sigma(1, 2, 4, 7)$$
> $$C(x, y, z,) = \Sigma(3, 5, 6, 7)$$
>
> Since there are three inputs and a total of eight minterms, we need a 3-to-8 line decoder. The implementation is shown in Fig. 5-11. The decoder generates the eight minterms for x, y, z. The OR gate for output S forms the sum of minterms 1, 2, 4, and 7. The OR gate for output C forms the sum of minterms 3, 5, 6, and 7.

A function with a long list of minterms requires an OR gate with a large number of inputs. A function F having a list of k minterms can be expressed in its

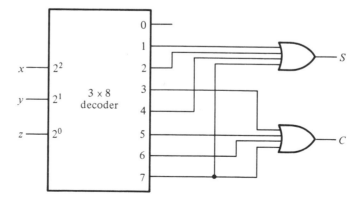

Figure 5-11   Implementation of a full-adder with a decoder

complemented form F' with $2^n - k$ minterms. If the number of minterms in a function is greater than $2^n/2$, then F' can be expressed with fewer minterms than required for F. In such a case, it is advantageous to use a NOR gate to sum the minterms of F'. The output of the NOR gate will generate the normal output F.

The decoder method can be used to implement any combinational circuit. However, its implementation must be compared with all other possible implementations to determine the best solution. In some cases this method may provide the best implementation, especially if the combinational circuit has many outputs and if each output function (or its complement) is expressed with a small number of minterms.

Demultiplexers

Some IC decoders are constructed with NAND gates. Since a NAND gate produces the AND operation with an inverted output, it becomes more economical to generate the decoder minterms in their complemented form. Most, if not all, IC decoders include one or more *enable* inputs to control the circuit operation. A 2-to-4 line decoder with an enable input constructed with NAND gates is shown in Fig. 5-12. All outputs are equal to 1 if enable input E is 1, regardless of the values of inputs A and B. When the enable input is 0, the circuit operates as a decoder with complemented outputs. The truth table lists these conditions. The X's under A and B are don't-care conditions. Normal decoder operation occurs only with $E = 0$, and the outputs are selected when they are in the 0 state.

The block diagram of the decoder is shown in Fig. 5-13(a). The small circle at input E indicates that the decoder is enabled when $E = 0$. The small circles at the outputs indicate that all outputs are complemented.

A decoder with an enable input can function as a demultiplexer. A *demultiplexer* is a circuit that receives information on a single line and transmits this information on one of 2^n possible output lines. The selection of a specific output

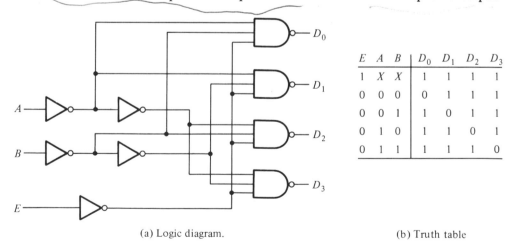

E	A	B	D_0	D_1	D_2	D_3
1	X	X	1	1	1	1
0	0	0	0	1	1	1
0	0	1	1	0	1	1
0	1	0	1	1	0	1
0	1	1	1	1	1	0

(a) Logic diagram.   (b) Truth table

Figure 5-12   A 2-to-4 line decoder with enable (E) input

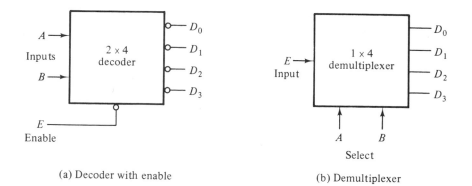

(a) Decoder with enable   (b) Demultiplexer

Figure 5-13 Block diagrams for the circuit of Fig. 5-12

line is controlled by the bit values of n selection lines. The decoder of Fig. 5-12 can function as a demultiplexer if the E line is taken as a data input line and lines A and B are taken as the selection lines. This is shown in Fig. 5-13(b). The single input variable E has a path to all four outputs, but the input information is directed to only one of the output lines, as specified by the binary value of the two selection lines A and B. This can be verified from the truth table of this circuit, shown in Fig. 5-12(b). For example, if the selection lines $AB = 10$, output D_2 will be the same as the input value E, while all other outputs are maintained at 1. Because decoder and demultiplexer operations are obtained from the same circuit, a decoder with an enable input is referred to as a *decoder/demultiplexer*. It is the enable input that makes the circuit a demultiplexer; the decoder itself can use AND, NAND, or NOR gates.

Decoder/demultiplexer circuits can be connected together to form a larger decoder circuit. Figure 5-14 shows two 3×8 decoders with enable inputs connected to form a 4×16 decoder. When $w = 0$, the top decoder is enabled and the

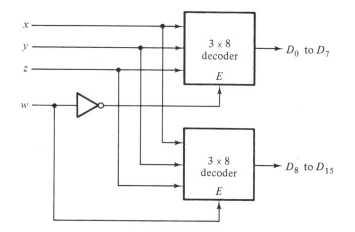

Figure 5-14 A 4×16 decoder constructed with two 3×8 decoders

other is disabled. The bottom decoder outputs are all 0's, and the top eight outputs generate minterms 0000 to 0111. When $w = 1$, the enable conditions are reversed; the bottom decoder outputs generate minterms 1000 to 1111, while the outputs of the top decoder are all 0's. This example demonstrates the usefulness of enable inputs in ICs. In general, enable lines are a convenient feature for connecting two or more IC packages for the purpose of expanding the digital function into a similar function with more inputs and outputs.

Encoders

An *encoder* is a digital function that produces a reverse operation from that of a decoder. An encoder has 2^n (or less) input lines and n output lines. The output lines generate the binary code for the 2^n input variables. An example of an encoder is shown in Fig. 5-15. The octal-to-binary encoder consists of eight inputs, one for each of the eight digits, and three outputs that generate the corresponding binary number. It is constructed with OR gates whose inputs can be determined from the truth table given in Table 5-4. The low-order output bit z is 1 if the input octal digit is odd. Output y is 1 for octal digits 2, 3, 6, or 7. Output x is a 1 for octal digits 4, 5, 6, or 7. Note that D_0 is not connected to any OR gate; the binary output must be all 0's in this case. An all 0's output is also obtained when all inputs are all 0's. This discrepancy can be resolved by providing one more output to indicate the fact that all inputs are not 0's.

The encoder in Fig. 5-15 assumes that only one input line can be equal to 1 at any time; otherwise the circuit has no meaning. Note that the circuit has eight inputs and could have $2^8 = 256$ possible input combinations. Only eight of these combinations have any meaning. The other input combinations are don't-care conditions.

Encoders of this type (Fig. 5-15) are not available in IC packages, since they can be easily constructed with OR gates. The type of encoder available in IC form

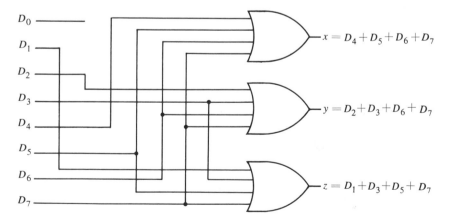

Figure 5-15   Octal-to-binary encoder

TABLE 5-4 Truth table of octal-to-binary encoder

Inputs								Outputs		
D_0	D_1	D_2	D_3	D_4	D_5	D_6	D_7	x	y	z
1	0	0	0	0	0	0	0	0	0	0
0	1	0	0	0	0	0	0	0	0	1
0	0	1	0	0	0	0	0	0	1	0
0	0	0	1	0	0	0	0	0	1	1
0	0	0	0	1	0	0	0	1	0	0
0	0	0	0	0	1	0	0	1	0	1
0	0	0	0	0	0	1	0	1	1	0
0	0	0	0	0	0	0	1	1	1	1

is called a *priority encoder*.* These encoders establish an input priority to ensure that only the highest-priority input line is encoded. Thus, in Table 5-4, if priority is given to an input with a higher subscript number over one with a lower subscript number, then if both D_2 and D_5 are logic-1 simultaneously, the output will be 101 because D_5 has a higher priority over D_2. Of course, the truth table of a priority encoder is different from the one in Table 5-4 (see Problem 5-21).

5-6 MULTIPLEXERS

Multiplexing means transmitting a large number of information units over a smaller number of channels or lines. A *digital multiplexer* is a combinational circuit that selects binary information from one of many input lines and directs it to a single output line The selection of a particular input line is controlled by a set of selection lines. Normally, there are 2^n input lines and n selection lines whose bit combinations determine which input is selected.

A 4-line to 1-line multiplexer is shown in Fig. 5-16. Each of the four input lines, I_0 to I_3, is applied to one input of an AND gate. Selection lines s_1 and s_0 are decoded to select a particular AND gate. The function table in the figure lists the input-to-output path for each possible bit combination of the selection lines. When this MSI function is used in the design of a digital system, it is represented in block diagram form as shown in Fig. 5-16(c). To demonstrate the circuit operation, consider the case when $s_1s_0 = 10$. The AND gate associated with input I_2 has two of its inputs equal to 1 and the third input connected to I_2. The other three AND gates have at least one input equal to 0, which makes their output equal to 0. The OR-gate output is now equal to the value of I_2, thus providing a path from the selected input to the output. A multiplexer is also called a *data selector*, since it selects one of many inputs and steers the binary information to the output line.

*For example, IC type 74148.

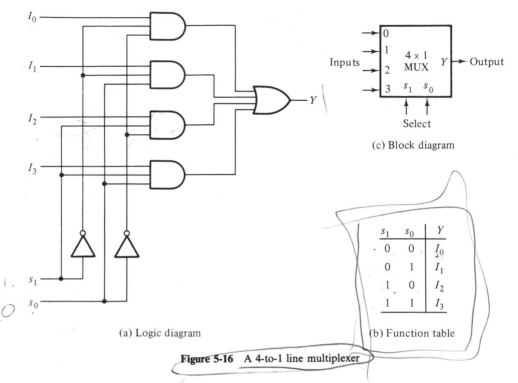

(a) Logic diagram

(c) Block diagram

s_1	s_0	Y
0	0	I_0
0	1	I_1
1	0	I_2
1	1	I_3

(b) Function table

Figure 5-16 A 4-to-1 line multiplexer

The AND gates and inverters in the multiplexer resemble a decoder circuit and, indeed, they decode the input selection lines. In general, a 2^n-to-1 line multiplexer is constructed from an n-to-2^n decoder by adding to it 2^n input lines, one to each AND gate. The outputs of the AND gates are applied to a single OR gate to provide the 1-line output. The size of a multiplexer is specified by the number 2^n of its input lines and the single output line. It is then implied that it also contains n selection lines. A multiplexer is often abbreviated as MUX.

As in decoders, multiplexer ICs may have an *enable* input to control the operation of the unit. When the enable input is in a given binary state, the outputs are disabled, and when it is in the other state (the enable state), the circuit functions as a normal multiplexer. The enable input (sometimes called *strobe*) can be used to expand two or more multiplexer ICs to a digital multiplexer with a larger number of inputs.

In some cases two or more multiplexers are enclosed within one IC package. The selection and enable inputs in multiple-unit ICs may be common to all multiplexers. As an illustration, a quadruple 2-line to 1-line multiplexer IC is shown in Fig. 5-17.* It has four multiplexers, each capable of selecting one of two input lines. Output Y_1 can be selected to be equal to either A_1 or B_1. Similarly, output Y_2 may have the value of A_2 or B_2, and so on. One input selection line, S,

*This is similar to IC type 74157.

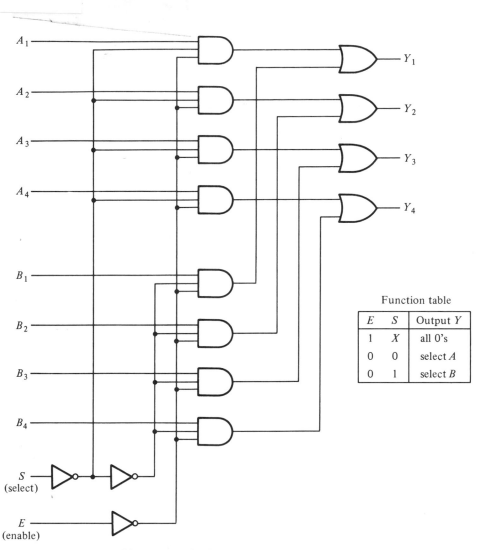

Function table

E	S	Output Y
1	X	all 0's
0	0	select A
0	1	select B

Figure 5-17 Quadruple 2-to-1 line multiplexers

suffices to select one of two lines in all four multiplexers. The control input E enables the multiplexers in the 0 state and disables them in the 1 state. Although the circuit contains four multiplexers, we may think of it as a circuit that selects one in a pair of 4-input lines. As shown in the function table, the unit is selected when $E = 0$. Then, if $S = 0$, the four A inputs have a path to the outputs. On the other hand, if $S = 1$, the four B inputs are selected. The outputs have all 0's when $E = 1$, regardless of the value of S.

The multiplexer is a very useful MSI function and has a multitude of applications. It is used for connecting two or more sources to a single destination among computer units, and it is useful for constructing a common bus system.

These and other uses of the multiplexer are discussed in later chapters in conjunction with their particular applications. Here we demonstrate the general properties of this device and show that it can be used to implement any Boolean function.

Boolean Function Implementation

It was shown in the previous section that a decoder can be used to implement a Boolean function by employing an external OR gate. A quick reference to the multiplexer of Fig. 5-16 reveals that it is essentially a decoder with the OR gate already available. The minterms out of the decoder to be chosen can be controlled with the input lines. The minterms to be included with the function being implemented are chosen by making their corresponding input lines equal to 1, those minterms not included in the function are disabled by making their input lines equal to 0. This gives a method for implementing any Boolean function of n variables with a 2^n-to-1 multiplexer. However, it is possible to do better than that.

If we have a Boolean function of $n + 1$ variables, we take n of these variables and connect them to the selection lines of a multiplexer. The remaining single variable of the function is used for the inputs of the multiplexer. If A is this single variable, the inputs of the multiplexer are chosen to be either A or A' or 1 or 0. By judicious use of these four values for the inputs and by connecting the other variables to the selection lines, one can implement any Boolean function with a multiplexer. In this way it is possible to generate any function of $n + 1$ variables with a 2^n-to-1 multiplexer.

To demonstrate this procedure with a concrete example, consider the function of three variables:

$$F(A, B, C) = \Sigma(1, 3, 5, 6)$$

The function can be implemented with a 4-to-1 multiplexer as shown in Fig. 5-18. Two of the variables, B and C are applied to the selection lines in that order, i.e., B is connected to s_1 and C to s_0. The inputs of the multiplexer are 0, 1, A, and A'. When $BC = 00$, output $F = 0$ since $I_0 = 0$. Therefore, both minterms $m_0 = A'B'C'$ and $m_4 = AB'C'$ produce a 0 output, since the output is 0 when $BC = 00$ regardless of the value of A. When $BC = 01$, output $F = 1$, since $I_1 = 1$. Therefore, both minterms $m_1 = A'B'C$ and $m_5 = AB'C$ produce a 1 output, since the output is 1 when $BC = 01$ regardless of the value of A. When $BC = 10$, input I_2 is selected. Since A is connected to this input, the output will be equal to 1 only for minterm $m_6 = ABC'$, but not for minterm $m_2 = A'BC'$, because when $A' = 1$, then $A = 0$, and since $I_2 = 0$, we have $F = 0$. Finally, when $BC = 11$, input I_3 is selected. Since A' is connected to this input, the output will be equal to 1 only for minterm $m_3 = A'BC$, but not for $m_7 = ABC$. This information is summarized in Fig. 5-18(b), which is the truth table of the function we want to implement.

The above discussion shows by analysis that the multiplexer implements the required function. We now present a general procedure for implementing any Boolean function of n variables with a 2^{n-1}-to-1 multiplexer.

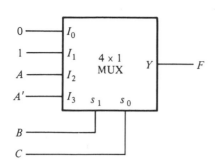

(a) Multiplexer implementation

Minterm	A	B	C	F
0	0	0	0	0
1	0	0	1	1
2	0	1	0	0
3	0	1	1	1
4	1	0	0	0
5	1	0	1	1
6	1	1	0	1
7	1	1	1	0

(b) Truth table

	I_0	I_1	I_2	I_3
A'	0	①	2	③
A	4	⑤	⑥	7
	0	1	A	A'

(c) Implementation table

Figure 5-18 Implementing $F(A, B, C) = \Sigma(1, 3, 5, 6)$ with a multiplexer

First, express the function in its sum of minterms form. Assume that the ordered sequence of variables chosen for the minterms is $ABCD \ldots$, where A is the leftmost variable in the ordered sequence of n variables and $BCD \ldots$ are the remaining $n - 1$ variables. Connect the $n - 1$ variables to the selection lines of the multiplexer with B connected to the high-order selection line, C to the next lower selection line, and so on down to the last variable, which is connected to the lowest-order selection line s_0. Consider now the single variable A. Since this variable is in the highest-order position in the sequence of variables, it will be complemented in minterms 0 to $(2^n/2) - 1$ which comprise the first half in the list of minterms. The second half of the minterms will have their A variable uncomplemented. For a three-variable function, A, B, C, we have eight minterms. Variable A is complemented in minterms 0 to 3 and uncomplemented in minterms 4 to 7.

List the inputs of the multiplexer and under them list all the minterms in two rows. The first row lists all those minterms where A is complemented, and the second row all the minterms with A uncomplemented, as shown in Fig. 5-18(c). Circle all the minterms of the function and inspect each column separately.

If the two minterms in a column are not circled, apply 0 to the corresponding multiplexer input.

If the two minterms are circled, apply 1 to the corresponding multiplexer input.

179

If the bottom minterm is circled and the top is not circled, apply A to the corresponding multiplexer input.

If the top minterm is circled and the bottom is not circled, apply A' to the corresponding multiplexer input.

This procedure follows from the conditions established during the previous analysis.

Figure 5-18(c) shows the implementation table for the Boolean function:

$$F(A, B, C) = \Sigma(1, 3, 5, 6)$$

from which we obtain the multiplexer connections of Fig. 5-18(a). Note that B must be connected to s_1 and C to s_0.

It is not necessary to choose the leftmost variable in the ordered sequence of a variable list for the inputs to the multiplexer. In fact, we can choose any one of the variables for the inputs of the multiplexer, provided we modify the multiplexer implementation table. Suppose we want to implement the same function with a multiplexer, but using variables A and B for selection lines s_1 and s_0, and variable C for the inputs of the multiplexer. Variable C is complemented in the even-numbered minterms and uncomplemented in the odd-numbered minterms, since it is the last variable in the sequence of listed variables. The arrangement of the two minterm rows in this case must be as shown in Fig. 5-19(a). By circling the minterms of the function and using the rules stated above, we obtain the multiplexer connection for implementing the function as in Fig. 5-19(b).

In a similar fashion, it is possible to use any single variable of the function for use in the multiplexer inputs. One can formulate various combinations for implementing a Boolean function with multiplexers. In any case, all the input variables, except one, are applied to the selection lines. The remaining single variable , or its complement, or 0 or 1, are then applied to the inputs of the multiplexer.

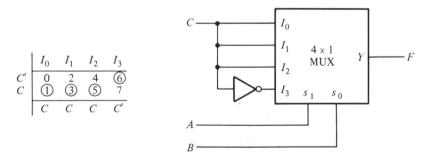

(a) Implementation table   (b) Multiplexer connection

Figure 5-19   Alternate implementation for $F(A, B, C) = \Sigma(1, 3, 5, 6)$

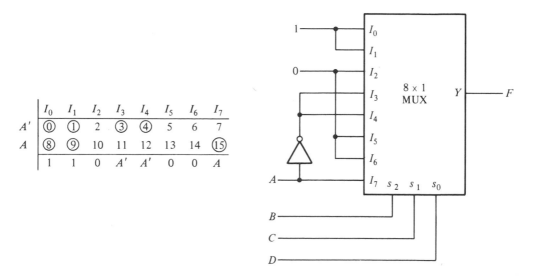

	I_0	I_1	I_2	I_3	I_4	I_5	I_6	I_7
A'	⓪	①	2	③	④	5	6	7
A	⑧	⑨	10	11	12	13	14	⑮
	1	1	0	A'	A'	0	0	A

Figure 5-20   Implementing $F(A, B, C\ D) = \Sigma(0, 1, 3, 4, 8, 9, 15)$

EXAMPLE 5-4: Implement the following function with a multiplexer:

$$F(A, B, C, D) = \Sigma(0, 1, 3, 4, 8, 9, 15)$$

This is a four-variable function and therefore we need a multiplexer with three selection lines and eight inputs. We choose to apply variables B, C, and D to the selection lines. The implementation table is then as shown in Fig. 5-20. The first half of the minterms are associated with A' and the second half with A. By circling the minterms of the function and applying the rules for finding values for the multiplexer inputs, we obtain the implementation shown.

Let us now compare the multiplexer method with the decoder method for implementing combinational circuits. The decoder method requires an OR gate for each output function, but only one decoder is needed to generate all minterms. The multiplexer method uses smaller-size units but requires one multiplexer for each output function. It would seem reasonable to assume that combinational circuits with a small number of outputs should be implemented with multiplexers. Combinational circuits with many output functions would probably use fewer ICs with the decoder method.

Although multiplexers and decoders may be used in the implementation of combinational circuits, it must be realized that decoders are mostly used for decoding binary information and multiplexers are mostly used to form a selected path between multiple sources and a single destination. They should be considered when designing small, special combinational circuits which are not otherwise

181

available as MSI functions. For large combinational circuits with multiple inputs and outputs, there is a more suitable IC component, and it is presented in the following section.

5-7 READ-ONLY MEMORY (ROM)

We saw in Section 5-5 that a decoder generates the 2^n minterms of the n input variables. By inserting OR gates to sum the minterms of Boolean functions, we were able to generate any desired combinational circuit. A read-only memory (ROM) is a device that includes both the decoder and the OR gates within a single IC package. The connections between the outputs of the decoder and the inputs of the OR gates can be specified for each particular configuration by "programming" the ROM. The ROM is very often used to implement a complex combinational circuit in one IC package and thus eliminate all interconnecting wires.

A ROM is essentially a memory (or storage) device in which a fixed set of binary information is stored. The binary information must first be specified by the user and is then embedded in the unit to form the required interconnection pattern. ROMs come with special internal links that can be fused or broken. The desired interconnection for a particular application requires that certain links be fused to form the required circuit paths. Once a pattern is established for a ROM, it remains fixed even when power is turned off and then on again.

A block diagram of a ROM is shown in Fig. 5-21. It consists of n input lines and m output lines. Each bit combination of the input variables is called an *address*. Each bit combination that comes out of the output lines is called a *word*. The number of bits per word is equal to the number of output lines m. An address is essentially a binary number that denotes one of the minterms of n variables. The number of distinct addresses possible with n input variables is 2^n. An output word can be selected by a unique address, and since there are 2^n distinct addresses in a ROM, there are 2^n distinct words which are said to be stored in the unit. The word available on the output lines at any given time depends on the address value applied to the input lines. A ROM is characterized by the number of words 2^n and

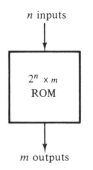

Figure 5-21 ROM block diagram

the number of bits per word m. This terminology is used because of the similarity between the read-only memory and the read-write memory which is presented in Section 7-7.

Consider a 32×8 ROM. The unit consists of 32 words of 8 bits each. This means that there are eight output lines and that there are 32 distinct words stored in the unit, each of which may be applied to the output lines. The particular word selected that is presently available on the output lines is determined from the five input lines. There are only five inputs in a 32×8 ROM because $2^5 = 32$, and with five variables we can specify 32 addresses or minterms. For each address input, there is a unique selected word. Thus, if the input address is 00000, word number 0 is selected and it appears on the output lines. If the input address is 11111, word number 31 is selected and applied to the output lines. In between, there are 30 other addresses that can select the other 30 words.

The number of addressed words in a ROM is determined from the fact that n input lines are needed to specify 2^n words. A ROM is sometimes specified by the total number of bits it contains, which is $2^n \times m$. For example, a 2048-bit ROM may be organized as 512 words of 4 bits each. This means that the unit has 4 output lines and 9 input lines to specify $2^9 = 512$ words. The total number of bits stored in the unit is $512 \times 4 = 2048$.

Internally, the ROM is a combinational circuit with AND gates connected as a decoder and a number of OR gates equal to the number of outputs in the unit. Figure 5-22 shows the internal logic construction of a 32×4 ROM. The five input

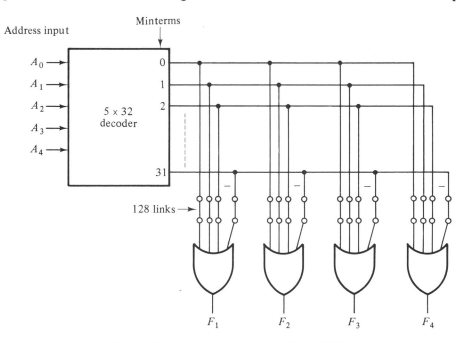

Figure 5-22 Logic construction of a 32×4 ROM

variables are decoded into 32 lines by means of 32 AND gates and 5 inverters. Each output of the decoder represents one of the minterms of a function of five variables. Each one of the 32 addresses selects one and only one output from the decoder. The address is a 5-bit number applied to the inputs, and the selected minterm out of the decoder is the one marked with the equivalent decimal number. The 32 outputs of the decoder are connected through *links* to each OR gate. Only four of these links are shown in the diagram, but actually each OR gate has 32 inputs and each input goes through a link that can be broken as desired.

The ROM is a two-level implementation in sum of minterms form. It does not have to be an AND-OR implementation, but it can be any other possible two-level minterm implementation. The second level is usually a wired-logic connection (see Section 3-7) to facilitate the fusing of links.

ROMs have many important applications in the design of digital computer systems. Their use for implementing complex combinational circuits is just one of these applications. Other uses of ROMs are presented in other parts of the book in conjunction with their particular applications.

Combinational Logic Implementation

From the logic diagram of the ROM, it is clear that each output provides the sum of all the minterms of the n input variables. Remember that any Boolean function can be expressed in sum-of-minterms form. By breaking the links of those minterms not included in the function, each ROM output can be made to represent the Boolean function of one of the output variables in the combinational circuit. For an n-input, m-output combinational circuit, we need a $2^n \times m$ ROM. The opening of the links is referred to as *programming* the ROM. The designer need only specify a ROM program table that gives the information for the required paths in the ROM. The actual programming is a hardware procedure which follows the specifications listed in the program table.

Let us clarify the process with a specific example. The truth table in Fig. 5-23(a) specifies a combinational circuit with two inputs and two outputs. The Boolean functions can be expressed in sum of minterms:

$$F_1(A_1, A_0) = \Sigma(1, 2, 3)$$
$$F_2(A_1, A_0) = \Sigma(0, 2)$$

When a combinational circuit is implemented by means of a ROM, the functions must be expressed in sum of minterms or, better yet, by a truth table. If the output functions are simplified, we find that the circuit needs only one OR gate and an inverter. Obviously, this is too simple a combinational circuit to be implemented with a ROM. The advantage of a ROM is in complex combinational circuits. This example merely demonstrates the procedure and should not be considered in a practical situation.

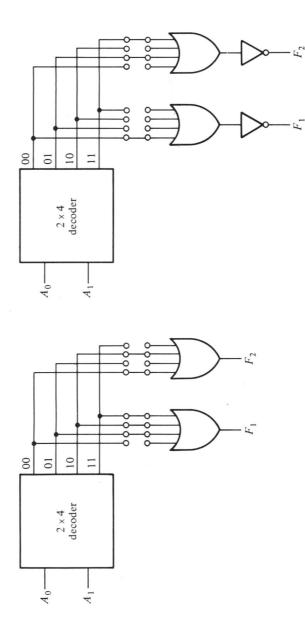

A_1	A_0	F_1	F_2
0	0	0	1
0	1	1	0
1	0	1	1
1	1	1	0

(a) Truth table

(b) ROM with AND-OR gates

(c) ROM with AND-OR-INVERT gates

Figure 5-23 Combinational-circuit implementation with a 4×2 ROM

The ROM that implements the combinational circuit must have two inputs and two outputs; so its size must be 4×2. Figure 5-23(b) shows the internal construction of such a ROM. It is now necessary to determine which of the eight available links must be broken and which should be left in place. This can be easily done from the output functions listed in the truth table. Those minterms that specify an output of 0 should not have a path to the output through the OR gate. Thus, for this particular case the truth table shows three 0's, and their corresponding links to the OR gates must be removed. It is obvious that we must assume here that an open input to an OR gate behaves as a 0 input.

Some ROM units come with an inverter after each of the OR gates and, as a consequence, they are specified as having initially all 0's at their outputs. The programming procedure in such ROMs requires that we open the link paths of the minterms (or addresses) that specify an output of 1 in the truth table. The output of the OR gate will then generate the complement of the function, but the inverter placed after the OR gate complements the function once more to provide the normal output. This is shown in the ROM of Fig. 5-23(c).

The previous example demonstrates the general procedure for implementing any combinational circuit with a ROM. From the number of inputs and outputs in the combinational circuit, we first determine the size of ROM required. Then we must obtain the programming truth table of the ROM; no other manipulation or simplification is required. The 0's (or 1's) in the output functions of the truth table directly specify those links that must be removed to provide the required combinational circuit in sum of minterms form.

In practice, when one designs a circuit by means of a ROM, it is not necessary to show the internal gate connections of links inside the unit as was done in Fig. 5-23. This was shown here for demonstration purposes only. All the designer has to do is specify the particular ROM (or its designation number) and provide the ROM truth table as in Fig. 5-23(a). The truth table gives all the information for programming the ROM. No internal logic diagram is needed to accompany the truth table.

TABLE 5-5   Truth table for circuit of Example 5-5

Inputs			Outputs						Decimal
A_2	A_1	A_0	B_5	B_4	B_3	B_2	B_1	B_0	
0	0	0	0	0	0	0	0	0	0
0	0	1	0	0	0	0	0	1	1
0	1	0	0	0	0	1	0	0	4
0	1	1	0	0	1	0	0	1	9
1	0	0	0	1	0	0	0	0	16
1	0	1	0	1	1	0	0	1	25
1	1	0	1	0	0	1	0	0	36
1	1	1	1	1	0	0	0	1	49

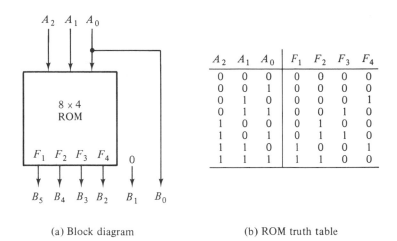

A_2	A_1	A_0	F_1	F_2	F_3	F_4
0	0	0	0	0	0	0
0	0	1	0	0	0	0
0	1	0	0	0	0	1
0	1	1	0	0	1	0
1	0	0	0	1	0	0
1	0	1	0	1	1	0
1	1	0	1	0	0	1
1	1	1	1	1	0	0

(a) Block diagram   (b) ROM truth table

Figure 5-24 ROM implementation of Example 5-5

EXAMPLE 5-5: Design a combinational circuit using a ROM. The circuit accepts a 3-bit number and generates an output binary number equal to the square of the input number.

The first step is to derive the truth table for the combinational circuit. In most cases this is all that is needed. In some cases we can fit a smaller truth table for the ROM by using certain properties in the truth table of the combinational circuit. Table 5-5 is the truth table for the combinational circuit. Three inputs and six outputs are needed to accommodate all possible numbers. We note that output B_0 is always equal to input A_0; so there is no need to generate B_0 with a ROM since it is equal to an input variable. Moreover, output B_1 is always 0, so this output is always known. We actually need to generate only four outputs with the ROM; the other two are easily obtained. The minimum size ROM needed must have three inputs and four outputs. Three inputs specify eight words, so the ROM size must be 8×4. The ROM implementation is shown in Fig. 5-24. The three inputs specify eight words of four bits each. The other two outputs of the combinational circuit are equal to 0 and A_0. The truth table in Fig. 5-24 specifies all the information needed for programming the ROM, and the block diagram shows the required connections.

Types of ROMs

The required paths in a ROM may be programmed in two different ways. The first is called *mask programming* and is done by the manufacturer during the last fabrication process of the unit. The procedure for fabricating a ROM requires that the customer fill out the truth table he wishes the ROM to satisfy. The truth table may be submitted on a special form provided by the manufacturer. More often, it is submitted on paper tape or punch cards in the format specified on the data sheet of the particular ROM. The manufacturer makes the corresponding mask for the paths to produce the 1's and 0's according to the customer's truth table. This procedure is costly because the vendor charges the customer a special fee for custom masking a ROM. For this reason, mask programming is economical only if large quantities of the same ROM configuration are to be manufactured.

For small quantities, it is more economical to use a second type of ROM called a *programmable read-only memory* or PROM. When ordered, PROM units contain all 0's (or all 1's) in every bit of the stored words. The links in the PROM are broken by application of current pulses through the output terminals. A broken link defines one binary state and an unbroken link represents the other state. This allows the user to program the unit in his own laboratory to achieve the desired relationship between input addresses and stored words. Special units called *PROM programmers* are available commercially to facilitate this procedure. In any case, all procedures for programming ROMs are *hardware* procedures even though the word *programming* is used.

The hardware procedure for programming ROMs or PROMs is irreversible and, once programmed the fixed pattern is permanent and cannot be altered. Once a bit pattern has been established, the unit must be discarded if the bit pattern is to be changed. A third type of unit available is called *erasable PROM* or EPROM. EPROMs can be restructured to the initial value (all 0's or all 1's) even though they have been changed previously. When an EPROM is placed under a special ultraviolet light for a given period of time, the short-wave radiation discharges the internal gates that serve as contacts. After erasure, the ROM returns to its initial state and can be reprogrammed. Certain ROMs can be erased with electrical signals instead of ultraviolet light, and these are sometimes called *electrically alterable ROMs* or EAROMs.

The function of a ROM can be interpreted in two different ways. The first interpretation is of a unit that implements any combinational circuit. From this point of view, each output terminal is considered separately as the output of a Boolean function expressed in sum of minterms. The second interpretation considers the ROM to be a storage unit having a fixed pattern of bit strings called *words*. From this point of view, the inputs specify an *address* to a specific stored word which is then applied to the outputs. For example, the ROM of Fig. 5-24 has three address lines which specify eight stored words as given by the truth table. Each word is four bits long. This is the reason why the unit is given the name *read-only memory*. *Memory* is commonly used to designate a storage unit. *Read* is commonly used to signify that the contents of a word specified by an address in a storage unit is placed at the output terminals. Thus, a ROM is a memory unit with a fixed word pattern that can be read out upon application of a given address. The bit pattern in the ROM is permanent and cannot be changed during normal operation.

ROMs are widely used to implement complex combinational circuits directly from their truth tables. They are useful for converting from one binary code to another (such as ASCII to EBCDIC and vice versa), for arithmetic functions such as multipliers, for display of characters in a cathode-ray tube, and in many other applications requiring a large number of inputs and outputs. They are also employed in the design of control units of digital systems. As such, they are used to store fixed bit patterns that represent the sequence of control variables needed to enable the various operations in the system. A control unit that utilizes a ROM to store binary control information is called a *microprogrammed control unit*.

5-8 PROGRAMMABLE LOGIC ARRAY (PLA)

A combinational circuit may occasionally have don't-care conditions. When implemented with a ROM, a don't-care condition becomes an address input that will never occur. The words at the don't-care addresses need not be programmed and may be left in their original state (all 0's or all 1's). The result is that not all the bit patterns available in the ROM are used, which may be considered a waste of available equipment.

Consider, for example, a combinational circuit that converts a 12-bit card code to a 6-bit internal alphanumeric code as listed in Table 1-5. The input card code consists of 12 lines designated by 0, 1, 2, . . . , 9, 11, 12. The size of the ROM for implementing the code converter must be 4096×6, since there are 12 inputs and 6 outputs. There are only 47 valid entries for the card code; all other input combinations are don't-care conditions. Thus only 47 words of the 4096 available are used. The remaining 4049 words of ROM are not used and are thus wasted.

For cases where the number of don't-care conditions is excessive, it is more economical to use a second type of LSI component called *programmable logic array* or PLA. A PLA is similar to a ROM in concept; however, the PLA does not provide full decoding of the variables and does not generate all the minterms as in the ROM. In the PLA, the decoder is replaced by a group of AND gates, each of which can be programmed to generate a product term of the input variables. The AND and OR gates inside the PLA are initially fabricated with links among them. The specific Boolean functions are implemented in sum of products form by opening appropriate links and leaving the desired connections.

A block diagram of the PLA is shown in Fig. 5-25. It consists of n inputs, m outputs, k product terms, and m sum terms. The product terms constitute a group of k AND gates and the sum terms constitute a group of m OR gates. Links are inserted between all n inputs and their complement values to each of the AND gates. Links are also provided between the outputs of the AND gates and the inputs of the OR gates. Another set of links in the output inverters allows the

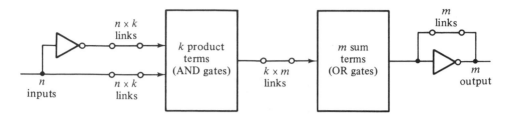

Figure 5-25 PLA block diagram

output function to be generated either in the AND-OR form or in the AND-OR-INVERT form. With the inverter link in place, the inverter is bypassed, giving an AND-OR implementation. With the link broken, the inverter becomes part of the circuit and the function is implemented in the AND-OR-INVERT form.

The size of the PLA is specified by the number of inputs, the number of product terms, and the number of outputs (the number of sum terms is equal to the number of outputs). A typical PLA has 16 inputs, 48 product terms, and 8 outputs.* The number of programmed links is $2n \times k + k \times m + m$, whereas that of a ROM is $2^n \times m$.

Figure 5-26 shows the internal construction of a specific PLA. It has three inputs, three product terms, and two outputs. Such a PLA is too small to be available commerically; it is presented here merely for demonstration purposes. Each input and its complement are connected through links to the inputs of all AND gates. The outputs of the AND gates are connected through links to each input of the OR gates. Two more links are provided with the output inverters. By breaking selected links and leaving others in place, it is possible to implement Boolean functions in their sum of products form.

As with a ROM, the PLA may be mask-programmable or field programmable. With a mask-programmable PLA, the customer must submit a PLA program table to the manufacturer. This table is used by the vendor to produce a custom-made PLA that has the required internal paths between inputs and outputs. A second type of PLA available is called a *field programmable logic array* or FPLA. The FPLA can be programmed by the user by means of certain recommended procedures. Commercial hardware programmer units are available for use in conjunction with certain FPLAs.

PLA Program Table

The use of a PLA must be considered for combinational circuits that have a large number of inputs and outputs. It is superior to a ROM for circuits that have a large number of don't-care conditions. The example presented below demonstrates

*TTL IC type 82S100.

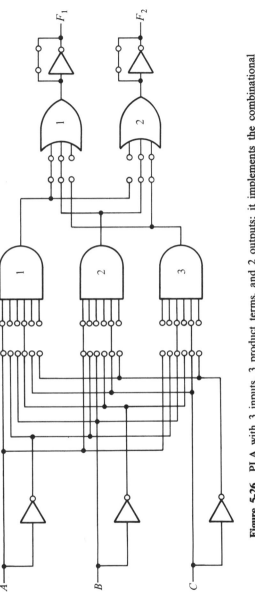

Figure 5-26 PLA with 3 inputs, 3 product terms, and 2 outputs; it implements the combinational circuit specified in Fig. 5-27

191

how a PLA is programmed. Bear in mind when going through the example that such a simple circuit will not require a PLA because it can be implemented more economically with SSI gates.

Consider the truth table of the combinational circuit, shown in Fig. 5-27(a). Although a ROM implements a combinational circuit in its sum of minterms form, a PLA implements the functions in their sum of products form. Each product term in the expression requires an AND gate. Since the number of AND gates in a PLA is finite, it is necessary to simplify the function to a minimum number of product terms in order to minimize the number of AND gates used. The simplified functions in sum of products are obtained from the maps of Fig. 5-27(b):

$$F_1 = AB' + AC$$

$$F_2 = AC + BC$$

There are three distinct product terms in this combinational circuit: AB', AC, and BC. The circuit has three inputs and two outputs; so the PLA of Fig. 5-26 can be used to implement this combinational circuit.

Programming the PLA means that we specify the paths in its AND-OR-NOT pattern. A typical PLA program table is shown in Fig. 5-27(c). It consists of three columns. The first column lists the product terms numerically. The second column specifies the required paths between inputs and AND gates. The third column specifies the paths between the AND gates and the OR gates. Under each output variable, we write a T (for true) if the output inverter is to be bypassed, and C (for complement) if the function is to be complemented with the output inverter. The Boolean terms listed at the left are not part of the table; they are included for reference only.

For each product term, the inputs are marked with 1, 0, or – (dash). If a variable in the product term appears in its normal form (unprimed), the corresponding input variable is marked with a 1. If it appears complemented (primed), the corresponding input variable is marked with a 0. If the variable is absent in the product term, it is marked with a dash. Each product term is associated with an AND gate. The paths between the inputs and the AND gates are specified under the column heading *inputs*. A 1 in the input column specifies a path from the corresponding input to the input of the AND gate that forms the product term. A 0 in the input column specifies a path from the corresponding complemented input to the input of the AND gate. A dash specifies no connection. The appropriate links are broken, and the ones left in place form the desired paths, as shown in Fig. 5-26. It is assumed that the open terminals in the AND gate behave like a 1 input.

The paths between the AND and OR gates are specified under the column heading *outputs*. The output variables are marked with 1's for all those product terms that formulate the function. In the example of Fig. 5-27, we have:

$$F_1 = AB' + AC$$

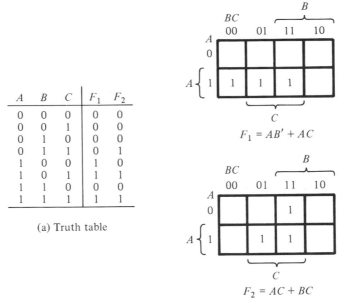

A	B	C	F_1	F_2
0	0	0	0	0
0	0	1	0	0
0	1	0	0	0
0	1	1	0	1
1	0	0	1	0
1	0	1	1	1
1	1	0	0	0
1	1	1	1	1

(a) Truth table

$F_1 = AB' + AC$

$F_2 = AC + BC$

(b) Map simplification

	Product term	Inputs A	B	C	Outputs F_1	F_2
AB'	1	1	0	—	1	—
AC	2	1	—	1	1	1
BC	3	—	1	1	—	1
		T	T		T/C	

(c) PLA program table

Figure 5-27 Steps required in PLA implementation

so F_1 is marked with 1's for product terms 1 and 2 and with a dash for product term 3. Each product term that has a 1 in the output column requires a path from the corresponding AND gate to the output OR gate. Those marked with a dash specify no connection. Finally, a T (true) output dictates that the link across the output inverter remains in place, and a C (complement) specifies that the corresponding link be broken. The internal paths of the PLA for this circuit are shown in Fig. 5-26. It is assumed that an open terminal in an OR gate behaves like a 0, and that a short circuit across the output inverter does not damage the circuit.

When designing a digital system with a PLA, there is no need to show the internal connections of the unit as was done in Fig. 5-26. All that is needed is a PLA program table from which the PLA can be programmed to supply the appropriate paths.

When implementing a combinational circuit with PLA, careful investigation must be undertaken in order to reduce the total number of distinct product terms, since a given PLA would have a finite number of AND terms. This can be done by simplifying each function to a minimum number of terms. The number of literals in a term is not important since we have available all input variables. Both the true value and the complement of the function should be simplified to see which one can be expressed with fewer product terms and which one provides product terms that are common to other functions.

EXAMPLE 5-6: A combinational circuit is defined by the functions:

$$F_1(A, B, C) = \Sigma(3, 5, 6, 7)$$
$$F_2(A, B, C) = \Sigma(0, 2, 4, 7)$$

Implement the circuit with a PLA having three inputs, four product terms, and two outputs.

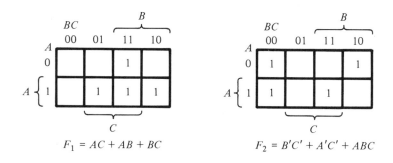

$$F_1 = AC + AB + BC \qquad\qquad F_2 = B'C' + A'C' + ABC$$

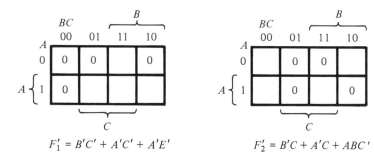

$$F_1' = B'C' + A'C' + A'E' \qquad\qquad F_2' = B'C + A'C + ABC'$$

PLA program table

Product term		Inputs			Output	
		A	B	C	F_1	F_2
$B'C'$	1	—	0	0	1	1
$A'C'$	2	0	—	0	1	1
$A'B'$	3	0	0	—	1	—
ABC	4	1	1	1	—	1
					C	T	T/C

Figure 5-28   Solution to Example 5-6

The two functions are simplified in the maps of Fig. 5-28. Both the true values and the complements of the functions are simplified. The combinations that gives a minimum number of product terms are:

$$F_1 = (B'C' + A'C' + A'B')'$$
$$F_2 = B'C' + A'C' + ABC$$

This gives only four distinct product terms: $B'C'$, $A'C'$, $A'B'$, and ABC. The PLA program table for this combination is shown in Fig. 5-28. Note that output F_1 is the normal (or true) output even though a C is marked under it. This is because F_1' is generated *prior to* the output inverter. The inverter complements the function to produce F_1 in the output.

The combinational circuit for this example is too small for practical implementation with a PLA. It was presented here merely for demonstration purposes. A typical commercial PLA would have over 10 inputs and about 50 product terms. The simplification of Boolean functions with so many variables should be carried out by means of a tabulation method or other computer-assisted simplification method. This is where a computer program may aid in the design of complex digital systems. The computer program should simplify each function of the combinational circuit and its complement to a minimum number of terms. The program then selects a minimum number of distinct terms that cover all functions in their true or complement form.

5-9 CONCLUDING REMARKS

This chapter presented a variety of design methods for combinational circuits. It also presented and explained a number of MSI and LSI circuits that can be used when designing more complicated digital systems. The emphasis here was on combinational logic MSI and LSI functions. Sequential logic MSI functions are discussed in Chapter 7. These MSI and LSI digital functions are the basic building blocks from which digital systems and digital computers are constructed.

The MSI functions presented here and others available commercially are described in data books or catalogs. IC data books contain exact descriptions of many MSI and other integrated circuits. Some of these data books are listed in the following References.

MSI and LSI circuits can be used in a variety of applications. Some of these applications were discussed throughout the chapter, some are included in Problems, and others will be found in succeeding chapters in conjunction with their particular applications. Resourceful designers may find many other applications to suit their particular needs. Manufacturers of integrated circuits publish numerous *application notes* to suggest possible utilization of their products. A list of available application notes can be obtained by writing to manufacturers directly or by inquiring of their local representatives.

REFERENCES

1. Mano, M. M., *Computer System Architecture*, 2nd ed. Englewood Cliffs, N.J.: Prentice-Hall, Inc., 1982.

2. Morris, R. L., and J. R. Miller, eds., *Designing with TTL Integrated Circuits*. New York: McGraw-Hill Book Co., 1971.

3. Blakeslee, T. R., *Digital Design with Standard MSI and LSI*. New York: John Wiley & Sons, 1975.

4. Barna A., and D. I. Porat, *Integrated Circuits in Digital Electronics*. New York: John Wiley & Sons, 1973.

5. Lee, S. C., *Digital Circuits and Logic Design*, Englewood Cliffs, N. J.: Prentice-Hall, Inc., 1976.

6. Semiconductor Manufacturers Data Books (Consult latest edition):
    (a) *The TTL Data Book for Design Engineers*. Dallas, Texas: Texas Instruments, Inc.
    (b) *The Fairchild Semiconductor TTL Data Book*. Mountain View, Calif.: Fairchild Semiconductor.
    (c) *Digital Integrated Circuits*. Santa Clara, Calif.: National Semiconductor Corp.
    (d) *Signetics Digital, Linear, MOS*. Sunnyvale, Calif.: Signetics.
    (e) *MECL Integrated Circuits Data Book*. Phoenix, Ariz.: Motorola Semiconductor Products, Inc.
    (f) *RCA Solid State Data Book Series*. Somerville, N. J.: RCA Solid State Div.

PROBLEMS

5-1.   Design an excess-3-to-BCD code converter using a 4-bit full-adders MSI circuit.

5-2.   Using four MSI circuits, construct a binary parallel adder to add two 16-bit binary numbers. Label all carries between the MSI circuits.

5-3.   Using 4 exclusive-OR gates and a 4-bit full-adders MSI circuit, construct a 4-bit parallel adder/subtractor. Use an input select variable V so that when $V = 0$, the circuit adds and when $V = 1$, the circuit subtracts. (*Hint*: Use 2's complement subtraction.)

5-4.   Derive the two-level equation for the output carry C_5 shown in the look-ahead carry generator of Fig. 5-5.

5-5.   (a) Using the AND-OR-INVERT implementation procedure described in Section

3-7, show that the output carry in a full-adder circuit can be expressed as:

$$C_{i+1} = G_i + P_i C_i = (G'_i P'_i + G'_i C'_i)'$$

(b) IC type 74182 is a look-ahead carry generator MSI circuit that generates the carries with AND-OR-INVERT gates. The MSI circuit assumes that the input terminals have the complements of the G's, the P's, and of C_1. Derive the Boolean functions for the look-ahead carries C_2, C_3, and C_4 in this IC. (*Hint*: Use the equation-substitution method to derive the carries in terms of C'_1.)

5-6.   (a) Redefine the carry propagate and carry generate as follows:

$$P_i = A_i + B_i$$
$$G_i = A_i B_i$$

Show that the output carry and output sum of a full-adder becomes:

$$C_{i+1} = (C'_i G'_i + P'_i)' = G_i + P_i C_i$$
$$S_i = (P_i G'_i) \oplus C_i$$

(b) The logic diagram of the first stage of a 4-bit parallel adder as implemented in IC type 74283 is shown in Fig. P5-6. Identify the P'_i and G'_i terminals as defined in (a) and show that the circuit implements a full-adder circuit.

(c) Obtain the output carries C_3 and C_4 as a function of P'_1, P'_2, P'_3, G'_1, G'_2, G'_3, and C'_1 in AND-OR-INVERT form, and draw the two-level look-ahead circuit for this IC. [*Hint*: Use the equation-substitution method as done in the text when deriving Fig. 5-4, but use the AND-OR-INVERT function given in (a) for C_{i+1}.]

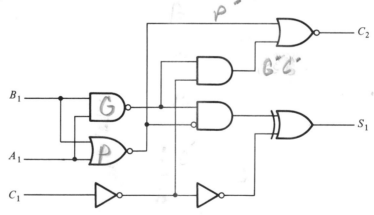

Figure P5-6   First stage of a parallel adder

5-7.   (a) Assume that the exclusive-OR gate has a propagation delay of 20 ns and that the AND or OR gates have a propagation delay of 10 ns. What is the total propagation delay time in the 4-bit adder of Fig. 5-5?

(b) Assume that C_5 is propagated in the box of Fig. 5-5 at the same time as the other carries (see problem 5-4). What will be the propagation delay time of the 16-bit adder of problem 5-2?

5-8.   Design a binary multiplier that multiplies a 4-bit number $B = b_3b_2b_1b_0$ by a 3-bit number $A = a_2a_1a_0$ to form the product $C = c_6c_5c_4c_3c_2c_1c_0$. This can be done with 12 gates and two 4-bit parallel adders. The AND gates are used to form the products of pairs of bits. For example, the product of a_0 and b_0 can be generated by ANDing a_0 with b_0. The partial products formed by the AND gates are summed with the parallel adders.

5-9.   How many don't-care inputs are there in a BCD adder?

5-10. Design a combinational circuit that generates the 9's complement of a BCD digit.

5-11. Design a decimal arithmetic unit with two selection variables, V_1 and V_0, and two BCD digits, A and B. The unit should have four arithmetic operations which depend on the values of the selection variables as shown below.

V_1	V_0	Output function
0	0	$A + $ 9's complement of B
0	1	$A + B$
1	0	$A + $ 10's complement of B
1	1	$A + 1$ (add 1 to A)

Use MSI functions in the design and the 9's complementer of problem 5-10.

5-12. It is necessary to design a decimal adder for two digits represented in the excess-3 code (Table 1-2). Show that the correction after adding the two digits with a 4-bit binary adder is as follows:

(a) The output carry is equal to the carry out of the binary adder.

(b) If output carry = 1, add 0011.

(c) If output carry = 0, add 1101.

Construct the adder with two 4-bit binary adders and an inverter.

5-13. Design a circuit that compares two 4-bit numbers, A and B, to check if they are equal. The circuit has one output x, so that $x = 1$ if $A = B$, and $x = 0$ if $A \neq B$.

5-14. The 74L85 IC is a 4-bit magnitude comparator similar to that in Fig. 5-7, except that it has three more inputs and internal circuits that perform the equivalent logic as shown in Fig. P5-14. With these ICs, numbers of greater length may be compared by connecting comparators in cascade. The $A < B$, $A > B$, and $A = B$ outputs of a stage handling less-significant bits are connected to the corresponding $A < B$, $A > B$, and $A = B$ inputs of the next stage handling more-significant bits. The stage that handles the least-significant bits must be a circuit as shown in Fig. 5-7. If the 74L85 IC is used, a 1 must be applied to the $A = B$ input and a 0 to the $A < B$ and $A > B$ inputs in the IC that handles the four least-significant bits. Using one circuit as in Fig. 5-7 and one 74L85 IC, obtain a circuit to compare two 8-bit numbers. Justify the circuit operation.

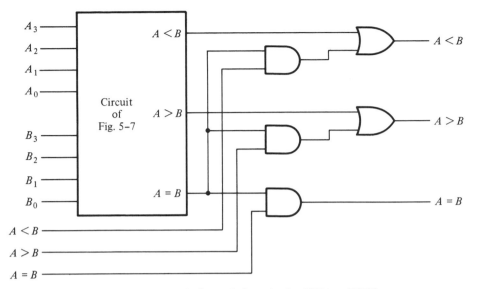

Figure P5-14 Logically equivalent circuit of IC type 74L85

5-15. Modify the BCD-to-decimal decoder of Fig. 5-10 to give an output of all 0's when any invalid input combination occurs.

5-16. Design a BCD-to-excess-3 code converter with a BCD-to-decimal decoder and four OR gates.

5-17. A combinational circuit is defined by the following three functions:

$$F_1 = x'y' + xyz'$$
$$F_2 = x' + y$$
$$F_3 = xy + x'y'$$

Design the circuit with a decoder and external gates.

5-18. A combinational circuit is defined by the following two functions:

$$F_1(x, y) = \Sigma(0, 3)$$
$$F_2(x, y) = \Sigma(1, 2, 3)$$

Implement the combinational circuit by means of the decoder shown in Fig. 5-12 and external NAND gates.

5-19. Construct a 5×32 decoder with four 3×8 decoder/demultiplexers and a 2×4 decoder. Use a block diagram construction as in Fig. 5-14.

5-20. Draw the logic diagram of a 2-line to 4-line decoder/demultiplexer using NOR gates only.

5-21. Specify the truth table of an octal-to-binary priority encoder. Provide an output to indicate if at least one of the inputs is a 1. The table can be listed with 9 rows, and some of the inputs will have don't-care values.

5-22. Design a 4-line to 2-line priority encoder. Include an output E to indicate that at least one input is a 1.

5-23. Implement the Boolean function of Example 5-4 with an 8×1 multiplexer with A, B, and D connected to selection lines s_2, s_1, and s_0, respectively.

5-24. Implement the combinational circuit specified in problem 5-17 with a dual 4-line to 1-line multiplexers, an OR gate, and inverter.

5-25. Obtain an 8×1 multiplexer with a dual 4-line to 1-line multiplexers having separate enable inputs but common selection lines. Use a block diagram construction.

5-26. Implement a full-adder circuit with multiplexers.

5-27. The 32×6 ROM together with the 2^0 line as shown in Fig. P5-27 converts a 6-bit binary number to its corresponding 2-digit BCD number. For example, binary 100001 converts to BCD 011 0011 (decimal 33). Specify the truth table for the ROM.

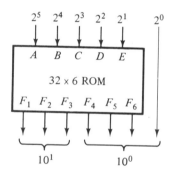

Figure P5-27   Binary-to-decimal converter

5-28. Prove that a 32×8 ROM can be used to implement a circuit that generates the binary square of an input 5-bit number with $B_0 = A_0$ and $B_1 = 0$ as in Fig. 5-24(a). Draw a block diagram of the circuit and list the first four and the last four entries of the ROM truth table.

5-29. What size ROM would it take to implement:
(a) A BCD adder/subtractor with a control input to select between the addition and subtraction.
(b) A binary multiplier that multiplies two 4-bit numbers.
(c) Dual 4-line to 1-line multiplexers with common selection inputs.

5-30. Each output inverter in the PLA of Fig. 5-26 is replaced by an exclusive-OR gate. Each exclusive-OR gate has two inputs. One input is connected to the output of the

OR gate, and the other input is connected through links to a signal equivalent to either 0 or 1. Show how to select the true/complement output in this configuration.

5-31. Derive the PLA program table for a combinational circuit that squares a 3-bit number. Minimize the number of product terms. (See Fig. 5-24 for the equivalent ROM implementation.)

5-32. List the PLA program table for the BCD-to-excess-3 code converter defined in Section 4-5.

Synchronous Sequential Logic

6-1 INTRODUCTION

The digital circuits considered thus far have been combinational, i.e., the outputs at any instant of time are entirely dependent upon the inputs present at that time. Although every digital system is likely to have combinational circuits, most systems encountered in practice also include memory elements, which require that the system be described in terms of *sequential logic*.

A block diagram of a sequential circuit is shown in Fig. 6-1. It consists of a combinational circuit to which memory elements are connected to form a feedback path. The memory elements are devices capable of storing binary information within them. The binary information stored in the memory elements at any given time defines the *state* of the sequential circuit. The sequential circuit receives binary information from external inputs. These inputs, together with the present state of the memory elements, determine the binary value at the output terminals. They also determine the condition for changing the state in the memory elements. The block diagram demonstrates that the external outputs in a sequential circuit are a function not only of external inputs but also of the present state of the memory elements. The next state of the memory elements is also a function of external inputs and the present state. Thus, a sequential circuit is specified by a time sequence of inputs, outputs, and internal states.

There are two main types of sequential circuits. Their classification depends on the timing of their signals. A *synchronous* sequential circuit is a system whose behavior can be defined from the knowledge of its signals at discrete instants of time. The behavior of an *asynchronous* sequential circuit depends upon the order in which its input signals change and can be affected at any instant of time. The memory elements commonly used in asynchronous sequential circuits are time-delay devices. The memory capability of a time-delay device is due to the fact that it takes a finite time for the signal to propagate through the device. In practice, the internal propagation delay of logic gates is of sufficient duration to produce the

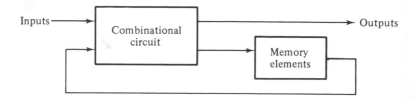

Figure 6-1 Block diagram of a sequential circuit

needed delay, so that physical time-delay units may be unnecessary. In gate-type asynchronous systems, the memory elements of Fig. 6-1 consist of logic gates whose propagation delays constitute the required memory. Thus, an asynchronous sequential circuit may be regarded as a combinational circuit with feedback. Because of the feedback among logic gates, an asynchronous sequential circuit may, at times, become unstable. The instability problem imposes many difficulties on the designer. Asynchronous sequential circuits are presented in Chapter 9.

A synchronous sequential logic system, by definition, must employ signals that affect the memory elements only at discrete instants of time. One way of achieving this goal is to use pulses of limited duration throughout the system so that one pulse amplitude represents logic-1 and another pulse amplitude (or the absence of a pulse) represents logic-0. The difficulty with a system of pulses is that any two pulses arriving from separate independent sources to the inputs of the same gate will exhibit unpredictable delays, will separate the pulses slightly, and will result in unreliable operation.

Practical synchronous sequential logic systems use fixed amplitudes such as voltage levels for the binary signals. Synchronization is achieved by a timing device called a *master-clock generator* which generates a periodic train of *clock pulses*. The clock pulses are distributed throughout the system in such a way that memory elements are affected only with the arrival of the synchronization pulse. In practice, the clock pulses are applied into AND gates together with the signals that specify the required change in memory elements. The AND gate outputs can transmit signals only at instants which coincide with the arrival of clock pulses. Synchronous sequential circuits that use clock pulses in the inputs of memory elements are called *clocked sequential circuits*. Clocked sequential circuits are the type encountered most frequently. They do not manifest instability problems and their timing is easily broken down into independent discrete steps, each of which is considered separately. The sequential circuits discussed in this chapter are exclusively of the clocked type.

The memory elements used in clocked sequential circuits are called *flip-flops*. These circuits are binary cells capable of storing one bit of information. A flip-flop circuit has two outputs, one for the normal value and one for the complement value of the bit stored in it. Binary information can enter a flip-flop in a variety of ways, a fact which gives rise to different types of flip-flops. In the next section we examine the various types of flip-flops and define their logical properties.

6-2 FLIP-FLOPS

A flip-flop circuit can maintain a binary state indefinitely (as long as power is delivered to the circuit) until directed by an input signal to switch states. The major differences among various types of flip-flops are in the number of inputs they possess and in the manner in which the inputs affect the binary state. The most common types of flip-flops are discussed below.

Basic Flip-Flop Circuit

It was mentioned in Sections 4-7 and 4-8 that a flip-flop circuit can be constructed from two NAND gates or two NOR gates. These constructions are shown in the logic diagrams of Figs. 6-2 and 6-3. Each circuit forms a basic flip-flop upon which other more complicated types can be built. The cross-coupled connection from the output of one gate to the input of the other gate constitutes a feedback path. For this reason, the circuits are classified as asynchronous sequential circuits. Each flip-flop has two outputs, Q and Q', and two inputs, *set* and *reset*. This type of flip-flop is sometimes called a *direct-coupled RS* flip-flop or *SR latch*. The R and S are the first letters of the two input names.

To analyze the operation of the circuit of Fig. 6-2, we must remember that the output of a NOR gate is 0 if any input is 1, and that the output is 1 only when all inputs are 0. As a starting point, assume that the set input is 1 and the reset input is 0. Since gate 2 has an input of 1, its output Q' must be 0, which puts both inputs of gate 1 at 0, so that output Q is 1. When the set input is returned to 0, the outputs remain the same, because output Q remains a 1, leaving one input of gate 2 at 1. That causes output Q' to stay at 0, which leaves both inputs of gate number 1 at 0, so that output Q is a 1. In the same manner it is possible to show that a 1 in the reset input changes output Q to 0 and Q' to 1. When the reset input returns to 0, the outputs do not change.

When a 1 is applied to both the set and the reset inputs, both Q and Q' outputs go to 0. This condition violates the fact that outputs Q and Q' are the complements of each other. In normal operation this condition must be avoided by making sure that 1's are not applied to both inputs simultaneously.

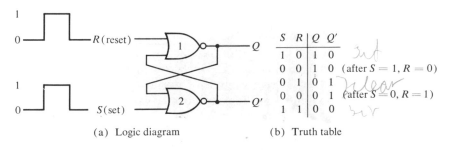

S	R	Q	Q'	
1	0	1	0	
0	0	1	0	(after $S = 1, R = 0$)
0	1	0	1	
0	0	0	1	(after $S = 0, R = 1$)
1	1	0	0	

(a) Logic diagram   (b) Truth table

Figure 6-2 Basic flip-flop circuit with NOR gates

204

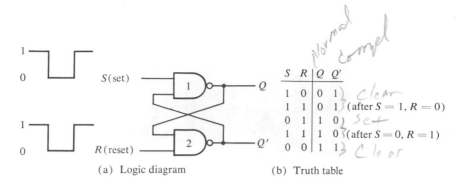

(a) Logic diagram   (b) Truth table

Figure 6-3 Basic flip-flop circuit with NAND gates

A flip-flop has two useful states. When $Q = 1$ and $Q' = 0$, it is in the *set state* (or 1-state). When $Q = 0$ and $Q' = 1$, it is in the *clear state* (or 0-state). The outputs Q and Q' are complements of each other and are referred to as the normal and complement outputs, respectively. The binary state of the flip-flop is taken to be the value of the normal output.

Under normal operation, both inputs remain at 0 unless the state of the flip-flop has to be changed. The application of a momentary 1 to the set input causes the flip-flop to go to the set state. The set input must go back to 0 before a 1 is applied to reset input. A momentary 1 applied to the reset input causes the flip-flop to go the clear state. When both inputs are initially 0, a 1 applied to the set input while the flip-flop is in the set state or a 1 applied to the reset input while the flip-flop is in the clear state leaves the outputs unchanged. When a 1 is applied to both the set and the reset inputs, both outputs go to 0. This state is undefined and is usually avoided. If both inputs now go to 0, the state of the flip-flop is indeterminate and depends on which input remains a 1 longer before the transition to 0.

The NAND basic flip-flop circuit of Fig. 6-3 operates with both inputs normally at 1 unless the state of the flip-flop has to be changed. The application of a momentary 0 to the set input causes output Q to go to 1 and Q' to go to 0, thus putting the flip-flop into the set state. After the set input returns to 1, a momentary 0 to the reset input causes a transition to the clear state. When both inputs go to 0, both outputs go to 1—a condition avoided in normal flip-flop operation.

Clocked *RS* Flip-Flop

The basic flip-flop as it stands is an asynchronous sequential circuit. By adding gates to the inputs of the basic circuit, the flip-flop can be made to respond to input levels during the occurrence of a clock pulse. The clocked *RS* flip-flop shown in Fig. 6-4(a) consists of a basic NOR flip-flop and two AND gates. The outputs of the two AND gates remain at 0 as long as the clock pulse (abbreviated *CP*) is 0, regardless of the S and R input values. When the clock pulse goes to 1, information from the S and R inputs is allowed to reach the basic flip-flop. The set state is reached with $S = 1$, $R = 0$, and $CP = 1$. To change to the clear state, the

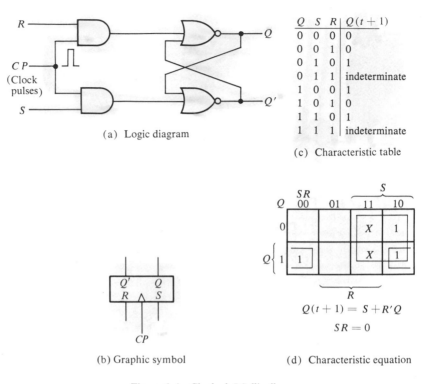

Q	S	R	$Q(t+1)$
0	0	0	0
0	0	1	0
0	1	0	1
0	1	1	indeterminate
1	0	0	1
1	0	1	0
1	1	0	1
1	1	1	indeterminate

(a) Logic diagram

(c) Characteristic table

(b) Graphic symbol

(d) Characteristic equation

$$Q(t+1) = S + R'Q$$
$$SR = 0$$

Figure 6-4 Clocked *RS* flip-flop

inputs must be $S = 0$, $R = 1$, and $CP = 1$. With both $S = 1$ and $R = 1$, the occurrence of a clock pulse causes both outputs to momentarily go to 0. When the pulse is removed, the state of the flip-flop is indeterminate, i.e., either state may result, depending on whether the set or the reset input of the basic flip-flop remains a 1 longer before the transition to 0 at the end of the pulse.

The graphic symbol for the clocked *RS* flip-flop is shown in Fig. 6-4(b). It has three inputs: *S*, *R*, and *CP*. The *CP* input is not written within the box because it is recognized from the marked small triangle. The triangle is a symbol for a *dynamic indicator* and denotes the fact that the flip-flop responds to an input clock *transition* from a low-level (binary 0) to a high-level (binary 1) signal. The outputs of the flip-flop are marked with *Q* and *Q'* *within* the box. The flip-flop can be assigned a different variable name even though *Q* is written inside the box. In that case the letter chosen for the flip-flop variable is marked *outside* the box along the output line. The state of the flip-flop is determined from the value of its normal output *Q*. If one wishes to obtain the complement of the normal output, it is not necessary to insert an inverter, because the complemented value is available directly from output *Q'*.

The characteristic table for the flip-flop is shown in Fig. 6-4(c). This table summarizes the operation of the flip-flop in a tabular form. *Q* is the binary state of the flip-flop at a given time (referred to as *present state*), the *S* and *R* columns give the possible values of the inputs, and $Q(t + 1)$ is the state of the flip-flop after the occurrence of a clock pulse (referred to as *next state*).

The characteristic equation of the flip-flop is derived in the map of Fig. 6-4(d). This equation specifies the value of the next state as a function of the present state and the inputs. The characteristic equation is an algebraic expression for the binary information of the characteristic table. The two indeterminate states are marked by X's in the map, since they may result in either a 1 or a 0. However, the relation $SR = 0$ must be included as part of the characteristic equation to specify that both S and R cannot equal 1 simultaneously.

D Flip-Flop

The D flip-flop shown in Fig. 6-5 is a modification of the clocked RS flip-flop. NAND gates 1 and 2 form a basic flip-flop and gates 3 and 4 modify it into a clocked RS flip-flop. The D input goes directly to the S input, and its complement, through gate 5, is applied to the R input. As long as the clock pulse input is at 0, gates 3 and 4 have a 1 in their outputs, regardless of the value of the other inputs. This conforms to the requirement that the two inputs of a basic NAND flip-flop (Fig. 6-3) remain initially at the 1 level. The D input is sampled during the occurrence of a clock pulse. If it is 1, the output of gate 3 goes to 0, switching the flip-flop to the set state (unless it was already set). If it is 0, the output of gate 4 goes to 0, switching the flip-flop to the clear state.

The D flip-flop receives the designation from its ability to transfer "data" into a flip-flop. It is basically an RS flip-flop with an inverter in the R input. The

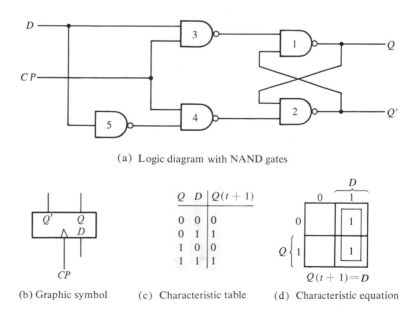

(a) Logic diagram with NAND gates

(b) Graphic symbol

(c) Characteristic table

Q	D	$Q(t + 1)$
0	0	0
0	1	1
1	0	0
1	1	1

(d) Characteristic equation

$$Q(t + 1) = D$$

Figure 6-5 Clocked D flip-flop

added inverter reduces the number of inputs from two to one. This type of flip-flop is sometimes called a *gated D-latch*. The *CP* input is often given the variable designation *G* (for *gate*) to indicate that this input enables the gated latch to make possible the data entry into the flip-flop.

The symbol for a clocked *D* flip-flop is shown in Fig. 6-5(b). The characteristic table is listed in part (c) and the characteristic equation is derived in part (d). The characteristic equation shows that the next state of the flip-flop is the same as the *D* input and is independent of the value of the present state.

JK Flip-Flop

A *JK* flip-flop is a refinement of the *RS* flip-flop in that the indeterminate state of the *RS* type is defined in the *JK* type. Inputs *J* and *K* behave like inputs *S* and *R* to set and clear the flip-flop (note that in a *JK* flip-flop, the letter *J* is for *set* and the letter *K* is for *clear*). When inputs are applied to both *J* and *K* simultaneously, the flip-flop switches to its complement state, that is, if $Q = 1$, it switches to $Q = 0$, and vice versa.

A clocked *JK* flip-flop is shown in Fig. 6-6(a). Output *Q* is ANDed with *K* and *CP* inputs so that the flip-flop is cleared during a clock pulse only if *Q* was previously 1. Similarly, output *Q'* is ANDed with *J* and *CP* inputs so that the flip-flop is set with a clock pulse only if *Q'* was previously 1.

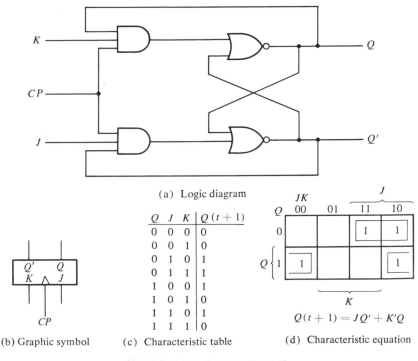

(a) Logic diagram

(b) Graphic symbol

(c) Characteristic table

Q	J	K	$Q(t+1)$
0	0	0	0
0	0	1	0
0	1	0	1
0	1	1	1
1	0	0	1
1	0	1	0
1	1	0	1
1	1	1	0

$$Q(t+1) = JQ' + K'Q$$

(d) Characteristic equation

Figure 6-6 Clocked *JK* flip-flop

As shown in the characteristic table in Fig. 6-6(c), the *JK* flip-flop behaves like an *RS* flip-flop, except when both *J* and *K* are equal to 1. When both *J* and *K* are 1, the clock pulse is transmitted through one AND gate only—the one whose input is connected to the flip-flop output which is presently equal to 1. Thus, if $Q = 1$, the output of the upper AND gate becomes 1 upon application of a clock pulse, and the flip-flop is cleared. If $Q' = 1$, the output of the lower AND gate becomes a 1 and the flip-flop is set. In either case, the output state of the flip-flop is complemented.

The inputs in the graphic symbol for the *JK* flip-flop must be marked with a *J* (under *Q*) and *K* (under *Q'*). The characteristic equation is given in Fig. 6-4(d) and is derived from the map of the characteristic table.

Note that because of the feedback connection in the *JK* flip-flop, a *CP* signal which remains a 1 (while $J = K = 1$) after the outputs have been complemented once will cause repeated and continuous transitions of the outputs. To avoid this undesirable operation, the clock pulses must have a time duration which is shorter than the propagation delay through the flip-flop. This is a restrictive requirement, since the operation of the circuit depends on the width of the pulses. For this reason, *JK* flip-flops are never constructed as shown in Fig. 6-6(a). The restriction on the pulse width can be eliminated with a master-slave or edge-triggered construction, as discussed in the next section. The same reasoning applies to the *T* flip-flop presented below.

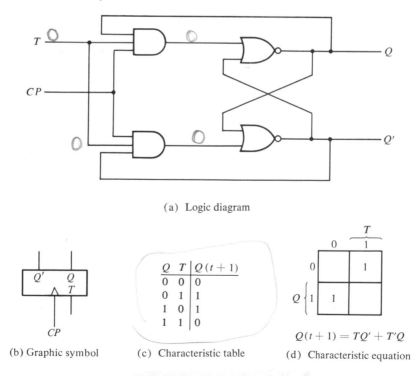

(a) Logic diagram

(b) Graphic symbol

(c) Characteristic table

Q	T	Q(t + 1)
0	0	0
0	1	1
1	0	1
1	1	0

(d) Characteristic equation

$$Q(t + 1) = TQ' + T'Q$$

Figure 6-7 Clocked *T* flip-flop

T Flip-Flop

The T flip-flop is a single-input version of the JK flip-flop. As shown in Fig. 6-7(a), the T flip-flop is obtained from a JK type if both inputs are tied together. The designation T comes from the ability of the flip-flop to "toggle," or change state. Regardless of the present state of the flip-flop, it assumes the complement state when the clock pulse occurs while input T is logic-1. The symbol, characteristic table, and characteristic equation of the T flip-flop are shown in Fig. 6-7, parts (b), (c), and (d), respectively.

The flip-flops introduced in this section are the most common types available commercially. The analysis and design procedures developed in this chapter are applicable for any clocked flip-flop once its characteristic table is defined.

6-3   TRIGGERING OF FLIP-FLOPS

The state of a flip-flop is switched by a momentary change in the input signal. This momentary change is called a *trigger* and the transition it causes is said to trigger the flip-flop. Asynchronous flip-flops, such as the basic circuits of Figs. 6-2 and 6-3, require an input trigger defined by a change of signal *level*. This level must be returned to its initial value (0 in the NOR and 1 in the NAND flip-flop) before a second trigger is applied. Clocked flip-flops are triggered by *pulses*. A pulse starts from an initial value of 0, goes momentarily to 1, and after a short time, returns to its initial 0 value. The time interval from the application of the pulse until the output transition occurs is a critical factor that needs further investigation.

As seen from the block diagram of Fig. 6-1, a sequential circuit has a feedback path between the combinational circuit and the memory elements. This path can produce instability if the outputs of memory elements (flip-flops) are changing while the outputs of the combinational circuit that go to flip-flop inputs are being sampled by the clock pulse. This timing problem can be prevented if the outputs of flip-flops do not start changing until the pulse input has returned to 0. To ensure such an operation, a flip-flop must have a signal propagation delay from input to output in excess of the pulse duration. This delay is usually very difficult to control if the designer depends entirely on the propagation delay of logic gates. One way of ensuring the proper delay is to include within the flip-flop circuit a physical delay unit having a delay equal to or greater than the pulse duration. A better way to solve the feedback timing problem is to make the flip-flop sensitive to the pulse *transition* rather than the pulse duration.

A clock pulse may be either positive or negative. A positive clock source remains at 0 during the interval between pulses and goes to 1 during the occurrence of a pulse. The pulse goes through two signal transitions: from 0 to 1 and the return from 1 to 0. As shown in Fig. 6-8, the positive transition is defined as the *positive edge* and the negative transition as the *negative edge*. This definition applies also to negative pulses.

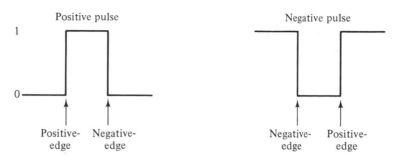

Positive pulse   Negative pulse

Positive-   Negative-   Negative-   Positive-
edge   edge   edge   edge

Figure 6-8 Definition of clock pulse transition

The clocked flip-flops introduced in Section 6-2 are triggered during the positive edge of the pulse, and the state transition starts as soon as the pulse reaches the logic-1 level. The new state of the flip-flop may appear at the output terminals while the input pulse is still 1. If the other inputs of the flip-flop change while the clock is still 1, the flip-flop will start responding to these new values and a new output state may occur. When this happens, the output of one flip-flop cannot be applied to the inputs of another flip-flop when both are triggered by the same clock pulse. However, if we can make the flip-flop respond to the positive (or negative) edge transition *only*, instead of the entire pulse duration, then the multiple-transition problem can be eliminated.

One way to make the flip-flop respond only to a pulse transition is to use capacitive coupling. In this configuration, an *RC* (resistor-capacitor) circuit is inserted in the clock input of the flip-flop. This circuit generates a spike in response to a momentary change of input signal. A positive edge emerges from such a circuit with a positive spike, and a negative edge emerges with a negative spike. Edge triggering is achieved by designing the flip-flop to neglect one spike and trigger on the occurrence of the other spike. Another way to achieve edge triggering is to use a master-slave or edge-triggered flip-flop as discussed below.

Master-Slave Flip-Flop

A master-slave flip-flop is constructed from two separate flip-flops. One circuit serves as a master and the other as a slave, and the overall circuit is referred to as a *master-slave flip-flop*. The logic diagram of an *RS* master-slave flip-flop is shown in Fig. 6-9. It consists of a master flip-flop, a slave flip-flop, and an inverter. When clock pulse *CP* is 0, the output of the inverter is 1. Since the clock input of the slave is 1, the flip-flop is enabled and output *Q* is equal to *Y*, while *Q′* is equal to *Y′*. The master flip-flop is disabled because *CP* = 0. When the pulse becomes 1, the information then at the external *R* and *S* inputs is transmitted to the master flip-flop. The slave flip-flop, however, is isolated as long as the pulse is at its 1 level, because the output of the inverter is 0. When the pulse returns to 0, the master flip-flop is isolated, which prevents the external inputs from affecting it. The slave flip-flop then goes to the same state as the master flip-flop.

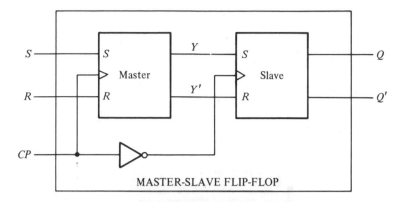

Figure 6-9   Logic diagram of master-slave flip-flop

The timing relationships shown in Fig. 6-10 illustrate the sequence of events that occur in a master-slave flip-flop. Assume that the flip-flop is in the clear state prior to the occurrence of a pulse, so that $Y = 0$ and $Q = 0$. The input conditions are $S = 1$, $R = 0$, and the next clock pulse should change the flip-flop to the set state with $Q = 1$. During the pulse transition from 0 to 1, the master flip-flop is set and changes Y to 1. The slave flip-flop is not affected because its CP input is 0. Since the master flip-flop is an internal circuit, its change of state is not noticeable in the outputs Q and Q'. When the pulse returns to 0, the information from the master is allowed to pass through to the slave, making the external output $Q = 1$. Note that the external S input can be changed at the same time that the pulse goes through its negative edge transition. This is because, once the CP reaches 0, the master is disabled and its R and S inputs have no influence until the next clock pulse occurs. Thus, in a master-slave flip-flop, it is possible to switch the output of the flip-flop and its input information with the same clock pulse. It must be realized that the S input could come from the output of another master-slave flip-flop that was switched with the same clock pulse.

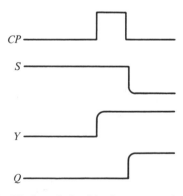

Figure 6-10   Timing relationships in a master-slave flip-flop

The behavior of the master-slave flip-flop just described dictates that the state changes in all flip-flops coincide with the negative edge transition of the pulse. However, some IC master-slave flip-flops change output states in the positive edge transition of clock pulses. This happens in flip-flops that have an additional inverter between the *CP* terminal and the input of the master. Such flip-flops are triggered with negative pulses (see Fig. 6-8), so that the negative edge of the pulse affects the master and the positive edge affects the slave and the output terminals.

The master-slave combination can be constructed for any type of flip-flop by adding a clocked *RS* flip-flop with an inverted clock to form the slave. An example of a master-slave *JK* flip-flop constructed with NAND gates is shown in Fig. 6-11. It consists of two flip-flops; gates 1 through 4 form the master flip-flop, and gates 5 through 8 form the slave flip-flop. The information present at the *J* and *K* inputs is transmitted to the master flip-flop on the positive edge of a clock pulse and is held there until the negative edge of the clock pulse occurs, after which it is allowed to pass through to the slave flip-flop. The clock input is normally 0, which keeps the outputs of gates 1 and 2 at the 1 level. This prevents the *J* and *K* inputs from affecting the master flip-flop. The slave flip-flop is a clocked *RS* type, with the master flip-flop supplying the inputs and the clock input being inverted by gate 9. When the clock is 0, the output of gate 9 is 1, so that output *Q* is equal to *Y*, and *Q'* is equal to *Y'*. When the positive edge of a clock pulse occurs, the master flip-flop is affected and may switch states. The slave flip-flop is isolated as long as the clock is at the 1 level, because the output of gate 9 provides a 1 to both inputs of the NAND basic flip-flop of gates 7 and 8. When the clock input returns to 0, the master flip-flop is isolated from the *J* and *K* inputs and the slave flip-flop goes to the same state as the master flip-flop.

Now consider a digital system containing many master-slave flip-flops, with the outputs of some flip-flops going to the inputs of other flip-flops. Assume that clock pulse inputs to all flip-flops are synchronized (occur at the same time). At the beginning of each clock pulse, some of the master elements change state, but all

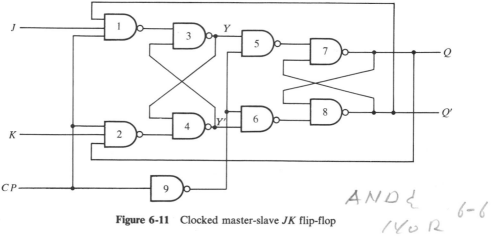

Figure 6-11   Clocked master-slave *JK* flip-flop

flip-flop outputs remain at their previous values. After the clock pulse returns to 0, some of the outputs change state, but none of these new states have an effect on any of the master elements until the next clock pulse. Thus the states of flip-flops in the system can be changed simultaneously during the same clock pulse, even though outputs of flip-flops are connected to inputs of flip-flops. This is possible because the new state appears at the output terminals only after the clock pulse has returned to 0. Therefore, the binary content of one flip-flop can be transferred to a second flip-flop and the content of the second transferred to the first, and both transfers can occur during the same clock pulse.

Edge-Triggered Flip-Flop

Another type of flip-flop that synchronizes the state changes during a clock pulse transition is the *edge-triggered* flip-flop. In this type of flip-flop, output transitions occur at a specific level of the clock pulse. When the pulse input level exceeds this threshold level, the inputs are locked out and the flip-flop is therefore unresponsive to further changes in inputs until the clock pulse returns to 0 and another pulse occurs. Some edge-triggered flip-flops cause a transition on the positive edge of the pulse, and others cause a transition on the negative edge of the pulse.

The logic diagram of a D-type positive-edge-triggered flip-flop is shown in Fig. 6-12. It consists of three basic flip-flops of the type shown in Fig. 6-3. NAND gates 1 and 2 make up one basic flip-flop and gates 3 and 4 another. The third basic flip-flop comprising gates 5 and 6 provides the outputs to the circuit. Inputs S and R of the third basic flip-flop must be maintained at logic-1 for the outputs to remain in their steady-state values. When $S = 0$ and $R = 1$, the output goes to the set state with $Q = 1$. When $S = 1$ and $R = 0$, the output goes to the clear state

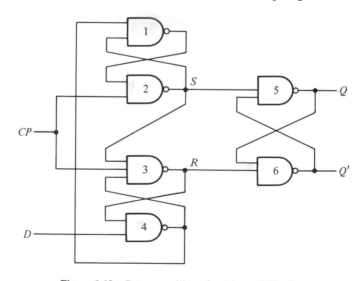

Figure 6-12 D-type positive-edge-triggered flip-flop

with $Q = 0$. Inputs S and R are determined from the states of the other two basic flip-flops. These two basic flip-flops respond to the external inputs D (data) and CP (clock pulse).

The operation of the circuit is explained in Fig. 6-13, where gates 1–4 are redrawn to show all possible transitions. Outputs S and R from gates 2 and 3 go to gates 5 and 6, as shown in Fig. 6-12, to provide the actual outputs of the flip-flop. Figure 6-13(a) shows the binary values at the outputs of the four gates when $CP = 0$. Input D may be equal to 0 or 1. In either case, a CP of 0 causes the outputs of gates 2 and 3 to go to 1, thus making $S = R = 1$, which is the condition for a steady-state output. When $D = 0$, gate 4 has a 1 output, which causes the

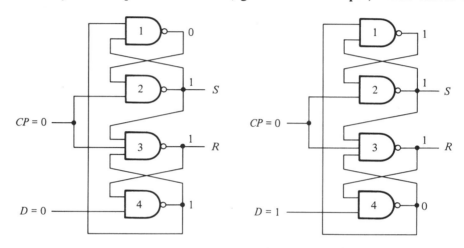

(a) With $CP = 0$

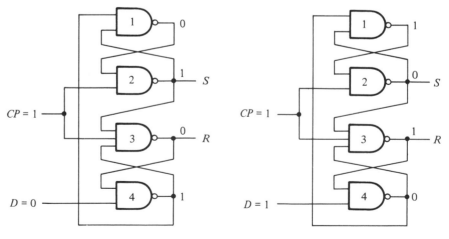

(b) With $CP = 1$

Figure 6-13   Operation of the D-type edge-triggered flip-flop

output of gate 1 to go to 0. When $D = 1$, gate 4 goes to 0, which causes the output of gate 1 to go to 1. These are the two possible conditions when the CP terminal, being 0, disables any changes at the outputs of the flip-flop, no matter what the value of D happens to be.

There is a definite time, called the *setup* time, in which the D input must be maintained at a constant value prior to the application of the pulse. The setup time is equal to the propagation delay through gates 4 and 1 since a change in D causes a change in the outputs of these two gates. Assume now that D does not change during the setup time and that input CP becomes 1. This situation is depicted in Fig. 6-13(b). If $D = 0$ when CP becomes 1, then S remains 1 but R changes to 0. This causes the output of the flip-flop Q to go to 0 (in Fig. 6-12). If now, while $CP = 1$, there is a change in the D input, the output of gate 4 will remain at 1 (even if D goes to 1), since one of the gate inputs comes from R which is maintained at 0. Only when CP returns to 0 can the output of gate 4 change; but then both R and S become 1, disabling any changes in the output of the flip-flop. However, there is a definite time, called the *hold time*, that the D input must not change after the application of the positive-going transition of the pulse. The hold time is equal to the propagation delay of gate 3, since it must be ensured that R becomes 0 in order to maintain the output of gate 4 at 1, regardless of the value of D.

If $D = 1$ when $CP = 1$, then S changes to 0 but R remains at 1, which causes the output of the flip-flop Q to go to 1. A change in D while $CP = 1$ does not alter S and R because gate 1 is maintained at 1 by the 0 signal from S. When CP goes to zero, both S and R go to 1 to prevent the output from undergoing any changes.

In summary, when the input clock pulse makes a positive-going transition, the value of D is transferred to Q. Changes in D when CP is maintained at a steady 1 value do not affect Q. Moreover, a negative pulse transition does not affect the output, nor does it when $CP = 0$. Hence, the edge-triggered flip-flop eliminates any feedback problems in sequential circuits just as a master-slave flip-flop does. The setup time and hold time must be taken into consideration when using this type of flip-flop.

When using different types of flip-flops in the same sequential circuit, one must ensure that all flip-flop outputs make their transitions at the same time, i.e., during either the negative edge or the positive edge of the pulse. Those flip-flops that behave opposite from the adopted polarity transition can be changed easily by the addition of inverters in their clock inputs. An alternate procedure is to provide both positive and negative pulses (by means of an inverter), and then apply the positive pulses to flip-flops that trigger during the negative edge and negative pulses to flip-flops that trigger during the positive edge, or vice versa.

Direct Inputs

Flip-flops available in IC packages sometimes provide special inputs for setting or clearing the flip-flop asynchronously. These inputs are usually called *direct preset* and *direct clear*. They affect the flip-flop on a positive (or negative) value of the

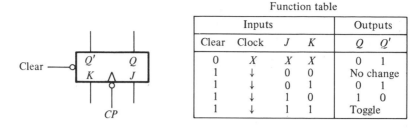

Function table

Inputs				Outputs	
Clear	Clock	J	K	Q	Q'
0	X	X	X	0	1
1	↓	0	0	No change	
1	↓	0	1	0	1
1	↓	1	0	1	0
1	↓	1	1	Toggle	

Figure 6-14 *JK* flip-flop with direct clear

input signal without the need for a clock pulse. These inputs are useful for bringing all flip-flops to an initial state prior to their clocked operation. For example, after power is turned on in a digital system, the states of its flip-flops are indeterminate. A *clear* switch clears all the flip-flops to an initial cleared state and a *start* switch begins the system's clocked operation. The clear switch must clear all flip-flops asynchronously without the need for a pulse.

The graphic symbol of a master-slave flip-flop with direct clear is shown in Fig. 6-14. The clock or *CP* input has a circle under the small triangle to indicate that the outputs change during the negative transition of the pulse. (The absence of the small circle would indicate a positive-edge-triggered flip-flop.) The direct clear input also has a small circle to indicate that, normally, this input must be maintained at 1. If the clear input is maintained at 0, the flip-flop remains cleared, regardless of the other inputs or the clock pulse. The function table specifies the circuit operation. The *X*'s are don't-care conditions which indicate that a 0 in the direct clear input disables all other inputs. Only when the clear input is 1 would a negative transition of the clock have an effect on the outputs. The outputs do not change if $J = K = 0$. The flip-flop toggles or complements when $J = K = 1$. Some flip-flops may also have a direct preset input which sets the output Q to 1 (and Q' to 0) asynchronously.

When direct asynchronous inputs are available in a master-slave flip-flop, they must connect to both the master and the slave in order to override the other inputs and the clock. A direct clear in the *JK* master-slave flip-flop of Fig. 6-10 is connected to the inputs of gates 1, 4, and 8. A direct clear in the *D* edge-triggered flip-flop of Fig. 6-12 is connected to the inputs of gates 2 and 6.

6-4 ANALYSIS OF CLOCKED SEQUENTIAL CIRCUITS

The behavior of a sequential circuit is determined from the inputs, the outputs, and the states of its flip-flops. Both the outputs and the next state are a function of the inputs and the present state. The analysis of sequential circuits consists of obtaining a table or a diagram for the time sequence of inputs, outputs, and internal states. It is also possible to write Boolean expressions that describe the behavior of sequential circuits. However, these expressions must include the necessary time sequence either directly or indirectly.

A logic diagram is recognized as the circuit of a sequential circuit if it includes flip-flops. The flip-flops may be of any type and the logic diagram may or may not include combinational gates. In this section, we first introduce a specific example of a clocked sequential circuit and then present various methods for describing the behavior of sequential circuits. The specific example will be used throughout the discussion to illustrate the various methods.

An Example of a Sequential Circuit

An example of a clocked sequential circuit is shown in Fig. 6-15. It has one input variable x, one output variable y, and two clocked RS flip-flops labeled A and B. The cross-connections from outputs of flip-flops to inputs of gates are not shown by line drawings so as to facilitate the tracing of the circuit. Instead, the connections are recognized from the letter symbol marked in each input. For example, the input marked x' in gate 1 designates an input from the complement of x. The second input marked A designates a connection to the normal output of flip-flop A.

We shall assume negative edge triggering in both flip-flops and in the source that produces the external input x. Therefore, the signals for a given present state are available during the time from the termination of a clock pulse to the termination of the next clock pulse, at which time the circuit goes to the next state.

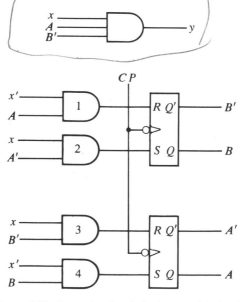

Figure 6-15   Example of a clocked sequential circuit

State Table

The time sequence of inputs, outputs, and flip-flop states may be enumerated in a *state table.** The state table for the circuit of Fig. 6-15 is shown in Table 6-1. It consists of three sections labeled *present state*, *next state*, and *output*. The *present state* designates the states of flip-flops before the occurrence of a clock pulse. The *next state* shows the states of flip-flops after the application of a clock pulse, and the *output* section lists the values of the output variables during the present state. Both the next state and output sections have two columns, one for $x = 0$ and the other for $x = 1$.

TABLE 6-1 State table for circuit of Fig. 6-15

Present State	Next state		Output	
	$x = 0$	$x = 1$	$x = 0$	$x = 1$
AB	AB	AB	y	y
00	00	01	0	0
01	11	01	0	0
10	10	00	0	1
11	10	11	0	0

The derivation of the state table starts from an assumed initial state. The initial state of most practical sequential circuits is defined to be the state with 0's in all flip-flops. Some sequential circuits have a different initial state and some have none at all. In either case, the analysis can always start from any arbitrary state. In this example, we start deriving the state table from the initial state 00.

When the present state is 00, $A = 0$ and $B = 0$. From the logic diagram, we see that with both flip-flops cleared and $x = 0$, none of the AND gates produce a logic-1 signal. Therefore, the next state remains unchanged. With $AB = 00$ and $x = 1$, gate 2 produces a logic-1 signal at the S input of flip-flop B and gate 3 produces a logic-1 signal at the R input of flip-flop A. When a clock pulse triggers the flip-flops, A is cleared and B is set, making the next state 01. This information is listed in the first row of the state table.

In a similar manner, we can derive the next state starting from the other three possible present states. In general, the next state is a function of the inputs, the present state, and the type of flip-flop used. With RS flip-flops, for example, we must remember that a 1 in input S sets the flip-flop and a 1 in input R clears the flip-flop, regardless of its previous state. A 0 in both the S and R inputs leaves the

*Switching circuit theory books call this table a *transition table*. They reserve the name *state table* for a table with internal states represented by arbitrary symbols.

flip-flop unchanged, whereas a 1 in both the S and R inputs shows a bad design and an indeterminate state table.

The entries for the output section are easier to derive. In this example, output y is equal to 1 only when $x = 1$, $A = 1$, and $B = 0$. Therefore, the output columns are marked with 0's, except when the present state is 10 and input $x = 1$, for which y is marked with a 1.

The state table of any sequential circuit is obtained by the same procedure used in the example. In general, a sequential circuit with m flip-flops and n input variables will have 2^m rows, one for each state. The next state and output sections each will have 2^n columns, one for each input combination.

The external outputs of a sequential circuit may come from logic gates or from memory elements. The output section in the state table is necessary only if there are outputs from logic gates. Any external output taken directly from a flip-flop is already listed in the present state column of the state table. Therefore, the output section of the state table can be excluded if there are no external outputs from logic gates.

State Diagram

The information available in a state table may be represented graphically in a *state diagram*. In this diagram, a state is represented by a circle, and the transition between states is indicated by directed lines connecting the circles. The state diagram of the sequential circuit of Fig. 6-15 is shown in Fig. 6-16. The binary number inside each circle identifies the state the circle represents. The directed lines are labeled with two binary numbers separated by a /. The input value that causes the state transition is labeled first; the number after the symbol / gives the value of the output during the present state. For example, the directed line from state 00 to 01 is labeled 1/0, meaning that the sequential circuit is in a present state 00 while $x = 1$ and $y = 0$, and that on the termination of the next clock pulse, the

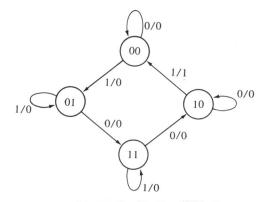

Figure 6-16   State diagram for the circuit of Fig. 6-15

circuit goes to next state 01. A directed line connecting a circle with itself indicates that no change of state occurs. The state diagram provides the same information as the state table and is obtained directly from Table 6-1.

There is no difference between a state table and a state diagram except in the manner of representation. The state table is easier to derive from a given logic diagram and the state diagram follows directly from a state table. The state diagram gives a pictorial view of state transitions and is in a form suitable for human interpretation of the circuit operation. The state diagram is often used as the initial design specification of a sequential circuit.

State Equations

A *state equation* (also known as an *application equation*) is an algebraic expression that specifies the conditions for a flip-flop state transition. The left side of the equation denotes the next state of a flip-flop and the right side, a Boolean function that specifies the present state conditions that make the next state equal to 1. A state equation is similar in form to a flip-flop characteristic equation, except that it specifies the next state conditions in terms of external input variables and other flip-flop values. The state equation is derived directly from a state table. For example, the state equation for flip-flop A is derived from inspection of Table 6-1. From the next state columns, we note that flip-flop A goes to the 1 state four times: when $x = 0$ and $AB = 01$ or 10 or 11, or when $x = 1$ and $AB = 11$. This can be expressed algebraically in a state equation as follows:

$$A(t + 1) = (A'B + AB' + AB)x' + ABx$$

The right-hand side of the state equation is a Boolean function for a *present state*. When this function is equal to 1, the occurrence of a clock pulse causes flip-flop A to have a next state of 1. When the function is equal to 0, the clock pulse causes A to have a next state of 0. The left side of the equation identifies the flip-flop by its letter symbol, followed by the time function designation $(t + 1)$, to emphasize that this value is to be reached by the flip-flop one pulse sequence later.

The state equation is a Boolean function with time included. It is applicable only in clock sequential circuits, since $A(t + 1)$ is defined to change value with the occurrence of a clock pulse at discrete instants of time.

The state equation for flip-flop A is simplified by means of a map as shown in Fig. 6-17(a). With some algebraic manipulation, the function can be expressed in the following form:

$$A(t + 1) = Bx' + (B'x)'A$$

If we let $Bx' = S$ and $B'x = R$, we obtain the relationship:

$$A(t + 1) = S + R'A$$

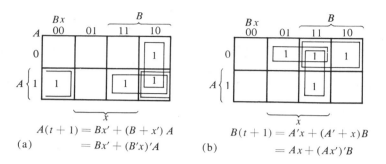

$$A(t+1) = Bx' + (B+x')A$$
$$= Bx' + (B'x)'A$$

(a)

$$B(t+1) = A'x + (A'+x)B$$
$$= Ax + (Ax')'B$$

(b)

Figure 6-17 State equations for flip-flops A and B

which is the characteristic equation of an RS flip-flop [Fig. 6-4(d)]. This relationship between the state equation and the flip-flop characteristic equation can be justified from inspection of the logic diagram of Fig. 6-15. In it we see that the S input of flip-flop A is equal to the Boolean function Bx' and the R input is equal to $B'x$. Substituting these functions into the flip-flop characteristic equation results in its state equation for this sequential circuit.

The state equation for a flip-flop in a sequential circuit may be derived from a state table or from a logic diagram. The derivation from the state table consists of obtaining the Boolean function specifying the conditions that make the next state of the flip-flop a 1. The derivation from a logic diagram consists of obtaining the functions of the flip-flop inputs and substituting them into the flip-flop characteristic equation.

The derivation of the state equation for flip-flop B from the state table is shown in the map of Fig. 6-17(b). The 1's marked in the map are the present state and input combinations that cause the flip-flop to go to a next state of 1. These conditions are obtained directly from Table 6-1. The simplified form obtained in the map is manipulated algebraically, and the state equation obtained is:

$$B(t+1) = A'x + (Ax')'B$$

The state equation can be derived directly from the logic diagram. From Fig. 6-15, we see that the signal for input S of flip-flop B is generated by the function $A'x$ and the signal for input R by the function Ax'. Substituting $S = A'x$ and $R = Ax'$ into an RS flip-flop characteristic equation given by:

$$B(t+1) = S + R'B$$

we obtain the state equation derived above.

The state equations of all flip-flops, together with the output functions, fully specify a sequential circuit. They represent, algebraically, the same information a state table represents in tabular form and a state diagram represents in graphical form.

Flip-flop Input Functions

The logic diagram of a sequential circuit consists of memory elements and gates. The type of flip-flops and their characteristic table specify the logical properties of the memory elements. The interconnections among the gates form a combinational circuit and may be specified algebraically with Boolean functions. Thus, knowledge of the type of flip-flops and a list of the Boolean functions of the combinational circuit provide all the information needed to draw the logic diagram of a sequential circuit. The part of the combinational circuit that generates external outputs is described algebraically by the *circuit output functions*. The part of the circuit that generates the inputs to flip-flops are described algebraically by a set of Boolean functions called *flip-flop input functions* or sometimes *input equations*.

We shall adopt the convention of using two letters to designate a flip-flop input variable: the first to designate the name of the input and the second the name of the flip-flop. As an example, consider the following flip-flop input functions:

$$JA = BC'x + B'Cx'$$
$$KA = B + y$$

JA and KA designate two Boolean variables. The first letter in each denotes the J and K input, respectively, of a JK flip-flop. The second letter A is the symbol name of the flip-flop. The right side of each equation is a Boolean function for the corresponding flip-flop input variable. The implementation of the two input functions is shown in the logic diagram of Fig. 6-18. The JK flip-flop has an output symbol A and two inputs labeled J and K. The combinational circuit drawn in the diagram is the implementation of the algebraic expression given by the input functions. The outputs of the combinational circuit are denoted by JA and KA in the input functions and go to the J and K inputs, respectively, of flip-flop A.

From this example, we see that a flip-flop input function is an algebraic expression for a combinational circuit. The two-letter designation is a variable

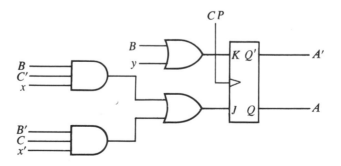

Figure 6-18 Implementation of the flip-flop input functions
$JA = BC'x + B'Cx'$ and $KA = B + y$

name for an *output* of the combinational circuit. This output is always connected to the *input* (designated by the first letter) of a flip-flop (designated by the second letter).

The sequential circuit of Fig. 6-15 has one input x, one output y, and two RS flip-flops denoted by A and B. The logic diagram can be expressed algebraically with four flip-flop input functions and one circuit output function as follows:

$$SA = Bx' \qquad RA = B'x$$
$$SB = A'x \qquad RB = Ax'$$
$$y = AB'x$$

This set of Boolean functions fully specifies the logic diagram. Variables SA and RA specify an RS flip-flop labeled A; variables SB and RB specify a second RS flip-flop labeled B. Variable y denotes the output. The Boolean expressions for the variables specify the combinational circuit part of the sequential circuit.

The flip-flop input functions constitute a convenient algebraic form for specifying a logic diagram of a sequential circuit. They imply the type of flip-flop from the first letter of the input variable and they fully specify the combinational circuit that drives the flip-flop. Time is not included explicitly in these equations but is implied from the clock pulse operation. It is sometimes convenient to specify a sequential circuit algebraically with circuit output functions and flip-flop input functions instead of drawing the logic diagram.

6-5 STATE REDUCTION AND ASSIGNMENT

The analysis of sequential circuits starts from a circuit diagram and culminates in a state table or diagram. The design of a sequential circuit starts from a set of specifications and culminates in a logic diagram. Design procedures are presented starting from Section 6-7. This section discusses certain properties of sequential circuits that may be used to reduce the number of gates and flip-flops during the design.

State Reduction*

Any design process must consider the problem of minimizing the cost of the final circuit. The two most obvious cost reductions are reductions in the number of flip-flops and the number of gates. Because these two items seem the most obvious, they have been extensively studied and investigated. In fact, a large portion of the subject of switching theory is concerned with finding algorithms for minimizing the number of flip-flops and gates in sequential circuits.

The reduction of the number of flip-flops in a sequential circuit is referred to as the *state reduction* problem. State reduction algorithms are concerned with

*Further discussion and more examples of state reduction can be found in Section 9-5.

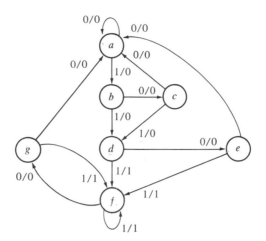

Figure 6-19 State diagram

procedures for reducing the number of states in a state table while keeping the external input-output requirements unchanged. Since m flip-flops produce 2^m states, a reduction in the number of states may (or may not) result in a reduction in the number of flip-flops. An unpredictable effect in reducing the number of flip-flops is that sometimes the equivalent circuit (with less flip-flops) may require more combinational gates.

We shall illustrate the need for state reduction with an example. We start with a sequential circuit whose specification is given in the state diagram of Fig. 6-19. In this example, only the input-output sequences are important; the internal states are used merely to provide the required sequences. For this reason, the states marked inside the circles are denoted by letter symbols instead of by their binary values. This is in contrast to a binary counter, where the binary value sequence of the states themselves are taken as the outputs.

There are an infinite number of input sequences that may be applied to the circuit; each results in a unique output sequence. As an example, consider the input sequence 01010110100 starting from the initial state a. Each input of 0 or 1 produces an output of 0 or 1 and causes the circuit to go to the next state. From the state diagram, we obtain the output and state sequence for the given input sequence as follows: With the circuit in initial state a, an input of 0 produces an output of 0 and the circuit remains in state a. With present state a and input of 1, the output is 0 and the next state is b. With present state b and input of 0, the output is 0 and next state is c. Continuing this process, we find the complete sequence to be as follows:

state		a	a	b	c	d	e	f	f	g	f	g	a
input		0	1	0	1	0	1	1	0	1	0	0	
output		0	0	0	0	0	1	1	0	1	0	0	

In each column, we have the present state, input value, and output value. The next state is written on top of the next column. It is important to realize that in this circuit the states themselves are of secondary importance because we are interested only in output sequences caused by input sequences.

Now let us assume that we have found a sequential circuit whose state diagram has less than seven states and we wish to compare it with the circuit whose state diagram is given by Fig. 6-19. If identical input sequences are applied to the two circuits and identical outputs occur for all input sequences, then the two circuits are said to be equivalent (as far as the input-output is concerned) and one may be replaced by the other. The problem of state reduction is to find ways of reducing the number of states in a sequential circuit without altering the input-output relationships.

We shall now proceed to reduce the number of states for this example. First, we need the state table; it is more convenient to apply procedures for state reduction here than in state diagrams. The state table of the circuit is listed in Table 6-2 and is obtained directly from the state diagram of Fig. 6-19.

TABLE 6-2   State table

Present state	Next state $x = 0$	$x = 1$	Output $x = 0$	$x = 1$
a	a	b	0	0
b	c	d	0	0
c	a	d	0	0
d	e	f	0	1
e	a	f	0	1
f	g	f	0	1
g	a	f	0	1

An algorithm for the state reduction of a completely specified state table is given here without proof: "Two states are said to be equivalent if, for each member of the set of inputs, they give exactly the same output and send the circuit either to the same state or to an equivalent state. When two states are equivalent, one of them can be removed without altering the input-output relationships."

We shall apply this algorithm to Table 6-2. Going through the state table, we look for two present states that go to the same next state and have the same output for both input combinations. States g and e are two such states; they both go to states a and f and have outputs of 0 and 1 for $x = 0$ and $x = 1$, respectively. Therefore, states g and e are equivalent; one can be removed. The procedure of removing a state and replacing it by its equivalent is demonstrated in Table 6-3. The row with present state g is crossed out and state g is replaced by state e each time it occurs in the next state columns.

TABLE 6-3 Reducing the state table

	Next state		Output	
Present state	$x = 0$	$x = 1$	$x = 0$	$x = 1$
a	a	b	0	0
b	c	d	0	0
c	a	d	0	0
d	e	$\not f d$	0	1
e	a	$\not f d$	0	1
$\not f$	$\not g e$	f	0	1
$\not g$	a	f	0	1

Present state f now has next states e and f and outputs 0 and 1 for $x = 0$ and $x = 1$, respectively. The same next states and outputs appear in the row with present state d. Therefore, states f and d are equivalent; state f can be removed and replaced by d. The final reduced table is shown in Table 6-4. The state diagram for the reduced table consists of only five states and is shown in Fig. 6-20. This state diagram satisfies the original input-output specifications and will produce the required output sequence for any given input sequence. The following list derived from the state diagram of Fig. 6-20 is for the input sequence used previously. We note that the same output sequence results although the state sequence is different:

state	a	a	b	c	d	e	d	d	e	d	e	a
input	0	1	0	1	0	1	1	0	1	0	0	
output	0	0	0	0	0	1	1	0	1	0	0	

In fact, this sequence is exactly the same as that obtained for Fig. 6-19, if we replace e by g and d by f.

TABLE 6-4 Reduced state table

	Next state		Output	
Present state	$x = 0$	$x = 1$	$x = 0$	$x = 1$
a	a	b	0	0
b	c	d	0	0
c	a	d	0	0
d	e	d	0	1
e	a	d	0	1

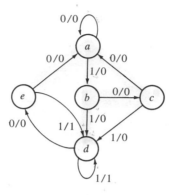

Figure 6-20 Reduced state diagram

It is worth noting that the reduction in the number of states of a sequential circuit is possible if one is interested only in external input-output relationships. When external outputs are taken directly from flip-flops, the outputs must be independent of the number of states before state reduction algorithms are applied.

The sequential circuit of this example was reduced from seven to five states. In either case, the representation of the states with physical components requires that we use three flip-flops, because m flip-flops can represent up to 2^m distinct states. With three flip-flops, we can formulate up to eight binary states denoted by binary numbers 000 through 111, with each bit designating the state of one flip-flop. If the state table of Table 6-2 is used, we must assign binary values to seven states; the remaining state is unused. If the state table of Table 6-4 is used, only five states need binary assignment, and we are left with three unused states. Unused states are treated as don't-care conditions during the design of the circuit. Since don't-care conditions usually help in obtaining a simpler Boolean function, it is more likely that the circuit with five states will require fewer combinational gates than the one with seven states. In any case, the reduction from seven to five states does not reduce the number of flip-flops. In general, reducing the number of states in a state table is likely to result in a circuit with less equipment. However, the fact that a state table has been reduced to fewer states does not guarantee a saving in the number of flip-flops or the number of gates.

State Assignment

The cost of the combinational circuit part of a sequential circuit can be reduced by using the known simplification methods for combinational circuits. However, there is another factor, known as the *state assignment* problem, that comes into play in minimizing the combinational gates. State assignment procedures are concerned with methods for assigning binary values to states in such a way as to reduce the cost of the combinational circuit that drives the flip-flops. This is particularly helpful when a sequential circuit is viewed from its external input-output terminals. Such a circuit may follow a sequence of internal states, but the binary values of the

TABLE 6-5 Three possible binary state assignments

State	Assignment 1	Assignment 2	Assignment 3
a	001	000	000
b	010	010	100
c	011	011	010
d	100	101	101
e	101	111	011

TABLE 6-6 Reduced state table with binary assignment 1

Present state	Next state		Output	
	$x = 0$	$x = 1$	$x = 0$	$x = 1$
001	001	010	0	0
010	011	100	0	0
011	001	100	0	0
100	101	100	0	1
101	001	100	0	1

individual states may be of no consequence as long as the circuit produces the required sequence of outputs for any given sequence of inputs. This does not apply to circuits whose external outputs are taken directly from flip-flops with binary sequences fully specified.

The binary state assignment alternatives available can be demonstrated in conjunction with the sequential circuit specified in Table 6-4. Remember that, in this example, the binary values of the states are immaterial as long as their sequence maintains the proper input-output relationships. For this reason, any binary number assignment is satisfactory as long as each state is assigned a unique number. Three examples of possible binary assignments are shown in Table 6-5 for the five states of the reduced table. Assignment 1 is a straight binary assignment for the sequence of states from *a* through *e*. The other two assignments are chosen arbitrarily. In fact, there are 140 different distinct assignments for this circuit (11).

Table 6-6 is the reduced state table with binary assignment 1 substituted for the letter symbols of the five states.* It is obvious that a different binary assignment will result in a state table with different binary values for the states, while the input-output relationships remain the same. The binary form of the state table is used to derive the combinational circuit part of the sequential circuit. The complexity of the combinational circuit obtained depends on the binary state assignment chosen. The design of the sequential circuit presented in this section is completed in Example 6-1 of Section 6-7.

*A state table with binary assignment is sometimes called a *transition table*.

Various procedures have been suggested that lead to a particular binary assignment from the many available. The most common criterion is that the chosen assignment should result in a simple combinational circuit for the flip-flop inputs. However, to date, there are no state assignment procedures that guarantee a minimal-cost combinational circuit. State assignment is one of the challenging problems of switching theory. The interested reader will find a rich and growing literature on this topic. Techniques for dealing with the state assignment problem are beyond the scope of this book.

6-6 FLIP-FLOP EXCITATION TABLES

The characteristic tables for the various flip-flops were presented in Section 6-2. A characteristic table defines the logical property of the flip-flop and completely characterizes its operation. Integrated-circuit flip-flops are sometimes defined by a characteristic table tabulated somewhat differently. This second form of the characteristic tables for RS, JK, D, and T flip-flops is shown in Table 6-7. They represent the same information as the characteristic tables of Figs. 6-4(c) through 6-7(c).

Table 6-7 defines the state of each flip-flop as a function of its inputs and previous state. $Q(t)$ refers to the present state and $Q(t + 1)$ to the next state after the occurrence of a clock pulse. The characteristic table for the RS flip-flop shows that the next state is equal to the present state when inputs S and R are both 0. When the R input is equal to 1, the next clock pulse clears the flip-flop. When the S input is equal to 1, the next clock pulse sets the flip-flop. The question mark for the next state when S and R are both equal to 1 simultaneously designates an indeterminate next state.

TABLE 6-7   Flip-flop characteristic tables

S	R	$Q(t + 1)$
0	0	$Q(t)$
0	1	0
1	0	1
1	1	?

(a) RS

J	K	$Q(t + 1)$
0	0	$Q(t)$
0	1	0
1	0	1
1	1	$Q'(t)$

(b) JK

D	$Q(t + 1)$
0	0
1	1

(c) D

T	$Q(t + 1)$
0	$Q(t)$
1	$Q'(t)$

(d) T

The table for the *JK* flip-flop is the same as that for the *RS* when *J* and *K* are replaced by *S* and *R*, respectively, except for the indeterminate case. When both *J* and *K* are equal to 1, the next state is equal to the complement of the present state, i.e., $Q(t + 1) = Q'(t)$. The next state of the *D* flip-flop is completely dependent on the input *D* and independent of the present state. The next state of the *T* flip-flop is the same as the present state if $T = 0$ and complemented if $T = 1$.

The characteristic table is useful for analysis and for defining the operation of the flip-flop. It specifies the next state when the inputs and present state are known. During the design process we usually know the transition from present state to next state and wish to find the flip-flop input conditions that will cause the required transition. For this reason, we need a table that lists the required inputs for a given change of state. Such a list is called an *excitation table*.

Table 6-8 presents the excitation tables for the four flip-flops. Each table consists of two columns, $Q(t)$ and $Q(t + 1)$, and a column for each input to show how the required transition is achieved. There are four possible transitions from present state to next state. The required input conditions for each of the four transitions are derived from the information available in the characteristic table. The symbol *X* in the tables represents a don't-care condition, i.e., it does not matter whether the input is 1 or 0.

RS Flip-flop

The excitation table for the *RS* flip-flop is shown in Table 6-8(a). The first row shows the flip-flop in the 0-state at time *t*. It is desired to leave it in the 0-state after the occurrence of the pulse. From the characteristic table, we find that if *S*

TABLE 6-8   Flip-flop excitation tables

$Q(t)$	$Q(t + 1)$	*S*	*R*
0	0	0	X
0	1	1	0
1	0	0	1
1	1	X	0

(a) *RS*

$Q(t)$	$Q(t + 1)$	*J*	*K*
0	0	0	X
0	1	1	X
1	0	X	1
1	1	X	0

(b) *JK*

$Q(t)$	$Q(t + 1)$	*D*
0	0	0
0	1	1
1	0	0
1	1	1

(c) *D*

P.S   N.S

$Q(t)$	$Q(t + 1)$	*T*
0	0	0
0	1	1
1	0	1
1	1	0

(d) *T*

and R are both 0, the flip-flop will not change state. Therefore, both S and R inputs should be 0. However, it really doesn't matter if R is made a 1 when the pulse occurs, since it results in leaving the flip-flop in the 0-state. Thus, R can be 1 or 0 and the flip-flop will remain in the 0-state at $t + 1$. Therefore, the entry under R is marked by the don't-care condition X.

If the flip-flop is in the 0-state and it is desired to have it go to the 1-state, then from the characteristic table, we find that the only way to make $Q(t + 1)$ equal to 1 is to make $S = 1$ and $R = 0$. If the flip-flop is to have a transition from the 1-state to the 0-state, we must have $S = 0$ and $R = 1$.

The last condition that may occur is for the flip-flop to be in the 1-state and remain in the 1-state. Certainly R must be 0; we do not want to clear the flip-flop. However, S may be either a 0 or a 1. If it is 0, the flip-flop does not change and remains in the 1-state; if it is 1, it sets the flip-flop to the 1-state as desired. Therefore, S is listed as a don't-care condition.

JK Flip-Flop

The excitation table for the JK flip-flop is shown in Table 6-8(b). When both present state and next state are 0, the J input must remain at 0 and the K input can be either 0 or 1. Similarly, when both present state and next state are 1, the K input must remain at 0 while the J input can be 0 or 1. If the flip-flop is to have a transition from the 0-state to the 1-state, J must be equal to 1 since the J input sets the flip-flop. However, input K may be either 0 or a 1. If $K = 0$, the $J = 1$ condition sets the flip-flop as required; if $K = 1$ and $J = 1$, the flip-flop is complemented and goes from the 0-state to the 1-state as required. Therefore the K input is marked with a don't-care condition for the 0-to-1 transition. For a transition from the 1-state to the 0-state, we must have $K = 1$, since the K input clears the flip-flop. However, the J input may be either 0 or 1, since $J = 0$ has no effect, and $J = 1$ together with $K = 1$ complements the flip-flop with a resultant transition from the 1-state to the 0-state.

The excitation table for the JK flip-flop illustrates the advantage of using this type when designing sequential circuits. The fact that it has so many don't-care conditions indicates that the combinational circuits for the input functions are likely to be simpler because don't-care terms usually simplify a function.

D Flip-Flop

The excitation table for the D flip-flop is shown in Table 6-8(c). From the characteristic table, Table 6-7(c), we note that the next state is always equal to the D input and independent of the present state. Therefore, D must be 0 if $Q(t + 1)$ has to be 0, and 1 if $Q(t + 1)$ has to be 1, regardless of the value of $Q(t)$.

T Flip-Flop

The excitation table for the T flip-flop is shown in Table 6-8(d). From the characteristic table, Table 6-7(d), we find that when input $T = 1$, the state of the flip-flop is complemented; when $T = 0$, the state of the flip-flop remains unchanged. Therefore, when the state of the flip-flop must remain the same, the requirement is that $T = 0$. When the state of the flip-flop has to be complemented, T must equal 1.

Other Flip-Flops

The design procedure to be described in this chapter can be used with any flip-flop. It is necessary that the flip-flop characteristic table, from which it is possible to develop a new excitation table, be known. The excitation table is then used to determine the flip-flop input functions, as explained in the next section.

6-7 DESIGN PROCEDURE

The design of a clocked sequential circuit starts from a set of specifications and culminates in a logic diagram or a list of Boolean functions from which the logic diagram can be obtained. In contrast to a combinational circuit, which is fully specified by a truth table, a sequential circuit requires a state table for its specification. The first step in the design of sequential circuits is to obtain a state table or an equivalent representation, such as a state diagram or state equations.

A synchronous sequential circuit is made up of flip-flops and combinational gates. The design of the circuit consists of choosing the flip-flops and then finding a combinational gate structure which, together with the flip-flops, produces a circuit that fulfills the stated specifications. The number of flip-flops is determined from the number of states needed in the circuit. The combinational circuit is derived from the state table by methods presented in this chapter. In fact, once the type and number of flip-flops are determined, the design process involves a transformation from the sequential circuit problem into a combinational circuit problem. In this way the techniques of combinational circuit design can be applied.

This section presents a procedure for the design of sequential circuits. Although intended to serve as a guide for the beginner, this procedure can be shortened with experience. The procedure is first summarized by a list of consecutive recommended steps as follows:

1. The word description of the circuit behavior is stated. This may be accompanied by a state diagram, a timing diagram, or other pertinent information.

2. From the given information about the circuit, obtain the state table.

3. The number of states may be reduced by state reduction methods if the sequential circuit can be characterized by input-output relationships independent of the number of states.

4. Assign binary values to each state if the state table obtained in step 2 or 3 contains letter symbols.

5. Determine the number of flip-flops needed and assign a letter symbol to each.

6. Choose the type of flip-flop to be used.

7. From the state table, derive the circuit excitation and output tables.

8. Using the map or any other simplification method, derive the circuit output functions and the flip-flop input functions.

9. Draw the logic diagram.

The word specification of the circuit behavior usually assumes that the reader is familiar with digital logic terminology. It is necessary that the designer use intuition and experience to arrive at the correct interpretation of the circuit specifications, because word descriptions may be incomplete and inexact. However, once such a specification has been set down and the state table obtained, it is possible to make use of the formal procedure to design the circuit.

The reduction of the number of states and the assignment of binary values to the states were discussed in Section 6-5. The examples that follow assume that the number of states and the binary assignment for the states are known. As a consequence, steps 3 and 4 of the design will not be considered in subsequent discussions.

It has already been mentioned that the number of flip-flops is determined from the number of states. A circuit may have unused binary states if the total number of states is less than 2^m. The unused states are taken as don't-care conditions during the design of the combinational circuit part of the circuit.

The type of flip-flop to be used may be included in the design specifications or may depend on what is available to the designer. Many digital systems are constructed entirely with JK flip-flops because they are the most versatile available. When many types of flip-flops are available, it is advisable to use the RS or D flip-flop for applications requiring transfer of data (such as shift registers), the T type for applications involving complementation (such as binary counters), and the JK type for general applications.

The external output information is specified in the output section of the state table. From it we can derive the circuit output functions. The excitation table for the circuit is similar to that of the individual flip-flops, except that the input conditions are dictated by the information available in the present state and next state columns of the state table. The method of obtaining the excitation table and the simplified flip-flop input functions is best illustrated by an example.

We wish to design the clocked sequential circuit whose state diagram is given in Fig. 6-21. The type of flip-flop to be used is JK.

The state diagram consists of four states with binary values already assigned. Since the directed lines are marked with a single binary digit without a /, we conclude that there is one input variable and no output variables. (The state of the flip-flops may be considered the outputs of the circuit.) The two flip-flops needed to represent the four states are designated A and B. The input variable is designated x.

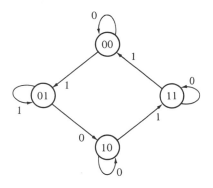

Figure 6-21 State diagram

The state table for this circuit, derived from the state diagram, is shown in Table 6-9. Note that there is no output section for this circuit. We shall now show the procedure for obtaining the excitation table and the combinational gate structure.

The derivation of the excitation table is facilitated if we arrange the state table in a different form. This form is shown in Table 6-10, where the present state and input variables are arranged in the form of a truth table. The next state value for each present state and input conditions is copied from Table 6-9. The excitation table of a circuit is a list of flip-flop input conditions that will cause the required state transitions and is a function of the type of flip-flop used. Since this example specified JK flip-flops, we need columns for the J and K inputs of flip-flops A (denoted by JA and KA) and B (denoted by JB and KB).

The excitation table for the JK flip-flop was derived in Table 6-8(b). This table is now used to derive the excitation table of the circuit. For example, in the first row of Table 6-10 we have a transition for flip-flop A from 0 in the present state to 0 in the next state. In Table 6-8(b) we find that a transition of states from 0 to 0 requires that input $J = 0$ and input $K = X$. So 0 and X are copied in the first row under JA and KA, respectively. Since the first row also shows a transition for flip-flop B from 0 in the present state to 0 in the next state, 0 and X are copied

TABLE 6-9 State table

Present state		Next state			
		$x = 0$		$x = 1$	
A	B	A	B	A	B
0	0	0	0	0	1
0	1	1	0	0	1
1	0	1	0	1	1
1	1	1	1	0	0

TABLE 6-10 Excitation table

Inputs of combinational circuit			Next state		Outputs of combinational circuit			
Present state		Input			Flip-flop inputs			
A	B	x	A	B	JA	KA	JB	KB
0	0	0	0	0	0	X	0	X
0	0	1	0	1	0	X	1	X
0	1	0	1	0	1	X	X	1
0	1	1	0	1	0	X	X	0
1	0	0	1	0	X	0	0	X
1	0	1	1	1	X	0	1	X
1	1	0	1	1	X	0	X	0
1	1	1	0	0	X	1	X	1

in the first row under JB and KB. The second row of Table 6-10 shows a transition for flip-flop B from 0 in the present state to 1 in the next state. From Table 6-8(b) we find that a transition from 0 to 1 requires that input $J = 1$ and input $K = X$. So 1 and X are copied in the second row under JB and KB, respectively. This process is continued for each row of the table and for each flip-flop, with the input conditions as specified in Table 6-8(b) being copied into the proper row of the particular flip-flop being considered.

Let us now pause and consider the information available in an excitation table such as Table 6-10. We know that a sequential circuit consists of a number of flip-flops and a combinational circuit. Figure 6-22 shows the two JK flip-flops needed for the circuit and a box to represent the combinational circuit. From the block diagram, it is clear that the outputs of the combinational circuit go to flip-flop inputs and external outputs (if specified). The inputs to the combinational circuit are the external inputs and the present state values of the flip-flops. Moreover, the Boolean functions that specify a combinational circuit are derived from a truth table that shows the input-output relations of the circuit. The truth table that describes the combinational circuit is available in the excitation table. The combinational circuit *inputs* are specified under the present state and input columns, and the combinational circuit *outputs* are specified under the flip-flop input columns. Thus, an excitation table transforms a state diagram to the truth table needed for the design of the combinational circuit part of the sequential circuit.

The simplified Boolean functions for the combinational circuit can now be derived. The inputs are the variables A, B, and x; the outputs are the variables JA, KA, JB, and KB. The information from the truth table is transferred into the maps

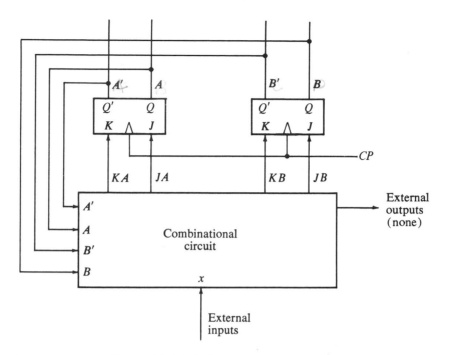

Figure 6-22 Block diagram of sequential circuit

of Fig. 6-23, where the four simplified flip-flop input functions are derived:

$$JA = Bx' \qquad KA = Bx$$
$$JB = x \qquad KB = A \odot x$$

The logic diagram is drawn in Fig. 6-24 and consists of two flip-flops, two AND gates, one equivalence gate, and one inverter.

  With some experience, it is possible to reduce the amount of work involved in the design of the combinational circuit. For example, it is possible to obtain the information for the maps of Fig. 6-23 directly from Table 6-9, without having to derive Table 6-10. This is done by systematically going through each present state and input combination in Table 6-9 and comparing it with the binary values of the corresponding next state. The required input conditions as specified by the flip-flop excitation in Table 6-8 is then determined. Instead of inserting the 0, 1, or X thus obtained into the excitation table, it can be written down directly into the appropriate square of the appropriate map.

  The excitation table of a sequential circuit with m flip-flops, k inputs per flip-flop, and n external inputs consists of $m + n$ columns for the present state and input variables and up to 2^{m+n} rows listed in some convenient binary count. The next state section has m columns, one for each flip-flop. The flip-flop input values are listed in mk columns, one for each input of each flip-flop. If the circuit contains j outputs, the table must include j columns. The truth table of the

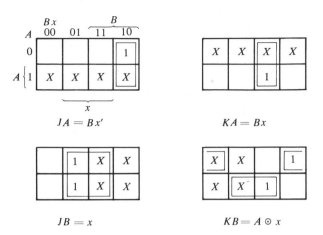

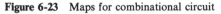

Figure 6-23 Maps for combinational circuit

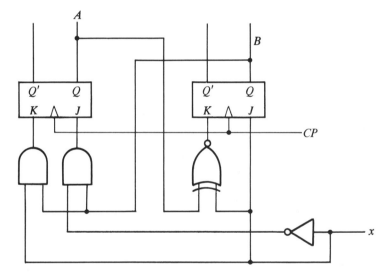

Figure 6-24 Logic diagram of sequential circuit

combinational circuit is taken from the excitation table by considering the $m + n$ present state and input columns as *inputs* and the $mk + j$ flip-flop input values and external outputs as *outputs*.

Design with Unused States

A circuit with m flip-flops would have 2^m states. There are occasions when a sequential circuit may use less than this maximum number of states. States that are not used in specifying the sequential circuit are not listed in the state table. When simplifying the input functions to flip-flops, the unused states can be treated as don't-care conditions.

238

TABLE 6-11   Excitation table for Example 6-1

Present state			Input	Next state			Flip-flop inputs						Output
A	B	C	x	A	B	C	SA	RA	SB	RB	SC	RC	y
0	0	1	0	0	0	1	0	X	0	X	X	0	0
0	0	1	1	0	1	0	0	X	1	0	0	1	0
0	1	0	0	0	1	1	0	X	X	0	1	0	0
0	1	0	1	1	0	0	1	0	0	1	0	X	0
0	1	1	0	0	0	1	0	X	0	1	X	0	0
0	1	1	1	1	0	0	1	0	0	1	0	1	0
1	0	0	0	1	0	1	X	0	0	X	1	0	0
1	0	0	1	1	0	0	X	0	0	X	0	X	1
1	0	1	0	0	0	1	0	1	0	X	X	0	0
1	0	1	1	1	0	0	X	0	0	X	0	1	1

EXAMPLE 6-1: Complete the design of the sequential circuit presented in Section 6-5. Use the reduced state table with assignment 1 as given in Table 6-6. The circuit is to employ *RS* flip-flops.

The state table of Table 6-6 is redrawn in Table 6-11 in the form convenient for obtaining the excitation table. The flip-flop input conditions are derived from the present state and next state columns of the state table. Since *RS* flip-flops are used, we need to refer to Table 6-8(a) for the excitation conditions of this type of flip-flop. The three flip-flops are given variable names *A*, *B*, and *C*. The input variable is *x* and the output variable is *y*. The excitation table of the circuit provides all the information needed for the design.

There are three unused states in this circuit: binary states 000, 110, and 111. When an input of 0 or 1 is included with these unused states, we obtain six don't-care minterms: 0, 1, 12, 13, 14, and 15. These six binary combinations are not listed in the table under present state and input and are treated as don't-care terms.

The combinational circuit part of the sequential circuit is simplified in the maps of Fig. 6-25. There are seven maps in the diagram. Six maps are for simplifying the input functions for the three *RS* flip-flops. The seventh map is for simplifying the output *y*. Each map has six *X*'s in the squares of the don't-care minterms 0, 1, 2, 13, 14, and 15. The other don't-care terms in the maps come from the *X*'s in the flip-flop input columns of the table. The simplified functions are listed under each map. The logic diagram obtained from these Boolean functions is drawn in Fig. 6-26.

One factor neglected up to this point in the design is the initial state of a sequential circuit. When power is first turned on in a digital system, one does not

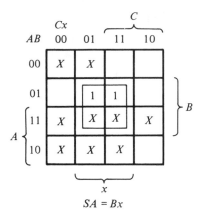

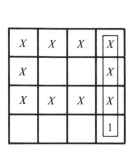

$SA = Bx$

$RA = Cx'$

$SB = A'B'x$

$RB = BC + Bx$

$SC = x'$

$RC = x$

$y = Ax$

Figure 6-25 Maps for simplifying the sequential circuit of Example 6-1

know in what state the flip-flops will settle. It is customary to provide a *master-re-set* input whose purpose is to initialize the states of all flip-flops in the system. Typically, the master reset is a signal applied to all flip-flops asynchronously before the clocked operations start. In most cases flip-flops are cleared to 0 by the master-reset signal, but some may be set to 1. For example, the circuit of Fig. 6-26 may initially be reset to a state $ABC = 001$, since state 000 is not a valid state for this circuit.

But what if a circuit is not reset to an initial valid state? Or worse, what if, because of a noise signal or any other unforeseen reason, the circuit finds itself in

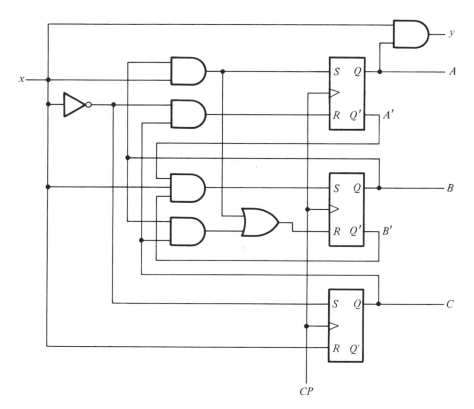

Figure 6-26 Logic diagram for Example 6-1

one of its invalid states? In that case it is necessary to ensure that the circuit eventually goes into one of the valid states so it can resume normal operation. Otherwise, if the sequential circuit circulates among invalid states, there will be no way to bring it back to its intended sequence of state transitions. Although one can assume that this undesirable condition is not supposed to occur, a careful designer must ensure that this situation never occurs.

It was stated previously that unused states in a sequential circuit can be treated as don't-care conditions. Once the circuit is designed, the m flip-flops in the system can be in any one of 2^m possible states. If some of these states were taken as don't-care conditions, the circuit must be investigated to determine the effect of these unused states. The next state from invalid states can be determined from the analysis of the circuit. In any case, it is always wise to analyze a circuit obtained from a design to ensure that no mistakes were made during the design process.

> **EXAMPLE 6-2:** Analyze the sequential circuit obtained in Example 6-1 and determine the effect of the unused states.
>
> The unused states are 000, 110, and 111. The analysis of the circuit is done by the method outlined in Section 6-4. The maps of

Fig. 6-25 may also help in the analysis. What is needed here is to start with the circuit diagram of Fig. 6-26 and derive the state table or diagram. If the derived state table is identical to Table 6-6 (or the state-table part of Table 6-11), then we know that the design is correct. In addition, we must determine the next states from the unused states 000, 110, and 111.

The maps of Fig. 6-25 can help in finding the next state from each of the unused states. Take, for instance, the unused state 000. If the circuit, for some reason, happens to be in the present state 000, an input $x = 0$ will transfer the circuit to some next state and an input $x = 1$ will transfer it to another (or the same) next state. We first investigate minterm $ABCx = 0000$. From the maps, we see that this minterm is not included in any function except for SC, i.e., the set input of flip-flop C. Therefore, flip-flops A and B will not change but flip-flop C will be set to 1. Since the present state is $ABC = 000$, the next state will be $ABC = 001$. The maps also show that minterm $ABCx = 0001$ is included in the functions for SB and RC. Therefore, B will be set and C will be cleared. Starting with $ABC = 000$ and setting B, we obtain the next state $ABC = 010$ (C is already cleared). Investigation of the map for output y shows that y will be 0 for these two minterms.

The result of the analysis procedure is shown in the state diagram of Fig. 6-27. The circuit operates as intended, as long as it stays within the states 001, 010, 011, 100, and 101. If it ever finds itself in one of the invalid states 000, 110, or 111, it goes to one of the valid states within one or two clock pulses. Thus the circuit is self-starting and self-correcting, since it eventually goes to a valid state from which it continues to operate as required.

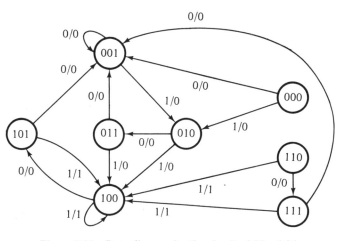

Figure 6-27 State diagram for the circuit of Fig. 6-26

An undesirable situation would have occurred if the next state of 110 for $x = 1$ happened to be 111 and the next state of 111 for $x = 0$ or 1 happened to be 110. Then, if the circuit starts from 110 or 111, it will circulate and stay between these two states forever. Unused states that cause such undesirable behavior should be avoided; if they are found to exist, the circuit should be redesigned. This can be done most easily by specifying a valid next state for any unused state that is found to circulate among invalid states.

6-8 DESIGN OF COUNTERS

A sequential circuit that goes through a prescribed sequence of states upon the application of input pulses is called a *counter*. The input pulses, called *count pulses*, may be clock pulses, or they may originate from an external source and may occur at prescribed intervals of time or at random. In a counter, the sequence of states may follow a binary count or any other sequence of states. Counters are found in almost all equipment containing digital logic. They are used for counting the number of occurrences of an event and are useful for generating timing sequences to control operations in a digital system.

Of the various sequences a counter may follow, the straight binary sequence is the simplest and most straightforward. A counter that follows the binary sequence is called a *binary counter*. An n-bit binary counter consists of n flip-flops and can count in binary from 0 to $2^n - 1$. As an example, the state diagram of a 3-bit counter is shown in Fig. 6-28. As seen from the binary states indicated inside the circles, the flip-flop outputs repeat the binary count sequence with a return to 000 after 111. The directed lines between circles are not marked with input-output values as in other state diagrams. Remember that state transitions in clocked sequential circuits occur during a clock pulse; the flip-flops remain in their present states if no pulse occurs. For this reason, the clock pulse variable *CP* does not

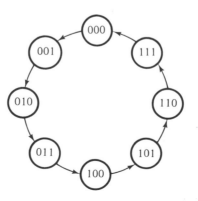

Figure 6-28   State diagram of a 3-bit binary counter

appear explicitly as an input variable in a state diagram or state table. From this point of view, the state diagram of a counter does not have to show input-output values along the directed lines. The only input to the circuit is the count pulse, and the outputs are directly specified by the present states of the flip-flops. The next state of a counter depends entirely on its present state, and the state transition occurs every time the pulse occurs. Because of this property, a counter is completely specified by a list of the *count sequence*, i.e., the sequence of binary states that it undergoes.

The count sequence of a 3-bit binary counter is given in Table 6-12. The next number in the sequence represents the next state reached by the circuit upon the application of a count pulse. The count sequence repeats after it reaches the last value, so that state 000 is the next state after 111. The count sequence gives all the information needed to design the circuit. It is not necessary to list the next states in a separate column because they can be read from the next number in the sequence. The design of counters follows the same procedure as that outlined in Section 6-7, except that the excitation table can be obtained directly from the count sequence.

TABLE 6-12 Excitation table for a 3-bit binary counter

Count sequence			Flip-flop inputs		
A_2	A_1	A_0	TA_2	TA_1	TA_0
0	0	0	0	0	1
0	0	1	0	1	1
0	1	0	0	0	1
0	1	1	1	1	1
1	0	0	0	0	1
1	0	1	0	1	1
1	1	0	0	0	1
1	1	1	1	1	1

Table 6-12 is the excitation table for the 3-bit binary counter. The three flip-flops are given variable designations A_2, A_1, and A_0. Binary counters are most efficiently constructed with T flip-flops (or JK flip-flop with J and K tied together). The flip-flop excitation for the T inputs is derived from the excitation table of the T flip-flop and from inspection of the state transition from a given count (present state) to the next below it (next state). As an illustration, consider the flip-flop input entries for row 001. The present state here is 001 and the next state is 010, which is the next count in the sequence. Comparing these two counts, we note that A_2 goes from 0 to 0; so TA_2 is marked with a 0 because flip-flop A_2 must remain unchanged when a clock pulse occurs. A_1 goes from 0 to 1; so TA_1 is marked with a 1 because this flip-flop must be complemented in the next clock pulse. Similarly, A_0 goes from 1 to 0, indicating that it must be complemented; so TA_0 is marked

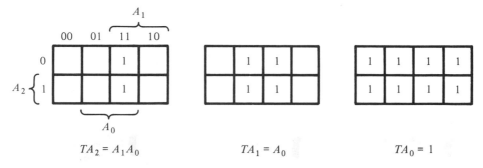

$$TA_2 = A_1 A_0 \qquad\qquad TA_1 = A_0 \qquad\qquad TA_0 = 1$$

Figure 6-29 Maps for a 3-bit binary counter

with a 1. The last row with present state 111 is compared with the first count 000 which is its next state. Going from all 1's to all 0's requires that all three flip-flops be complemented.

The flip-flop input functions from the excitation tables are simplified in the maps of Fig. 6-29. The Boolean functions listed under each map specify the combinational-circuit part of the counter. Including these functions with the three flip-flops, we obtain the logic diagram of the counter as shown in Fig. 6-30.

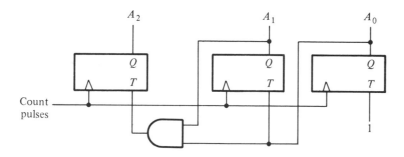

Figure 6-30 Logic diagram of a 3-bit binary counter

A counter with n flip-flops may have a binary sequence of less than 2^n numbers. A BCD counter counts the binary sequence from 0000 to 1001 and returns to 0000 to repeat the sequence. Other counters may follow an arbitrary sequence which may not be the straight binary sequence. In any case, the design procedure is the same. The count sequence is listed and the excitation table is obtained by comparing a present count with the next count listed below it. A tabulated count sequence always assumes a repeated count, so that the next state of the last entry is the first count listed.

EXAMPLE 6-3: Design a counter that has a repeated sequence of six states as listed in Table 6-13.

In this sequence, flip-flops B and C repeat the binary count 00, 01, 10, while flip-flop A alternates between 0 and 1 every three

245

TABLE 6-13 Excitation table for Example 6-3

Count sequence			Flip-flop inputs					
A	B	C	JA	KA	JB	KB	JC	KC
0	0	0	0	X	0	X	1	X
0	0	1	0	X	1	X	X	1
0	1	0	1	X	X	1	0	X
1	0	0	X	0	0	X	1	X
1	0	1	X	0	1	X	X	1
1	1	0	X	1	X	1	0	X

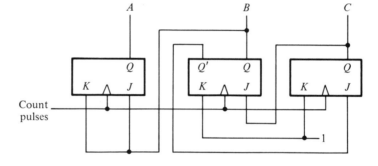

(a) Logic diagram of counter.

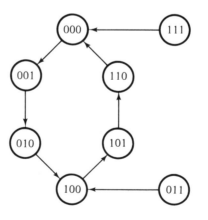

(b) State diagram of counter.

Figure 6-31 Solution to Example 6-3

counts. The count sequence for *A, B, C* is not straight binary and two states, 011 and 111, are not used. The choice of *JK* flip-flops results in the excitation table of Table 6-13. Inputs *KB* and *KC* have only 1's and *X*'s in their columns, so these inputs are always 1. The other flip-flop input functions can be simplified using minterms 3 and 7 as don't-care conditions. The simplified functions are:

$$JA = B \qquad KA = B$$
$$JB = C \qquad KB = 1$$
$$JC = B' \qquad KC = 1$$

The logic diagram of the counter is shown in Fig. 6-31(a). Since there are two unused states, we analyze the circuit to determine their effect. The state diagram so obtained is drawn in Fig. 6-31(b). If the circuit ever goes to an invalid state, the next count pulse transfers it to one of the valid states, and it continues to count correctly. Thus the counter is self-starting. A self-starting counter is one that can start from any state but eventually reaches the normal count sequence.

6-9 DESIGN WITH STATE EQUATIONS

A sequential circuit can be designed by means of state equations rather than an excitation table. As shown in Section 6-4, a state equation is an algebraic expression that gives the conditions for the next state as a function of the present state and input variables. The state equations of a sequential circuit express in algebraic form the same information which is expressed in tabular form in a state table.

The state equation method is convenient when the circuit is already specified in this form or when the state equations are easily derived from the state table. This is the preferred method when *D* flip-flops are used. The method may sometimes be convenient to use with *JK* flip-flops. The application of this procedure to circuits with *RS* or *T* flip-flops is possible but involves a considerable amount of algebraic manipulation. Here we will show the application of this method to sequential circuits employing *D* or *JK* flip-flops. The starting point in each case is the flip-flop characteristic equation derived in Section 6-2.

Sequential Circuits with *D* Flip-flops

The characteristic equation of the *D* flip-flop is derived in Fig. 6-5(d):

$$Q(t + 1) = D$$

This equation states that the next state of the flip-flop is equal to the present value of its D input and is independent of the value of the present state. This means that the entries for the next state in the state table are exactly the same as the D inputs. Therefore, it is not necessary to derive the flip-flop input conditions for the excitation table because this information is already available in the next state columns.

Take, for example, the excitation table of Table 6-10. The next state column for A has four 1's, and so does the column for the next state of B. To design this circuit with D flip-flops, we write the state equations and equate them to the corresponding D inputs:

$$A(t + 1) = DA(A, B, x) = \Sigma(2, 4, 5, 6)$$
$$B(t + 1) = DB(A, B, x) = \Sigma(1, 3, 5, 6)$$

where DA and DB are the flip-flop input functions for D flip-flops A and B, respectively, and each function is expressed as the sum of four minterms. The simplified functions can be obtained by means of two three-variable maps. The simplified flip-flop input functions are:

$$DA = AB' + Bx'$$
$$DB = A'x + B'x + ABx'$$

If there are unused states in the sequential circuit, they must be considered, together with the inputs, as don't-care combinations. The don't-care minterms thus obtained can be used to simplify the state equations of the D flip-flop input functions.

> **EXAMPLE 6-4:** Design a sequential circuit with four flip-flops, A, B, C, and D. The next states of B, C, and D are equal to the present states of A, B, and C, respectively. The next state of A is equal to the exclusive-OR of the present states of C and D.
>
> From the statement of the problem, it is convenient to first write the state equations for the circuit:
>
> $$A(t + 1) = C \oplus D$$
> $$B(t + 1) = A$$
> $$C(t + 1) = B$$
> $$D(t + 1) = C$$
>
> This circuit specifies a *feedback shift register*. In a feedback shift register, each flip-flop transfers or shifts its content to the next flip-flop when a clock pulse occurs, but the next state of the first flip-flop (A in this case) is some function of the present state of other flip-flops. Since the state equations are very simple, the most convenient flip-flop to use is the D type.

The flip-flop input functions for this circuit are taken directly from the state equations, with the next state variable replaced by the flip-flop input variable:

$$DA = C \oplus D$$
$$DB = A$$
$$DC = B$$
$$DD = C$$

The circuit can be constructed with four D flip-flops and one exclusive-OR gate.

State Equations with JK Flip-flops*

The characteristic equation for the JK flip-flop is derived in Fig. 6-6(d):

$$Q(t + 1) = (J)Q' + (K')Q$$

Input variables J and K are enclosed in parentheses so as not to confuse the AND terms of the characteristic equation with the two-letter convention which has been used to represent the flip-flop input variables.

The sequential circuit can be derived directly from the state equations without having to draw the excitation table. This is done by means of a matching process between the state equation for each flip-flop and the general characteristic equation of the JK flip-flop. The matching process consists of manipulating each state equation until it is in the form of the characteristic equation. Once this is done, the functions for inputs J and K can be extracted and simplified. This must be done for each state equation listed, and its flip-flop variable name A, B, C, etc., must replace the letter Q in the characteristic equation.

A given state equation for $Q(t + 1)$ may be already expressed as a function of Q and Q'. More often, either Q or Q' or both would be absent in the Boolean expression. It is then necessary to manipulate the expression algebraically until both Q and Q' are included in the expression. The following example demonstrates all the possibilities that may be encountered.

EXAMPLE 6-5: Design a sequential circuit with JK flip-flops to satisfy the following state equations:

$$A(t + 1) = A'B'CD + A'B'C + ACD + AC'D'$$
$$B(t + 1) = A'C + CD' + A'BC'$$
$$C(t + 1) = B$$
$$D(t + 1) = D'$$

*This part may be omitted without loss of continuity.

The input functions for flip-flop A are derived by this method by arranging the state equation and matching it with the characteristic equation as follows:

$$A(t + 1) = (B'CD + B'C)A' + (CD + C'D')A$$
$$= (J)A' + (K')A$$

From the equality of the two equations, we deduce the input functions for flip-flop A to be:

$$J = B'CD + B'C = B'C$$
$$K = (CD + C'D')' = CD' + C'D$$

The state equation for flip-flop B can be arranged as follows:

$$B(t + 1) = (A'C + CD') + (A'C')B$$

However, this form is not suitable for matching with the characteristic equation because the variable B' is missing. If the first quantity in parentheses is ANDed with $(B' + B)$, the equation remains the same but with the variable B' included. Thus:

$$B(t + 1) = (A'C + CD')(B' + B) + (A'C')B$$
$$= (A'C + CD')B' + (A'C + CD' + A'C')B$$
$$= (J)B' + (K')B$$

From the equality of the two equations, we deduce the input functions for flip-flop B:

$$J = A'C + CD'$$
$$K = (A'C + CD' + A'C')' = AC' + AD$$

The state equation for flip-flop C can be manipulated as follows:

$$C(t + 1) = B = B(C' + C) = BC' + BC$$
$$= (J)C' + (K')C$$

The input functions for flip-flop C are:

$$J = B$$
$$K = B'$$

Finally, the state equation for flip-flop D may be manipulated for the purpose of matching as follows:

$$D(t + 1) = D' = 1.D' + 0.D$$
$$= (J)D' + (K')D$$

REFERENCES *251*

which gives the input function:

$$J = K = 1$$

The derived input functions can be accumulated and listed together. The two-letter convention to designate the flip-flop input variable, not used in the above derivation, is used below:

$$JA = B'C \qquad KA = CD' + C'D$$
$$JB = A'C + CD' \qquad KB = AC' + AD$$
$$JC = B \qquad KC = B'$$
$$JD = 1 \qquad KD = 1$$

The design procedure introduced here is an alternative method for determining the flip-flop input functions of a sequential circuit when JK flip-flops are employed. To use this procedure when a state diagram or state table is initially specified, it is necessary that the state equations be derived by the procedure outlined in Section 6-4. The state-equation method for finding flip-flop input functions can be extended to cover unused states which are considered as don't-care conditions. The don't-care minterms are written in the form of a state equation and manipulated until they are in the form of the characteristic equation for the particular flip-flop considered. The J and K functions in the don't-care state equation are then taken as don't-care minterms when simplifying the input functions for a particular flip-flop.

REFERENCES

1. Marcus, M. P., *Switching Circuits for Engineers*, 3rd ed. Englewood Cliffs, N.J.: Prentice-Hall, 1975.

2. McCluskey, E. J., *Introduction to the Theory of Switching Circuits*. New York: McGraw-Hill Book Co., 1965.

3. Miller, R. E., *Switching Theory*, two volumes. New York: John Wiley and Sons, 1965.

4. Krieger, M., *Basic Switching Circuit Theory*. New York: The Macmillan Co., 1967.

5. Hill, F. J., and G. R. Peterson, *Introduction to Switching Theory and Logical Design*. 3rd ed. New York: John Wiley and Sons, 1981.

6. Givone, D. D., *Introduction to Switching Circuit Theory*. New York: McGraw-Hill Book Co., 1970.

7. Kohavi, Z., *Switching and Finite Automata Theory*, 2nd ed. New York: McGraw-Hill Book Co., 1978.

8. Phister M., *The Logical Design of Digital Computers*. New York: John Wiley and Sons, 1958.

9. Paull, M. C., and S. H. Unger, "Minimizing the Number of States in Incompletely Specified Sequential Switching Functions." *IRE Trans. on Electronic Computers*, Vol. EC-8, No. 3 (September 1959), 356–66.

10. Hartmanis, J., "On the State Assignment Problem for Sequential Machines I." *IRE Trans. on Electronic Computers*, Vol. EC-10, No. 2 (June 1961), 157–65.

11. McCluskey, E. J., and S. H. Unger, "A Note on the Number of Internal Assignments for Sequential Circuits." *IRE Trans. on Electronic Computer*, Vol. EC-8, No. 4 (December 1959), 439–40.

PROBLEMS

6-1. Show the logic diagram of a clocked *RS* flip-flop with four NAND gates.

6-2. Show the logic diagram of a clocked *D* flip-flop with AND and NOR gates.

6-3. Show that the clocked *D* flip-flop of Fig. 6-5(a) can be reduced by one gate.

6-4. Consider a *JK'* flip-flop, i.e., a *JK* flip-flop with an inverter between external input *K'* and internal input *K*.
    (a) Obtain the flip-flop characteristic table.
    (b) Obtain the characteristic equation.
    (c) Show that tying the two external inputs together forms a *D* flip-flop.

6-5. A set-dominate flip-flop has a set and a reset input. It differs from a conventional *RS* flip-flop in that an attempt to simultaneously set and reset results in setting the flip-flop.
    (a) Obtain the characteristic table and characteristic equation for the set-dominate flip-flop.
    (b) Obtain a logic diagram for an asynchronous set-dominate flip-flop.

6-6. Obtain the logic diagram of a master-slave *JK* flip-flop with AND and NOR gates. Include a provision for setting and clearing the flip-flop asynchronously (without a clock).

6-7. This problem investigates the operation of the master-slave *JK* flip-flop through the binary transition in the internal gates of Fig. 6-11. Evaluate the binary values (0 or 1) in the outputs of the nine gates when the inputs to the circuit go through the following sequence:
    (a) $CP = 0$, $Y = 0$, $Q = 0$, and $J = K = 1$.
    (b) After CP goes to 1 (Y should go to 1; Q remains at 0).
    (c) After CP goes to 0 and immediately after that J goes to 0 (Q should go to 1; Y is unaffected).
    (d) After CP goes to 1 again (Y should go to 0).
    (e) After CP goes back to 0 and immediately after that K goes to 0 (Q should go to 0).
    (f) All succeeding pulses have no effect as long as J and K remain at 0.

6-8. Draw the logic diagram (showing all gates) of a master-slave *D* flip-flop. Use NAND gates.

6-9. Connect an asynchronous clear terminal to the inputs of gates 2 and 6 of the flip-flop in Fig. 6-12.

(a) Show that when the clear input is 0, the flip-flop is cleared, and remains cleared, regardless of the values of *CP* and *D* inputs.

(b) Show that when the clear input is 1, it has no effect on the normal clocked operations.

6-10. The full-adder of Fig. P6-10 receives two external inputs x and y; the third input z comes from the output of a *D* flip-flop. The carry output is transferred to the flip-flop every clock pulse. The external *S* output gives the sum of x, y, and z. Obtain the state table and state diagram of the sequential circuit.

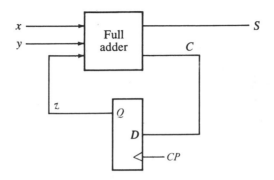

Figure P6-10

6-11. Derive the state table and state diagram of the sequential circuit of Fig. P6-11. What is the function of the circuit?

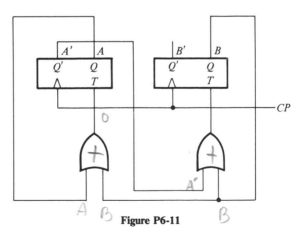

Figure P6-11

6-12. A sequential circuit has four flip-flops *A*, *B*, *C*, *D* and an input x. It is described by the following state equations:

$$A(t + 1) = (CD' + C'D)x + (CD + C'D')x'$$
$$B(t + 1) = A$$
$$C(t + 1) = B$$
$$D(t + 1) = C$$

(a) Obtain the sequence of states when $x = 1$, starting from state $ABCD = 0001$.

(b) Obtain the sequence of states when $x = 0$, starting from state $ABCD = 0000$.

6-13. A sequential circuit has two flip-flops (A and B), two inputs (x and y), and an output (z). The flip-flop input functions and the circuit output function are as follows:

$$JA = xB + y'B' \qquad KA = xy'B'$$
$$JB = xA' \qquad KB = xy' + A$$
$$z = xyA + x'y'B$$

Obtain the logic diagram, state table, state diagram, and state equations.

6-14. Reduce the number of states in the following state table and tabulate the reduced state table.

Present state	Next state		Output	
	$x = 0$	$x = 1$	$x = 0$	$x = 1$
a	f	b	0	0
b	d	c	0	0
c	f	e	0	0
d	g	a	1	0
e	d	c	0	0
f	f	b	1	1
g	g	h	0	1
h	g	a	1	0

6-15. Starting from state a of the state table in problem 6-14, find the output sequence generated with an input sequence 01110010011.

6-16. Repeat problem 6-15 using the reduced table of problem 6-14. Show that the same output sequence is obtained.

6-17. Substitute binary assignment 2 of Table 6-5 to the states in Table 6-4 and obtain the binary state table. Repeat with binary assignment 3.

6-18. Obtain the excitation table of the JK' flip-flop described in problem 6-4.

6-19. Obtain the excitation table of the set-dominate flip-flop described in problem 6-5.

6-20. A sequential circuit has one input and one output. The state diagram is shown in Fig. P6-20. Design the sequential circuit with (a) T flip-flops, (b) RS flip-flops, and (c) JK flip-flops.

6-21. Design the circuit of a 4-bit register that converts the binary number stored in the register to its 2's complement value when input $x = 1$. The flip-flops of the register are of the RST type. This flip-flop has three inputs: two inputs have RS capabilities and one has a T capability. The RS inputs are used to transfer the 4-bit number when an input $y = 1$. Use the T input for the conversion.

6-22. Repeat Example 6-1 with binary assignment 3 of Table 6-5. Use JK flip-flops.

6-23. Design a BCD counter with JK flip-flops.

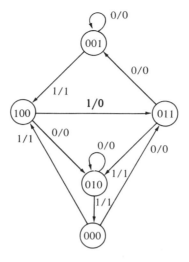

Figure P6-20

6-24. Design a counter that counts the decimal digits according to the 2, 4, 2, 1 code (Table 1-2). Use T flip-flops.

6-25. Design the binary counters having the following repeated binary sequence. Use JK flip-flops.
    (a) 0, 1, 2
    (b) 0, 1, 2, 3, 4
    (c) 0, 1, 2, 3, 4, 5, 6

6-26. Design a counter with the following binary sequence: 0, 1, 3, 2, 6, 4, 5, 7 and repeat. Use RS flip-flops.

6-27. Design a counter with the following binary sequence: 0, 1, 3, 7, 6, 4 and repeat. Use T flip-flops.

6-28. Design a counter with the following binary sequence: 0, 4, 2, 1, 6 and repeat. Use JK flip-flops.

6-29. Repeat Example 6-5 using D flip-flops.

6-30. Verify the circuit obtained in Example 6-5 by using the excitation table method.

6-31. Design the sequential circuit described by the following state equations. Use JK flip-flops.
$$A(t + 1) = xAB + yA'C + xy$$
$$B(t + 1) = xAC + y'BC'$$
$$C(t + 1) = x'B + yAB'$$

6-32. (a) Derive the state equations for the sequential circuit specified by Table 6-6, Section 6-5. List the don't-care terms. (b) Derive the flip-flop input functions from the state equations (and don't-care terms) using the method outlined in Example 6-5. Use JK flip-flops.

Registers, Counters, and the Memory Unit

7

7-1 INTRODUCTION

A clocked sequential circuit consists of a group of flip-flops and combinational gates connected to form a feedback path. The flip-flops are essential because, in their absence, the circuit reduces to a purely combinational circuit (provided there is no feedback path). A circuit with only flip-flops is considered a sequential circuit even in the absence of combinational gates.

An MSI circuit that contains storage cells within it is, by definition, a sequential circuit. MSI circuits that include flip-flops or other storage cells are usually classified by the function they perform rather than by the name "sequential circuit." These MSI circuits are classified in one of three categories: registers, counters, or random-access memory. This chapter presents various registers and counters available in IC form and explains their operation. The organization of the random-access memory is also presented.

A *register* is a group of binary storage cells suitable for holding binary information. A group of flip-flops constitutes a register, since each flip-flop is a binary cell capable of storing one bit of information. An *n*-bit register has a group of *n* flip-flops and is capable of storing any binary information containing *n* bits. In addition to the flip-flops, a register may have combinational gates that perform certain data-processing tasks. In its broadest definition, a register consists of a group of flip-flops and gates that effect their transition. The flip-flops hold binary information and the gates control when and how new information is transferred into the register.

Counters were introduced in Section 6-8. A counter is essentially a register that goes through a predetermined sequence of states upon the application of input pulses. The gates in a counter are connected in such a way as to produce a prescribed sequence of binary states in the register. Although counters are a special type of register, it is common to differentiate them by giving them a special name.

A memory unit is a collection of storage cells together with associated circuits needed to transfer information in and out of storage. A random-access memory

(RAM) differs from a read-only memory (ROM) in that a RAM can transfer the stored information out (read) and is also capable of receiving new information in for storage (write). A more appropriate name for such a memory would be *read-write memory*.

Registers, counters, and memories are extensively used in the design of digital systems in general and digital computers in particular. Registers can also be used to facilitate the design of sequential circuits. Counters are useful for generating timing variables to sequence and control the operations in a digital system. Memories are essential for storage of programs and data in a digital computer. Knowledge of the operation of these components is indispensable for the understanding of the organization and design of digital systems.

7-2 REGISTERS

Various types of registers are available in MSI circuits. The simplest possible register is one that consists of only flip-flops without any external gates. Figure 7-1 shows such a register constructed with four D-type flip-flops and a common clock pulse input. The clock pulse input, CP, enables all flip-flops so that the information presently available at the four inputs can be transferred into the 4-bit register. The four outputs can be sampled to obtain the information presently stored in the register.

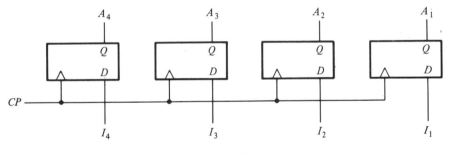

Figure 7-1 4-bit register

The way that the flip-flops in a register are triggered is of primary importance. If the flip-flops are constructed with gated D-type latches as in Fig. 6-5, then information present at a data (D) input is transferred to the Q output when the enable (CP) is 1, and the Q output follows the input data as long as the CP signal remains 1. When CP goes to 0, the information that was present at the data input just before the transition is retained at the Q output. In other words, the flip-flops are sensitive to the pulse duration, and the register is enabled for as long as $CP = 1$. A register that responds to the pulse duration is commonly called a *gated latch*, and the CP input is frequently labeled with the variable G (instead of CP). Latches are suitable for use as temporary storage of binary information that is to be transferred to an external destination. They should not be used in the design of sequential circuits that have feedback connections.

As explained in Section 6-3, a flip-flop can be used in the design of clocked sequential circuits provided it is sensitive to the pulse transition rather than the pulse duration. This means that the flip-flops in the register must be of the edge-triggered or master-slave type. Normally, it is not possible to distinguish from a logic diagram whether a flip-flop is a gated latch, edge-triggered, or master-slave, because the graphic symbols for all three are the same. The distinction must be made from the name given to the unit. A group of flip-flops sensitive to pulse duration is usually called a *latch*, whereas a group of flip-flops sensitive to pulse transition is called a *register*.* A register can always replace a latch, but the converse should be done with caution to make sure that outputs from a latch never go to other flip-flop inputs that are triggered with the same common clock pulse. In subsequent discussions, we will always assume that any group of flip-flops drawn constitutes a *register* and that all flip-flops are of the edge-triggered or master-slave type. If the register is sensitive to the pulse duration, it will be referred to as a *latch*.

Register with Parallel Load

The transfer of new information into a register is referred to as *loading* the register. If all the bits of the register are loaded simultaneously with a single clock pulse, we say that the loading is done in parallel. A pulse applied to the *CP* input of the register of Fig. 7-1 will load all four inputs in parallel. In this configuration, the clock pulse must be inhibited from the *CP* terminal if the content of the register must be left unchanged. In other words, the *CP* input acts as an enable signal which controls the loading of new information into the register. When *CP* goes to 1, the input information is loaded into the register. If *CP* remains at 0, the content of the register is not changed. Note that the change of state in the outputs occurs at the positive edge of the pulse. If a flip-flop changes state at the negative edge, there will be a small circle under the triangle symbol in the *CP* input of the flip-flop.

Most digital systems have a master-clock generator that supplies a continuous train of clock pulses. All clock pulses are applied to all flip-flops and registers in the system. The master-clock generator acts like a pump that supplies a constant beat to all parts of the system. A separate control signal then decides what specific clock pulses will have an effect on a particular register. In such a system, the clock pulses must be ANDed with the control signal, and the output of the AND gate is then applied to the *CP* terminal of the register shown in Fig. 7-1. When the control signal is 0, the output of the AND gate is 0, and the stored information in the register remains unchanged. Only when the control signal is a 1 does the clock pulse pass through the AND gate and into the *CP* terminal for new information to be loaded into the register. Such a control variable is called a *load* control input.

*For example, IC type 7475 is a 4-bit latch, whereas type 74175 is a 4-bit register.

Inserting an AND gate in the path of clock pulses means that logic is performed with clock pulses. The insertion of logic gates produces propagation delays between the master-clock generator and the clock inputs of flip-flops. To fully synchronize the system, we must ensure that all clock pulses arrive at the same time to all inputs of all flip-flops so that they can all change simultaneously. Performing logic with clock pulses inserts variable delays and may throw the system out of synchronism. For this reason, it is advisable (but not necessary, as long as the delays are taken into consideration) to apply clock pulses directly to all flip-flops and control the operation of the register with other inputs, such as the R and S inputs of an RS flip-flop.

A 4-bit register with a load control input using RS flip-flops is shown in Fig. 7-2. The CP input of the register receives continuous synchronized pulses which are applied to all flip-flops. The inverter in the CP path causes all flip-flops to be triggered by the negative edge of the incoming pulses. The purpose of the inverter

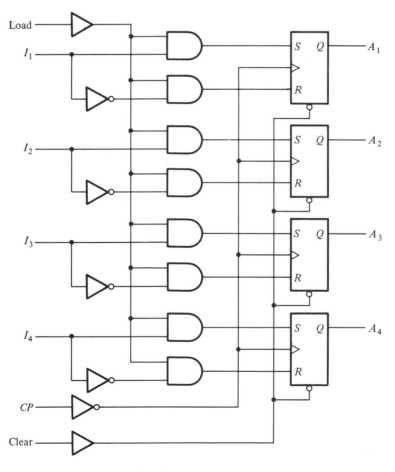

Figure 7-2 4-bit register with parallel load

is to reduce the loading of the master-clock generator. This is because the *CP* input is connected to only one gate (the inverter) instead of the four-gate inputs that would have been required if the connections were made directly into the flip-flop clock inputs (marked with small triangles).

The *clear* input goes to a special terminal in each flip-flop through a noninverting buffer gate. When this terminal goes to 0, the flip-flop is cleared asynchronously. The clear input is useful for clearing the register to all 0's prior to its clocked operation. The clear input must be maintained at 1 during normal clocked operations (see Fig. 6-14).

The *load* input goes through a buffer gate (to reduce loading) and through a series of AND gates to the *R* and *S* inputs of each flip-flop. Although clock pulses

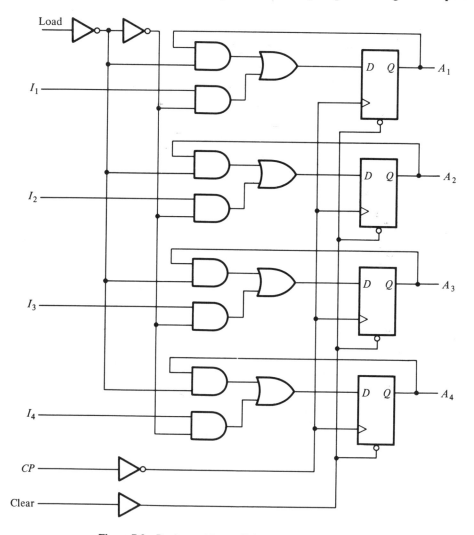

Figure 7-3   Register with parallel load using *D* flip-flops

are continuously present, it is the load input that controls the operation of the register. The two AND gates and the inverter associated with each input I determine the values of R and S. If the load input is 0, both R and S are 0, and no change of state occurs with any clock pulse. Thus, the load input is a control variable which can prevent any information change in the register as long as its input is 0. When the load control goes to 1, inputs I_1 through I_4 specify what binary information is loaded into the register on the next clock pulse. For each I that is equal to 1, the corresponding flip-flop inputs are $S = 1$, $R = 0$. For each I that is equal to 0, the corresponding flip-flop inputs are $S = 0$, $R = 1$. Thus, the input value is transferred into the register provided the load input is 1, the clear input is 1, and a clock pulse goes from 1 to 0. This type of transfer is called a *parallel-load* transfer because all bits of the register are loaded simultaneously. If the buffer gate associated with the load input is changed to an inverter gate, then the register is loaded when the load input is 0 and inhibited when the load input is 1.

A register with parallel load can be constructed with D flip-flops as shown in Fig. 7-3. The clock and clear inputs are the same as before. When the load input is 1, the I inputs are transferred into the register on the next clock pulse. When the load input is 0, the circuit inputs are inhibited and the D flip-flops are reloaded with their present value, thus maintaining the content of the register. The feedback connection in each flip-flop is necessary when D type is used because a D flip-flop does not have a "no-change" input condition. With each clock pulse, the D input determines the next state of the output. To leave the output unchanged, it is necessary to make the D input equal to the present Q output in each flip-flop.

Sequential Logic Implementation

We saw in Chapter 6 that a clocked sequential circuit consists of a group of flip-flops and combinational gates. Since registers are readily available as MSI circuits, it becomes convenient at times to employ a register as part of the sequential circuit. A block diagram of a sequential circuit that uses a register is shown in Fig. 7-4. The present state of the register and the external inputs determine the next state of the register and the values of external outputs. Part of

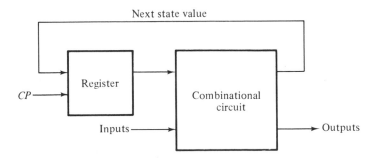

Figure 7-4 Block diagram of a sequential circuit

the combinational circuit determines the next state and the other part generates the outputs. The next state value from the combinational circuit is loaded into the register with a clock pulse. If the register has a load input, it must be set to 1; otherwise, if the register has no load input (as in Fig. 7-1), the next state value will be transferred automatically every clock pulse.

The combinational circuit part of a sequential circuit can be implemented by any of the methods discussed in Chapter 5. It can be constructed with SSI gates, with ROM, or with a programmable logic array (PLA). By using a register, it is possible to reduce the design of a sequential circuit to that of a combinational circuit connected to a register.

EXAMPLE 7-1: Design the sequential circuit whose state table is listed in Fig. 7-5(a).

The state table specifies two flip-flops A_1 and A_2, one input x, and one output y. The next state and output information is obtained directly from the table:

$$A_1(t + 1) = \Sigma(4, 6)$$
$$A_2(t + 1) = \Sigma(1, 2, 5, 6)$$
$$y(A_1, A_2, x) = \Sigma(3, 7)$$

The minterm values are for variables A_1, A_2, and x, which are the present state and input variables. The functions for the next state and output can be simplified by means of maps to give:

$$A_1(t + 1) = A_1 x'$$
$$A_2(t + 1) = A_2 \oplus x$$
$$y = A_2 x$$

The logic diagram is shown in Fig. 7-5(b).

Present state A_1	A_2	Input x	Next state A_1	A_2	Output y
0	0	0	0	0	0
0	0	1	0	1	0
0	1	0	0	1	0
0	1	1	0	0	1
1	0	0	1	0	0
1	0	1	0	1	0
1	1	0	1	1	0
1	1	1	0	0	1

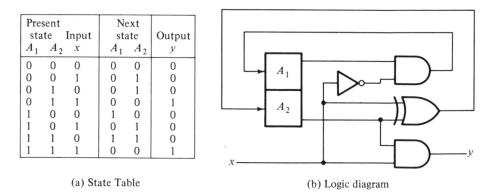

(a) State Table   (b) Logic diagram

Figure 7-5   Example of sequential-circuit implementation

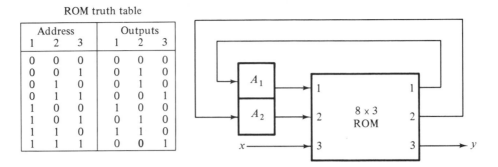

ROM truth table

Address			Outputs		
1	2	3	1	2	3
0	0	0	0	0	0
0	0	1	0	1	0
0	1	0	0	1	0
0	1	1	0	0	1
1	0	0	1	0	0
1	0	1	0	1	0
1	1	0	1	1	0
1	1	1	0	0	1

Figure 7-6 Sequential circuit using a register and a ROM

EXAMPLE 7-2: Repeat Example 7-1, but now use a ROM and a register.

The ROM can be used to implement the combinational circuit and the register will provide the flip-flops. The number of inputs to the ROM is equal to the number of flip-flops plus the number of external inputs. The number of outputs of the ROM is equal to the number of flip-flops plus the number of external outputs. In this case we have three inputs and three outputs for the ROM; so its size must be 8 × 3. The implementation is shown in Fig. 7-6. The ROM truth table is identical to the state table with "present state" and "inputs" specifying the address of ROM and "next state" and "outputs" specifying the ROM outputs. The next state values must be connected from the ROM outputs to the register inputs.

7-3 SHIFT REGISTERS

A register capable of shifting its binary information either to the right or to the left is called a *shift register*. The logical configuration of a shift register consists of a chain of flip-flops connected in cascade, with the output of one flip-flop connected to the input of the next flip-flop. All flip-flops receive a common clock pulse which causes the shift from one stage to the next.

The simplest possible shift register is one that uses only flip-flops, as shown in Fig. 7-7. The Q output of a given flip-flop is connected to the D input of the flip-flop at its right. Each clock pulse shifts the contents of the register one bit position to the right. The *serial input* determines what goes into the leftmost flip-flop during the shift. The *serial output* is taken from the output of the rightmost flip-flop prior to the application of a pulse. Although this register shifts its contents to the right, if we turn the page upside down, we find that the register shifts its contents to the left. Thus a unidirectional shift register can function either as a shift-right or as a shift-left register.

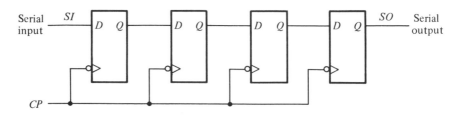

Figure 7-7 Shift register

The register in Fig. 7-7 shifts its contents with every clock pulse during the negative edge of the pulse transition. (This is indicated by the small circle associated with the clock input in all flip-flops.) If we want to control the shift so that it occurs only with certain pulses but not with others, we must control the *CP* input of the register. It will be shown later that the shift operations can be controlled through the *D* inputs of the flip-flops rather than through the *CP* input. If, however, the shift register in Fig. 7-7 is used, the shift can easily be controlled by means of an external AND gate as shown below.

Serial Transfer

A digital system is said to operate in a serial mode when information is transferred and manipulated one bit at a time. The content of one register is transferred to another by shifting the bits from one register to the other. The information is transferred one bit at a time by shifting the bits out of the source register into the destination register.

The serial transfer of information from register *A* to register *B* is done with shift registers, as shown in the block diagram of Fig. 7-8(a). The serial output (*SO*) of register *A* goes to the serial input (*SI*) of register *B*. To prevent the loss of information stored in the source register, the *A* register is made to circulate its information by connecting the serial output to its serial input terminal. The initial content of register *B* is shifted out through its serial output and is lost unless it is transferred to a third shift register. The shift-control input determines when and by how many times the registers are shifted. This is done by the AND gate that allows clock pulses to pass into the *CP* terminals only when the shift-control is 1.

Suppose the shift registers have four bits each. The control unit that supervises the transfer must be designed in such a way that it enables the shift registers, through the shift-control signal, for a fixed time duration equal to four clock pulses. This is shown in the timing diagram of Fig. 7-8(b). The shift-control signal is synchronized with the clock and changes value just after the negative edge of a clock pulse. The next four clock pulses find the shift-control signal in the 1 state, so the output of the AND gate connected to the *CP* terminals produces the four pulses T_1, T_2, T_3, and T_4. The fourth pulse changes the shift control to 0 and the shift registers are disabled.

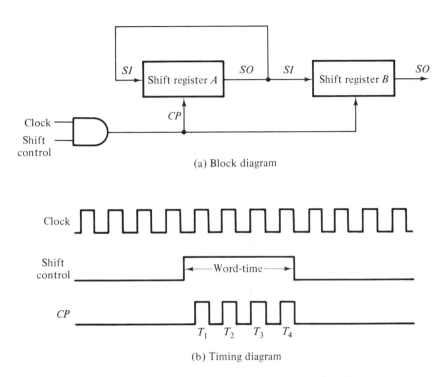

(a) Block diagram

(b) Timing diagram

Figure 7-8 Serial transfer from register A to register B

Assume that the binary content of A before the shift is 1011 and that of B, 0010. The serial transfer from A to B will occur in four steps as shown in Table 7-1. After the first pulse T_1, the rightmost bit of A is shifted into the leftmost bit of B and, at the same time, this bit is circulated into the leftmost position of A. The other bits of A and B are shifted once to the right. The previous serial output from B is lost and its value changes from 0 to 1. The next three pulses perform identical operations, shifting the bits of A into B, one at a time. After the fourth shift, the shift control goes to 0 and both registers A and B have the value 1011. Thus, the content of A is transferred into B while the content of A remains unchanged.

TABLE 7-1 Serial transfer example

Timing pulse	Shift register A				Shift register B				Serial output of B
Initial value	1	0	1	1	0	0	1	0	0
After T_1	1	1	0	1	1	0	0	1	1
After T_2	1	1	1	0	1	1	0	0	0
After T_3	0	1	1	1	0	1	1	0	0
After T_4	1	0	1	1	1	0	1	1	1

The difference between serial and parallel modes of operation should be apparent from this example. In the parallel mode, information is available from all bits of a register and all bits can be transferred simultaneously during one clock pulse. In the serial mode, the registers have a single serial input and a single serial output. The information is transferred one bit at a time while the registers are shifted in the same direction.

Computers may operate in a serial mode, a parallel mode, or in a combination of both. Serial operations are slower because of the time it takes to transfer information in and out of shift registers. Serial computers, however, require less hardware to perform operations because one common circuit can be used over and over again to manipulate the bits coming out of shift registers in a sequential manner. The time interval between clock pulses is called the *bit time*, and the time required to shift the entire contents of a shift register is called the *word time*. These timing sequences are generated by the control section of the system. In a parallel computer, control signals are enabled during one clock pulse interval. Transfers into registers are in parallel, and they occur upon application of a single clock pulse. In a serial computer, control signals must be maintained for a period equal to one word time. The pulse applied every bit time transfers the result of the operation, one at a time, into a shift register. Most computers operate in a parallel mode because this is a faster mode of operation.

Bidirectional Shift Register with Parallel Load

Shift registers can be used for converting serial data to parallel data, and vice versa. If we have access to all the flip-flop outputs of a shift register, then information entered serially by shifting can be taken out in parallel from the outputs of the flip-flops. If a parallel load capability is added to a shift register, then data entered in parallel can be taken out in serial fashion by shifting the data stored in the register.

Some shift registers provide the necessary input and output terminals for parallel transfer. They may also have both shift-right and shift-left capabilities. The most general shift register has all the capabilities listed below. Others may have only some of these functions, with at least one shift operation.

1. A *clear* control to clear the register to 0.

2. A *CP* input for clock pulses to synchronize all operations.

3. A *shift-right* control to enable the shift-right operation and the *serial input* and *output* lines associated with the shift-right.

4. A *shift-left* control to enable the shift-left operation and the *serial input* and *output* lines associated with the shift-left.

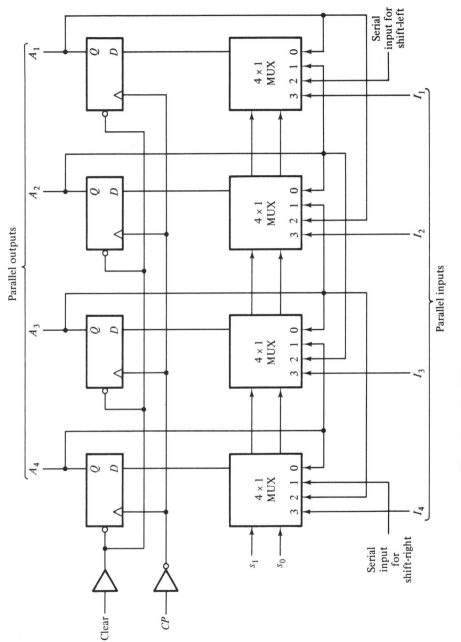

Figure 7-9 4-bit bidirectional shift register with parallel load

5. A *parallel-load* control to enable a parallel transfer and the n input lines associated with the parallel transfer.

6. n parallel output lines.

7. A control state that leaves the information in the register unchanged even though clock pulses are continuously applied.

A register capable of shifting both right and left is called a *bidirectional shift register*. One that can shift in only one direction is called a *unidirectional shift register*. If the register has both shift and parallel-load capabilities, it is called a *shift register with parallel load*.

The diagram of a shift register that has all the capabilities listed above is shown in Fig. 7-9.* It consists of four D flip-flops, although RS flip-flops could be used provided an inverter is inserted between the S and R terminals. The four multiplexers (MUX) are part of the register and are drawn here in block diagram form. (See Fig. 5-16 for the logic diagram of the multiplexer.) The four multiplexers have two common selection variables, s_1 and s_0. Input 0 in each MUX is selected when $s_1 s_0 = 00$, input 1 is selected when $s_1 s_0 = 01$, and similarly for the other two inputs to the multiplexers.

The s_1 and s_0 inputs control the mode of operation of the register as specified in the function entries of Table 7-2. When $s_1 s_0 = 00$, the present value of the register is applied to the D inputs of the flip-flops. This condition forms a path from the output of each flip-flop into the input of the same flip-flop. The next clock pulse transfers into each flip-flop the binary value it held previously, and no change of state occurs. When $s_1 s_0 = 01$, terminals 1 of the multiplexer inputs have a path to the D inputs of the flip-flops. This causes a shift-right operation, with the serial input transferred into flip-flop A_4. When $s_1 s_0 = 10$, a shift-left operation results, with the other serial input going into flip-flop A_1. Finally, when $s_1 s_0 = 11$, the binary information on the parallel input lines is transferred into the register simultaneously during the next clock pulse.

TABLE 7-2   Function table for the register of Fig. 7-9

Mode control		Register operation
s_1	s_0	
0	0	No change
0	1	Shift right
1	0	Shift left
1	1	Parallel load

*This is similar to IC type 74194.

A bidirectional shift register with parallel load is a general-purpose register capable of performing three operations: shift left, shift right, and parallel load. Not all shift registers available in MSI circuits have all these capabilities. The particular application dictates the choice of one MSI shift register over another.

Serial Addition

Operations in digital computers are mostly done in parallel because this is a faster mode of operation. Serial operations are slower but require less equipment. To demonstrate the serial mode of operation, we present here the design of a serial adder. The parallel counterpart was discussed in Section 5-2.

The two binary numbers to be added serially are stored in two shift registers. Bits are added one pair at a time, sequentially, through a single full-adder (FA) circuit, as shown in Fig. 7-10. The carry out of the full-adder is transferred to a D flip-flop. The output of this flip-flop is then used as an input carry for the next pair of significant bits. The two shift registers are shifted to the right for one word-time period. The sum bits from the S output of the full-adder could be transferred into a third shift register. By shifting the sum into A while the bits of A are shifted out, it is possible to use one register for storing both the augend and the sum bits. The serial input (SI) of register B is able to receive a new binary number while the addend bits are shifted out during the addition.

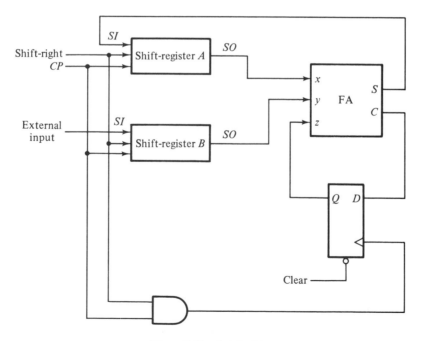

Figure 7-10   Serial adder

The operation of the serial adder is as follows. Initially, the A register holds the augend, the B register holds the addend, and the carry flip-flop is cleared to 0. The serial outputs (SO) of A and B provide a pair of significant bits for the full-adder at x and y. Output Q of the flip-flop gives the input carry at z. The shift-right control enables both registers and the carry flip-flop; so at the next clock pulse, both registers are shifted once to the right, the sum bit from S enters the leftmost flip-flop of A, and the output carry is transferred into flip-flop Q. The shift-right control enables the registers for a number of clock pulses equal to the number of bits in the registers. For each succeeding clock pulse, a new sum bit is transferred to A, a new carry is transferred to Q, and both registers are shifted once to the right. This process continues until the shift-right control is disabled. Thus, the addition is accomplished by passing each pair of bits together with the previous carry through a single full-adder circuit and transferring the sum, one bit at a time, into register A.

If a new number has to be added to the contents of register A, this number must be first transferred serially into register B. Repeating the process once more will add the second number to the previous number in A.

Comparing the serial adder with the parallel adder described in Section 5-2, we note the following differences. The parallel adder must use registers with parallel-load capability, whereas the serial adder uses shift registers. The number of full-adder circuits in the parallel adder is equal to the number of bits in the binary numbers, whereas the serial adder requires only one full-adder circuit and a carry flip-flop. Excluding the registers, the parallel adder is a purely combinational circuit, whereas the serial adder is a sequential circuit. The sequential circuit in the serial adder consists of a full-adder circuit and a flip-flop that stores the output carry. This is typical in serial operations because the result of a bit-time operation may depend not only on the present inputs but also on previous inputs.

To show that bit-time operations in serial computers may require a sequential circuit, we will redesign the serial adder by considering it a sequential circuit.

> *EXAMPLE 7-3:* Design a serial adder using a sequential-logic procedure.
>
> First, we must stipulate that two shift registers are available to store the binary numbers to be added serially. The serial outputs from the registers are designated by variables x and y. The sequential circuit to be designed will not include the shift registers; they will be inserted later to show the complete unit. The sequential circuit proper has two inputs, x and y, that provide a pair of significant bits, an output S that generates the sum bit, and flip-flop Q for storing the carry. The present state of Q provides the present value of the carry. The clock pulse that shifts the registers enables flip-flop Q to load the next carry. This carry is then used with the next pair of bits in x and y. The state table that specifies the sequential circuit is given in Table 7-3.

TABLE 7-3   Excitation table for a serial adder

Present state	Inputs		Next state	Output	Flip-flop inputs	
Q	x	y	Q	S	JQ	KQ
0	0	0	0	0	0	X
0	0	1	0	1	0	X
0	1	0	0	1	0	X
0	1	1	1	0	1	X
1	0	0	0	1	X	1
1	0	1	1	0	X	0
1	1	0	1	0	X	0
1	1	1	1	1	X	0

The present state of Q is the present value of the carry. The present carry in Q is added together with inputs x and y to produce the sum bit in output S. The next state of Q is equivalent to the output carry. Note that the state table entries are identical to the entries in a full-adder truth table, except that the input carry is now the present state of Q and the output carry is now the next state of Q.

If we use a D flip-flop for Q, we obtain the same circuit as in Fig. 7-10 because the input requirements of the D input are the same as the next state values. If we use a JK flip-flop for Q, we obtain the input excitation requirements listed in Table 7-3. The three Boolean functions of interest are the flip-flop input functions for JQ and KQ and output S. These functions are specified in the excitation table

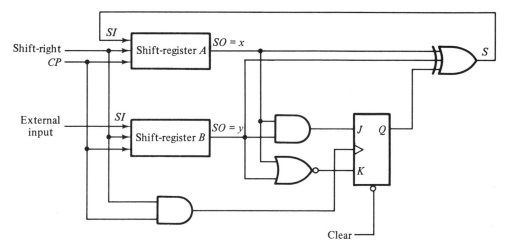

Figure 7-11   Second form of a serial adder

271

and can be simplified by means of maps:

$$JQ = xy$$
$$KQ = x'y' = (x + y)'$$
$$S = x \oplus y \oplus Q$$

As shown in Fig. 7-11, the circuit consists of three gates and a JK flip-flop. The two shift registers are also included in the diagram to show the complete serial adder. Note that output S is a function not only of x and y but also of the present state of Q. The next state of Q is a function of the present values of x and y that come out of the serial outputs of the shift registers.

7-4 RIPPLE COUNTERS

MSI counters come in two categories: ripple counters and synchronous counters. In a ripple counter, the flip-flop output transition serves as a source for triggering other flip-flops. In other words, the CP inputs of all flip-flops (except the first) are triggered not by the incoming pulses but rather by the transition that occurs in other flip-flops. In a synchronous counter, the input pulses are applied to all CP inputs of all flip-flops. The change of state of a particular flip-flop is dependent on the present state of other flip-flops. Synchronous MSI counters are discussed in the next section. Here we present some common MSI ripple counters and explain their operation.

Binary Ripple Counter

A binary ripple counter consists of a series connection of complementing flip-flops (T or JK type), with the output of each flip-flop connected to the CP input of the next higher-order flip-flop. The flip-flop holding the least significant bit receives the incoming count pulses. The diagram of a 4-bit binary ripple counter is shown in Fig. 7-12. All J and K inputs are equal to 1. The small circle in the CP input indicates that the flip-flop complements during a negative-going transition or when

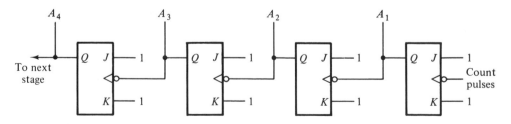

Figure 7-12 4-bit binary ripple counter

TABLE 7-4 Count sequence for a binary ripple counter

Count sequence				Conditions for complementing flip-flops	
A_4	A_3	A_2	A_1		
0	0	0	0	Complement A_1	
0	0	0	1	Complement A_1	A_1 will go from 1 to 0 and complement A_2
0	0	1	0	Complement A_1	
0	0	1	1	Complement A_1	A_1 will go from 1 to 0 and complement A_2; A_2 will go from 1 to 0 and complement A_3
0	1	0	0	Complement A_1	
0	1	0	1	Complement A_1	A_1 will go from 1 to 0 and complement A_2
0	1	1	0	Complement A_1	
0	1	1	1	Complement A_1	A_1 will go from 1 to 0 and complement A_2; A_2 will go from 1 to 0 and complement A_3; A_3 will go from 1 to 0 and complement A_4
1	0	0	0	and so on . . .	

the output to which it is connected goes from 1 to 0. To understand the operation of the binary counter, refer to its count sequence given in Table 7-4. It is obvious that the lowest-order bit A_1 must be complemented with each count pulse. Every time A_1 goes from 1 to 0, it complements A_2. Every time A_2 goes from 1 to 0, it complements A_3, and so on. For example, take the transition from count 0111 to 1000. The arrows in the table emphasize the transitions in this case. A_1 is complemented with the count pulse. Since A_1 goes from 1 to 0, it triggers A_2 and complements it. As a result, A_2 goes from 1 to 0, which in turn complements A_3. A_3 now goes from 1 to 0, which complements A_4. The output transition of A_4, if connected to a next stage, will not trigger the next flip-flop since it goes from 0 to 1. The flip-flops change one at a time in rapid succession, and the signal propagates through the counter in a *ripple* fashion. Ripple counters are sometimes called *asynchronous counters*.

A binary counter with a reverse count is called a binary *down-counter*. In a down-counter, the binary count is decremented by 1 with every input count pulse. The count of a 4-bit down-counter starts from binary 15 and continues to binary counts 14, 13, 12, . . . , 0 and then back to 15. The circuit of Fig. 7-12 will function as a binary down-counter if the outputs are taken from the complement terminals Q' of all flip-flops. If only the normal outputs of flip-flops are available, the circuit must be modified slightly as described below.

A list of the count sequence of a count-down binary counter shows that the lowest-order bit must be complemented with every count pulse. Any other bit in the sequence is complemented if its previous lower-order bit goes from 0 to 1. Therefore, the diagram of a binary down-counter looks the same as in Fig. 7-12, provided all flip-flops trigger on the positive edge of the pulse. (The small circles in the *CP* inputs must be absent.) If negative-edge-triggered flip-flops are used, then the *CP* input of each flip-flop must be connected to the Q' output of the previous flip-flop. Then when Q goes from 0 to 1, Q' will go from 1 to 0 and complement the next flip-flop as required.

BCD Ripple Counter

A decimal counter follows a sequence of ten states and returns to 0 after the count of 9. Such a counter must have at least four flip-flops to represent each decimal digit, since a decimal digit is represented by a binary code with at least four bits. The sequence of states in a decimal counter is dictated by the binary code used to represent a decimal digit. If BCD is used, the sequence of states is as shown in the state diagram of Fig. 7-13. This is similar to a binary counter, except that the state after 1001 (code for decimal digit 9) is 0000 (code for decimal digit 0).

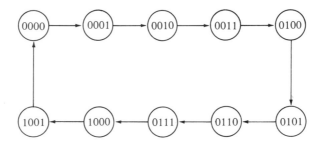

Figure 7-13 State diagram of a decimal BCD counter

The design of a decimal ripple counter or of any ripple counter not following the binary sequence is not a straightforward procedure. The formal tools of logic design can serve only as a guide. A satisfactory end product requires the ingenuity and imagination of the designer.

The logic diagram of a BCD ripple counter is shown in Fig. 7-14.* The four outputs are designated by the letter symbol Q with a numeric subscript equal to the binary weight of the corresponding bit in the BCD code. The flip-flops trigger on the negative edge, i.e., when the *CP* signal goes from 1 to 0. Note that the output of Q_1 is applied to the *CP* inputs of both Q_2 and Q_8 and the output of Q_2 is applied to the *CP* input of Q_4. The *J* and *K* inputs are connected either to a permanent 1 signal or to outputs of flip-flops, as shown in the diagram.

A ripple counter is an asynchronous sequential circuit and cannot be described by Boolean equations developed for describing clocked sequential circuits. Signals that affect the flip-flop transition depend on the order in which they change from 1 to 0. The operation of the counter can be explained by a list of conditions for flip-flop transitions. These conditions are derived from the logic diagram and from knowledge of how a *JK* flip-flop operates. Remember that when the *CP*

*This circuit is similar to IC type 7490.

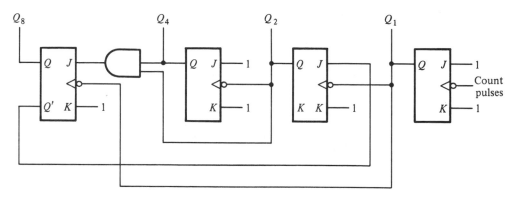

Figure 7-14 Logic diagram of a BCD ripple counter

input goes from 1 to 0, the flip-flop is set if $J = 1$, is cleared if $K = 1$, is complemented if $J = K = 1$, and is left unchanged if $J = K = 0$. The following are the conditions for each flip-flop state transition:

1. Q_1 is complemented on the negative edge of every count pulse.

2. Q_2 is complemented if $Q_8 = 0$ and Q_1 goes from 1 to 0. Q_2 is cleared if $Q_8 = 1$ and Q_1 goes from 1 to 0.

3. Q_4 is complemented when Q_2 goes from 1 to 0.

4. Q_8 is complemented when $Q_4 Q_2 = 11$ and Q_1 goes from 1 to 0. Q_8 is cleared if either Q_4 or Q_2 is 0 and Q_1 goes from 1 to 0.

To verify that these conditions result in the sequence required by a BCD ripple counter, it is necessary to verify that the flip-flop transitions indeed follow a sequence of states as specified by the state diagram of Fig. 7-13. Another way to verify the operation of the counter is to derive the timing diagram for each flip-flop from the conditions listed above. This diagram is shown in Fig. 7-15 with the

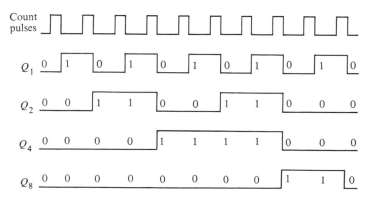

Figure 7-15 Timing diagram for the decimal counter of Fig. 7-14

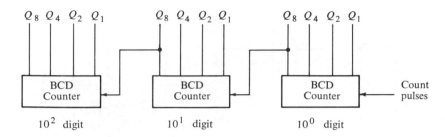

Figure 7-16 Block diagram of a 3-decade decimal BCD counter

binary states listed after each clock pulse. Q_1 changes state after each clock pulse. Q_2 complements every time Q_1 goes from 1 to 0 as long as $Q_8 = 0$. When Q_8 becomes 1, Q_2 remains cleared at 0. Q_4 complements every time Q_2 goes from 1 to 0. Q_8 remains cleared as long as Q_2 or Q_4 is 0. When both Q_2 and Q_4 become 1's, Q_8 complements when Q_1 goes from 1 to 0. Q_8 is cleared on the next transition of Q_1.

The BCD counter of Fig. 7-14 is a *decade* counter, since it counts from 0 to 9. To count in decimal from 0 to 99, we need a two-decade counter. To count from 0 to 999, we need a three-decade counter. Multiple-decade counters can be constructed by connecting BCD counters in cascade, one for each decade. A three-decade counter is shown in Fig. 7-16. The inputs to the second and third decades come from Q_8 of the previous decade. When Q_8 in one decade goes from 1 to 0, it triggers the count for the next higher-order decade while its own decade goes from 9 to 0. For instance, the count after 399 will be 400.

7-5 SYNCHRONOUS COUNTERS

Synchronous counters are distinguished from ripple counters in that clock pulses are applied to the *CP* inputs of *all* flip-flops. The common pulse triggers all the flip-flops simultaneously, rather than one at a time in succession as in a ripple counter. The decision whether a flip-flop is to be complemented or not is determined from the values of the J and K inputs at the time of the pulse. If $J = K = 0$, the flip-flop remains unchanged. If $J = K = 1$, the flip-flop complements.

A design procedure for any type of synchronous counter was presented in Section 6-8. The design of a 3-bit binary counter was carried out in detail and is illustrated in Fig. 6-30. In this section, we present some typical MSI synchronous counters and explain their operation. It must be realized that there is no need to design a counter if it is already available commerically in IC form.

Binary Counter

The design of synchronous binary counters is so simple that there is no need to go through a rigorous sequential-logic design process. In a synchronous binary counter, the flip-flop in the lowest-order position is complemented with every pulse.

This means that its J and K inputs must be maintained at logic-1. A flip-flop in any other position is complemented with a pulse provided all the bits in the lower-order positions are equal to 1, because the lower-order bits (when all 1's) will change to 0's on the next count pulse. The binary count dictates that the next higher-order bit be complemented. For example, if the present state of a 4-bit counter is $A_4A_3A_2A_1 = 0011$, the next count will be 0100. A_1 is always complemented. A_2 is complemented because the present state of $A_1 = 1$. A_3 is complemented because the present state of $A_2A_1 = 11$. But A_4 is not complemented because the present state of $A_3A_2A_1 = 011$, which does not give an all-1's condition.

Synchronous binary counters have a regular pattern and can easily be constructed with complementing flip-flops and gates. The regular pattern can be clearly seen from the 4-bit counter depicted in Fig. 7-17. The CP terminals of all flip-flops are connected to a common clock-pulse source. The first stage A_1 has its J and K equal to 1 if the counter is enabled. The other J and K inputs are equal to 1 if all previous low-order bits are equal to 1 and the count is enabled. The chain of AND gates generates the required logic for the J and K inputs in each stage. The counter can be extended to any number of stages, with each stage having an additional flip-flop and an AND gate that gives an output of 1 if all previous flip-flop outputs are 1's.

Note that the flip-flops trigger on the negative edge of the pulse. This is not essential here as it was with the ripple counter. The counter could also be triggered on the positive edge of the pulse.

Binary Up-Down Counter

In a synchronous count-down binary counter, the flip-flop in the lowest-order position is complemented with every pulse. A flip-flop in any other position is complemented with a pulse provided all the lower-order bits are equal to 0. For example, if the present state of a 4-bit count-down binary counter is $A_4A_3A_2A_1 = 1100$, the next count will be 1011. A_1 is always complemented. A_2 is complemented because the present state of $A_1 = 0$. A_3 is complemented because the present state of $A_2A_1 = 00$. But A_4 is not complemented because the present state of $A_3A_2A_1 = 100$, which is not an all-0's condition.

A count-down binary counter can be constructed as shown in Fig. 7-17, except that the inputs to the AND gates must come from the complement outputs Q' and not from the normal outputs Q of the previous flip-flops. The two operations can be combined in one circuit. A binary counter capable of counting either up or down is shown in Fig. 7-18. The T flip-flops employed in this circuit may be considered as JK flip-flops with the J and K terminals tied together. When the *up* input control is 1, the circuit counts up, since the T inputs are determined from the previous values of the normal outputs in Q. When the *down* input control is 1, the circuit counts down, since the complement outputs Q' determine the states of the T inputs. When both the *up* and *down* signals are 0's, the register does not change state but remains in the same count.

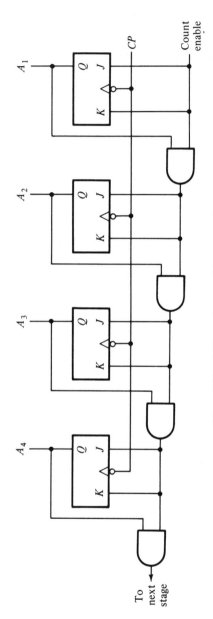

Figure 7-17 4-bit synchronous binary counter

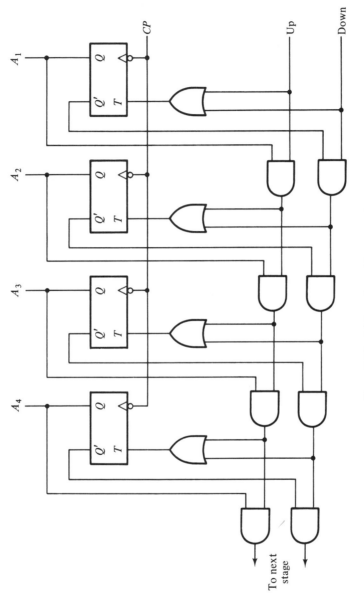

Figure 7-18 4-bit up-down binary counter

279

BCD Counter

A BCD counter counts in binary-coded decimal from 0000 to 1001 and back to 0000. Because of the return to 0 after a count of 9, a BCD counter does not have a regular pattern as in a straight binary count. To derive the circuit of a BCD synchronous counter, it is necessary to go through a design procedure as discussed in Section 6-8.

The count sequence of a BCD counter is given in Table 7-5. The excitation for the T flip-flops is obtained from the count sequence. An output y is also shown in the table. This output is equal to 1 when the counter present state is 1001. In this way, y can enable the count of the next-higher-order decade while the same pulse switches the present decade from 1001 to 0000.

The flip-flop input functions from the excitation table can be simplified by means of maps. The unused states for minterms 10 to 15 are taken as don't-care terms. The simplified functions are listed below:

$$TQ_1 = 1$$
$$TQ_2 = Q_8'Q_1$$
$$TQ_4 = Q_2Q_1$$
$$TQ_8 = Q_8Q_1 + Q_4Q_2Q_1$$
$$y = Q_8Q_1$$

The circuit can be easily drawn with four T flip-flops, five AND gates, and one OR gate.

Synchronous BCD counters can be cascaded to form a counter for decimal numbers of any length. The cascading is done as in Fig. 7-16, except that output y must be connected to the count input of the next-higher-order decade.

TABLE 7-5 Excitation table for a BCD counter

Count sequence				Flip-flop inputs				Output carry
Q_8	Q_4	Q_2	Q_1	TQ_8	TQ_4	TQ_2	TQ_1	y
0	0	0	0	0	0	0	1	0
0	0	0	1	0	0	1	1	0
0	0	1	0	0	0	0	1	0
0	0	1	1	0	1	1	1	0
0	1	0	0	0	0	0	1	0
0	1	0	1	0	0	1	1	0
0	1	1	0	0	0	0	1	0
0	1	1	1	1	1	1	1	0
1	0	0	0	0	0	0	1	0
1	0	0	1	1	0	0	1	1

Binary Counter with Parallel Load

Counters employed in digital systems quite often require a parallel-load capability for transferring an initial binary number prior to the count operation. Figure 7-19 shows the logic diagram of a register that has a parallel-load capability and can also operate as a counter.* The input load control, when equal to 1, disables the count sequence and causes a transfer of data from inputs I_1 through I_4 into flip-flops A_1 through A_4, respectively. If the load input is 0 and the count input control is 1, the circuit operates as a counter. The clock pulses then cause the state of the flip-flops to change according to the binary count sequence. If both control inputs are 0, clock pulses do not change the state of the register.

The carry-out terminal becomes a 1 if all flip-flops are equal to 1 while the count input is enabled. This is the condition for complementing the flip-flop holding the next-higher-order bit. This output is useful for expanding the counter to more than four bits. The speed of the counter is increased if this carry is generated directly from the outputs of all four flip-flops instead of going through a chain of AND gates. Similarly, each flip-flop is associated with an AND gate that receives all previous flip-flop outputs directly to determine when the flip-flop should be complemented.

The operation of the counter is summarized in Table 7-6. The four control inputs: clear, CP, load, and count determine the next output state. The clear input is asynchronous and, when equal to 0, causes the counter to be cleared to all 0's, regardless of the presence of clock pulses or other inputs. This is indicated in the table by the X entries, which symbolize don't-care conditions for the other inputs, so their value can be either 0 or 1. The clear input must go to the 1 state for the clocked operations listed in the next three entries in the table. With the load and count inputs both at 0, the outputs do not change, whether a pulse is applied in the CP terminal or not. A load input of 1 causes a transfer from inputs I_1–I_4 into the register during the positive edge of an input pulse. The input information is loaded into the register regardless of the value of the count input, because the count input is inhibited when the load input is 1. If the load input is maintained at 0, the count input controls the operation of the counter. The outputs change to the next binary count on the positive-edge transition of every clock pulse, but no change of state occurs if the count input is 0.

The 4-bit counter shown in Fig. 7-19 can be enclosed in one IC package. Two ICs are necessary for the construction of an 8-bit counter; four ICs for a 16-bit counter; and so on. The carry output of one IC must be connected to the count input of the IC holding the four next-higher-order bits of the counter.

Counters with parallel-load capability having a specified number of bits are very useful in the design of digital systems. Later we will refer to them as registers with load and increment capabilities. The *increment* function is an operation that adds 1 to the present content of a register. By enabling the count control during one clock pulse period, the content of the register can be incremented by 1.

*This is similar but not identical to IC type 74161.

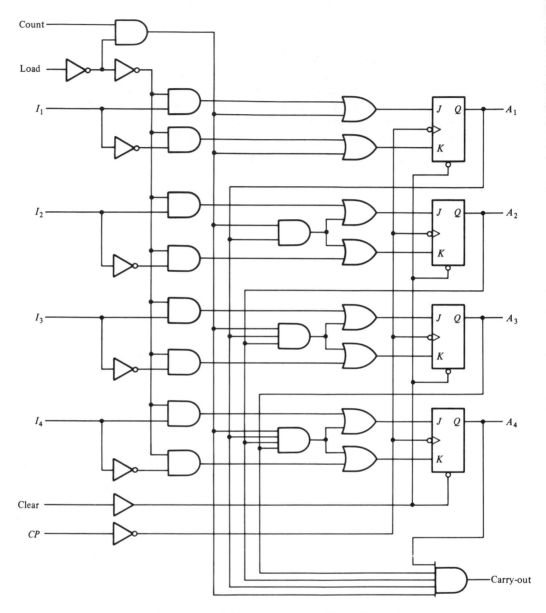

Figure 7-19 4-bit binary counter with parallel load

TABLE 7-6 Function table for the counter of Fig. 7-19

Clear	CP	Load	Count	Function
0	X	X	X	Clear to 0
1	X	0	0	No change
1	↑	1	X	Load inputs
1	↑	0	1	Count next binary state

A counter with parallel load can be used to generate any desired number of count sequences. A modulo-N (abbreviated mod N) counter is a counter that goes through a repeated sequence of N counts. For example, a 4-bit binary counter is a mod-16 counter. A BCD counter is a mod-10 counter. In some applications, one may not be concerned with the particular N states that a mod-N counter uses. If this is the case, then a counter with parallel load can be used to construct any mod-N counter, with N being any value desired. This is shown in the following example.

EXAMPLE 7-4: Construct a mod-6 counter using the MSI circuit specified in Fig. 7-19.

Figure 7-20 shows four ways in which a counter with parallel load can be used to generate a sequence of six counts. In each case the count control is set to 1 to enable the count through the pulses in the *CP* input. We also use the facts that the load control inhibits the count and that the clear operation is independent of other control inputs.

The AND gate in Fig. 7-20(a) detects the occurrence of state 0101 in the output. When the counter is in this state, the load input is enabled and an all-0's input is loaded into the register. Thus, the counter goes through binary states 0, 1, 2, 3, 4, and 5 and then returns to 0. This produces a sequence of six counts.

The clear input of the register is asynchronous, i.e., it does not depend on the clock. In Fig. 7-20(b), the NAND gate detects the count of 0110, but as soon as this count occurs, the register is cleared. The count 0110 has no chance of staying on for any appreciable time because the register goes immediately to 0. A momentary spike occurs in output A_2 as the count goes from 0101 to 0110 and immediately to 0000. This momentary spike may be undesirable and for this reason this configuration is not recommended. If the counter has a synchronous clear input, it would be possible to clear the counter with the clock after an occurrence of the 0101 count.

Instead of using the first six counts, we may want to choose the last six counts from 10 to 15. In this case it is possible to take advantage of the output carry to load a number in the register. In Fig. 7-20(c), the counter starts with count 1010 and continues to 1111. The output carry generated during the last state enables the load control, which then loads the input which is set at 1010.

It is also possible to choose any intermediate count of six states. The mod-6 counter of Fig. 7-20(d) goes through the count sequence 3, 4, 5, 6, 7, and 8. When the last count 1000 is reached, output A_4 goes to 1 and the load control is enabled. This loads into the register the value of 0011, and the binary count continues from this state.

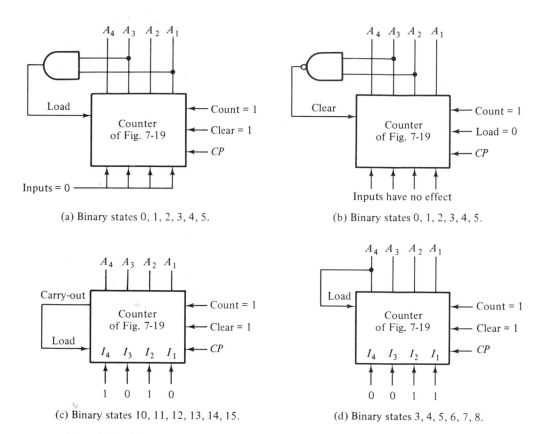

(a) Binary states 0, 1, 2, 3, 4, 5.

(b) Binary states 0, 1, 2, 3, 4, 5.

(c) Binary states 10, 11, 12, 13, 14, 15.

(d) Binary states 3, 4, 5, 6, 7, 8.

Figure 7-20 Four ways to achieve a mod-6 counter using a counter with parallel load

7-6 TIMING SEQUENCES

The sequence of operations in a digital system are specified by a control unit. The control unit that supervises the operations in a digital system would normally consist of timing signals that determine the time sequence in which the operations are executed. The timing sequences in the control unit can be easily generated by means of counters or shift registers. This section demonstrates the use of these MSI functions in the generation of timing signals for a control unit.

Word-time Generation

First, we demonstrate a circuit that generates the required timing signal for serial mode of operation. Serial transfer of information was discussed in Section 7-3, with an example depicted in Fig. 7-8. The control unit in a serial computer must generate a *word-time* signal that stays on for a number of pulses equal to the number of bits in the shift registers. The word-time signal can be generated by means of a counter that counts the required number of pulses.

Assume that the word-time signal to be generated must stay on for a period of eight clock pulses. Figure 7-21(a) shows a counter circuit that accomplishes this task. Initially, the 3-bit counter is cleared to 0. A start signal will set flip-flop Q. The output of this flip-flop supplies the word-time control and also enables the counter. After the count of eight pulses, the flip-flop is reset and Q goes to 0. The timing diagram of Fig. 7-21(b) demonstrates the operation of the circuit. The start signal is synchronized with the clock and stays on for one clock pulse period. After Q is set to 1, the counter starts counting the clock pulses. When the counter reaches the count of 7 (binary 111), it sends a stop signal to the reset input of the flip-flop. The stop signal becomes a 1 after the negative-edge transition of pulse 7. The next clock pulse switches the counter to the 000 state and also clears Q. Now the counter is disabled and the word-time signal stays at 0. Note that the word-time control stays on for a period of eight pulses. Note also that the stop signal in this circuit can be used to start another word-count control in another circuit just as the start signal is used in this circuit.

Timing Signals

In a parallel mode of operation, a single clock pulse can specify the time at which an operation should be executed. The control unit in a digital system that operates in the parallel mode must generate timing signals that stay on for only one clock

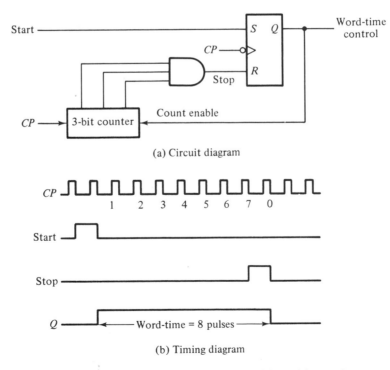

(a) Circuit diagram

(b) Timing diagram

Figure 7-21 Generation of a word-time control for serial operations

pulse period, but these timing signals must be distinguished from each other.

Timing signals that control the sequence of operations in a digital system can be generated with a shift register or a counter with a decoder. A *ring counter* is a circular shift register with only one flip-flop being set at any particular time; all others are cleared. The single bit is shifted from one flip-flop to the other to produce the sequence of timing signals. Figure 7-22(a) shows a 4-bit shift register connected as a ring counter. The initial value of the register is 1000, which produces the variable T_0. The single bit is shifted right with every clock pulse and circulates back from T_3 to T_0. Each flip-flop is in the 1 state once every four clock pulses and produces one of the four timing signals shown in Fig. 7-22(c). Each output becomes a 1 after the negative-edge transition of a clock pulse and remains 1 during the next clock pulse.

The timing signals can be generated also by continuously enabling a 2-bit counter that goes through four distinct states. The decoder shown in Fig. 7-22(b) decodes the four states of the counter and generates the required sequence of timing signals.

The timing signals, when enabled by the clock pulses, will provide multiple-phase clock pulses. For example, if T_0 is ANDed with CP, the output of the AND gate will generate clock pulses at one-fourth the frequency of the master-clock pulses. Multiple-phase clock pulses can be used for controlling different registers with different time scales.

To generate 2^n timing signals, we need either a shift register with 2^n flip-flops or an n-bit counter together with an n-to-2^n line decoder. For example, 16 timing signals can be generated with a 16-bit shift register connected as a ring counter or with a 4-bit counter and a 4-to-16 line decoder. In the first case, we need 16 flip-flops. In the second case, we need four flip-flops and 16 4-input AND gates for the decoder. It is also possible to generate the timing signals with a combination of a shift register and a decoder. In this way, the number of flip-flops is less than in a ring counter, and the decoder requires only 2-input gates. This combination is sometimes called a *Johnson counter*.

Johnson Counter

A k-bit ring counter circulates a single bit among the flip-flops to provide k distinguishable states. The number of states can be doubled if the shift register is connected as a *switch-tail* ring counter. A switch-tail ring counter is a circular shift register with the complement output of the last flip-flop connected to the input of the first flip-flop. Figure 7-23(a) shows such a shift register. The circular connection is made from the complement output of the rightmost flip-flop to the input of the leftmost flip-flop. The register shifts its contents once to the right with every clock pulse, and at the same time, the complement value of the E flip-flop is transferred into the A flip-flop. Starting from a cleared state, the switch-tail ring counter goes through a sequence of eight states as listed in Fig. 7-23(b). In general,

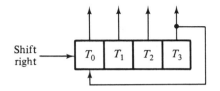

(a) Ring-counter (initial value = 1000)

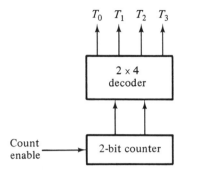

(b) Counter and decoder

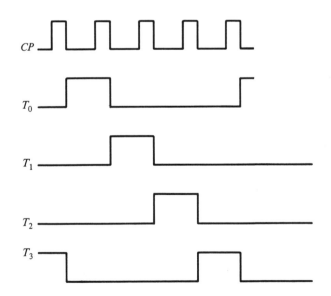

(c) Sequence of four timing signals

Figure 7-22 Generation of timing signals

a k-bit switch-tail ring counter will go through a sequence of $2k$ states. Starting from all 0's, each shift operation inserts 1's from the left until the register is filled with all 1's. In the following sequences, 0's are inserted from the left until the register is again filled with all 0's.

A Johnson counter is a k-bit switch-tail ring counter with $2k$ decoding gates to provide outputs for $2k$ timing signals. The decoding gates are not shown in Fig. 7-23 but are specified in the last column of the table. The eight AND gates listed in the table, when connected to the circuit, will complete the construction of the Johnson counter. Since each gate is enabled during one particular state sequence, the outputs of the gates generate eight timing sequences in succession.

The decoding of a k-bit switch-tail ring counter to obtain $2k$ timing sequences follows a regular pattern. The all-0's state is decoded by taking the complement of the two extreme flip-flop outputs. The all-1's state is decoded by taking the normal outputs of the two extreme flip-flops. All other states are decoded from an adjacent 1, 0 or 0, 1 pattern in the sequence. For example, sequence 7 has an adjacent 0, 1 pattern in flip-flops B and C. The decoded output is then obtained by taking the complement of B and the normal output of C, or $B'C$.

One disadvantage of the circuit in Fig. 7-23(a) is that, if it finds itself in an unused state, it will persist in moving from one invalid state to another and never

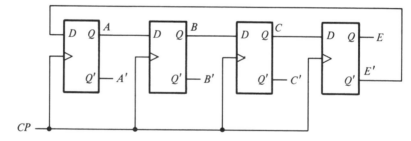

(a) 4-stage switch-tail ring counter

Sequence number	Flip-flop outputs				AND gate required for output
	A	B	C	E	
1	0	0	0	0	$A'E'$
2	1	0	0	0	AB'
3	1	1	0	0	BC'
4	1	1	1	0	CE'
5	1	1	1	1	AE
6	0	1	1	1	$A'B$
7	0	0	1	1	$B'C$
8	0	0	0	1	$C'E$

(b) Count sequence and required decoding.

Figure 7-23 Construction of a Johnson counter

find its way to a valid state. This difficulty can be corrected by modifying the circuit to avoid this undesirable condition. One correcting procedure is to disconnect the output from flip-flop B that goes to the D input of flip-flop C, and instead enable the input of flip-flop C by the function:*

$$DC = (A + C)B$$

where DC is the flip-flop input function for the D input of flip-flop C.

Johnson counters can be constructed for any number of timing sequences. The number of flip-flops needed is one-half the number of timing signals. The number of decoding gates is equal to the number of timing signals and only 2-input gates are employed.

7-7   THE MEMORY UNIT

The registers in a digital computer may be classified as either operational or storage type. An *operational* register is capable of storing binary information in its flip-flops and, in addition, has combinational gates capable of data-processing tasks. A *storage* register is used solely for temporary storage of binary information. This information cannot be altered when transferred in and out of the register. A *memory unit* is a collection of storage registers together with the associated circuits needed to transfer information in and out of the registers. The storage registers in a memory unit are called *memory registers*.

The bulk of the registers in a digital computer are memory registers, to which information is transferred for storage and from which information is available when needed for processing. Comparatively few operational registers are found in the processor unit. When data processing takes place, the information from selected registers in the memory unit is first transferred to the operational registers in the processor unit. Intermediate and final results obtained in the operational registers are transferred back to selected memory registers. Similarly, binary information received from input devices is first stored in memory registers; information transferred to output devices is taken from registers in the memory unit.

The component that forms the binary cells of registers in a memory unit must have certain basic properties, the most important of which are: (1) It must have a reliable two-state property for binary representation. (2) It must be small in size. (3) The cost per bit of storage should be as low as possible. (4) The time of access to a memory register should be reasonably fast. Examples of memory unit components are magnetic cores, semiconductor ICs, and magnetic surfaces on tapes, drums, or disks.

A memory unit stores binary information in groups called *words*, each word being stored in a memory register. A word in memory is an entity of n bits that moves in and out of storage as a unit. A memory word may represent an operand,

*This is the way it is done in IC type 4022.

an instruction, a group of alphanumeric characters, or any binary-coded information. The communication between a memory unit and its environment is achieved through two control signals and two external registers. The control signals specify the direction of transfer required, that is, whether a word is to be stored in a memory register or whether a word previously stored is to be transferred out of a memory register. One external register specifies the particular memory register chosen out of the thousands available; the other specifies the particular bit configuration of the word in question. The control signals and the registers are shown in the block diagram of Fig. 7-24.

The memory *address register* specifies the memory word selected. Each word in memory is assigned a number identification starting from 0 up to the maximum number of words available. To communicate with a specific memory word, its location number, or *address*, is transferred to the address register. The internal circuits of the memory unit accept this address from the register and open the paths needed to select the word called. An address register with n bits can specify up to 2^n memory words. Computer memory units can range from 1024 words, requiring an address register of 10 bits, to $1,048,576 = 2^{20}$ words, requiring a 20-bit address register.

The two control signals applied to the memory unit are called *read* and *write*. A write signal specifies a transfer-in function; a read signal specifies a transfer-out function. Each is referenced from the memory unit. Upon accepting one of the control signals, the internal control circuits inside the memory unit provide the

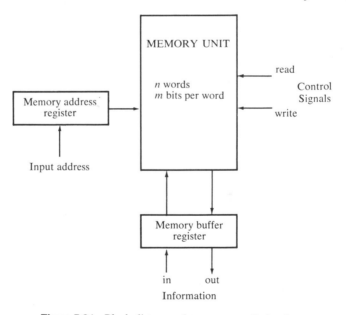

Figure 7-24   Block diagram of a memory unit showing communication with environment

desired function. Certain types of storage units, because of their component characteristics, destroy the information stored in a cell when the bit in that cell is read out. Such a unit is said to be a destructive read-out memory, as opposed to a nondestructive memory where the information remains in the cell after it is read out. In either case, the old information is always destroyed when new information is written. The sequence of internal control in a destructive read-out memory must provide control signals that will cause the word to be restored into its binary cells if the application calls for a nondestructive function.

The information transfer to and from registers in memory and the external environment is communicated through one common register called the memory *buffer register* (other names are *information register* and *storage register*). When the memory unit receives a *write* control signal, the internal control interprets the contents of the buffer register to be the bit configuration of the word to be stored in a memory register. With a *read* control signal, the internal control sends the word from a memory register into the buffer register. In each case the contents of the address register specify the particular memory register referenced for writing or reading.

Let us summarize the information transfer characteristics of a memory unit by an example. Consider a memory unit of 1024 words with eight bits per word. To specify 1024 words, we need an address of ten bits, since $2^{10} = 1024$. Therefore, the address register must contain ten flip-flops. The buffer register must have eight flip-flops to store the contents of words transferred into and out of memory. The memory unit has 1024 registers with assigned address numbers from 0 to 1023.

Figure 7-25 shows the initial contents of three registers: memory address register (MAR), memory buffer register (MBR), and the memory register addressed

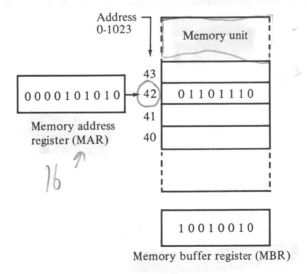

Figure 7-25   Initial values of registers

by MAR. Since the equivalent binary number in MAR is decimal 42, the memory register addressed by MAR is the one with address number 42.

The sequence of operations needed to communicate with the memory unit for the purpose of transferring a word out to the MBR is:

1. Transfer the address bits of the selected word into MAR.

2. Activate the *read* control input.

The result of the read operation is depicted in Fig. 7-26(a). The binary information presently stored in memory register 42 is transferred into MBR.

The sequence of operations needed to store a new word into memory is:

1. Transfer the address bits of the selected word into MAR.

2. Transfer the data bits of the word into MBR.

3. Activate the *write* control input.

The result of the write operation is depicted in Fig. 7-26(b). The data bits from MBR are stored in memory register 42.

In the above example, we assumed a memory unit with nondestructive read-out property. Such memories can be constructed with semiconductor ICs. They retain the information in the memory register when the register is sampled during the reading process so that no loss of information occurs. Another component commonly used in memory units is the magnetic core. A magnetic core characteristically has destructive read-out, i.e., it loses the stored binary information during the reading process. Examples of semiconductor and magnetic-core memories are presented in Section 7-8.

Because of its destructive read-out property, a magnetic-core memory must provide additional control functions to restore the word into the memory register.

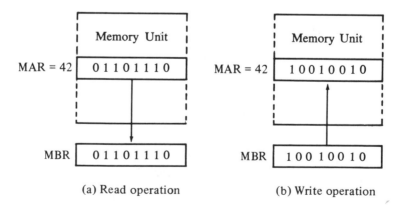

(a) Read operation   (b) Write operation

Figure 7-26   Information transfer during read and write operations

A read control signal applied to a magnetic-core memory transfers the content of the addressed word into an external register and, at the same time, the memory register is automatically cleared. The sequence of internal control in a magnetic-core memory then provides appropriate signals to cause the restoration of the word into the memory register. The information transfer in a magnetic-core memory during a read operation is depicted in Fig. 7-27. A destructive read operation transfers the selected word into MBR but leaves the memory register with all 0's. Normal memory operation requires that the content of the selected word remain in memory after a read operation. Therefore, it is necessary to go through a *restore* operation that writes the value in MBR into the selected memory register. During the restore operation, the contents of MAR and MBR must remain unchanged.

A write control input applied to a magnetic-core memory causes a transfer of information as depicted in Fig. 7-28. To transfer new information into a selected register, the old information must first be erased by clearing all the bits of the word to 0. After this is done, the content of MBR can be transferred to the selected word. MAR must not change during the operation to ensure that the same selected word that is cleared is the one that receives the new information.

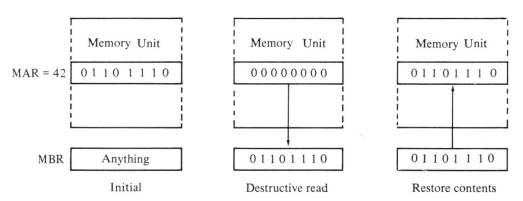

Figure 7-27   Information transfer in a magnetic-core memory during a read operation

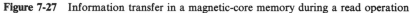

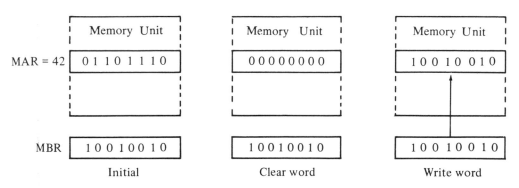

Figure 7-28   Information transfer in a magnetic-core memory during a write operation

A magnetic-core memory requires two half-cycles either for reading or writing. The time it takes for the memory to go through both half-cycles is called the *memory-cycle* time.

The mode of access of a memory system is determined by the type of components used. In a *random-access* memory, the registers may be thought of as being separated in space, with each register occupying one particular spatial location as in a magnetic-core memory. In a *sequential-access* memory, the information stored in some medium is not immediately accessible but is available only at certain intervals of time. A magnetic-tape unit is of this type. Each memory location passes the read and write heads in turn, but information is read out only when the requested word has been reached. The *access time* of a memory is the time required to select a word and either read or write it. In a random-access memory, the access time is always the same regardless of the word's particular location in space. In a sequential memory, the access time depends on the position of the word at the time of request. If the word is just emerging from storage at the time it is requested, the access time is just the time necessary to read or write it. But, if the word happens to be in the last position, the access time also includes the time required for all the other words to move past the terminals. Thus, the access time in a sequential memory is variable.

Memory units whose components lose stored information with time or when the power is turned off are said to be *volatile*. A semiconductor memory unit is of this category since its binary cells need external power to maintain the needed signals. In contrast, a nonvolatile memory unit, such as magnetic core or magnetic disk, retains its stored information after removal of power. This is because the stored information in magnetic components is manifested by the direction of magnetization, which is retained when power is turned off. A nonvolatile property is desirable in digital computers because many useful programs are left permanently in the memory unit. When power is turned off and then on again, the previously stored programs and other information are not lost but continue to reside in memory.

7-8 EXAMPLES OF RANDOM-ACCESS MEMORIES

The internal construction of two different types of random-access memories are presented diagramatically in this section. The first is constructed with flip-flops and gates and the second with magnetic cores. To be able to include the entire memory unit in one diagram, a limited storage capacity must be used. For this reason, the memory units presented here have a small capacity of 12 bits arranged in four words of three bits each. Commercial random-access memories may have a capacity of thousands of words and each word may range somewhere between 8 and 64 bits. The logical construction of large-capacity memory units would be a direct extension of the configuration shown here.

Integrated-circuit Memory

The internal construction of a random-access memory of *m* words with *n* bits per word consists of $m \times n$ binary storage cells and the associated logic for selecting individual words. The binary storage cell is the basic building block of a memory unit. The equivalent logic of a binary cell that stores one bit of information is shown in Fig. 7-29. Although the cell is shown to include gates and a flip-flop, internally it is constructed with two transistors having multiple inputs. A binary storage cell must be very small in order to be able to pack as many cells as possible in the small area available in the integrated-circuit chip. The binary cell has three inputs and one output. The select input enables the cell for reading or writing. The read/write input determines the cell operation when it is selected. A 1 in the read/write input forms a path from the flip-flop to the output terminal. The information in the input terminal is transferred into the flip-flop when the read/write control is 0. Note that the flip-flop operates without clock pulses and that its purpose is to store the information bit in the binary cell.

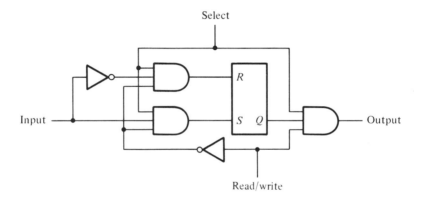

(a) Logic diagram

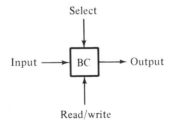

(b) Block diagram

Figure 7-29 Memory cell

Integrated-circuit memories sometimes have a single line for the read and write control. One binary state in the single line specifies a read operation and the other state specifies a write operation. In addition, one or more enable lines are included to provide means for selecting the IC and for expanding several packages into a memory unit with a larger number of words. The logical construction of a IC RAM is shown in Fig. 7-30. It consists of 4 words of 3 bits each, for a total of 12 binary cells. The small boxes labeled BC represent a binary cell, and the three inputs and one output in each BC are as specified in the diagram of Fig. 7-29.

The two address input lines go through an internal 2-to-4 line decoder. The decoder is enabled with the memory-enable input. When the memory enable is 0,

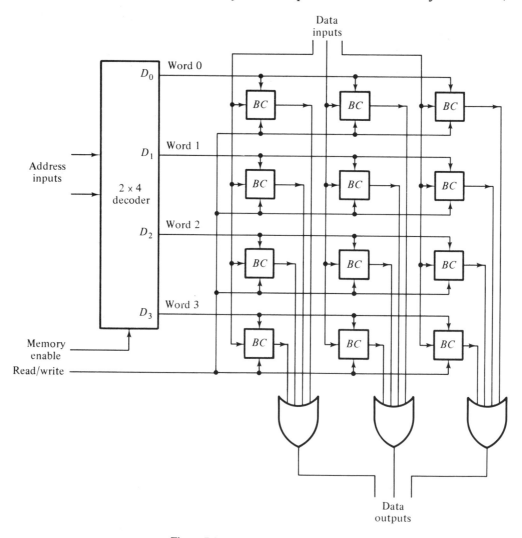

Figure 7-30   Integrated-circuit memory

all the outputs of the decoder are 0 and none of the memory words are selected. With the memory enable at 1, one of the four words is selected, depending on the value of the two address lines. Now, with the read/write control at 1, the bits of the selected word go through the three OR gates to the output terminals. The nonselected binary cells produce 0's in the inputs of the OR gates and have no effect on the outputs. With the read/write control at 0, the information available on the input lines is transferred into the binary cells of the selected word. The nonselected binary cells in the other words are disabled by their selection inputs and their previous values remain unchanged. With the memory-enable control at 0, the contents of all cells in the memory remain unchanged, regardless of the value of the read/write control.

IC RAMs are constructed internally with cells having a wired-OR capability. This eliminates the need for the OR gates in the diagram. The external output lines can also form wired logic to facilitate the connection of two or more IC packages to form a memory unit with a larger number of words.

Magnetic-core Memory

A magnetic-core memory uses magnetic cores to store binary information. A magnetic core is a doughnut-shaped toroid made of magnetic material. In contrast to a semiconductor flip-flop that needs only one physical quantity such as voltage for its operation, a magnetic core employs three physical quantities: current, magnetic flux, and voltage. The signal that excites the core is a *current* pulse in a wire passing through the core. The binary information stored is represented by the direction of *magnetic flux* within the core. The output binary information is extracted from a wire linking the core in the form of a *voltage* pulse.

The physical property that makes a magnetic core suitable for binary storage is its hysteresis loop, shown in Fig. 7-31(c). This is a plot of current vs magnetic flux, and it has the shape of a square loop. With zero current, a flux which is either positive (counterclockwise direction) or negative (clockwise direction) remains in the magnetized core. One direction, say counterclockwise magnetization, is used to represent a 1 and the other to represent a 0.

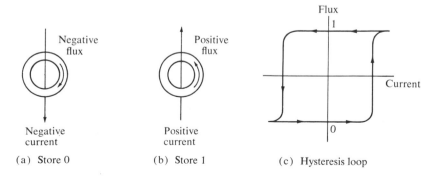

(a) Store 0   (b) Store 1   (c) Hysteresis loop

Figure 7-31 Storing a bit into a magnetic core

A pulse of current applied to the winding through the core can shift the direction of magnetization. As shown in Fig. 7-31(a), current in the downward direction produces flux in the clockwise direction, causing the core to go to the 0 state. Figure 7-31(b) shows the current and flux directions for storing a 1. The path that the flux takes when the current pulse is applied is indicated by arrows in the hysteresis loop.

Reading out the binary information stored in the core is complicated by the fact that flux cannot be detected when it is not changing. However, if flux is changing with respect to time, it induces a voltage in a wire that links the core. Thus, read-out could be accomplished by applying a current in the negative direction as shown in Fig. 7-32. If the core is in the 1 state, the current reverses the direction of magnetization, and the resulting change of flux produces a voltage pulse in the sense wire. If the core is already in the 0 state, the negative current leaves the core magnetized in the same direction, causing a very slight disturbance of magnetic flux which results in a very small output voltage in the sense wire. Note that this is a destructive read-out, since the read current always returns the core to the 0 state. The previously stored value is lost.

Figure 7-33 shows the organization of a magnetic-core memory containing four words with three bits each. Comparing it with the IC memory unit of Fig. 7-30, we note that the binary cell now is a magnetic core and the wires linking it. The excitation of the core is accomplished by means of a current pulse generated in a driver (DR). The output information goes through a sense amplifier (SA) whose outputs set corresponding flip-flops in the buffer register. Three wires link each core. The word wire is excited by a word driver and goes through the three cores of a word. A bit wire is excited by a bit driver and goes through four cores in the same bit position. The sense wire links the same cores as the bit wire and is applied to a sense amplifier that shapes the voltage pulse when a 1 is read and rejects the small disturbance when a 0 is read.

During a read operation, a word-driver current pulse is applied to the cores of the word selected by the decoder. The read current is in the negative direction (Fig. 7-32) and causes all cores of the selected word to go to the 0 state, regardless of their previous state. Cores which previously contained a 1 switch their flux and

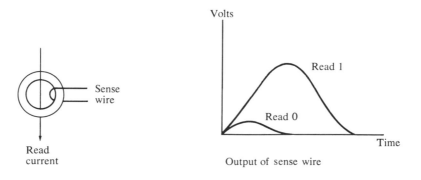

Figure 7-32   Reading a bit from a magnetic core

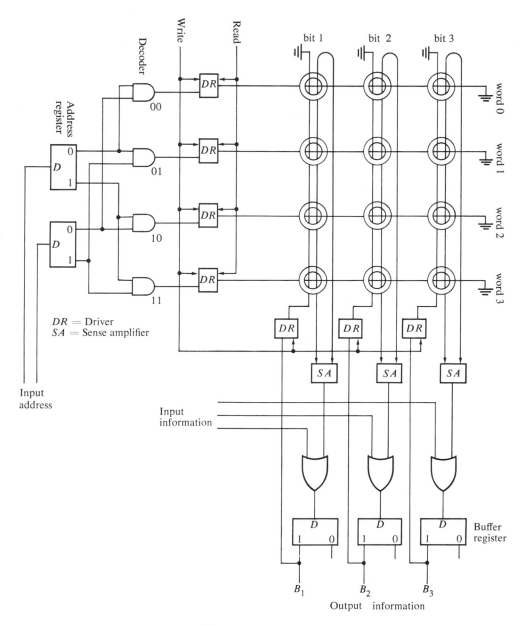

Figure 7-33 Magnetic-core memory unit

induce a voltage into their sense wire. The flux of cores which already contained a 0 is not changed. The voltage pulse on a sense wire of cores with a previous 1 is amplified in the sense amplifier and sets the corresponding flip-flop in the buffer register.

During a write operation, the buffer register holds the information to be stored in the word specified by the address register. We assume that all cores in the selected word are initially cleared, i.e., all are in the 0 state so that cores requiring a 1 need to undergo a change of state. A current pulse is generated simultaneously in the word driver selected by the decoder and in the bit driver, whose corresponding buffer register flip-flop contains a 1. Both currents are in the positive direction, but their magnitude is only half that needed to switch the flux to the 1 state. This half-current by itself is too small to change the direction of magnetization. But the sum of two half-currents is enough to switch the direction of magnetization to the 1 state. A core switches to the 1 state only if there is a coincidence of two half-currents from a word driver and a bit driver. The direction of magnetization of a core does not change if it receives only half-current from one of the drivers. The result is that the magnetization of cores is switched to the 1 state only if the word and bit wires intersect, that is, only in the selected word and only in the bit position in which the buffer register is a 1.

The read and write operations described above are incomplete, because the information stored in the selected word is destroyed by the reading process and the write operation works properly only if the cores are initially cleared. As mentioned in Section 7-7, a read operation must be followed by another cycle that restores the values previously stored in the cores. A write operation is preceded by a cycle that clears the cores of the selected word.

The restore operation during a read cycle is equivalent to a write operation which, in effect, writes the previously read information from the buffer register back into the word selected. The clear operation during a write cycle is equivalent to a read operation which destroys the stored information but prevents the read information from reaching the buffer register by inhibiting the sense amplifier. Restore and clear cycles are normally initiated by the memory internal control, so that the memory unit appears to the outside as having a nondestructive read-out property.

REFERENCES

1. *The TTL Data Book for Design Engineers*. Dallas, Texas: Texas Instruments, Inc., 1976.

2. Blakeslee, T. R., *Digital Design with Standard MSI and LSI*. New York: John Wiley & Sons, 1975.

3. Barna A., and D. I. Porat, *Integrated Circuits in Digital Electronics*. New York: John Wiley & Sons, 1973.

4. Taub, H., and D. Schilling, *Digital Integrated Electronics*. New York: McGraw-Hill Book Co., 1977.

5. Grinich, V. H., and H. G. Jackson, *Introduction to Integrated Electronics*. New York: McGraw-Hill Book Co., 1975.

6. Kostopoulos, G. K., *Digital Engineering*. New York: McGraw-Hill Book Co., 1975.

7. Scott, N. R., *Electronic Computer Technology*. New York: McGraw-Hill Book Co., 1970, chap. 10.

8. Kline, R. M., *Digital Computer Design*. Englewood Cliffs, N.J.: Prentice-Hall, Inc., 1977, chap. 9.

PROBLEMS

7-1. The register of Fig. 7-1 transfers the input information into the flip-flops when the *CP* input goes through a positive-edge transition. Modify the circuit so that the input information is transferred into the register when a clock pulse goes through a negative-edge transition, provided a load input control is equal to binary 1.

7-2. The register of Fig. 7-3 loads the inputs during a negative transition of a clock pulse. What internal changes are necessary for the inputs to be loaded during the positive edge of a pulse?

7-3. Verify the circuit of Fig. 7-5 using maps to simplify the next-state equations.

7-4. Design the sequential circuit whose state table is given below using a 2-bit register and combinational gates.

Present state		Input	Next state	
A	B	x	A	B
0	0	0	0	0
0	0	1	0	1
0	1	0	1	0
0	1	1	0	1
1	0	0	1	0
1	0	1	1	1
1	1	0	1	0
1	1	1	0	1

7-5. Design a sequential circuit whose state diagram is given in Fig. 6-27 using a 3-bit register and a 16 × 4 ROM.

7-6. The content of a 4-bit shift register is initially 1101. The register is shifted six times to the right, with the serial input being 101101. What is the content of the register after each shift?

7-7. What is the difference between serial and parallel transfer? What type of register is used in each case?

7-8. The 4-bit bidirectional shift register of Fig. 7-9 is enclosed within one IC package.
      (a) Draw a block diagram of the IC showing all inputs and outputs.
      (b) Draw a block diagram using three ICs to produce a 12-bit bidirectional shift
      register.

7-9. The serial adder of Fig. 7-10 uses two 4-bit shift registers. Register A holds the
      binary number 0101 and register B holds 0111. The carry flip-flop Q is initially
      cleared. List the binary values in register A and flip-flop Q after each shift.

7-10. What changes are needed in the circuit of Fig. 7-11 to convert it to a circuit that
      subtracts the content of B from the content of A?

7-11. Design a serial counter; in other words, determine the circuit that must be included
      externally with a shift register in order to obtain a counter that operates in a serial
      fashion.

7-12. Draw the diagram of a 4-bit binary ripple counter using flip-flops that trigger on the
      positive edge.

7-13. A flip-flop has a 20-ns delay from the time its CP input goes from 1 to 0 to the time
      the output is complemented. What is the maximum delay in a 10-bit binary ripple
      counter that uses these flip-flops? What is the maximum frequency the counter can
      operate at reliably?

7-14. How many flip-flops must be complemented in a 10-bit binary ripple counter to
      reach the next count after 0111111111?

7-15. Draw the diagram of a 4-bit binary ripple down-counter using flip-flops that trigger
      on the (a) positive-edge transition and (b) negative-edge transition.

7-16. Draw a timing diagram similar to that in Fig. 7-15 for the binary ripple counter of
      Fig. 7-12.

7-17. Determine the next state for each of the six unused states in the BCD ripple counter
      of Fig. 7-14. Is the counter self-starting?

7-18. The ripple counter shown in Fig. P7-18 uses flip-flops that trigger on the negative-
      edge transition of the CP input. Determine the count sequence of the counter. Is the
      counter self-starting?

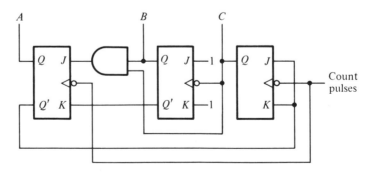

Figure P7-18   Ripple counter

7-19. What happens to the counter of Fig. 7-18 if both the up and down inputs are equal to 1 at the same time? Modify the circuit so that it will count up if this condition occurs.

7-20. Verify the flip-flop input functions of the synchronous BCD counter specified in Table 7-5. Draw the logic diagram of the BCD counter and include a count-enable control input.

7-21. Design a synchronous BCD counter with JK flip-flops.

7-22. Show the external connections of four IC binary counters with parallel load (Fig. 7-19) to produce a 16-bit binary counter. Use a block diagram for each IC.

7-23. Construct a BCD counter using the MSI circuit of Fig. 7-19.

7-24. Construct a mod-12 counter using the MSI circuit specified in Fig. 7-19. Give four alternatives.

7-25. Using two MSI circuits as specified in Fig. 7-19, construct a binary counter that counts from 0 to binary 64.

7-26. Using the *stop* variable from Fig. 7-21 as a start signal, construct a second word-time control that stays on for a period of 16 clock pulses.

7-27. Show that an n-bit binary counter connected to an n-to-2^n line decoder is equivalent to a ring counter with 2^n flip-flops. Draw the block diagrams of both circuits for $n = 3$. How many timing signals are generated?

7-28. Include an enable input to the decoder of Fig. 7-22(b) and connect it to the clock pulses. Draw the timing signals that are now generated at the outputs of the decoder.

7-29. Complete the design of the Johnson counter of Fig. 7-23, showing the outputs of the eight timing signals.

7-30. (a) List the eight unused states in the switch-tail ring counter of Fig. 7-23. Determine the next state for each unused state and show that, if the circuit finds itself in an invalid state, it does not return to a valid state. (b) Modify the circuit as recommended in the text and show that (1) the circuit produces the same sequence of states as listed in Fig. 7-23(b), and (2) the circuit reaches a valid state from any one of the unused states.

7-31. Construct a Johnson counter with ten timing signals.

7-32. (a) The memory unit of Fig. 7-24 has a capacity of 8192 words of 32 bits per word. How many flip-flops are needed for the memory address register and memory buffer register? (b) How many words will the memory unit contain if the address register has 15 bits?

7-33. When the number of words to be selected in a memory is too large, it is convenient to use a binary storage cell with two select inputs: one X (horizontal) and one Y (vertical) select input. Both X and Y must be enabled to select the cell.
(a) Draw a binary cell similar to that in Fig. 7-29 with X and Y select inputs.
(b) Show how two 4×16 decoders can be used to select a word in a 256-word memory.

7-34. (a) Draw a block diagram of the 4×3 memory of Fig. 7-30, showing all inputs and outputs. (b) Construct an 8×3 memory using two such units. Use a block diagram construction.

7-35. It is required to construct a memory with 256 words, 16 bits per word, organized as in Fig. 7-33. Cores are available in a matrix of 16 rows and 16 columns.

   (a) How many matrices are needed?

   (b) How many flip-flops are in the address and buffer registers?

   (c) How many cores receive current during a read cycle?

   (d) How many cores receive at least half-current during a write cycle?

Algorithmic
State
Machines (ASM)

8

8-1 INTRODUCTION

The binary information stored in a digital system can be classified as either data or control information. Data are discrete elements of information that are manipulated to perform arithmetic, logic, shift, and other similar data-processing tasks. These operations are implemented with digital components such as adders, decoders, multiplexers, counters, and shift registers. Control information provides command signals that supervise the various operations in the data section in order to accomplish the desired data-processing tasks. The logic design of a digital system can be divided into two distinct parts. One part is concerned with the design of the digital circuits that perform the data-processing operations. The other part is concerned with the design of the control circuit that supervises the operations and their sequence.

The relationship between the control logic and the data processor in a digital system is shown in Fig. 8-1. The data processor subsystem manipulates data in registers according to the system's requirements. The control logic initiates properly sequenced commands to the data processor. The control logic uses status conditions from the data processor to serve as decision variables for determining the sequence of control signals.

The control logic that generates the signals for sequencing the operations in the data processor is a sequential circuit whose internal states dictate the control commands for the system. At any given time, the state of the sequential control initiates a prescribed set of commands. Depending on status conditions and other external inputs, the sequential control goes to the next state to initiate other operations. The digital circuits that act as the control logic provide a time sequence of signals for initiating the operations in the data processor and also determine the next state of the control subsystem itself.

The control sequence and data-processing tasks of a digital system are specified by means of a hardware algorithm. An algorithm consists of a finite number of procedural steps that specify how to obtain a solution to a problem. A hardware

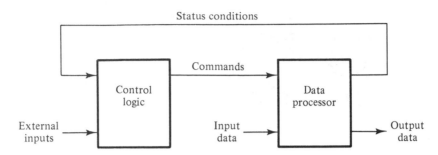

Status conditions

Commands

Control
logic

Data
processor

External
inputs

Input
data

Output
data

Figure 8-1 Control and data processor interaction

algorithm is a procedure for implementing the problem with a given piece of equipment. The most challenging and creative part of digital design is the formulation of hardware algorithms for achieving required objectives.

A flowchart is a convenient way to specify the sequence of procedural steps and decision paths for an algorithm. A flowchart for a hardware algorithm translates the word statement to an information diagram that enumerates the sequence of operations together with the conditions necessary for their execution. A special flowchart that has been developed specifically to define digital hardware algorithms is called an *algorithmic state machine* (ASM) chart. A *state machine* is another term for a sequential circuit, which is the basic structure of a digital system.

The ASM chart resembles a conventional flowchart but is interpreted somewhat differently. A conventional flowchart describes the sequence of procedural steps and decision paths for an algorithm without concern for their time relationship. The ASM chart describes the sequence of events as well as the timing relationship between the states of a sequential controller and the events that occur while going from one state to the next. It is specifically adapted to specify accurately the control sequence and data-processing operations in a digital system, taking into consideration the constraints of digital hardware.

This chapter presents a method of digital logic design using the ASM chart. The various blocks that make up the chart are first defined. The timing relationship between the blocks is then explained by example. Various ways of implementing the control logic are discussed together with examples of ASM charts and the corresponding digital systems that they represent.

8-2 ASM CHART

The ASM chart is a special type of flowchart suitable for describing the sequential operations in a digital system. The chart is composed of three basic elements: the state box, the decision box, and the conditional box. A state in the control sequence is indicated by a state box, as shown in Fig. 8-2. The shape of the state box is a rectangle within which are written register operations or output signal names that the control generates while being in this state. The state is given a symbolic name,

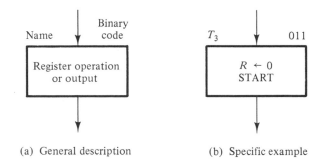

(a) General description   (b) Specific example

Figure 8-2 State box

which is placed at the upper left corner of the box. The binary code assigned to the state is placed at the upper right corner. Figure 8-2(b) shows a specific example of a state box. The state has the symbolic name T_3, and the binary code assigned to it is 011. Inside the box is written the register operation $R \leftarrow 0$, which indicates that register R is to be cleared to 0 when the system is in state T_3. The START name inside the box may indicate, for example, an output signal that starts a certain operation.

The decision box describes the effect of an input on the control subsystem. It has a diamond-shaped box with two or more exit paths, as shown in Fig. 8-3. The input condition to be tested is written inside the box. One exit path is taken if the condition is true and another when the condition is false. When an input condition is assigned a binary value, the two paths are indicated by 1 and 0.

The state and decision boxes are familiar from use in conventional flowcharts. The third element, the conditional box, is unique to the ASM chart. The oval shape of the conditional box is shown in Fig. 8-4. The rounded corners differentiate it from the state box. The input path to the conditional box must come from one of the exit paths of a decision box. The register operations or outputs listed inside the conditional box are generated during a given state provided that the input condition is satisfied. Figure 8-5 shows an example with a conditional box. The control generates a START output signal when in state T_1. While in state T_1, the control checks the status of input E. If $E = 1$, then R is cleared to 0; otherwise, R remains unchanged. In either case, the next state is T_2.

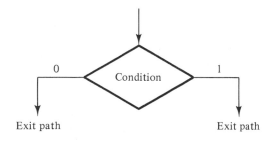

Figure 8-3 Decision box

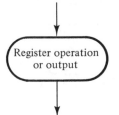

Figure 8-4   Conditional box

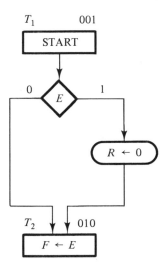

Figure 8-5   Example with conditional box

ASM Block

An ASM block is a structure consisting of one state box and all the decision and conditional boxes connected to its exit path. An ASM block has one entrance and any number of exit paths represented by the structure of the decision boxes. An ASM chart consists of one or more interconnected blocks. An example of an ASM block is shown in Fig. 8-6. Associated with state T_1 are two decision boxes and one conditional box. The diagram distinguishes the block with dashed lines around the entire structure, but this is not usually done, since the ASM chart uniquely defines each block from its structure. A state box without any decision or conditional boxes constitutes a simple block.

Each block in the ASM chart describes the state of the system during one clock pulse interval. The operations within the state and conditional boxes in Fig. 8-6 are executed with a common clock pulse while the system is in state T_1. The same clock

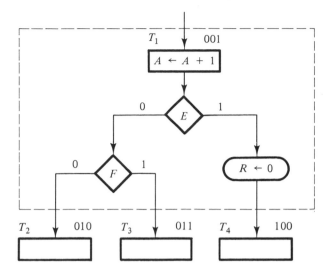

Figure 8-6 ASM block

pulse also transfers the system controller to one of the next states, T_2, T_3, or T_4, as dictated by the binary values of E and F.

The ASM chart is very similar to a state diagram. Each state block is equivalent to a state in a sequential circuit. The decision box is equivalent to the binary information written along the directed lines that connect two states in a state diagram. As a consequence, it is sometimes convenient to convert the chart into a state diagram and then use sequential circuit procedures to design the control logic. As an illustration, the ASM chart of Fig. 8-6 is drawn as a state diagram in Fig. 8-7. The three states are symbolized by circles with their binary value written inside each circle. The directed lines indicate the conditions that determine the next state. The unconditional and conditional operations that must be performed are not indicated in the state diagram.

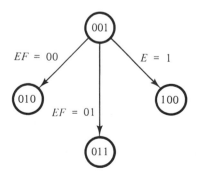

Figure 8-7 State diagram equivalent to the ASM chart of Fig. 8-6

TABLE 8-1 Symbolic notation for register operations

Symbolic notation	Description
$A \leftarrow B$	Transfer contents of register B into register A
$R \leftarrow 0$	Clear register R
$F \leftarrow 1$	Set flip-flop F to 1
$A \leftarrow A + 1$	Increment register A by 1 (count-up)
$A \leftarrow A - 1$	Decrement register A by 1 (count-down)
$A \leftarrow A + B$	Add contents of register B to register A

Register Operations

A digital system is quite often defined by the registers it contains and the operations that are performed on the data stored in them. A *register* in its broader sense includes storage registers, shift registers, counters, and single flip-flops. Examples of register operations are shift, increment, add, clear, and data transfer. It is sometimes convenient to adopt a suitable notation to describe the operations performed among the registers.

Table 8-1 gives examples of symbolic notation for some register operations. A register is designated by one or more capital letters such as A, B, or RA. The individual cells or flip-flops within an n-bit register are numbered in sequence from 1 to n or from 0 to $n - 1$. A single flip-flop is considered a 1-bit register. The transfer of data from one register to another is symbolized by a directed arrow that denotes a transfer of contents from the source register to the destination register. The register clear operation is symbolized by a transfer of 0 into the register. A single flip-flop can be set to 1 or cleared to 0. To increment a register by 1, it is necessary that the register be able to count-up as in a binary counter. The decrement operation requires a count-down counter. The contents of two registers can be added by means of an adder circuit. Some operations, such as the shift operation, do not have a known symbol. In such a case we will use the words "shift right R" to denote a shift right of register R.

8-3 TIMING CONSIDERATIONS

The timing for all registers and flip-flops in a digital system is controlled by a master clock generator. The clock pulses are applied not only to the registers of the data-processor subsection but also to all the flip-flops in the control logic. Inputs are also synchronized with the clock pulses because they are normally generated as outputs of another circuit that uses the same clock signals. If the input signal changes at an arbitrary time independent of the clock, we call it an asynchronous input. Asynchronous inputs may cause a variety of problems, as discussed in Chapter 9. To simplify the design, we will assume that all inputs are synchronized

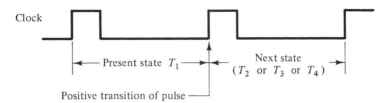

Clock

Present state T_1

Next state
(T_2 or T_3 or T_4)

Positive transition of pulse

Figure 8-8 Transition between states

with the clock and change state in response to an edge transition of the clock pulse. Similarly, any output that is a function of the present state and a synchronous input will also be synchronous.

The major difference between a conventional flowchart and an ASM chart is in interpreting the time relationship among the various operations. For example, if Fig. 8-6 were a conventional flowchart, then the listed operations would be considered to follow one after another in time sequence: Register A is first incremented and only then is E evaluated. If $E = 1$, then register R is cleared and control goes to state T_4. Otherwise, if $E = 0$, the next step is to evaluate F and go to state T_2 or T_3. In contrast, an ASM chart considers the entire block as one unit. All the operations that are specified within the block must occur in synchronism during the edge transition of the same clock pulse while the system changes from T_1 to the next state. This is presented pictorially in Fig. 8-8. We assume positive edge triggering of all flip-flops. The first positive transition of the clock transfers the control circuit into state T_1. While in state T_1, the control circuits check inputs E and F and generate appropriate signals accordingly. The following operations occur simultaneously during the next positive transition of the clock pulse:

1. Register A is incremented.

2. If $E = 1$, register R is cleared.

3. Depending on the values of E and F, control is transferred to next state, T_2 or T_3 or T_4.

Note that the operations in the data-processor subsection and the change of state in the control logic occur at the same time.

We will now demonstrate the time relationship between the components of an ASM chart by going over a specific design example. The example does not have any known application and is merely formulated to show the usefulness of the ASM Chart. We start from the initial specifications and proceed with the development of an appropriate ASM chart from which the digital hardware can be derived.

Design Example

We wish to design a digital system with two flip-flops E and F and one 4-bit binary counter A. The individual flip-flops in A are denoted by A_4, A_3, A_2, and A_1, with A_4

311

holding the most significant bit of the count. A start signal S initiates the system operation by clearing the counter A and flip-flop F. The counter is then incremented by 1 starting from the next clock pulse and continues to increment until the operations stop. Counter bits A_3 and A_4 determine the sequence of operations:

If $A_3 = 0$, E is cleared to 0 and the count continues.

If $A_3 = 1$, E is set to 1; then if $A_4 = 0$, the count continues, but if $A_4 = 1$, F is set to 1 on the next clock pulse and the system stops counting.

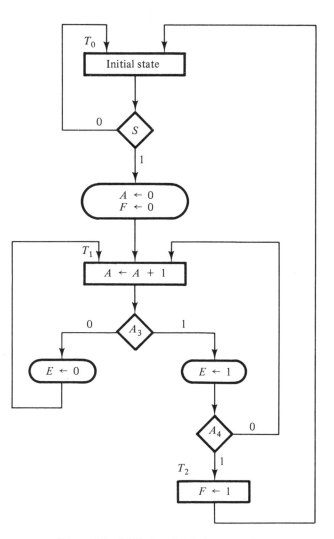

Figure 8-9   ASM chart for design example

ASM Chart

The ASM chart is shown in Fig. 8-9. When no operations are performed, the system is in the initial state T_0, waiting for the start signal S. When input S is equal to 1, counter A and flip-flop F are cleared to 0 and the controller goes to state T_1. Note the conditional box that follows the decision box for S. This means that the counter and flip-flop will be cleared during T_0 if $S = 1$, and at the same time, control transfers to state T_1. The block associated with state T_1 has two decision boxes and two conditional boxes. The counter is incremented with every clock pulse. At the same time, one of three possible operations occur during the same clock pulse transition:

Either E is cleared and control stays in state T_1 $(A_3 = 0)$;

or E is set and control stays in state T_1 $(A_3 A_4 = 10)$;

or E is set and control goes to state T_2 $(A_3 A_4 = 11)$.

When the control is in state T_2, flip-flop F is set to 1 and the circuit goes back to its initial state, T_0.

The ASM chart consists of three states and three blocks. The block associated with T_0 consists of the state box, one decision box, and one conditional box. The block associated with T_2 consists of only the state box. The control logic has one external input, S, and two status inputs, A_3 and A_4.

Timing Sequence

Every block in an ASM chart specifies the operations that are to be performed during one common clock pulse. The operations specified within the state and conditional boxes in the block are performed in the data-processor subsection. The change from one state to the next is performed in the control logic. In order to appreciate the timing relationship involved, we will list the step-by-step sequence of operations after each clock pulse from the time the start signal occurs until the system goes back to its initial state.

Table 8-2 shows the binary values of the counter and the two flip-flops after every clock pulse. The table also shows separately the status of A_3 and A_4 as well as the present state of the controller. We start with state T_1 right after the input signal S has caused the counter and flip-flop F to be cleared. The value of E is assumed to be 1, because E is equal to 1 at T_0 (as shown at the end of the table) and because E does not change during the transition from T_0 to T_1. The system stays in state T_1 during the next thirteen clock pulses. Each pulse increments the counter and either clears or sets E. Note the relationship between the time at which A_3 becomes a 1 and the time at which E is set to 1. When $A = 0011$, the next clock pulse increments the counter to 0100, but that same clock pulse sees the value of A_3 as 0, so E is cleared. The next pulse changes the counter from 0100 to 0101, and now A_3 is

TABLE 8-2 Sequence of operations for design example

Counter				Flip-flops		Conditions	State
A_4	A_3	A_2	A_1	E	F		
0	0	0	0	1	0	$A_3 = 0, A_4 = 0$	T_1
0	0	0	1	0	0		
0	0	1	0	0	0		
0	0	1	1	0	0		
0	1	0	0	0	0	$A_3 = 1, A_4 = 0$	
0	1	0	1	1	0		
0	1	1	0	1	0		
0	1	1	1	1	0		
1	0	0	0	1	0	$A_3 = 0, A_4 = 1$	
1	0	0	1	0	0		
1	0	1	0	0	0		
1	0	1	1	0	0		
1	1	0	0	0	0	$A_3 = 1, A_4 = 1$	
1	1	0	1	1	0		T_2
1	1	0	1	1	1		T_0

initially equal to 1, so E is set to 1. Similarly, E is cleared to 0 not when the count goes from 0111 to 1000 but when it goes from 1000 to 1001, which is when A_3 is 0 in the present value of the counter.

When the count reaches 1100, both A_3 and A_4 are equal to 1. The next clock pulse increments A by 1, sets E to 1, and transfers control to state T_2. Control stays in T_2 for only one clock period. The pulse transition associated with T_2 sets flip-flop F to 1 and transfers control to state T_0. The system stays in the initial state T_0 as long as S is equal to 0.

From observation of Table 8-2 it may seem that the operations performed on E are delayed by one clock pulse. This is the difference between an ASM chart and a conventional flowchart. If Fig. 8-9 were a conventional flowchart, we would assume that A is first incremented and the incremented value would have been used to check the status of A_3. The operations that are performed in the digital hardware as specified by a block in the ASM chart occur during the same clock period and not in a sequence of operations following each other in time, as is usually interpreted in a conventional flowchart. Thus, the value of A_3 to be considered in the decision box is taken from the value of the counter in the present state and before it is incremented. This is because the decision box for E belongs with the same block as state T_1. The digital circuits in the control generate the signals for all the operations specified in the present block prior to the arrival of the next clock pulse. The next clock transition executes all the operations in the registers and flip-flops, including the flip-flops in the controller that determine the next state.

Data Processor

The ASM chart gives all the information necessary to design the digital system. The requirements for the design of the data-processor subsystem are specified inside the state and conditional boxes. The control logic is determined from the decision boxes and the required state transitions. A diagram showing the hardware for the design example is shown in Fig. 8-10. The control subsystem is shown with only its inputs and outputs. The detailed design of the control is considered in the next section. The data processor consists of a 4-bit binary counter, two flip-flops, and a number of gates. The counter is similar to the one shown in Fig. 7-17 except that additional

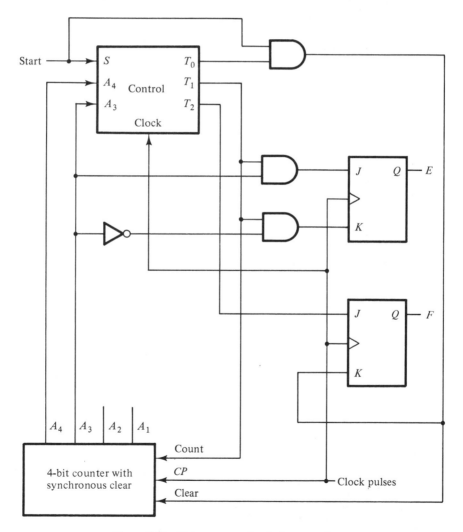

Figure 8-10   Data processor for design example

315

gates are required for the synchronous clear operation. The counter is incremented with every clock pulse when control is in state T_1. It is cleared only when control is at state T_0 and S is equal to 1. This conditional operation requires an AND gate to guarantee that both conditions are present. The other two conditional operations use two other AND gates for setting or clearing flip-flop E. Flip-flop F is set unconditionally during state T_2. Note that all flip-flops and registers including the flip-flops in the control use a common clock pulse source.

This example demonstrates a method of digital design using the ASM chart. The design of the data-processor subsystem requires an interpretation of the register operations and their implementation by means of the components introduced in Chapters 5 and 7 such as registers, counters, multiplexers, and adders. The design of the control subsystem requires the application of design procedures based on the theory of sequential logic. The next three sections present some of the alternatives that are available for designing the control logic.

8-4   CONTROL IMPLEMENTATION

The control section of a digital system is essentially a sequential circuit that can be designed by the procedure outlined in Chapter 6. However, in most cases this method is impractical because of the large number of states and inputs that a typical control circuit may have. Except for very simple controllers, the design method that uses state and excitation tables is cumbersome and difficult to manage. Experienced digital designers use specialized methods for control logic design that may be considered an extension of the classical sequential method combined with other simplified assumptions. Two of these specialized methods are presented in this section, and a third method is explained in Section 8-5. Another alternative is to use a ROM or PLA to design the control logic. This is covered in Section 8-6.

State Table

As mentioned previously, the ASM chart resembles a state diagram with each state box representing a state. The state diagram can be converted into a state table from which the sequential circuit of the controller can be designed. First we must assign binary values to each state in the ASM chart. For n flip-flops in the control sequential circuit, the ASM chart can accommodate up to 2^n states. A chart with three or four states requires a sequential circuit with two flip-flops. With five to eight states, there is a need for three flip-flops. Each combination of flip-flop values represents a binary number for one of the states.

A state table for a controller is a list of present states and inputs and their corresponding next states and outputs. In most cases there are many don't-care input conditions that must be included, so it is advisable to arrange the state table to take this into consideration. In order to clarify the procedure, we will illustrate by obtaining the state table of the controller defined in the example of the previous section.

TABLE 8-3   State table for control of Fig. 8-10

Present state symbol	Present state G_1	G_2	Inputs S	A_3	A_4	Next state G_1	G_2	Outputs T_0	T_1	T_2
T_0	0	0	0	X	X	0	0	1	0	0
T_0	0	0	1	X	X	0	1	1	0	0
T_1	0	1	X	0	X	0	1	0	1	0
T_1	0	1	X	1	0	0	1	0	1	0
T_1	0	1	X	1	1	1	1	0	1	0
T_2	1	1	X	X	X	0	0	0	0	1

The ASM chart of the design example is shown in Fig. 8-9. We assign the following binary values to the three states: $T_0 = 00$, $T_1 = 01$, $T_2 = 11$. Binary state 10 is not used and will be treated as a don't-care condition. The state table corresponding to the ASM chart is shown in Table 8-3. Two flip-flops are needed, and they are labeled G_1 and G_2. There are three inputs and three outputs. The inputs are taken from the conditions in the decision boxes. The outputs are equivalent to the present state of the control. Note that there is a row in the table for each possible transition between states. Initial state 00 goes to state 01 or stays in 00 depending on the value of input S. The other two inputs are marked with don't-care X's, as they do not determine the next state in this case. While the system is in binary state 00, the control provides an output labeled T_0 to initiate the required register operations. The transition from binary state 01 depends on inputs A_3 and A_4. The system goes to binary state 11 only if $A_3A_4 = 11$; otherwise, it remains in binary state 01. Finally, binary state 11 goes to 00 independently of the input variables.

This example demonstrates a state table for a sequential controller. Note again the large number of don't-care conditions under the inputs. The number of rows in the state table is equal to the number of distinct paths between the states in the ASM chart.

Logic Diagram with *JK* Flip-flops

The procedure for designing a sequential circuit starting from a state table is presented in Section 6-7. This procedure requires that we obtain the excitation table of the flip-flop inputs and then simplify the combinational-circuit part of the sequential circuit. If we apply this procedure to Table 8-3, we will need to use five-variable maps (see Fig. 3-11) to simplify the input functions. This is because there are five variables listed under the "present state" and "input" columns. Since this procedure was explained in Chapter 6, we will not show the detail work here. The flip-flop input functions obtained by this method, if we assume JK flip-flops, are:

$$JG_1 = G_2 A_3 A_4 \qquad JG_2 = S$$
$$KG_1 = 1 \qquad KG_2 = G_1$$

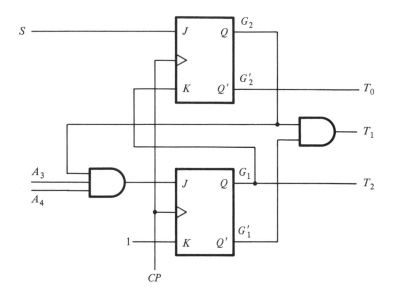

Figure 8-11   Logic diagram of control using JK flip-flops

To derive the three output functions, we can utilize the fact that binary state 10 is not used and obtain the following simplified functions:

$$T_0 = G_2'$$
$$T_1 = G_1'G_2$$
$$T_2 = G_1$$

The logic diagram of the control is shown in Fig. 8-11. This circuit replaces the control block in Fig. 8-10.

D Flip-Flops and Decoder

When the number of flip-flops plus inputs in a state table is greater than five, it is necessary to use large maps to simplify the input functions. This is cumbersome and difficult to achieve, as explained in Chapter 3. Therefore, it is necessary to find alternative ways to design controllers except when they are very simple. One possibility is to use D-type flip-flops and obtain the input functions directly from the state table without the need of an excitation table. This is because the next state is the same as the input requirement for the D flip-flops (see Section 6-9). To design the sequential circuit with D flip-flops, it is necessary to go over the next state column in the state table and derive all the conditions that must set each flip-flop to 1. From Table 8-3 we note that the next state column of G_1 has a single 1 in the fifth row. The D input of flip-flop G_1 must be equal to 1 during present state $T_1 = G_1'G_2$ when both inputs A_3 and A_4 are equal to 1. This is expressed with the D

flip-flop input function:

$$DG_1 = G_1'G_2A_3A_4$$

Similarly, the next state column of G_2 has four 1's, and the condition for setting this flip-flop is:

$$DG_2 = G_1'G_2'S + G_1'G_2$$

We can go one step further and insert a decoder at the output of the flip-flops to obtain the necessary three outputs, T_0, T_1, and T_2. Then, instead of using the flip-flop outputs as the present-state condition, we might as well use the outputs of the decoder to supply this information. The input functions to the D flip-flops can now be expressed as follows:

$$DG_1 = A_3A_4T_1$$
$$DG_2 = ST_0 + T_1$$

The alternative logic diagram is shown in Fig. 8-12. The decoder provides the three control outputs, and these outputs are also used to determine the next state of each flip-flop. The second control circuit requires more components than the first, but it has the advantage that it can be derived by inspection from the state table.

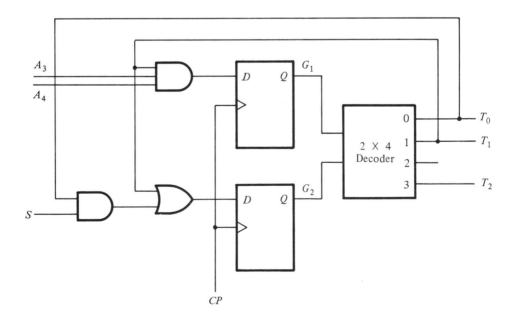

Figure 8-12   Alternate logic diagram of control using D flip-flops and a decoder

One Flip-Flop per State

Another possible method of control logic design is to use one flip-flop per state in the sequential circuit. Only one flip-flop is set at any particular time; all others are cleared to 0. The single bit is made to propagate from one flip-flop to the other under the control of decision logic. In such an array, each flip-flop represents a state that is activated only when the control bit is transferred to it.

It is obvious that this method does not use a minimum number of flip-flops for the sequential circuit. In fact, it uses a maximum number of flip-flops. For example, a sequential circuit with 12 states requires a minimum of four flip-flops. Yet by this method, the control circuit needs 12 flip-flops, one for each state.

A control organization that uses one flip-flop per state has the convenient characteristic that the circuit can be derived directly from the state diagram without the need of state or excitation tables. Consider for example the state diagram of Fig. 8-13. This diagram is equivalent to the ASM chart of the design example from Fig. 8-9 as far as the control-state transitions are concerned. Since the diagram has three states, we assign three flip-flops to the circuit and label them T_0, T_1, and T_2. The controller can be designed by inspection from the state diagram if D-type flip-flops are used. The Boolean function for setting the flip-flop is determined from the present state and the input conditions along the directed lines. For example, flip-flop T_0 is set with the next clock pulse if present state $T_2 = 1$ or if present state $T_0 = 1$ and input $S = 0$. This condition is defined by the flip-flop input function:

$$DT_0 = T_2 + S'T_0$$

where DT_0 designates the D input of flip-flop T_0. In fact, the condition for setting a flip-flop to 1 is obtained directly from the state diagram from the condition specified in the directed lines going into the corresponding flip-flop state ANDed with the previous flip-flop state. If there is more than one directed line going into a state, all conditions must be ORed. Using this procedure for the other two flip-flops, we obtain the input functions:

$$DT_1 = ST_0 + A_3'T_1 + A_3A_4'T_1 = ST_0 + (A_3A_4)'T_1$$
$$DT_2 = A_3A_4T_1$$

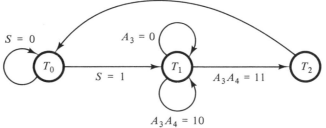

Figure 8-13   State diagram of controller

The logic diagram is shown in Fig. 8-14. It consists of three D flip-flops T_0, T_1, and T_2 and the associated gates specified by the input functions listed above.

Initially, flip-flop T_0 must be set to 1 and all other flip-flops cleared to 0 so that the flip-flop representing the initial state is equal to 1 and all other states equal to 0. Once started, the one flip-flop per state controller will propagate itself from state to state in the proper manner. For a register with a common asynchronous clear input, as shown in Fig. 8-14, all flip-flops including the Q output of T_0 are cleared to 0. Taking the output of T_0 from the complement output Q' provides the required initial 1 signal for T_0. In order to keep Q' as the output of T_0, it is necessary that the input function to the D input be complemented. This is done by the extra inverter that is placed at the D input of flip-flop T_0.

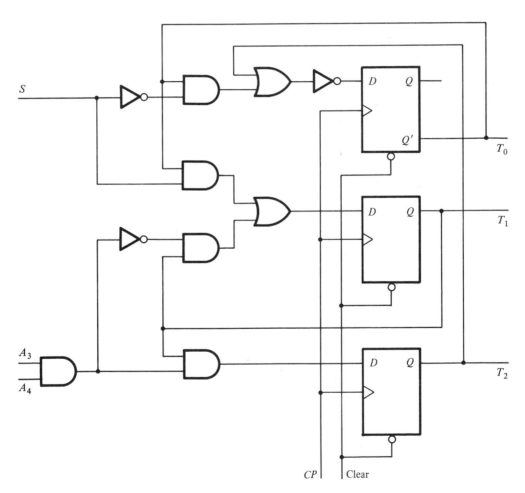

Figure 8-14   Third alternate logic diagram of control using one flip-flop per state

8-5 DESIGN WITH MULTIPLEXERS

One major goal of control-logic design is the development of a circuit that implements the desired control sequence in a logical and straightforward manner. The attempt to minimize the number of gates tends to produce an irregular network making it difficult for anyone but the designer to identify the sequence of events the control undergoes. As a consequence, it is difficult to alter, service, or maintain the equipment after the initial design. The sequence of states in the control should be clearly evident from the circuit configuration even if this requires additional components and results in a nonminimal circuit. The multiplexer method is such an implementation.

The control circuit shown in Fig. 8-12 consists of three components: the flip-flops that hold the binary state value, the decoder that generates the control outputs, and the gates that determine the next state. We now replace the gates with multiplexers and use a register for the individual flip-flops. This design method results in a regular pattern of three levels of components. The first level consists of multiplexers that determine the next state of the register. The second level contains a register that holds the present binary state. The third level has the decoder that provides a separate output for each control state.

Consider for example the ASM chart of Fig. 8-15. It consists of four states and four control inputs. The state boxes are left empty in this case because we are interested only in the control sequence, which is independent of the register operations. The binary assignment for each state is indicated at the upper right corner of the state boxes. The decision boxes specify the state transitions as a function of the four control inputs w, x, y, and z. The three-level control implementation is shown in Fig. 8-16. It consists of two multiplexers MUX1 and MUX2, a register with two flip-flops G_1 and G_2, and a decoder with four outputs. The outputs of the register are applied to the decoder inputs and also to the select inputs of the multiplexers. In this way, the present state of the register is used to select one of the inputs from each multiplexer. The outputs of the multiplexers are then applied to the D inputs of G_1 and G_2. The purpose of each multiplexer is to produce an input to its corresponding flip-flop equal to the binary value of the next state.

The inputs of the multiplexers are determined from the decision boxes and state transitions given in the ASM chart. For example, state 00 stays at 00 or goes to 01 depending on the value of input w. Since the next state of G_1 is 0 in either case, we place a signal equivalent to logic-0 in MUX1 input 0. The next state of G_2 is 0 if $w = 0$ and 1 if $w = 1$. Since the next state of G_2 is equal to w, we apply control input w to MUX2 input 0. What this means is that when the select inputs of the multiplexers are equal to present state 00, the outputs of the multiplexers provide the binary value that is transferred to the register during the next clock pulse.

To facilitate the evaluation of the multiplexer inputs, we prepare a table showing the input conditions for each possible transition in the ASM chart. Table 8-4 gives this information for the ASM chart of Fig. 8-15. There are two transitions from present state 00 or 01 and three transitions from present state 10 or 11. These

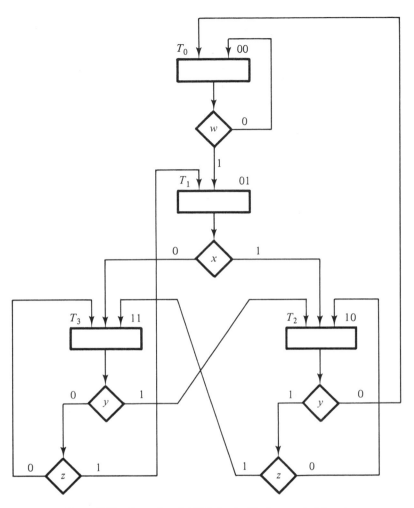

Figure 8-15 Example of ASM chart with four control inputs

are separated by horizontal lines across the table. The input conditions listed in the table are obtained from the decision boxes in the ASM chart. For example, from Fig. 8-15 we note that present state 01 will go to next state 10 if $x = 1$ or to next state 11 if $x = 0$. In the table we mark these input conditions as x and x', respectively. The two columns under "multiplexer inputs" in the table specify the input values that must be applied to MUX1 and MUX2. The multiplexer input for each present state is determined from the input conditions when the next state of the flip-flop is equal to 1. Thus, after present state 01, the next state of G_1 is always equal to 1 and the next state of G_2 is equal to the complement value of x. Therefore, the input of MUX1 is made equal to 1 and that of MUX2 to x' when the present state of the register is 01. As another example, after present state 10, the next state

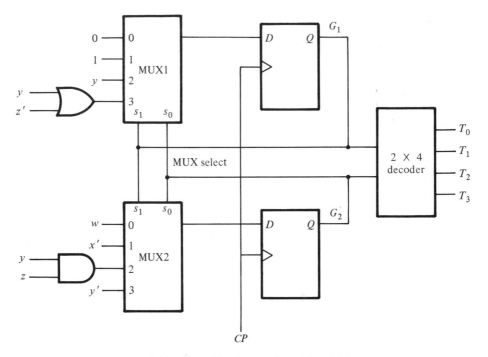

Figure 8-16 Control implementation with multiplexers

TABLE 8-4 Multiplexer input conditions

Present state		Next state		Input	Multiplexer inputs	
G_1	G_2	G_1	G_2	conditions	MUX1	MUX2
0	0	0	0	w'		
0	0	0	1	w	0	w
0	1	1	0	x		
0	1	1	1	x'	1	x'
1	0	0	0	y'		
1	0	1	0	yz'		
1	0	1	1	yz	$yz' + yz = y$	yz
1	1	0	1	$y'z$		
1	1	1	0	y		
1	1	1	1	$y'z'$	$y + y'z' = y + z'$	$y'z + y'z' = y'$

of G_1 must be equal to 1 if the input conditions are yz' or yz. When these two Boolean terms are ORed together and then simplified, we obtain the single binary variable y, as indicated in the table. The next state of G_2 is equal to 1 if the input conditions are $yz = 11$. If the next state of G_1 remains at 0 after a given present state, we place a 0 in the multiplexer input as shown in present state 00 for MUX1. If the next state of G_1 is always 1, we place a 1 in the multiplexer input as shown in present state 01 for MUX1. The other entries for MUX1 and MUX2 are derived in a similar manner. The multiplexer inputs from the table are then used in the control implementation of Fig. 8-16. Note that if the next state of a flip-flop is a function of two or more control variables, the multiplexer may require one or more gates in its input. Otherwise, the multiplexer input is equal to the control variable, or the complement of the control variable, or 0, or 1.

Design Example

We will demonstrate the multiplexer control implementation by means of a second design example. The example will also demonstrate the formulation of the ASM chart and the implementation of the data-processor subsystem.

The digital system to be designed consists of two registers $R1$ and $R2$ and a flip-flop E. The system counts the number of 1's in the number loaded into register $R1$ and sets register $R2$ to that number. For example, if the binary number loaded into $R1$ is 10111001, the circuit counts the five 1's in $R1$ and sets register $R2$ to the binary count 101. This is done by shifting each bit from register $R1$ one at a time into flip-flop E. The value in E is checked by the control, and each time it is equal to 1, register $R2$ is incremented by 1.

The control subsystem uses one external input S to start the operation and two status inputs E and Z from the data processor. E is the output of the flip-flop. Z is the output of a circuit that checks the contents of register $R1$ for all 0's. The circuit produces an output $Z = 1$ when $R1$ is equal to 0.

The ASM chart for the design example is shown in Fig. 8-17. The binary number is loaded into $R1$, and register $R2$ is set to an all 1's value. Note that a number with all 1's in a register when incremented produces a number with all 0's. In state T_1, register $R2$ is incremented and the content of $R1$ is examined. If the content is zero, then $Z = 1$, and it signifies that there are no 1's stored in the register; so the operation terminates with $R2$ equal to 0. If the content of $R1$ is not zero, then $Z = 0$, and it indicates that there are some 1's stored in the register. The number in $R1$ is shifted and its leftmost bit transferred into E. This is done as many times as necessary until a 1 is transferred into E. For every 1 detected in E, register $R2$ is incremented and register $R1$ is checked again for more 1's. The major loop is repeated until all the 1's in $R1$ are counted. Note that the state box of T_3 has no register operations but the block associated with it contains the decision box for E. Also note that the serial input to shift register $R1$ must be equal to 0 because we don't want to shift external 1's into $R1$.

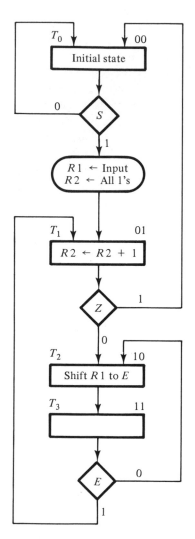

Figure 8-17 ASM chart for design example

The data-processor subsystem is shown in Fig. 8-18. The control has three inputs and four outputs. Only three outputs are used by the data processor. Register $R1$ is a shift register similar to the one shown in Fig. 7-9. Register $R2$ is a counter with parallel load similar to the one shown in Fig. 7-19. In order not to complicate the diagram, the clock pulses are not shown, but they must be applied to the two registers, the E flip-flop, and the flip-flops in the control. The circuit that checks for zero is a NOR gate. For example, if $R1$ is a four-bit register with outputs R_1, R_2, R_3, R_4, then Z is generated with the Boolean function

$$Z = R_1' R_2' R_3' R_4' = (R_1 + R_2 + R_3 + R_4)'$$

which is the NOR functions of all bits in the register.

326

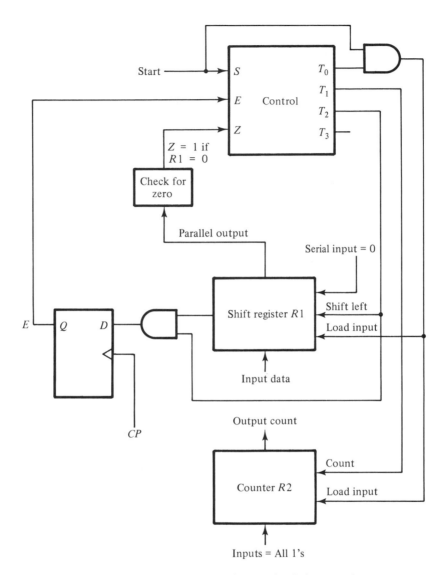

Figure 8-18 Data processor subsystem for design example

The multiplexer input conditions for the control are determined from Table 8-5. The input conditions are obtained from the ASM chart for each possible binary state transition. The binary assignment to each state is written at the upper right corner of the state boxes. The transition from present state 00 depends on S, from present state 01 depends on Z, and from present state 11 on E. Present state 10 goes to next state 11 unconditionally. The values under MUX1 and MUX2 in the table are determined from the input Boolean conditions for the next state of G_1 and G_2, respectively.

TABLE 8-5 Multiplexer input conditions for design example

Present state		Next state		Input conditions	Multiplexer inputs	
G_1	G_2	G_1	G_2		MUX1	MUX2
0	0	0	0	S'		
0	0	0	1	S	0	S
0	1	0	0	Z		
0	1	1	0	Z'	Z'	0
1	0	1	1	None	1	1
1	1	1	0	E'		
1	1	0	1	E	E'	E

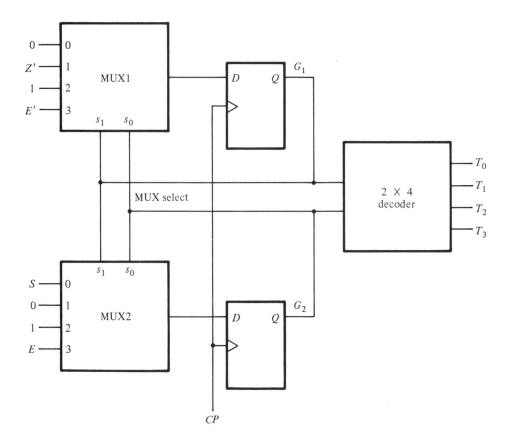

Figure 8-19 Control implementation of design example

The control implementation of the design example is shown in Fig. 8-19. This is a three-level implementation with the multiplexers in the first level. The inputs to the multiplexers are obtained from Table 8-5.

8-6 PLA CONTROL

We have seen from the examples presented in this chapter that the design of a control circuit is essentially a sequential logic problem. In Section 7-2 we showed that a sequential circuit can be constructed by means of a register connected to a combinational circuit. In Section 5-8 we investigated the programmable logic array (PLA) and showed that it can be used to implement any combinational circuit. Since the control logic is a sequential circuit, it is then possible to design the control circuit with a register connected to a PLA. The design of a PLA control requires that we obtain the state table of the circuit. The PLA method should be used if the state table contains many don't-care entries; otherwise, it may be advantageous to use a ROM instead of a PLA.

The PLA control will be demonstrated by means of a third design example. This example is an arithmetic circuit that multiplies two unsigned binary numbers and produces their binary product.

Binary Multiplier

The multiplication of two binary numbers is done with paper and pencil by successive additions and shifting. This process is best illustrated with a numerical example. Let us multiply the two binary numbers 10111 and 10011.

23	10111	multiplicand
19	10011	multiplier
	10111	
	10111	
	00000	
	00000	
	10111	
437	110110101	product

The process consists of looking at successive bits of the multiplier, least significant bit first. If the multiplier bit is a 1, the multiplicand is copied down; otherwise, 0's are copied down. The numbers copied down in successive lines are shifted one position to the left from the previous number. Finally, the numbers are added and their sum forms the product. Note that the product obtained from the multiplication of two binary numbers of n bits each can be up to $2n$ bits long.

When the above process is implemented with digital hardware, it is convenient to change the process slightly. First, instead of providing digital circuits to store and add simultaneously as many binary numbers as there are 1's in the multiplier, it is convenient to provide circuits for the summation of only two binary numbers and successively accumulate the partial products in a register. Second, instead of shifting the multiplicand to the left, the partial product is shifted to the right, which results in leaving the partial product and the multiplicand in the required relative positions. Third, when the corresponding bit of the multiplier is a 0, there is no need to add all 0's to the partial product, since this will not alter its value.

The data-processor subsystem for the binary multiplier is shown in Fig. 8-20. The multiplicand is stored in register B, the multiplier is stored in register Q, and the partial product is formed in register A. A parallel adder similar to the circuit shown in Fig. 5-1 is used to add the contents of register B to register A. The E flip-flop stores the carry after the addition. The P counter is initially set to hold a binary number equal to the number of bits in the multiplier. This counter is decremented after the formation of each partial product. When the content of the counter reaches zero, the product is formed in the double register A and Q and the process stops.

The control logic stays in an initial state until the start signal S becomes a 1. The system then performs the multiplication. The sum of A and B forms a partial product, which is transferred to A. The output carry from the addition whether 0 or 1 is transferred to E. Both the partial product in A and the multiplier in Q are shifted to the right. The least significant bit of A is shifted into the most significant position of Q; the carry from E is shifted into the most significant position of A; and 0 is shifted into E. After the shift-right operation, one bit of the partial product is transferred into Q while the multiplier bits in Q are shifted one position to the right. In this manner, the rightmost bit of register Q, designated by Q_1, always holds the bit of the multiplier that must be inspected next.

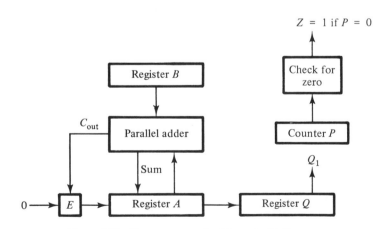

Figure 8-20   Data processor for binary multiplier

ASM Chart

The ASM chart for the binary multiplier is shown in Fig. 8-21. Initially, the multiplicand is in B and the multiplier in Q. The multiplication process is initiated when $S = 1$. Register A and flip-flop E are cleared and the sequence counter P is set to a binary number n, which is equal to the number of bits in the multiplier.

Next we enter a loop that keeps forming the partial products. The multiplier bit in Q_1 is checked, and if it is equal to 1, the multiplicand in B is added to the partial product in A. The carry from the addition is transferred to E. The partial product in A is left unchanged if $Q_1 = 0$. The P counter is decremented by 1 regardless of the value of Q_1. Registers E, A, and Q are combined into one composite register EAQ, which is then shifted once to the right to obtain a new partial product.

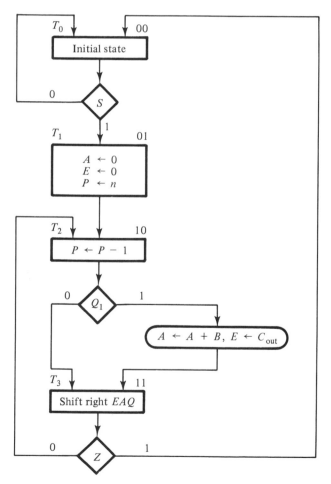

Figure 8-21   ASM chart for binary multiplier

Multiplicand $B = 10111$

	E	A	Q	P
Multiplier in Q	0	00000	10011	101
$Q_1 = 1$; add B		10111		
First partial product	0	10111		100
Shift right EAQ	0	01011	11001	
$Q_1 = 1$: add B		10111		
Second partial product	1	00010		011
Shift right EAQ	0	10001	01100	
$Q_1 = 0$; shift right EAQ	0	01000	10110	010
$Q_1 = 0$; shift right EAQ	0	00100	01011	001
$Q_1 = 1$; add B		10111		
Fifth partial product	0	11011		000
Shift right EAQ	0	01101	10101	
Final product in $AQ = 0110110101$				

Figure 8-22   Example of binary multiplication

The value in the P counter is checked after the formation of each partial product. If the content of P is not zero, control input Z is equal to 0 and the process is repeated to form a new partial product. The process stops when the P counter reaches 0 and the control input Z is equal to 1. Note that the partial product formed in A is shifted into Q one bit at a time and eventually replaces the multiplier. The final product is available in A and Q, with A holding the most significant bits and Q the least significant bits.

The previous numerical example is repeated in Fig. 8-22 to clarify the multiplication process. The procedure follows the steps outlined in the ASM chart.

PLA Control

The control for the binary multiplier has four states and three inputs. The binary state assignment is shown in the ASM chart over each state box. The three control inputs are S, Q_1, and Z. The design of a control unit with a PLA is similar to the design using D flip-flops and a decoder. The only difference is in the way the combinational circuit part of the control is implemented. The PLA essentially replaces the decoder and all the gates in the inputs of the flip-flops.

The block diagram of the PLA control is shown in Fig. 8-23. The PLA is connected to a register with two flip-flops, G_1 and G_2. The inputs to the PLA are the values of the present state of the register and the three control inputs. The outputs of the PLA provide the values for the next state in the register and the control output variables. There is one output for each present state and an additional output for the conditional operation $D = Q_1 T_2$. Since the PLA implements the control combinational circuit, we might as well include within it the gates for all

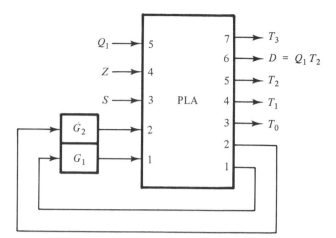

Figure 8-23 PLA control block diagram

conditional operations. In the binary multiplier there is a conditional operation to add B to A during state T_2 provided that $Q_1 = 1$. PLA output D will then activate this operation in the data processor.

At any given time, the present state of the register together with the input conditions determine the output values and the next state for the register. The next clock pulse initiates the register operations specified by the PLA outputs and transfers the next state value into the register. This provides a new control state and possibly different input values. Thus, the PLA acts as the combinational circuit part of the sequential circuit to generate the control outputs and the next state values for the register.

PLA Program Table

The internal organization of the PLA was presented in Section 5-8. It was also shown there how to obtain the PLA program table. The reader is advised to review this section to make sure that the meaning of a PLA program table is understood. The internal paths inside the PLA are constructed according to the specifications given in the program table. The design of a PLA control requires that we obtain the state table for the circuit. The state table gives essentially all the information required for obtaining the PLA program table.

The state table for the control subsystem of the binary multiplier is shown in Table 8-6. The present state is determined from flip-flops G_1 and G_2. The input variables for the control are S, Z, and Q_1. The next state of G_1 and G_2 may be a function of one of the input control variables, or it may be independent of any inputs. If an input variable does not influence the next state, we mark it with a don't-care condition, X. If there are two different transitions from the same present state, the present state is repeated in the table but the next states are assigned

TABLE 8-6 State table for control circuit

Present state		Inputs			Next state		Outputs				
G_1	G_2	S	Z	Q_1	G_1	G_2	T_0	T_1	T_2	D	T_3
0	0	0	X	X	0	0	1	0	0	0	0
0	0	1	X	X	0	1	1	0	0	0	0
0	1	X	X	X	1	0	0	1	0	0	0
1	0	X	X	0	1	1	0	0	1	0	0
1	0	X	X	1	1	1	0	0	1	1	0
1	1	X	0	X	1	0	0	0	0	0	1
1	1	X	1	X	0	0	0	0	0	0	1

different binary values. The table also lists all control outputs as a function of the present state. Note that input Q_1 does not affect the next state but only determines the value of output D during state T_2.

The PLA program table can be obtained directly from the state table without the need for simplification procedures. The PLA program table listed in Table 8-7 specifies seven product terms, one for each row in the state table. The input and output terminals are marked with numbers, and the variables applied to these numbered terminals are indicated in the block diagram of Fig. 8-23. The comments are not part of the table but are included for clarification.

According to the rules established in Section 5-8, a no connection for a PLA path is indicated by a dash (—) in the table. The X's in the state table designate don't-care conditions and imply no connection for the PLA. The 0's in the output columns also indicate no connections to the OR gates within the PLA. The translation from the state table to a PLA program table is very simple. The X's in the "input" columns and the 0's in the "next state" and "output" columns are changed to dashes, and all other entries remain the same. The inputs to the PLA are the same as the present state and inputs in the state table. The outputs of the PLA are the same as the next state and outputs in the state table.

TABLE 8-7 PLA program table

Product term	Inputs					Outputs							Comments	
	1	2	3	4	5	1	2	3	4	5	6	7		
1	0	0	0	—	—	—	—	1	—	—	—	—	$T_0 = 1$,	$S = 0$
2	0	0	1	—	—	—	1	1	—	—	—	—	$T_0 = 1$,	$S = 1$
3	0	1	—	—	—	1	—	—	1	—	—	—	$T_1 = 1$	
4	1	0	—	—	0	1	1	—	—	1	—	—	$T_2 = 1$,	$Q_1 = 0$
5	1	0	—	—	1	1	1	—	—	1	1	—	$T_2 = 1$,	$D = 1$,
6	1	1	—	0	—	1	—	—	—	—	—	1	$T_3 = 1$,	$Z = 0$
7	1	1	—	1	—	—	—	—	—	—	—	1	$T_3 = 1$,	$Z = 1$

The preceding example demonstrates the procedure for designing the control logic with a PLA. From the specifications of the system, we first obtain a state table for the controller. The number of states determines the number of flip-flops for the register. The PLA is then connected to the register and to the input and output variables. The PLA program table is obtained directly from the state table.

The examples introduced in this chapter demonstrate five methods of control-logic design. These should not be considered the only possible methods. A resourceful designer may be able to formulate a control configuration to suit a particular application. This configuration may consist of a combination of methods or may constitute a control organization other than the ones presented here.

REFERENCES

1. Clare, C. R., *Designing Logic Systems Using State Machines*. New York: McGraw-Hill Book Co., 1973.

2. Winkel, D., and F. Prosser, *The Art of Digital Design*. Englewood Cliffs, N.J.: Prentice-Hall, Inc., 1980.

3. Peatman, J. B., *Digital Hardware Design*. New York: McGraw-Hill Book Co., 1980.

4. Wiatrowski, C. A., and C. H. House, *Logic Circuits and Microcomputer Systems*. New York: McGraw-Hill Book Co., 1980.

5. Fletcher, W. I., *An Engineering Approach to Digital Design*. Englewood Cliffs, N.J.: Prentice-Hall, Inc., 1980.

6. Rhyne, V. T., *Fundamentals of Digital Systems Design*. Englewood Cliffs, N.J.: Prentice-Hall, Inc., 1973.

PROBLEMS

8-1. Draw the portion of an ASM chart that specifies a conditional operation to increment register R during state T_1 and transfer to state T_2 if control inputs z and y are equal to 1 and 0, respectively.

8-2. Show the eight exit paths in an ASM block emanating from the decision boxes that check the eight possible binary values of three control variables x, y, and z.

8-3. Obtain the ASM chart for the following state transitions:
    (a) If $x = 0$, control goes from state T_1 to state T_2; if $x = 1$, generate a conditional operation and go from T_1 to T_2.
    (b) If $x = 1$, control goes from T_1 to T_2 and then to T_3; if $x = 0$, control goes from T_1 to T_3.
    (c) Start from state T_1; then: if $xy = 00$, go to T_2; if $xy = 01$, go to T_3; if $xy = 10$, go to T_1; otherwise, go to T_3.

8-4.   Construct an ASM chart for a digital system that counts the number of people in a room. People enter the room from one door with a photocell that changes a signal x from 1 to 0 when the light is interrupted. They leave the room from a second door with a similar photocell with a signal y. Both x and y are synchronized with the clock, but they may stay on or off for more than one clock pulse period. The data processor subsystem consists of an up-down counter with a display of its contents.

8-5.   Explain how the ASM chart differs from a conventional flowchart. Using Fig. 8-5 as an illustration, show the difference in interpretation.

8-6.   Design the 4-bit counter with synchronous clear specified in Fig. 8-10.

8-7.   Using five-variable maps, derive the input Boolean functions to the JK flip-flops of Fig. 8-11.

8-8.   Design the control whose state table is given in Table 8-3 using two multiplexers, a register, and a decoder.

8-9.   Design the control of the design example of Section 8-5 by the method of one flip-flop per state.

8-10. The state diagram of a control unit is shown in Fig. P8-10. It has four states and two inputs, x and y.
       (a) Draw the equivalent ASM chart, leaving the state boxes empty.
       (b) Design the control with multiplexers.

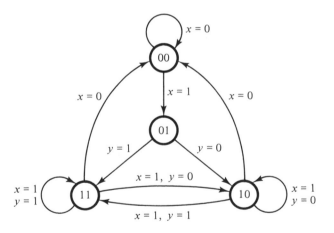

Figure P8-10   Control state diagram for problem 8-10

8-11. Assume that $R1$ in Fig. 8-18 is the 4-bit shift register shown in Fig. 7-9. Show how the shift and load inputs in Fig. 8-18 are to be connected to the s_1 and s_0 inputs of the shift register.

8-12. Design a digital system with three 4-bit registers, A, B, and C, to perform the following operations:
       1. Transfer two binary numbers to A and B when a start signal is enabled.

2. If $A < B$, shift-left the contents of A and transfer the result to register C.

3. If $A > B$, shift-right the contents of B and transfer the result to register C.

4. If $A = B$, transfer the number to register C unchanged.

8-13. Design a digital system that multiplies two binary numbers by the repeated addition method. For example, to multiply 5×4, the digital system evaluates the product by adding the multiplicand four times: $5 + 5 + 5 + 5 = 20$. Let the multiplicand be in register BR, the multiplier in register AR, and the product in register PR. An adder circuit adds the contents of BR to PR. A zero-detection circuit Z checks when AR becomes 0 after each time that it is decremented.

8-14. Prove that the multiplication of two n-bit numbers gives a product of length less than or equal to $2n$ bits.

8-15. In Fig. 8-20, the Q register holds the multiplier and the B register holds the multiplicand. Assume that each number consists of 15 bits.

(a) How many bits can be expected in the product, and where is it available?

(b) How many bits are in the P counter, and what is the binary number loaded into it initially?

(c) Design the circuit that checks for zero in the P counter.

8-16. List the contents of registers E, A, Q, and P similar to Fig. 8-22 during the process of multiplying the two numbers 11111 (multiplicand) and 10101 (multiplier).

8-17. Determine the time it takes to process the multiplication operation in the binary multiplier described in Section 8-6. Assume that the Q register has n bits and the clock period is t nanoseconds.

8-18. Design the control circuit of the binary multiplier specified by the ASM chart of Fig. 8-21 using each of the following methods:

(a) *JK* flip-flops and gates.

(b) *D* flip-flops and a decoder.

(c) Input multiplexers and a register.

(d) One flip-flop per state.

8-19. Design the control whose state table is given in Table 8-3 using the PLA method.

8-20. Consider the ASM chart of Fig. P8-20. The register operations are not specified, because we are interested only in designing the control logic.

(a) Draw the equivalent state diagram.

(b) Design the control with one flip-flop per state.

8-21. (a) Derive the state table for the ASM chart of Fig. P8-20.

(b) Design the control with three *D* flip-flops, a decoder, and gates.

(c) Design the control with a register and a PLA. List the PLA program table.

8-22. (a) Derive a table showing the multiplexer input conditions for the control specified in the ASM chart of Fig. P8-20.

(b) Design the control with three multiplexers, a register with three flip-flops, and a 3×8 decoder.

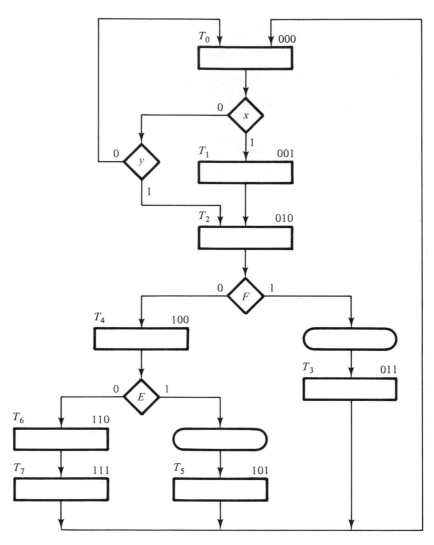

Figure P8-20 ASM chart for problems 8-20 through 8-22

Asynchronous
Sequential Logic

9

9-1 INTRODUCTION

A sequential circuit is specified by a time sequence of inputs, outputs, and internal states. In synchronous sequential circuits the change of internal state occurs in response to the synchronized clock pulses. Asynchronous sequential circuits do not use clock pulses. The change of internal state occurs when there is a change in the input variables. The memory elements in synchronous sequential circuits are clocked flip-flops. The memory elements in asynchronous sequential circuits are either unclocked flip-flops or time delay elements. The memory capability of a time delay device is due to the fact that it takes a finite time for the signal to propagate through digital gates. An asynchronous sequential circuit quite often resembles a combinational circuit with feedback.

The design of asynchronous sequential circuits is more difficult than that of synchronous circuits because of the timing problems involved in the feedback path. In a properly designed synchronous system, timing problems are eliminated by triggering all flip-flops with the pulse edge. The change from one state to the next occurs during the short time of the pulse transition. Since the asynchronous circuit does not use a clock, the state of the system is allowed to change immediately after the input changes. Care must be taken to ensure that each new state keeps the circuit in a stable condition even though a feedback path exists.

Asynchronous sequential circuits are useful in a variety of applications. They are used when speed of operation is important, especially in those cases where the digital system must respond quickly without having to wait for a clock pulse. They are more economical to use in small independent systems that require only a few components, as it may not be practical to go to the expense of providing a circuit for generating clock pulses. Asynchronous circuits are useful in applications where the input signals to the system may change at any time, independently of an internal clock. The communication between two units with each unit having its own independent clock must be done with asynchronous circuits. Digital designers often produce a mixed system where some part of the synchronous system has the characteristics of an asynchronous circuit. Knowledge of asynchronous sequential logic behavior is helpful in verifying that the total digital system is operating in the proper manner.

Figure 9-1 shows the block diagram of an asynchronous sequential circuit. It consists of a combinational circuit and delay elements connected to form feedback loops. There are n input variables, m output variables, and k internal states. The delay elements can be visualized as providing short-term memory for the sequential circuit. In a gate-type circuit, the propagation delay that exists in the combinational circuit path from input to output provides sufficient delay along the feedback loop so that no specific delay elements are actually inserted in the feedback path. The present state and next state variables in asynchronous sequential circuits are customarily called secondary variables and excitation variables, respectively. The excitation variables should not be confused with the excitable table used in the design of clocked sequential circuits.

When an input variable changes in value, the y secondary variables do not change instantaneously. It takes a certain amount of time for the signal to propagate from the input terminals through the combinational circuit to the Y excitation variables where new values are generated for the next state. These values propagate through the delay elements and become the new present state for the secondary variables. Note the distinction between the y's and the Y's. In the steady-state

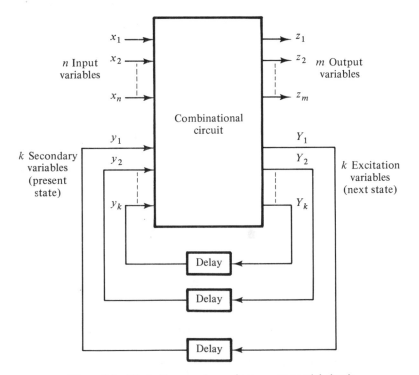

Figure 9-1 Block diagram of asynchronous sequential circuit

condition, they are the same, but during transition they are not. For a given value of input variables, the system is stable if the circuit reaches a steady-state condition with $y_i = Y_i$ for $i = 1, 2, \ldots, k$. Otherwise, the circuit is in a continuous transition and is said to be unstable. It is important to realize that a transition from one stable state to another occurs only in response to a change in an input variable. This is in contrast to synchronous systems, where the state transitions occur in response to the application of a clock pulse.

To ensure proper operation, asynchronous sequential circuits must be allowed to attain a stable state before the input is changed to a new value. Because of delays in the wires and the gate circuits, it is impossible to have two or more input variables change at exactly the same instant of time without an uncertainty as to which one changes first. Therefore, simultaneous changes of two or more variables are usually prohibited. This restriction means that only one input variable can change at any one time and the time between two input changes must be longer than the time it takes the circuit to reach a stable state. This type of operation is defined as *fundamental mode*. Fundamental-mode operation assumes that the input signals change one at a time and only when the circuit is in a stable condition.

9-2 ANALYSIS PROCEDURE

The analysis of asynchronous sequential circuits consists of obtaining a table or a diagram that describes the sequence of internal states and outputs as a function of changes in the input variables. A logic diagram manifests an asynchronous sequential circuit behavior if it has one or more feedback loops or if it includes unclocked flip-flops. In this section we will investigate the behavior of asynchronous sequential circuits that have feedback paths without employing flip-flops. Unclocked flip-flops are called latches, and their use in asynchronous sequential circuits will be explained in the next section.

The analysis procedure will be presented by means of three specific examples. The first example introduces the transition table. The second example defines the flow table. The third example investigates the stability of asynchronous sequential circuits.

Transition Table

An example of an asynchronous sequential circuit with only gates is shown in Fig. 9-2. The diagram clearly shows two feedback loops from the OR gate outputs back to the AND gate inputs. The circuit consists of one input variable, x, and two internal states. The internal states have two excitation variables, Y_1 and Y_2, and two secondary variables, y_1 and y_2. The delay associated with each feedback loop is obtained from the propagation delay between each y input and its corresponding Y output. Each logic gate in the path introduces a propagation delay of about 2 to 10 nanoseconds (see Table 2-8). The wires that conduct electrical signals introduce

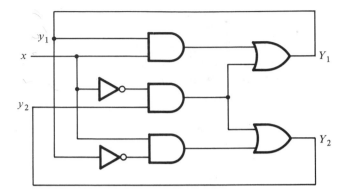

Figure 9-2 Example of asynchronous sequential circuit

approximately one nanosecond delay for each foot of wire. Thus, no additional external delay elements are necessary when the combinational circuit and the wires in the feedback path provide sufficient delay.

The analysis of the circuit starts by considering the excitation variables as outputs and the secondary variables as inputs. We then derive the Boolean expressions for the excitation variables as a function of the input and secondary variables. These can be readily obtained from the logic diagram.

$$Y_1 = xy_1 + x'y_2$$
$$Y_2 = xy_1' + x'y_2$$

The next step is to plot the Y_1 and Y_2 functions in a map as shown in Fig. 9-3(a) and (b). The encoded binary values of the y variables are used for labeling the rows, and the input x variable is used to designate the columns. This configuration results in a slightly different three-variable map from the one used in previous chapters. However, it is still a valid map, and this type of configuration is more

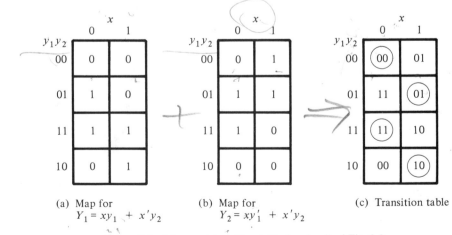

(a) Map for
$Y_1 = xy_1 + x'y_2$

(b) Map for
$Y_2 = xy_1' + x'y_2$

(c) Transition table

Figure 9-3 Maps and transition table for circuit of Fig. 9-2

convenient when dealing with asynchronous sequential circuits. Note that the variables belonging to the appropriate squares are not marked along the sides of the map as done in previous chapters.

The transition table shown in Fig. 9-3(c) is obtained from the maps by combining the binary values in corresponding squares. The transition table shows the value of $Y = Y_1 Y_2$ inside each square. The first bit of Y is obtained from the value of Y_1, and the second bit is obtained from the value of Y_2 in the same square position. For a state to be stable, the value of Y must be the same as that of $y = y_1 y_2$. Those entries in the transition table where $Y = y$ are circled, to indicate a stable condition. An uncircled entry represents an unstable state.

Now consider the effect of a change in the input variable. The square for $x = 0$ and $y = 00$ in the transition table shows that $Y = 00$. Since Y represents the next value of y, this is a stable condition. If x changes from 0 to 1 while $y = 00$, the circuit changes the value of Y to 01. This represents a temporary unstable condition because Y is not equal to the present value of y. What happens next is that as soon as the signal propagates to make $Y = 01$, the feedback path in the circuit causes a change in y to 01. This is manifested in the transition table by a transition from the first row ($y = 00$) to the second row, where $y = 01$. Now that $y = Y$, the circuit reaches a stable condition with an input of $x = 1$. In general, if a change in the input takes the circuit to an unstable state, the value of y will change (while x remains the same) until it reaches a stable (circled) state. Using this type of analysis for the remaining squares of the transition table we find that the circuit repeats the sequence of states 00, 01, 11, 10 when the input repeatedly alternates between 0 and 1.

Note the difference between a synchronous and an asynchronous sequential circuit. In a synchronous system, the present state is totally specified by the flip-flop values and does not change if the input changes while the clock pulse is inactive. In an asynchronous circuit the internal state can change immediately after a change in the input. Because of this, it is sometimes convenient to combine the internal state with the input value together and call it the *total state* of the circuit. The circuit whose transition table is shown in Fig. 9-3(c) has four stable total states, $y_1 y_2 x = 000$, 011, 110, and 101, and four unstable total states, 001, 010, 111, and 100.

The transition table of asynchronous sequential circuits is similar to the state table used for synchronous circuits. If we regard the secondary variables as the present state and the excitation variables as the next state, we obtain the state table as shown in Table 9-1. This table provides the same information as the transition

TABLE 9-1   State table for circuit of Fig. 9-2

Present state		Next state			
		$x = 0$		$x = 1$	
0	0	0	0	0	1
0	1	1	1	0	1
1	0	0	0	1	0
1	1	1	1	1	0

table. There is one restriction that applies to the asynchronous case but does not apply to the synchronous case. In the asynchronous transition table there usually is at least one next state entry which is the same as the present state value in each row. Otherwise, all the total states in that row will be unstable.

The procedure for obtaining a transition table from the circuit diagram of an asynchronous sequential circuit is as follows:

1. Determine all feedback loops in the circuit.

2. Designate the output of each feedback loop with variable Y_i and its corresponding input with y_i for $i = 1, 2, \ldots, k$ where k is the number of feedback loops in the circuit.

3. Derive the Boolean functions of all Y's as a function of the external inputs and the y's.

4. Plot each Y function in a map, using the y variables for the rows and the external inputs for the columns.

5. Combine all the maps into one table showing the value of $Y = Y_1 Y_2 \cdots Y_k$ inside each square.

6. Circle those values of Y in each square that are equal to the value of $y = y_1 y_2 \cdots y_k$ in the same row.

Once the transition table is available, the behavior of the circuit can be analyzed by observing the state transition as a function of changes in the input variables.

Flow Table

During the design of asynchronous sequential circuits it is more convenient to name the states by letter symbols without making specific reference to their binary values. Such a table is called a *flow table*. A flow table is similar to a transition table except that the internal states are symbolized with letters rather than binary numbers. The flow table also includes the output values of the circuit for each stable state.

Examples of flow tables are shown in Fig. 9-4. The one in Fig. 9-4(a) has four states designated by the letters a, b, c, d. It reduces to the transition table of Fig. 9-3(c) if we assign the following binary values to the states: $a = 00$, $b = 01$, $c = 11$, and $d = 10$. The table of Fig. 9-4(a) is called a *primitive* flow table because it has only one stable state in each row. Fig. 9-4(b) shows a flow table with more than one stable state in the same row. It has two states a and b, two inputs x_1 and x_2, and one output z. The binary value of the output variable is indicated inside the square next to the state symbol and is separated by a comma. From the flow table we observe the following behavior of the circuit. If $x_1 = 0$, the circuit is in state a. If x_1 goes to 1 while x_2 is 0, the circuit goes to state b. With inputs $x_1 x_2 = 11$, the circuit may be either in state a or state b. If in state a, the output is 0, and if in state b, the

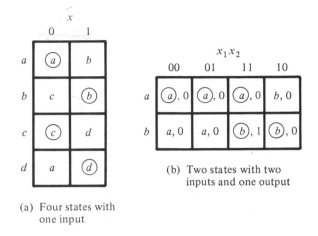

(a) Four states with one input

(b) Two states with two inputs and one output

Figure 9-4 Examples of flow tables

output is 1. State b is maintained if the inputs change from 10 to 11. The circuit stays in state a if the inputs change from 01 to 11. Remember that in fundamental mode, two input variables cannot change simultaneously, and therefore we do not allow a change of inputs from 00 to 11.

In order to obtain the circuit described by a flow table, it is necessary to assign to each state a distinct binary value. This assignment converts the flow table into a transition table from which we can derive the logic diagram. This is illustrated in Fig. 9-5 for the flow table of Fig. 9-4(b). We assign binary 0 to state a and binary 1 to state b. The result is the transition table of Fig. 9-5(a). The output map shown in Fig. 9-5(b) is obtained directly from the output values in the flow table. The excitation function Y and the output function z are simplified by means of the two maps. The logic diagram of the circuit is shown in Fig. 9-5(c).

This example demonstrates the procedure for obtaining the logic diagram from a given flow table. This procedure is not always as simple as in this example. There are several difficulties associated with the binary state assignment and with the output assigned to the unstable states. These problems are discussed in detail in the following sections.

Race Conditions

A *race* condition is said to exist in an asynchronous sequential circuit when two or more binary state variables change value in response to a change in an input variable. When unequal delays are encountered, a race condition may cause the state variables to change in an unpredictable manner. For example, if the state variables must change from 00 to 11, the difference in delays may cause the first variable to change faster than the second, with the result that the state variables change in sequence from 00 to 10 and then to 11. If the second variable changes

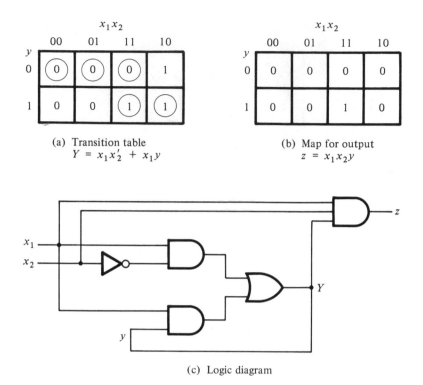

(a) Transition table
$Y = x_1x_2' + x_1y$

(b) Map for output
$z = x_1x_2y$

(c) Logic diagram

Figure 9-5 Derivation of circuit specified by the flow table of Fig. 9-4(b)

faster than the first, the state variables will change from 00 to 01 and then to 11. Thus the order by which the state variables change may not be known in advance. If the final stable state that the circuit reaches does not depend on the order in which the state variables change, the race is called a *noncritical* race. If it is possible to end up in two or more different stable states depending on the order in which the state variables change, then it is a *critical* race. For proper operation, critical races must be avoided.

The two examples in Fig. 9-6 illustrate noncritical races. We start with the total stable state $y_1y_2x = 000$ and then change the input from 0 to 1. The state variables must change from 00 to 11, which defines a race condition. The listed transitions under each table show three possible ways that the state variables may change. They can either change simultaneously from 00 to 11, or they may change in sequence from 00 to 01 and then to 11, or they may change in sequence from 00 to 10 and then to 11. In either case, the final stable state is the same which results in a noncritical race condition. In (a) the final total state is $y_1y_2x = 111$ and in (b) it is 011.

The transition tables of Fig. 9-7 illustrate critical races. Here again we start with the total stable state $y_1y_2x = 000$ and then change the input from 0 to 1. The

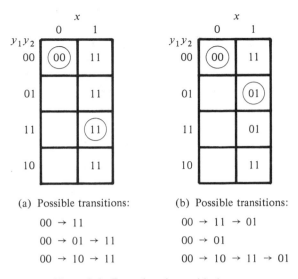

(a) Possible transitions:

$00 \rightarrow 11$

$00 \rightarrow 01 \rightarrow 11$

$00 \rightarrow 10 \rightarrow 11$

(b) Possible transitions:

$00 \rightarrow 11 \rightarrow 01$

$00 \rightarrow 01$

$00 \rightarrow 10 \rightarrow 11 \rightarrow 01$

Figure 9-6 Examples of noncritical races

state variables must change from 00 to 11. If they change simultaneously, the final total stable state is 111. In the transition table of part (a), if Y_2 changes to 1 before Y_1 because of unequal propagation delay, then the circuit goes to the total stable state 011 and remains there. On the other hand, if Y_1 changes first, the internal state becomes 10 and the circuit will remain in the stable total state 101. Hence the race is critical because the circuit goes to different stable states depending on the order in which the state variables change. The transition table of Fig. 9-7(b) illustrates

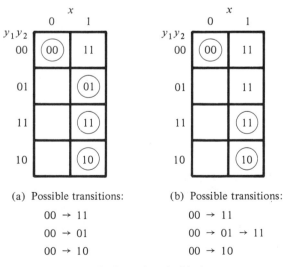

(a) Possible transitions:

$00 \rightarrow 11$

$00 \rightarrow 01$

$00 \rightarrow 10$

(b) Possible transitions:

$00 \rightarrow 11$

$00 \rightarrow 01 \rightarrow 11$

$00 \rightarrow 10$

Figure 9-7 Examples of critical races

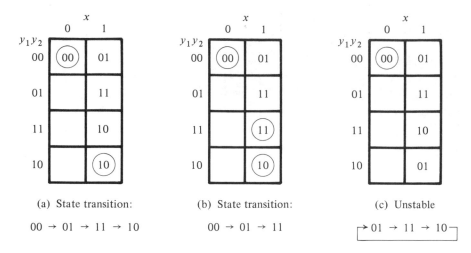

(a) State transition:

$00 \to 01 \to 11 \to 10$

(b) State transition:

$00 \to 01 \to 11$

(c) Unstable

$\rightarrow 01 \to 11 \to 10 \rightarrow$

Figure 9-8 Examples of cycles

another critical race where two possible transitions result in one final total state but the third possible transition goes to a different total state.

Races may be avoided by making a proper binary assignment to the state variables. The state variables must be assigned binary numbers in such a way that only one state variable can change at any one time when a state transition occurs in the flow table. The subject of race-free state assignment is discussed in Sec. 9-6.

Races can be avoided by directing the circuit through intermediate unstable states with a unique state-variable change. When a circuit goes through a unique sequence of unstable states, it is said to have a *cycle*. Figure 9-8 illustrates the occurrence of cycles. Again we start with $y_1 y_2 = 00$ and then change the input from 0 to 1. The transition table of part (a) gives a *unique* sequence that terminates in a total stable state 101. The table in (b) shows that even though the state variables change from 00 to 11, the cycle provides a unique transition from 00 to 01 and then to 11. Care must be taken when using a cycle that it terminates with a stable state. If a cycle does not terminate with a stable state, the circuit will keep going from one unstable state to another, making the entire circuit unstable. This is demonstrated in Fig. 9-8(c) and also in the following example.

Stability Considerations

Because of the feedback connection that exists in asynchronous sequential circuits, care must be taken to ensure that the circuit does not become unstable. An unstable condition will cause the circuit to oscillate between unstable states. The transition-table method of analysis can be useful in detecting the occurrence of instability.

Consider, for example, the circuit of Fig. 9-9(a). The excitation function is:

$$Y = (x_1 y)' x_2 = (x_1' + y') x_2 = x_1' x_2 + x_2 y'$$

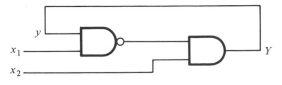

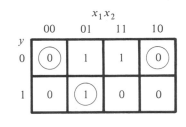

(a) Logic diagram

$x_1 x_2$

	00	01	11	10
y 0	⓪	1	1	⓪
1	0	①	0	0

(b) Transition table

Figure 9-9 Example of unstable circuit

The transition table for the circuit is shown in Fig. 9-9(b). Those values of Y that are equal to y are circled and represent stable states. The encircled entries indicate unstable conditions. Note that column 11 has no stable states. This means that with input $x_1 x_2$ fixed at 11, the values of Y and y are never the same. If $y = 0$, then $Y = 1$, which causes a transition to the second row of the table with $y = 1$ and $Y = 0$. This causes a transition back to the first row, with the result that the state variable alternates between 0 and 1 indefinitely as long as the input is 11.

The instability condition can be detected directly from the logic diagram. Let $x_1 = 1$, $x_2 = 1$, and $y = 1$. The output of the NAND gate is equal to 0, and the output of the AND gate is equal to 0, making Y equal to 0, with the result that $Y \neq y$. Now if $y = 0$, the output of the NAND gate is 1, the output of the AND gate is 1, making Y equal to 1, with the result that $Y \neq y$. If it is assumed that each gate has a propagation delay of 5 ns (including the wires) we will find that Y will be 0 for 10 ns and 1 for the next 10 ns. This will result in a square-wave waveform with a period of 20 ns. The frequency of oscillation is the reciprocal of the period and is equal to 50 MHz. Unless one is designing a square-wave generator, the instability that may occur in asynchronous sequential circuits is undesirable and must be avoided.

9-3 CIRCUITS WITH LATCHES

Historically, asynchronous sequential circuits were known and used before synchronous circuits were developed. The first practical digital systems were constructed with relays, which are more adaptable to asynchronous type operations. For this reason, the traditional method of asynchronous circuit configuration has been with components that are connected to form one or more feedback loops. As electronic digital circuits were developed, it was realized that the flip-flop circuit can be used as a memory element in sequential circuits. Asynchronous sequential circuits can be implemented by employing a basic flip-flop commonly referred to as an *SR latch*. The use of *SR* latches in asynchronous circuits produces a more orderly pattern, which may result in a reduction of the circuit complexity. An added advantage is that the circuit resembles the synchronous circuit in having distinct memory elements that store and specify the internal states.

In this section we will first explain the operation of the *SR* latch using the analysis technique introduced in the previous section. We will then proceed to give examples of analysis and implementation of asynchronous sequential circuits that employ *SR* latches.

SR Latch

The *SR* latch is a digital circuit with two inputs, *S* and *R*, and two cross-coupled NOR gates or two cross-coupled NAND gates. This circuit was introduced in Section 6-2 as a basic flip-flop from which other, more complicated flip-flop circuits were obtained. The cross-coupled NOR circuit is shown in Fig. 9-10(a). This circuit, and the truth table listed in Fig. 9-10(b), were taken directly from Fig. 6-2. In order

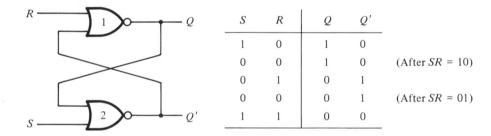

S	R	Q	Q'	
1	0	1	0	
0	0	1	0	(After SR = 10)
0	1	0	1	
0	0	0	1	(After SR = 01)
1	1	0	0	

(a) Crossed coupled circuit   (b) Truth table

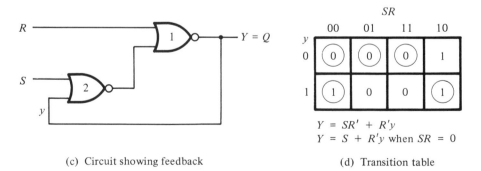

$$Y = SR' + R'y$$
$$Y = S + R'y \text{ when } SR = 0$$

(c) Circuit showing feedback   (d) Transition table

Figure 9-10   *SR* latch with NOR gates

to analyze the circuit by the transition table method, we redraw the circuit as shown in Fig. 9-10(c). Here we distinctly see a feedback path from the output of gate 1 to the input of gate 2. The output Q is identical to the excitation variable Y and the secondary variable y. The Boolean function for the output is:

$$Y = [(S + y)' + R]' = (S + y)R' = SR' + R'y$$

Plotting Y as in Fig. 9-10(d), we obtain the transition table for the circuit.

We can now investigate the behavior of the SR latch from the transition table. With $SR = 10$, the output $Q = Y = 1$ and the latch is said to be set. Changing S to 0 leaves the circuit in the set state. With $SR = 01$, the output $Q = Y = 0$ and the latch is said to be reset. A change of R back to 0 leaves the circuit in the reset state. These conditions are also listed in the truth table. The circuit exhibits some difficulty when both S and R are equal to 1. From the truth table we see that both Q and Q' are equal to 0, a condition that violates the requirement that these two outputs be the complement of each other. Moreover, from the transition table we note that going from $SR = 11$ to $SR = 00$ produces an unpredictable result. If S goes to 0 first, the output remains at 0, but if R goes to 0 first, the output goes to 1. In normal operation, we must make sure that 1's are not applied to both the S and R inputs simultaneously. This condition can be expressed by the Boolean function $SR = 0$, which states that the ANDing of S and R must always result in a 0.

Coming back to the excitation function, we note that when we OR the Boolean expression SR' with SR, the result is the single variable S.

$$SR' + SR = S(R' + R) = S$$

From this we deduce that $SR' = S$ when $SR = 0$. Therefore, the excitation function derived previously,

$$Y = SR' + R'y$$

can be expressed as

$$Y = S + R'y \quad \text{when } SR = 0$$

To analyze a circuit with an SR latch, we must first check that the Boolean condition $SR = 0$ holds at all times. We then use the reduced excitation function to analyze the circuit. However, if it is found that both S and R can be equal to 1 at the same time, then it is necessary to use the original excitation function.

The analysis of the SR latch with NAND gates is carried out in Fig. 9-11. The NAND latch operates with both inputs normally at 1 unless the state of the latch has to be changed. The application of 0 to R causes the output Q to go to 0, thus putting the latch in the reset state. After the R input returns to 1, a change of S to 0 causes a change to the set state. The condition to be avoided here is that both S and R not be 0 simultaneously. This condition is satisfied when $S'R' = 0$. The excita-

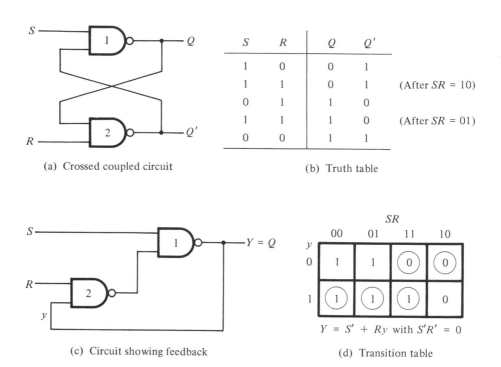

(a) Crossed coupled circuit

S	R	Q	Q'	
1	0	0	1	
1	1	0	1	(After $SR = 10$)
0	1	1	0	
1	1	1	0	(After $SR = 01$)
0	0	1	1	

(b) Truth table

(c) Circuit showing feedback

$Y = S' + Ry$ with $S'R' = 0$

(d) Transition table

Figure 9-11 SR latch with NAND gates

tion function for the circuit is

$$Y = [S(Ry)']' = S' + Ry$$

Comparing it with the excitation function of the NOR latch, we note that S has been replaced with S' and R' with R. Hence the input variables for the NAND latch require the complemented values of those used in the NOR latch. For this reason, the NAND latch is sometimes referred to as an $S'R'$ latch (or $\overline{S}$–$\overline{R}$ latch).

Analysis Example

Asynchronous sequential circuits can be constructed with the use of SR latches with or without external feedback paths. Of course, there is always a feedback loop within the latch itself. The analysis of a circuit with latches will be demonstrated by means of a specific example. From this example it will be possible to generalize the procedural steps necessary to analyze other, similar circuits.

The circuit shown in Fig. 9-12 has two SR latches with outputs Y_1 and Y_2. There are two inputs, x_1 and x_2, and two external feedback loops giving rise to the secondary variables y_1 and y_2. Note that this circuit resembles a conventional sequential circuit with latches behaving like flip-flops without clock pulses. The analysis of the circuit requires that we first obtain the Boolean functions for the S

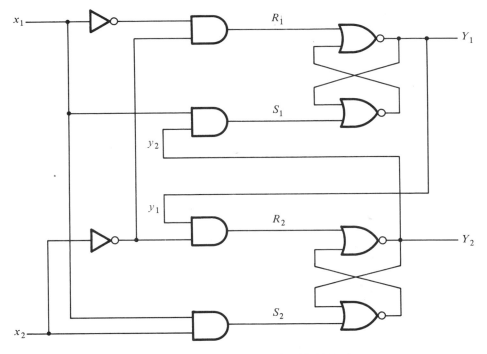

Figure 9-12 Example of a circuit with SR latches

and R inputs in each latch.

$$S_1 = x_1 y_2 \qquad S_2 = x_1 x_2$$
$$R_1 = x_1' x_2' \qquad R_2 = x_2' y_1$$

We then check whether the condition $SR = 0$ is satisfied to ensure proper operation.

$$S_1 R_1 = x_1 y_2 x_1' x_2' = 0$$
$$S_2 R_2 = x_1 x_2 x_2' y_1 = 0$$

The result is 0 because $x_1 x_1' = x_2 x_2' = 0$.

The next step is to derive the transition table of the circuit. Remember that the transition table specifies the value of Y as a function of y and x. The excitation functions are derived from the relation $Y = S + R'y$.

$$Y_1 = S_1 + R_1' y_1 = x_1 y_2 + (x_1 + x_2) y_1 = x_1 y_2 + x_1 y_1 + x_2 y_1$$
$$Y_2 = S_2 + R_2' y_2 = x_1 x_2 + (x_2 + y_1') y_2 = x_1 x_2 + x_2 y_2 + y_1' y_2$$

We now develop a composite map for $Y = Y_1 Y_2$. The y variables are assigned to the rows in the map, and the x variables are assigned to the columns as shown in Fig. 9-13. The Boolean functions of Y_1 and Y_2 as expressed above are used to plot the composite map for Y. The entries of Y in each row that have the same value as that

$$x_1 x_2$$

$y_1 y_2$	00	01	11	10
00	(00)	(00)	01	(00)
01	(01)	(01)	11	11
11	00	(11)	(11)	10
10	00	(10)	11	(10)

Figure 9-13 Transition table for circuit of Fig. 9-12

given to Y are circled and represent stable states. From investigation of the transition table we deduce that the circuit is stable. There is a critical race condition when the circuit is initially in total state $y_1 y_2 x_1 x_2 = 1101$ and x_2 changes from 1 to 0. If Y_1 changes to 0 before Y_2, the circuit goes to total state 0100 instead of 0000. However, with approximately equal delays in the gates and latches, this undesirable situation is not likely to occur.

The procedure for analyzing an asynchronous sequential circuit with SR latches can be summarized as follows:

1. Label each latch output with Y_i and its external feedback path (if any) with y_i for $i = 1, 2, \ldots, k$.

2. Derive the Boolean functions for the S_i and R_i inputs in each latch.

3. Check whether $SR = 0$ for each NOR latch or whether $S'R' = 0$ for each NAND latch. If this condition is not satisfied, there is a possibility that the circuit may not operate properly.

4. Evaluate $Y = S + R'y$ for each NOR latch or $Y = S' + Ry$ for each NAND latch.

5. Construct a map with the y's representing the rows and the x inputs representing the columns.

6. Plot the value of $Y = Y_1 Y_2 \cdots Y_k$ in the map.

7. Circle all stable states where $Y = y$. The resulting map is then the transition table.

Implementation Example

The implementation of a sequential circuit with SR latches is a procedure for obtaining the logic diagram from a given transition table. The procedure requires that we determine the Boolean functions for the S and R inputs of each latch. The logic diagram is then obtained by drawing the *SR* latches and the logic gates that implement the *S* and *R* functions. To demonstrate the procedure, we will repeat the implementation example of Fig. 9-5. The output circuit remains the same and will not be repeated again.

The transition table from Fig. 9-5(a) is duplicated in Fig. 9-14(a). The latch excitation table is shown in Fig. 9-14(b). Remember that the transition table resembles a state table with y representing the present state and Y the next state. Moreover, the excitation table for the *SR* latch is exactly the same as that of an *RS* flip-flop as listed previously in Table 6-8(a), except that y is replaced by $Q(t)$ and Y by $Q(t + 1)$. Thus, the excitation table for the *SR* latch is used in the design of asynchronous sequential circuits just as the *RS* flip-flop excitation table is used in

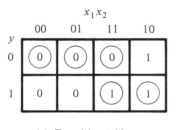

(a) Transition table
$$Y = x_1 x_2' + x_1 y$$

y	Y	S	R
0	0	0	X
0	1	1	0
1	0	0	1
1	1	X	0

(b) Latch excitation table

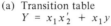

(c) Map for $S = x_1 x_2'$

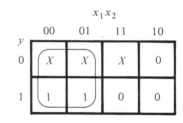

(d) Map for $R = x_1'$

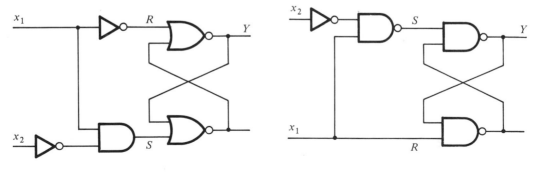

(e) Circuit with NOR latch   (f) Circuit with NAND latch

Figure 9-14   Derivation of latch circuit from a transition table

the design of synchronous sequential circuits as described in Section 6-7. From the information given in the transition table in Fig. 9-14(a) and from the latch excitation table conditions in Fig. 9-14(b) we can obtain the maps for the S and R inputs of the latch as shown in Fig. 9-14(c) and (d). For example, the square in the second row and third column ($yx_1x_2 = 111$) in Fig. 9-14(a) requires a transition from $y = 1$ to $Y = 1$. The excitation table specifies $S = X$, $R = 0$ for this change. Therefore, the corresponding square in the S map is marked with an X and the one in the R map with a 0. All other squares are filled with values in a similar manner. The maps are then used to derive the simplified Boolean functions.

$$S = x_1x_2' \quad \text{and} \quad R = x_1'$$

The logic diagram consists of an SR latch and the gates required to implement the S and R Boolean functions. The circuit is as shown in Fig. 9-14(e) when a NOR latch is used. With a NAND latch we must use the complemented values for S and R.

$$S = (x_1x_2')' \quad \text{and} \quad R = x_1$$

This circuit is shown in Fig. 9-14(f).

The general procedure for implementing a circuit with SR latches from a given transition table can now be summarized as follows:

1. Given a transition table that specifies the excitation function $Y = Y_1Y_2 \cdots Y_k$, derive a pair of maps for S_i and R_i for each $i = 1, 2, \ldots, k$. This is done by using the conditions specified in the latch excitation table of Fig. 9-14(b).

2. Derive the simplified Boolean functions for each S_i and R_i. Care must be taken not to make S_i and R_i equal to 1 in the same minterm square.

3. Draw the logic diagram using k latches together with the gates required to generate the S and R Boolean functions. For NOR latches use the S and R Boolean functions obtained in step 2. For NAND latches use the complemented values of those obtained in step 2.

Another useful example of latch implementation can be found in Section 9-7 in conjunction with Fig. 9-38.

Debounce Circuit

Input binary information in a digital system can be generated manually by means of mechanical switches. One position of the switch provides a voltage equivalent to logic 1, and the other position provides a second voltage equivalent to logic 0. Mechanical switches are also used to start, stop, or reset the digital system. When testing digital circuits in the laboratory, the input signals will normally come from switches. A common characteristic of a mechanical switch is that when the arm is thrown from one position to the other, the switch contact vibrates or bounces several

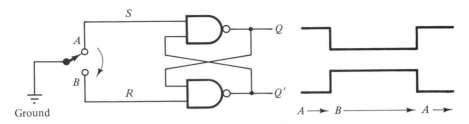

Figure 9-15 Debounce circuit

times before coming to a final rest. In a typical switch, the contact bounce may take several milliseconds to die out. This may cause the signal to oscillate between 1 and 0 because the switch contact is vibrating.

A debounce circuit is one that removes the series of pulses which result from a contact bounce and produces a single smooth transition of the binary signal from 0 to 1 or from 1 to 0. One such circuit consists of a single-pole double-throw switch connected to an SR latch as shown in Fig. 9-15. The center contact is connected to ground that provides a signal equivalent to logic 0. When one of the two contacts A or B is not connected to ground through the switch, it behaves like a logic 1 signal. A resistor is sometimes connected from each contact to a fixed voltage to provide a firm logic 1 signal. When the switch is thrown from position A to position B and back, the outputs of the latch produce a single pulse as shown, negative for Q and positive for Q'. The switch is usually a pushbutton whose contact rests in position A. When the pushbutton is depressed, it goes to position B and when released, it returns to position A.

The operation of the debounce circuit is as follows. When the switch rests in position A, we have the condition $S = 0$, $R = 1$ and $Q = 1$, $Q' = 0$ (see Fig. 9-11(b)). When the switch is moved to position B, the ground connection causes R to go to 0 while S becomes a 1 because contact A is open. This condition causes output Q to go to 0 and Q' to go to 1. After the switch makes an initial contact with B, it bounces several times, but for proper operation we must assume that it does not bounce back far enough to reach point A. The output of the latch will be unaffected by the contact bounce because Q' remains 1 (and Q remains 0) whether R is equal to 0 (contact with ground) or equal to 1 (no contact with ground). When the switch returns to position A, S becomes 0 and Q returns to 1. The output again will exhibit a smooth transition even if there is a contact bounce in position A.

9-4 DESIGN PROCEDURE

The design of an asynchronous sequential circuit starts from the statement of the problem and culminates in a logic diagram. There are a number of design steps that must be carried out in order to minimize the circuit complexity and to produce a stable circuit without critical races. Briefly, the design steps are as follows. A primitive flow table is obtained from the design specifications. The flow table is reduced to a minimum number of states. The states are then given a binary assignment from which we obtain the transition table. From the transition table we derive the logic diagram as a combinational circuit with feedback or as a circuit with *SR* latches.

The design process will be demonstrated by going through a specific example. Once this example is mastered, it will be easier to understand the design steps that are enumerated at the end of this section. Some of the steps require the application of formal procedures, and these are discussed in greater detail in the following sections.

Design Example

It is necessary to design a gated latch circuit with two inputs, G (gate) and D (data), and one output, Q. Binary information present at the D input is transferred to the Q output when G is equal to 1. The Q output will follow the D input as long as $G = 1$. When G goes to 0, the information that was present at the D input at the time the transition occurred is retained at the Q output. The gated latch is a memory element that accepts the value of D when $G = 1$ and retains this value after G goes to 0. Once $G = 0$, a change in D does not change the value of the output Q.

Primitive Flow Table

As defined previously, a primitive flow table is a flow table with only one stable total state in each row. Remember that a total state consists of the internal state combined with the input. The derivation of the primitive flow table can be facilitated if we first form a table with all possible total states in the system. This is shown in Table 9-2 for the gated latch. Each row in the table specifies a total state which consists of a letter designation for the internal state and a possible input combination for D and G. The output Q is also shown for each total state. We start with the two total states that have $G = 1$. From the design specifications we know that $Q = 0$ if $DG = 01$ and $Q = 1$ if $DG = 11$ because D must be equal to Q when $G = 1$. We assign these conditions to states a and b. When G goes to 0, the output depends on the last value of D. Thus if the transition of DG is from 01 to 00 to 10,

TABLE 9-2   Gated latch total states

State	Inputs D	G	Output Q	Comments
a	0	1	0	$D = Q$ because $G = 1$
b	1	1	1	$D = Q$ because $G = 1$
c	0	0	0	After state a or d
d	1	0	0	After state c
e	1	0	1	After state b or f
f	0	0	1	After state e

then Q must remain 0 because D is 0 at the time of the transition from 1 to 0 in G. If the transition of DG is from 11 to 10 to 00, then Q must remain 1. This information results in six different total states, as shown in the table. Note that simultaneous transitions of two input variables such as from 01 to 10 or from 11 to 00 are not allowed in fundamental mode operation.

The primitive flow table for the gated latch is shown in Fig. 9-16. It has one row for each state and one column for each input combination. First we fill in one square in each row belonging to the stable state in that row. These entries are determined from Table 9-2. For example, state a is stable and the output is 0 when the input is 01. This information is entered in the flow table in the first row and second column. Similarly, the other five stable states together with their output are entered in the corresponding input columns.

Next we note that since both inputs are not allowed to change simultaneously, we can enter dash marks in each row which differ in two or more variables from the input variables associated with the stable state. For example, the first row in the flow table shows a stable state with an input of 01. Since only one input can change at any given time, it can change to 00 or 11 but not to 10. Therefore, we enter two dashes in the 10 column of row a. This will eventually result in a don't-care condition for the next state and output in this square. Following this procedure, we fill in a second square in each row of the primitive flow table.

Next it is necessary to find values for two more squares in each row. The comments listed in Table 9-2 may help in deriving the necessary information. For example, state c is associated with input 00 and is reached after an input change from state a or d. Therefore, an unstable state c is shown in column 00 and rows a and d in the flow table. The output is marked with a dash to indicate a don't-care condition. The interpretation of this is that if the circuit is in stable state a and the

DG

	00	01	11	10
a	$c, -$	$\textcircled{a}, 0$	$b, -$	$-, -$
b	$-, -$	$a, -$	$\textcircled{b}, 1$	$e, -$
c	$\textcircled{c}, 0$	$a, -$	$-, -$	$d, -$
d	$c, -$	$-, -$	$b, -$	$\textcircled{d}, 0$
e	$f, -$	$-, -$	$b, -$	$\textcircled{e}, 1$
f	$\textcircled{f}, 1$	$a, -$	$-, -$	$e, -$

Figure 9-16 Primitive flow table

input changes from 01 to 00, the circuit first goes to an unstable next state c, which changes the present state value from a to c, causing a transition to the third row and first column of the flow table. The unstable state values for the other squares are determined in a similar manner. All outputs associated with unstable states are marked with a dash to indicate don't-care conditions. The assignment of actual values to the outputs is discussed further after the design example is completed.

Reduction of the Primitive Flow Table

The primitive flow table has only one stable state in each row. The table can be reduced to a smaller number of rows if two or more stable states are placed in the same row of the flow table. The grouping of stable states from separate rows into one common row is called *merging*. Merging a number of stable states in the same row means that the binary state variable which is ultimately assigned to the merged row will not change when the input variable changes. This is because in a primitive flow table the state variable changes every time the input changes, but in a reduced flow table, a change of input will not cause a change in the state variable if the next stable state is in the same row.

A formal procedure for reducing a flow table is given in the next section. In order to complete the design example without going through the formal procedure, we will apply the merging process by using a simplified version of the merging rules. Two or more rows in the primitive flow table can be merged into one row if there are nonconflicting states and outputs in each of the columns. Whenever one state symbol and don't-care entries are encountered in the same column, the state is listed in the merged row. Moreover, if the state is circled in one of the rows, it is also circled in the merged row. The output value is included with each stable state in the merged row.

We now apply these rules to the primitive flow table of Fig. 9-16. To see how this is done, the primitive flow table is separated in two parts of three rows each, as shown in Fig. 9-17(a). Each part shows three stable states that can be merged because there are no conflicting entries in each of the four columns. The first column shows state c in all the rows and 0 or a dash for the output. Since a dash represents a don't-care condition, it can be associated with any state or output. The two dashes in the first column can be taken as 0 output to make all three rows identical to a stable state c with a 0 output. The second column shows that the dashes can be assigned to correspond to a stable state a with a 0 output. Note that if the state is circled in one of the rows, it is also circled in the merged row. Similarly, the third column can be merged into an unstable state b with a don't-care output and the fourth column can be merged into stable state d and a 0 output. Thus the three rows a, c, and d can be merged into one row with three stable states and one unstable state as shown in the first row of Fig. 9-17(b). The second row of the reduced table results from the merging of rows b, e, and f of the primitive flow table. There are two ways that the reduced table can be drawn. The letter symbols for the states can be retained to show the relationship between the reduced and primitive

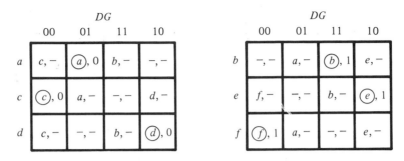

	DG 00	01	11	10
a	c, −	(a), 0	b, −	−, −
c	(c), 0	a, −	−, −	d, −
d	c, −	−, −	b, −	(d), 0

	DG 00	01	11	10
b	−, −	a, −	(b), 1	e, −
e	f, −	−, −	b, −	(e), 1
f	(f), 1	a, −	−, −	e, −

(a) States that are candidates for merging

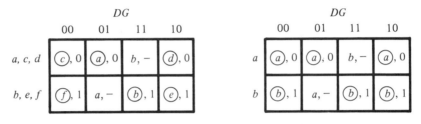

	DG 00	01	11	10
a, c, d	(c), 0	(a), 0	b, −	(d), 0
b, e, f	(f), 1	a, −	(b), 1	(e), 1

	DG 00	01	11	10
a	(a), 0	(a), 0	b, −	(a), 0
b	(b), 1	a, −	(b), 1	(b), 1

(b) Reduced table (two alternatives)

Figure 9-17 Reduction of the primitive flow table

flow tables. The other alternative is to define a common letter symbol for all the stable states of the merged rows. Thus states c and d are replaced by state a, and states e and f are replaced by state b. Both alternatives are shown in Fig. 9-17(b).

Transition Table and Logic Diagram

In order to obtain the circuit described by the reduced flow table, it is necessary to assign to each state a distinct binary value. This assignment converts the flow table into a transition table. In the general case, a binary state assignment must be made to ensure that the circuit will be free of critical races. The state assignment problem in asynchronous sequential circuits and ways to solve it are discussed in Section 9-6. Fortunately, there can be no critical races in a two-row flow table, and therefore we can finish the design of the gated latch prior to studying Section 9-6. Assigning 0 to state a and 1 to state b in the reduced flow table of Fig. 9-17(b), we obtain the transition table of Fig. 9-18(a). The transition table is in effect a map for the excitation variable Y. The simplified Boolean function for Y is then obtained from the map.

$$Y = DG + G'y$$

There are two don't-care outputs in the final reduced flow table. If we assign values

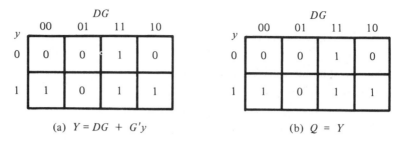

DG				
y	00	01	11	10
0	0	0	1	0
1	1	0	1	1

(a) $Y = DG + G'y$

DG				
y	00	01	11	10
0	0	0	1	0
1	1	0	1	1

(b) $Q = Y$

Figure 9-18 Transition table and output map for gated latch

to the output as shown in Fig. 9-18(b), it is possible to make output Q equal to the excitation function Y. If we assign the other possible values to the don't-care outputs, we can make output Q equal to y. In either case, the logic diagram of the gated latch is as shown in Fig. 9-19.

The diagram can be implemented also by means of an SR latch. Using the procedure outlines in Sec. 9-3, we first obtain the Boolean functions for S and R as shown in Fig. 9-20(a). The logic diagram with NAND gates is shown in Fig. 9-20(b). Note that the gated latch is a level-sensitive D-type flip-flop with the clock pulses applied to input G (see Fig. 6-5).

Assigning Outputs to Unstable States

The stable states in a flow table have specific output values associated with them. The unstable states have unspecified output entries designated by a dash. The output values for the unstable states must be chosen so that no momentary false outputs occur when the circuit switches between stable states. This means that if an output variable is not supposed to change as the result of a transition, then an unstable state that is a transient state between two stable states must have the same output value as the stable states. Consider, for example, the flow table of Fig. 9-21(a). A transition from stable state a to stable state b goes through the unstable state b. If the output assigned to the unstable b is a 1, then a momentary short pulse will appear on the output as the circuit shifts from an output of 0 in state a to an output of 1 for the unstable b and back to 0 when the circuit reaches stable state b.

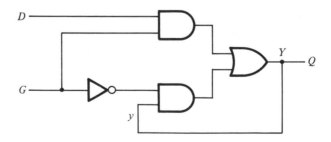

Figure 9-19 Gated latch logic diagram

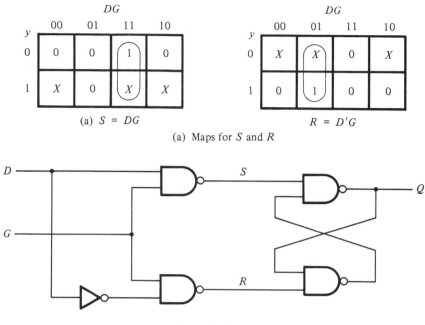

(a) $S = DG$

$R = D'G$

(a) Maps for S and R

(b) Logic diagram

Figure 9-20 Circuit with SR latch

Thus the output corresponding to unstable state b must be specified as 0 to avoid a momentary false output.

If an output variable is to change value as a result of a state change, then this variable is assigned a don't-care condition. For example, the transition from stable state b to stable state c in Fig. 9-21(a) changes the output from 0 to 1. If a 0 is entered as the output value for unstable c, then the change in the output variable will not take place until the end of the transition. If a 1 is entered, the change will take place at the start of the transition. Since it makes no difference when the output

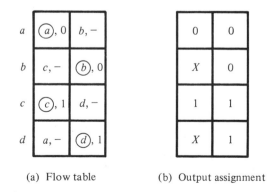

(a) Flow table   (b) Output assignment

Figure 9-21 Assigning output values to unstable states

363

change occurs, we place a don't-care entry for the output associated with unstable state *c*. Fig. 9-21(b) shows the output assignment for the flow table. It demonstrates the four possible combinations in output change that can occur. The procedure for making the assignment to outputs associated with unstable states can be summarized as follows:

1. Assign a 0 to an output variable associated with an unstable state that is a transient state between two stable states that have a 0 in the corresponding output variable.

2. Assign a 1 to an output variable associated with an unstable state that is a transient state between two stable states that have a 1 in the corresponding output variable.

3. Assign a don't-care condition to an output variable associated with an unstable state that is a transient state between two stable states that have different values (0 and 1 or 1 and 0) in the corresponding output variable.

Summary of Design Procedure

The design of asynchronous sequential circuits can be carried out by using the procedure illustrated in the previous example. Some of the design steps need further elaboration and are explained in the following sections. The procedural steps are as follows.

1. Obtain a primitive flow table from the given design specifications. This is the most difficult part of the design because it is necessary to use intuition and experience to arrive at the correct interpretation of the problem specifications.

2. Reduce the flow table by merging rows in the primitive flow table. A formal procedure for merging rows in the flow table is given in Sec. 9-5.

3. Assign binary state variables to each row of the reduced flow table to obtain the transition table. The procedure of state assignment that eliminates any possible critical races is given in Section 9-6.

4. Assign output values to the dashes associated with the unstable states to obtain the output maps. This procedure was explained above.

5. Simplify the Boolean functions of the excitation and output variables and draw the logic diagram as shown in Section 9-2. The logic diagram can be drawn using *SR* latches as shown in Section 9-3 and also at the end of Section 9-7.

9-5 REDUCTION OF STATE AND FLOW TABLES

The procedure for reducing the number of internal states in an asynchronous sequential circuit resembles the procedure that is used for synchronous circuits. An algorithm for state reduction of a completely specified state table is given in Section 6-5. We will review this algorithm and apply it to a state reduction method that uses an implication table. The algorithm and the implication table will then be modified to cover the state reduction of incompletely specified state tables. This modified algorithm will be used to explain the procedure for reducing the flow table of asynchronous sequential circuits.

Implication Table

The state reduction procedure for completely specified state tables is based on the algorithm that two states in a state table can be combined into one if they can be shown to be equivalent. Two states are equivalent if for each possible input they give exactly the same output and go to the same next states or to equivalent next states. Table 6-3 shows an example of equivalent states that have the same next states and outputs for each combination of inputs. There are occasions when a pair of states do not have the same next states but nonetheless go to equivalent next states. Consider, for example, the state table shown in Table 9-3. The present states a and b have the same output for the same input. Their next states are c and d for $x = 0$ and b and a for $x = 1$. If we can show that the pair of states (c, d) are equivalent, then the pair of states (a, b) will also be equivalent because they will have the same or equivalent next states. When this relationship exists, we say that (a, b) *imply* (c, d). Similarly, from the last two rows of Table 9-3 we find that the pair of states (c, d) imply the pair of states (a, b). The characteristic of equivalent states is that if (a, b) imply (c, d) and (c, d) imply (a, b), then both pairs of states are equivalent; that is, a and b are equivalent as well as c and d. As a consequence, the four rows of Table 9-3 can be reduced to two rows by combining a and b into one state and c and d into a second state.

The checking of each pair of states for possible equivalence in a table with a large number of states can be done systematically by means of an implication table. The implication table is a chart that consists of squares, one for every possible pair

TABLE 9-3 State table to demonstrate equivalent states

Present state	Next state $x = 0$	Next state $x = 1$	Output $x = 0$	Output $x = 1$
a	c	b	0	1
b	d	a	0	1
c	a	d	1	0
d	b	d	1	0

TABLE 9-4 State table to be reduced

Present state	Next state $x = 0$	$x = 1$	Output $x = 0$	$x = 1$
a	d	b	0	0
b	e	a	0	0
c	g	f	0	1
d	a	d	1	0
e	a	d	1	0
f	c	b	0	0
g	a	e	1	0

of states, that provide spaces for listing any possible implied states. By judicious use of the table, it is possible to determine all pairs of equivalent states. The state table of Table 9-4 will be used to illustrate this procedure. The implication table is shown in Fig. 9-22. On the left side along the vertical are listed all the states defined in the state table except the first, and across the bottom horizontally are listed all the states except the last. The result is a display of all possible combinations of two states with a square placed in the intersection of a row and a column where the two states can be tested for equivalence.

Two states that are not equivalent are marked with a cross ($\times$) in the corresponding square, while their equivalence is recorded with a check mark ($\checkmark$). Some of the squares have entries of implied states that must be further investigated to determine whether they are equivalent or not. The step-by-step procedure of filling in the squares is as follows. First we place a cross in any square corresponding to a pair of states whose outputs are not equal for every input. In this case, state

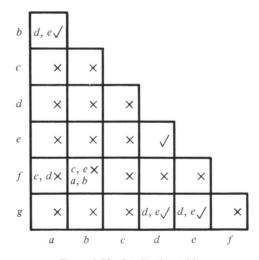

Figure 9-22 Implication table

c has a different output than any other state, so a cross is placed in the two squares of row *c* and the four squares of column *c*. There are nine other squares in this category in the implication table.

Next, we enter in the remaining squares the pairs of states that are implied by the pair of states representing the squares. We do that starting from the top square in the left column and going down and then proceeding with the next column to the right. From the state table we see that pair (a, b) imply (d, e), so (d, e) is recorded in the square defined by column *a* and row *b*. We proceed in this manner until the entire table is completed. Note that states (d, e) are equivalent because they go to the same next state and have the same output. Therefore, a check mark is recorded in the square defined by column *d* and row *e*, indicating that the two states are equivalent and independent of any implied pair.

The next step is to make successive passes through the table to determine whether any additional squares should be marked with a cross. A square in the table is crossed out if it contains at least one implied pair that is not equivalent. For example, the square defined by *a* and *f* is marked with a cross next to *c, d* because the pair (c, d) defines a square that contains a cross. This procedure is repeated until no additional squares can be crossed out. Finally, all the squares that have no crosses are recorded with check marks. These squares define pairs of equivalent states. In this example, the equivalent states are:

$$(a, b) \quad (d, e) \quad (d, g) \quad (e, g)$$

We now combine pairs of states into larger groups of equivalent states. The last three pairs can be combined into a set of three equivalent states (d, e, g) because each one of the states in the group is equivalent to the other two. The final partition of the states consists of the equivalent states found from the implication table together with all the remaining states in the state table which are not equivalent to any other state.

$$(a, b) \quad (c) \quad (d, e, g) \quad (f)$$

This means that Table 9-4 can be reduced from seven states to four states, one for each member of the above partition. The reduced table is obtained by replacing state *b* by *a* and states *e* and *g* by *d*. The reduced state table is shown in Table 9-5.

TABLE 9-5   Reduced state table

Present state	Next state $x = 0$	$x = 1$	Output $x = 0$	$x = 1$
a	d	a	0	0
c	d	f	0	1
d	a	d	1	0
f	c	a	0	0

Merging of the Flow Table

There are occasions when the state table for a sequential circuit is incompletely specified. This happens when certain combinations of inputs or input sequences may never occur because of external or internal constraints. In such a case, the next states and outputs that should have occurred if all inputs were possible are never attained and are regarded as don't-care conditions. Although synchronous sequential circuits may sometimes be represented by incompletely specified state tables, our interest here is with asynchronous sequential circuits where the primitive flow table is always incompletely specified.

Incompletely specified states can be combined to reduce the number of states in the flow table. Such states cannot be called equivalent, because the formal definition of equivalence requires that all outputs and next states be specified for all inputs. Instead, two incompletely specified states that can be combined are said to be *compatible*. Two states are compatible if for each possible input they have the same output whenever specified and their next states are compatible whenever they are specified. All don't-care conditions marked with dashes have no effect when searching for compatible states as they represent unspecified conditions.

The process that must be applied in order to find a suitable group of compatibles for the purpose of merging a flow table can be divided into three procedural steps.

1. Determine all compatible pairs by using the implication table.

2. Find the maximal compatibles using a merger diagram.

3. Find a minimal collection of compatibles that covers all the states and is closed.

The minimal collection of compatibles is then used to merge the rows of the flow table. We will now proceed to show and explain the three procedural steps using the primitive flow table from the design example in the previous section.

Compatible Pairs

The procedure for finding compatible pairs is illustrated in Fig. 9-23. The primitive flow table in (a) is the same as Fig. 9-16. The entries in each square represent the next state and output. The dashes represent the unspecified states or outputs. The implication table is used to find compatible states just as it is used to find equivalent states in the completely specified case. The only difference is that when comparing rows, we are at liberty to adjust the dashes to fit any desired condition.

Two states are compatible if in every column of the corresponding rows in the flow table there are identical or compatible states and if there is no conflict in the output values. For example, rows a and b in the flow table are found to be compatible but rows a and f will be compatible only if c and f are compatible.

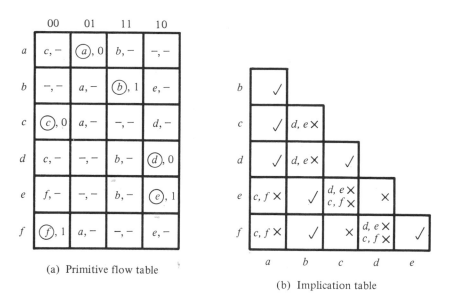

	00	01	11	10
a	c, −	ⓐ, 0	b, −	−, −
b	−, −	a, −	ⓑ, 1	e, −
c	ⓒ, 0	a, −	−, −	d, −
d	c, −	−, −	b, −	ⓓ, 0
e	f, −	−, −	b, −	ⓔ, 1
f	ⓕ, 1	a, −	−, −	e, −

(a) Primitive flow table

	a	b	c	d	e
b	✓				
c	✓	d, e ×			
d	✓	d, e ×	✓		
e	c, f ×	✓	d, e × c, f ×	×	
f	c, f ×	✓	×	d, e × c, f ×	✓

(b) Implication table

Figure 9-23 Flow and implication tables

However, rows c and f are not compatible because they have different outputs in the first column. This information is recorded in the implication table. A check mark designates a square whose pair of states are compatible. Those states that are not compatible are marked with a cross. The remaining squares are recorded with the implied pairs that need further investigation.

Once the initial implication table has been filled, it is scanned again to cross out the squares whose implied states are not compatible. The remaining squares that contain check marks define the compatible pairs. In the example of Fig. 9-23 the compatible pairs are:

$$(a, b) \quad (a, c) \quad (a, d) \quad (b, e) \quad (b, f) \quad (c, d) \quad (e, f)$$

Maximal Compatibles

Having found all the compatible pairs, the next step is to find larger sets of states that are compatible. The *maximal compatible* is a group of compatibles that contains all the possible combinations of compatible states. The maximal compatible can be obtained from a merger diagram as shown in Fig. 9-24. The merger diagram is a graph in which each state is represented by a dot placed along the circumference of a circle. Lines are drawn between any two corresponding dots that form a compatible pair. All possible compatibles can be obtained from the merger diagram by observing the geometrical patterns in which states are connected to each other. An isolated dot represents a state that is not compatible to any other state. A line represents a

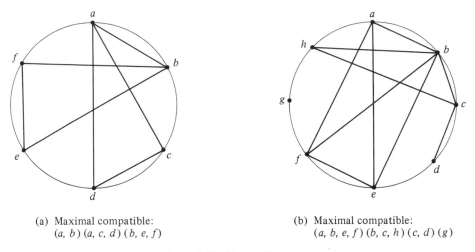

(a) Maximal compatible:
$(a, b) (a, c, d) (b, e, f)$

(b) Maximal compatible:
$(a, b, e, f) (b, c, h) (c, d) (g)$

Figure 9-24 Merger diagrams

compatible pair. A triangle constitutes a compatible with three states. An *n*-state compatible is represented in the merger diagram by an *n*-sided polygon with all its diagonals connected.

The merger diagram of Fig. 9-24(a) is obtained from the list of compatible pairs derived from the implication table of Fig. 9-23. There are seven straight lines connecting the dots, one for each compatible pair. The lines form a geometrical pattern consisting of two triangles connecting (a, c, d) and (b, e, f) and a line (a, b). The maximal compatibles are

$$(a, b) \quad (a, c, d) \quad (b, e, f)$$

Figure 9-24(b) shows the merger diagram of an 8-state flow table. The geometrical patterns are a rectangle with its two diagonals connected to form the 4-state compatible (a, b, e, f). A triangle (b, c, h), a line (c, d), and a single state *g* which is not compatible to any other state. The maximal compatibles are:

$$(a, b, e, f) \quad (b, c, h) \quad (c, d) \quad (g)$$

The maximal compatible set can be used to merge the flow table by assigning one row in the reduced table to each member of the set. However, quite often the maximal compatibles do not necessarily constitute the set of compatibles that is minimal. In many cases, it is possible to find a smaller collection of compatibles that will satisfy the condition for row merging.

Closed Covering Condition

The condition that must be satisfied for row merging is that the set of chosen compatibles must *cover* all the states and must be *closed*. The set will cover all the states if it includes all the states of the original state table. The closure condition is satisfied if there are no implied states or if the implied states are included within the set. A closed set of compatibles which covers all the states is called a *closed covering*. The closed covering condition will be explained by means of two examples.

Consider the maximal compatibles from Fig. 9-24(a). If we remove (a, b), we are left with a set of two compatibles:

$$(a, c, d) \quad (b, e, f)$$

All six states from the flow table in Fig. 9-23 are included in this set. This satisfies the covering condition. There are no implied states for (a, c), (a, d), (c, d), (b, e), (b, f), and (e, f), as seen from the implication table of Fig. 9-23(b), so the closure condition is also satisfied. Therefore, the primitive flow table can be merged into two rows, one for each of the compatibles. The detailed construction of the reduced table for this particular example was done in the previous section and is shown in Fig. 9-17(b).

The second example is from a primitive flow table (not shown) whose implication table is given in Fig. 9-25(a). The compatible pairs derived from the implication table are:

$$(a, b) \quad (a, d) \quad (b, c) \quad (c, d) \quad (c, e) \quad (d, e)$$

From the merger diagram of Fig. 9-25(b) we determine the maximal compatibles:

$$(a, b) \quad (a, d) \quad (b, c) \quad (c, d, e)$$

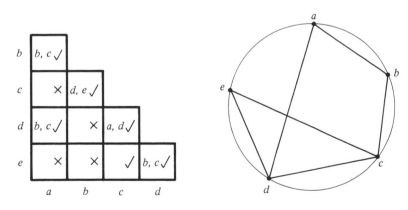

(a) Implication table   (b) Merger diagram

Compatibles:	(a, b)	(a, d)	(b, c)	(c, d, e)
Implied states:	(b, c)	(b, c)	(d, e)	(a, d) (b, c)

(c) Closure table

Figure 9-25 Choosing a set of compatibles

If we choose the two compatibles

$$(a, b) \quad (c, d, e)$$

the set will cover all five states of the original table. The closure condition can be checked by means of a closure table as shown in Fig. 9-25(c). The implied pairs listed for each compatible are taken directly from the implication table. The implied states for (a, b) are (b, c). But (b, c) is not included in the chosen set of (a, b) (c, d, e), so this set of compatibles is not closed. A set of compatibles that will satisfy the closed covering condition is

$$(a, d) \quad (b, c) \quad (c, d, e).$$

The set is covered because it contains all five states. Note that the same state can be repeated more than once. The closure condition is satisfied because the implied states are (b, c) (d, e) and (a, d), which are included in the set. The original flow table (not shown here) can be reduced from five rows to three rows by merging rows a and d, b and c, and c, d, and e. Note that an alternative satisfactory choice of closed covered compatibles would be (a, b) (b, c) (d, e). In general there may be more than one possible way of merging rows when reducing a primitive flow table.

9-6 RACE-FREE STATE ASSIGNMENT

Once a reduced flow table has been derived for an asynchronous sequential circuit, the next step in the design is to assign binary variables to each stable state. This assignment results in the transformation of the flow table into its equivalent transition table. The primary objective in choosing a proper binary state assignment is the prevention of critical races. The problem of critical races was demonstrated in Section 9-2 in conjunction with Fig. 9-7.

Critical races can be avoided by making a binary state assignment in such a way that only one variable changes at any given time when a state transition occurs in the flow table. To accomplish this, it is necessary that states between which transitions occur be given adjacent assignments. Two binary values are said to be adjacent if they differ in only one variable. For example, 010 and 011 are adjacent because they only differ in the third bit.

In order to ensure that a transition table has no critical races, it is necessary to test each possible transition between two stable states and verify that the binary state variables change one at a time. This is a tedious process, especially when there are many rows and columns in the table. To simplify matters, we will explain the procedure of binary state assignment by going through examples with only three and four rows in the flow table. These examples will demonstrate the general procedure that must be followed to ensure a race-free state assignment. The procedure can then be applied to flow tables with any number of rows and columns.

Three-Row Flow Table Example

The assignment of a single binary variable to a flow table with two rows does not impose critical race problems. A flow table with three rows requires an assignment of two binary variables. The assignment of binary values to the stable states may cause critical races if not done properly. Consider, for example, the reduced flow table of Fig. 9-26(a). The outputs have been omitted from the table for simplicity. Inspection of row *a* reveals that there is a transition from state *a* to state *b* in column 01 and from state *a* to state *c* in column 11. This information is transferred into a *transition diagram*, as shown in Fig. 9-26(b). The directed lines from *a* to *b* and from *a* to *c* represent the two transitions just mentioned. Similarly, the transitions from the other two rows are represented by directed lines in the transition diagram. The transition diagram is a pictorial representation of all required transitions between rows.

   To avoid critical races, we must find a binary state assignment such that only one binary variable changes during each state transition. An attempt to find such assignment is shown in the transition diagram. State *a* is assigned binary 00, and state *c* is assigned binary 11. This assignment will cause a critical race during the transition from *a* to *c* because there are two changes in the binary state variables. Note that the transition from *c* to *a* also causes a race condition, but it is noncritical.

   A race-free assignment can be obtained if we add an extra row to the flow table. The use of a fourth row does not increase the number of binary state variables, but it allows the formation of cycles between two stable states. Consider the modified flow table in Fig. 9-27. The first three rows represent the same conditions as the original three-row table. The fourth row, labeled *d*, is assigned the binary value 10, which is adjacent to both *a* and *c*. The transition from *a* to *c* must now go through *d*, with the result that the binary variables change from $a = 00$ to $d = 10$ to $c = 11$, thus avoiding a critical race. This is accomplished by changing row *a*, column 11 to *d* and row *d*, column 11 to *c*. Similarly, the transition from *c* to

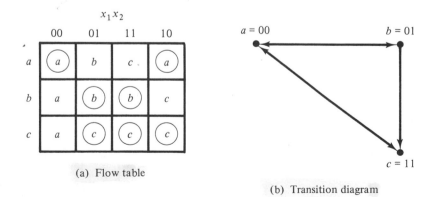

(a) Flow table

(b) Transition diagram

Figure 9-26   Three-row flow table example

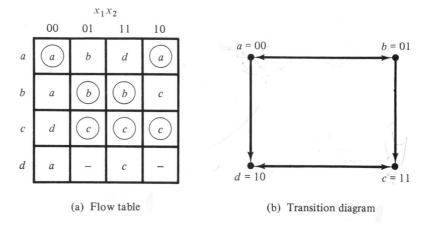

$x_1 x_2$

	00	01	11	10
a	(a)	b	d	(a)
b	a	(b)	(b)	c
c	d	(c)	(c)	(c)
d	a	–	c	–

(a) Flow table

a = 00   b = 01

d = 10   c = 11

(b) Transition diagram

Figure 9-27 Flow table with an extra row

a is shown to go through unstable state *d* even though column 00 constitutes a noncritical race.

The transition table corresponding to the flow table with the indicated binary state assignment is shown in Fig. 9-28. The two dashes in row *d* represent unspecified states that can be considered don't-care conditions. However, care must be taken not to assign 10 to these squares in order to avoid the possibility of an unwanted stable state being established in the fourth row.

This example demonstrates the use of an extra row in the flow table for the purpose of achieving a race-free assignment. The extra row is not assigned to any specific stable state but instead is used to convert a critical race into a cycle that goes through adjacent transitions between two stable states. Sometimes, just one extra row may not be sufficient to prevent critical races, and it may be necessary to add two or more extra rows in the flow table. This is demonstrated in the next example.

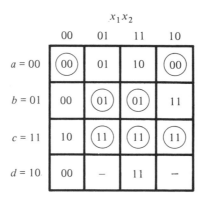

$x_1 x_2$

	00	01	11	10
a = 00	(00)	01	10	(00)
b = 01	00	(01)	(01)	11
c = 11	10	(11)	(11)	(11)
d = 10	00	–	11	–

Figure 9-28 Transition table

374

Four-Row Flow Table Example

A flow table with four rows requires a minimum of two state variables. Although race-free assignment is sometimes possible with only two binary state variables, in many cases the requirement of extra rows to avoid critical races will dictate the use of three binary state variables. Consider, for example, the flow table and its corresponding transition diagram, shown in Fig. 9-29. If there were no transitions in the diagonal direction (from b to d or from c to a), it would be possible to find an adjacent assignment for the remaining four transitions. With one or two diagonal transitions there is no way of assigning two binary variables that satisfy the adjacency requirement. Therefore, at least three binary state variables are needed.

Figure 9-30 shows a state assignment map which is suitable for any four-row flow table. States a, b, c, and d are the original states, and e, f, and g are extra states. States placed in adjacent squares in the map will have adjacent assignments. State b is assigned binary 001 and is adjacent to the other three original states. The transition from a to d must be directed through the extra state e to produce a cycle so that only one binary variable changes at a time. Similarly, the transition from c to a is directed through g and the transition from d to c goes through f. By using the assignment given by the map, the four-row table can be expanded to a seven-row table that is free of critical races, as shown in Fig. 9-31. Note that although the flow table has seven rows, there are only four stable states. The uncircled states in the three extra rows are there merely to provide a race-free transition between the stable states.

This example demonstrates a possible way of selecting extra rows in a flow table in order to achieve a race-free assignment. A state assignment map similar to the one used in Fig. 9-30(a) can be helpful in most cases. Sometimes it is possible to take advantage of unspecified entries in the flow table. Instead of adding rows to the table, it may be possible to eliminate critical races by directing some of the state transitions through the don't-care entries. The actual assignment is done by trial and error until a satisfactory assignment is found that resolves all critical races.

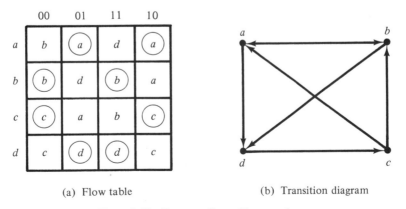

(a) Flow table   (b) Transition diagram

Figure 9-29   Four-row flow table example

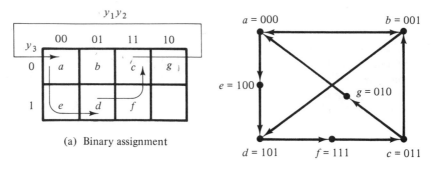

(a) Binary assignment

(b) Transition diagram

Figure 9-30 Choosing extra rows for the flow table

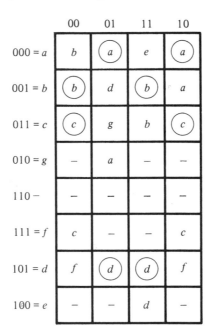

Figure 9-31 State assignment to modified flow table

Multiple-Row Method

The method for making race-free state assignment by adding extra rows in the flow table as demonstrated in the previous two examples is sometimes referred to as the *shared-row* method. There is a second method that is not as efficient but is easier to apply, called the *multiple-row* method. In the multiple-row assignment, each state in the original flow table is replaced by two or more combinations of state variables. The state assignment map of Fig. 9-32(a) shows a multiple-row assignment that can

$$y_2 y_3$$

y_1	00	01	11	10
0	a_1	b_1	c_1	d_1
1	c_2	d_2	a_2	b_2

(a) Binary assignment

	00	01	11	10
$000 = a_1$	b_1	(a_1)	d_1	(a_1)
$111 = a_2$	b_2	(a_2)	d_2	(a_2)
$001 = b_1$	(b_1)	d_2	(b_1)	a_1
$110 = b_2$	(b_2)	d_1	(b_2)	a_2
$011 = c_1$	(c_1)	a_2	b_1	(c_1)
$100 = c_2$	(c_2)	a_1	b_2	(c_2)
$010 = d_1$	c_1	(d_1)	(d_1)	c_1
$101 = d_2$	c_2	(d_2)	(d_2)	c_2

(b) Flow table

Figure 9-32   Multiple-row assignment

be used with any four-row flow table. There are two binary state variables for each stable state, each being the logical complement of each other. For example, the original state a is replaced with two equivalent states $a_1 = 000$ and $a_2 = 111$. The output values, not shown here, must be the same in a_1 and a_2. Note that a_1 is adjacent to b_1, c_2, and d_1 and a_2 is adjacent to c_1, b_2, and d_2, and similarly each state is adjacent to three states of different letter designation. The behavior of the circuit is the same whether the internal state is a_1 or a_2, and so on for the other states.

Figure 9-32(b) shows the multiple-row assignment for the original flow table of Fig. 9-29(a). The expanded table is formed by replacing each row of the original table with two rows. For example, row b is replaced by rows b_1 and b_2 and stable state b is entered in columns 00 and 11 in both rows b_1 and b_2. After all the stable states have been entered, the unstable states are filled in by reference to the assignment specified in the map of part (a). When choosing the next state for a given present state, a state which is adjacent to the present state is selected from the map. In the original table, the next states of b are a and d for inputs 10 and 01, respectively. In the expanded table, the next states for b_1 are a_1 and d_2 because these are the states adjacent to b_1. Similarly, the next states for b_2 are a_2 and d_1 because they are adjacent to b_2.

In the multiple-row assignment, the change from one stable state to another will always cause a change of only one binary state variable. Each stable state has two binary assignments with exactly the same output. At any given time, only one of the assignments is in use. For example, if we start with state a_1 and input 01 and then change the input to 11, 01, 00, and back to 01, the sequence of internal states will be a_1, d_1, c_1, and a_2. Although the circuit starts in state a_1 and terminates in state a_2, as far as the input–output relationship is concerned, the two states a_1 and a_2 are equivalent to state a of the original flow table.

9-7 HAZARDS

When designing asynchronous sequential circuits, care must be taken to conform with certain restrictions and precautions to ensure proper operation. The circuit must be operated in fundamental mode with only one input changing at any time and must be free of critical races. In addition, there is one more phenomenon, called *hazard*, that may cause the circuit to malfunction. Hazards are unwanted switching transients that may appear at the output of a circuit because different paths exhibit different propagation delays. Hazards occur in combinational circuits, where they may cause a temporary false output value. When this condition occurs in asynchronous sequential circuits, it may result in a transition to a wrong stable state. It is therefore necessary to check for possible hazards and determine whether they cause improper operations. Steps must then be taken to eliminate their effect.

Hazards in Combinational Circuits

A hazard is a condition where a single variable change produces a momentary output change when no output change should occur. The circuit of Fig. 9-33(a) demonstrates the occurrence of a hazard. Assume that all three inputs are initially equal to 1. This causes the output of gate 1 to be 1, that of gate 2 to be 0, and the output of the circuit to be equal to 1. Now consider a change of x_2 from 1 to 0. The output of gate 1 changes to 0 and that of gate 2 changes to 1 leaving the output at 1. However, the output may momentarily go to 0 if the propagation delay through the inverter is taken into consideration. The delay in the inverter may cause the output of gate 1 to change to 0 before the output of gate 2 changes to 1. In that case, both inputs of gate 3 are momentarily equal to 0, causing the output to go to 0 for the

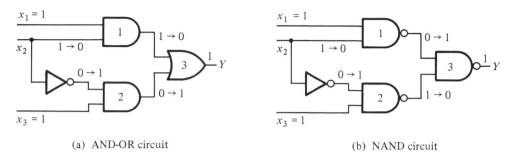

(a) AND-OR circuit   (b) NAND circuit

Figure 9-33   Circuits with hazards

short interval of time that the input signal from x_2 is delayed while it is propagating through the inverter circuit.

The circuit of Fig. 9-33(b) is a NAND implementation of the same Boolean function. It has a hazard for the same reason. Because gate 1 and 2 are NAND gates, their outputs are the complement of the outputs of the corresponding AND gates. When x_2 changes from 1 to 0, both inputs of gate 3 may be equal to 1, causing the output to produce a momentary change to 0 when it should have stayed at 1.

The two circuits shown in Fig. 9-33 implement the Boolean function in sum of products.

$$Y = x_1 x_2 + x_2' x_3$$

This type of implementation may cause the output to go to 0 when it should remain a 1. If the circuit is implemented in product of sums (see Section 3-5)

$$Y = (x_1 + x_2')(x_2 + x_3)$$

then the output may momentarily go to 1 when it should remain 0. The first case is referred to as *static 1-hazard* and the second case as *static 0-hazard*. A third type of hazard known as *dynamic hazard* causes the output to change three or more times when it should change from 1 to 0 or from 0 to 1. Figure 9-34 demonstrates the three types of hazards. When a circuit is implemented in sum of products with AND–OR gates or with NAND gates, the removal of static 1-hazard guarantees that no static 0-hazards or dynamic hazards will occur.

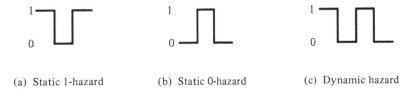

(a) Static 1-hazard   (b) Static 0-hazard   (c) Dynamic hazard

Figure 9-34   Types of hazards

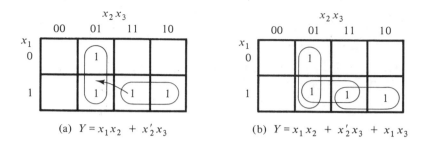

(a) $Y = x_1 x_2 + x_2' x_3$

(b) $Y = x_1 x_2 + x_2' x_3 + x_1 x_3$

Figure 9-35 Maps demonstrating a hazard and its removal

The occurrence of the hazard can be detected by inspecting the map of the particular circuit. To illustrate, consider the map in Fig. 9-35(a), which is a plot of the function implemented in Fig. 9-33. The change in x_2 from 1 to 0 moves the circuit from minterm 111 to minterm 101. The hazard exists because the change of input results in a different product term covering the two minterms. Minterm 111 is covered by the product term implemented in gate 1, and minterm 101 is covered by the product term implemented in gate 2 of Fig. 9-33. Whenever the circuit must move from one product term to another, there is a possibility of a momentary interval when neither term is equal to 1, giving rise to an undesirable 0 output.

The remedy for eliminating a hazard is to enclose the two minterms in question with another product term that overlaps both groupings. This is shown in the map of Fig. 9-35(b), where the two minterms that cause the hazard are combined into one product term. The hazard-free circuit obtained by this configuration is shown in Fig. 9-36. The extra gate in the circuit generates the product term $x_1 x_3$. In general, hazards in combinational circuits can be removed by covering any two minterms that may produce a hazard with a product term common to both. The removal of hazards requires the addition of redundant gates to the circuit.

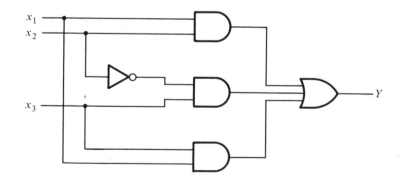

Figure 9-36 Hazard-free circuit

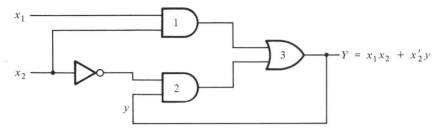

(a) Logic diagram

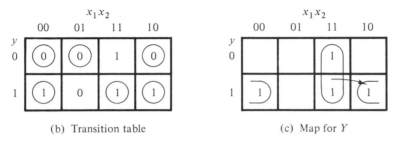

(b) Transition table

(c) Map for Y

Figure 9-37 Hazard in asynchronous sequential circuit

Hazards in Sequential Circuits

In normal combinational circuit design associated with synchronous sequential circuits, hazards are not of concern, since momentary erroneous signals are not generally troublesome. However, if a momentary incorrect signal is fed back in an asynchronous sequential circuit, it may cause the circuit to go to the wrong stable state. This is illustrated in the example of Fig. 9-37. If the circuit is in total stable state $yx_1x_2 = 111$ and input x_2 changes from 1 to 0, the next total stable state should be 110. However, because of the hazard, output Y may go to 0 momentarily. If this false signal feeds back into gate 2 before the output of the inverter goes to 1, the output of gate 2 will remain at 0 and the circuit will switch to the incorrect total stable state 010. This malfunction can be eliminated by adding an extra gate as done in Fig. 9-36.

Implementation with *SR* Latches

Another way to avoid static hazards in asynchronous sequential circuits is to implement the circuit with *SR* latches. A momentary 0 signal applied to the *S* or *R* inputs of a NOR latch will have no effect on the state of the circuit. Similarly, a momentary 1 signal applied to the *S* and *R* inputs of a NAND latch will have no effect on the state of the latch. In Fig. 9-33(b) we observed that a two-level sum of product expression implemented with NAND gates may have a static 1-hazard if both inputs of gate 3 go to 1, changing the output from 1 to 0 momentarily. But if gate 3 is part of a latch, the momentary 1 signal will have no effect on the output because a third input to the gate will come from the complemented side of the latch which will be equal to 0 and thus maintaining the output at 1. To clarify what was just said, consider a NAND SR latch with the following Boolean functions for S and R.

$$S = AB + CD$$
$$R = A'C$$

Since this is a NAND latch, we must apply the complemented values to the inputs.

$$S = (AB + CD)' = (AB)'(CD)'$$
$$R = (A'C)'$$

This implementation is shown in Fig. 9-38(a). S is generated with two NAND gates

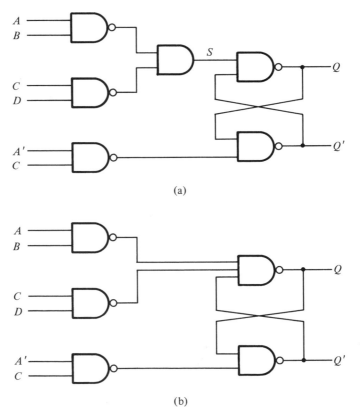

Figure 9-38 Latch implementation

and one AND gate. The Boolean function for output Q is:

$$Q = (Q'S)' = [Q'(AB)'(CD)']'$$

This function is generated in Fig. 9-38(b) with two levels of NAND gates. If output Q is equal to 1, then Q' is equal to 0. If two of the three inputs go momentarily to 1, the NAND gate associated with output Q will remain at 1 because Q' is maintained at 0.

Figure 9-38(b) shows a typical circuit that can be used to construct asynchronous sequential circuits. The two NAND gates forming the latch normally have two inputs. However, if the S or R functions contain two or more product terms when expressed in sum of products, then the corresponding NAND gate of the SR latch will have three or more inputs. Thus, the two terms in the original sum of products expression for S are AB and CD and each is implemented with a NAND gate whose output is applied to the input of the NAND latch. In this way, each state variable requires a two-level circuit of NAND gates. The first level consists of NAND gates that implement each product term in the original Boolean expression of S and R. The second level forms the cross-coupled connection of the SR latch with inputs that come from the outputs of each NAND gate in the first level.

Essential Hazards

Thus far we have considered what are known as static and dynamic hazards. There is another type of hazard that may occur in asynchronous sequential circuits, called *essential hazard*. An essential hazard is caused by unequal delays along two or more paths that originate from the same input. An excessive delay through an inverter circuit in comparison to the delay associated with the feedback path may cause such a hazard. Essential hazards cannot be corrected by adding redundant gates as in static hazards. The problem that they impose can be corrected by adjusting the amount of delay in the affected path. To avoid essential hazards, each feedback loop must be handled with individual care to ensure that the delay in the feedback path is long enough compared to delays of other signals that originate from the input terminals. This problem tends to be specialized, as it depends on the particular circuit used and the amount of delays that are encountered in its various paths.

9-8   DESIGN EXAMPLE

We are now in a position to examine a complete design example of an asynchronous sequential circuit. This example may serve as a reference for the design of other similar circuits. We will demonstrate the method of design by following the recommended procedural steps that were listed at the end of Section 9-4 and are repeated here:

1. State the design specifications.

2. Derive a primitive flow table.

3. Reduce the flow table by merging the rows.

4. Make a race-free binary state assignment.

5. Obtain the transition table and output map.

6. Obtain the logic diagram using *SR* latches.

Design Specifications

It is necessary to design a negative-edge-triggered T flip-flop. The circuit has two inputs, T (toggle) and C (clock), and one output, Q. The output state is complemented if $T = 1$ and the clock C changes from 1 to 0 (negative edge triggering). Otherwise, under any other input condition, the output Q remains unchanged. Although this circuit can be used as a flip-flop in clocked sequential circuits, the internal design of the flip-flop (as is the case with all other flip-flops) is an asynchronous problem.

Primitive Flow Table

The derivation of the primitive flow table can be facilitated if we first derive a table that lists all the possible total states in the circuit. This is shown in Table 9-6. We start with the input condition $TC = 11$ and assign to it state a. The circuit goes to state b and the output Q complements from 0 to 1 when C changes from 1 to 0 while T remains a 1. Another change in the output occurs when the circuit goes from state c to state d. In this case $T = 1$, C changes from 1 to 0, and the output Q complements from 1 to 0. The other four states in the table do not change the

TABLE 9-6 Specification of total states

State	Inputs T	C	Output Q	Comments
a	1	1	0	Initial output is 0
b	1	0	1	After state a
c	1	1	1	Initial output is 1
d	1	0	0	After state c
e	0	0	0	After states d or f
f	0	1	0	After states e or a
g	0	0	1	After states b or h
h	0	1	1	After states g or c

$$TC$$

	00	01	11	10
a	−, −	f, −	(a), 0	b, −
b	g, −	−, −	c, −	(b), 1
c	−, −	h, −	(c), 1	d, −
d	e, −	−, −	a, −	(d), 0
e	(e), 0	f, −	−, −	d, −
f	e, −	(f), 0	a, −	−, −
g	(g), 1	h, −	−, −	b, −
h	g, −	(h), 1	c, −	−, −

Figure 9-39 Primitive flow table

output, because T is equal to 0. If Q is initially 0, it stays at 0, and if initially at 1, it stays at 1 even though the clock input changes. This information results in six total states. Note that simultaneous transitions of two input variables, such as from 01 to 10, are not included, as they violate the condition for fundamental mode operation.

The primitive flow table is shown in Fig. 9-39. The information for the flow table can be obtained directly from the conditions listed in Table 9-6. We first fill in one square in each row belonging to the stable state in that row as listed in the table. Then we enter dashes in those squares whose input differs by two variables from the input corresponding to the stable state. The unstable conditions are then determined by utilizing the information listed under the comments in Table 9-6.

Merging of the Flow Table

The rows in the primitive flow table are merged by first obtaining all compatible pairs of states. This is done by means of the implication table shown in Fig. 9-40. The squares that contain check marks define the compatible pairs:

$$(a, f) \quad (b, g) \quad (b, h) \quad (c, h) \quad (d, e) \quad (d, f) \quad (e, f) \quad (g, h)$$

The maximal compatibles are obtained from the merger diagram shown in Fig. 9-41. The geometrical patterns that are recognized in the diagram consist of two

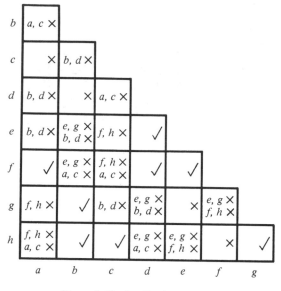

Figure 9-40 Implication table

triangles and two straight lines. The maximal compatible set is:

$$(a, f) \quad (b, g, h) \quad (c, h) \quad (d, e, f)$$

In this particular example, the minimal collection of compatibles is also the maximal compatible set. Note that the closed condition is satisfied because the set includes all the original eight states listed in the primitive flow table, although states h and f are repeated twice. The covering condition is also satisfied because all the compatible pairs have no implied states, as can be seen from the implication table.

The reduced flow table is shown in Fig. 9-42. The one shown in part (a) of the figure retains the original state symbols but merges the corresponding rows. For

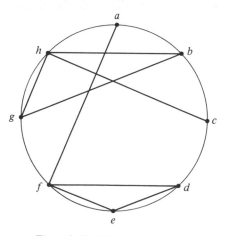

Figure 9-41 Merger diagram

386

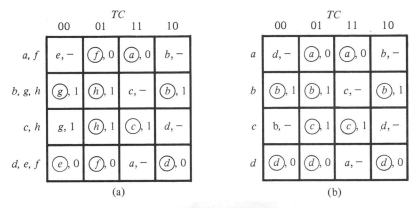

Figure 9-42 Reduced flow table

example, states a and f are compatible and are merged into one row that retains the original letter symbols of the states. Similarly, the other three compatible sets of states are used to merge the flow table into four rows, retaining the eight original letter symbols. The other alternative for drawing the merged flow table is shown in part (b) of the figure. Here we assign a common letter symbol to all the stable states in each merged row. Thus the symbol f is replaced by a, and g and h are replaced by b, and similarly for the other two rows. The second alternative shows clearly a four-state flow table with only four letter symbols for the states.

State Assignment and Transition Table

The next step in the design is to find a race-free binary assignment for the four stable states in the reduced flow table. In order to find a suitable adjacent assignment, we draw the transition diagram as shown in Fig. 9-43. For this example it is possible to obtain a suitable adjacent assignment without the need of extra states. This is because there are no diagonal lines in the transition diagram.

Substituting the binary assignment indicated in the transition diagram into the reduced flow table, we obtain the transition table shown in Fig. 9-44. The output map is obtained from the reduced flow table. The dashes in the output section are assigned values according to the rules established in Section 9-4.

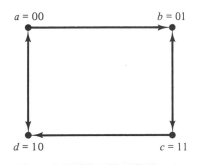

Figure 9-43 Transition diagram

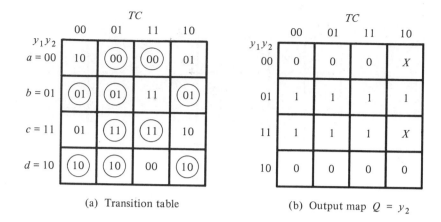

(a) Transition table

(b) Output map $Q = y_2$

Figure 9-44 Transition table and output map

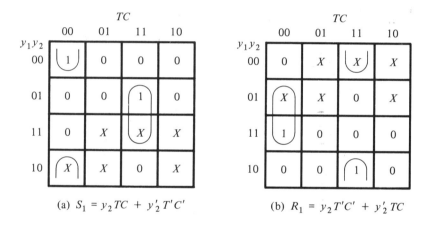

(a) $S_1 = y_2 TC + y_2' T'C'$

(b) $R_1 = y_2 T'C' + y_2' TC$

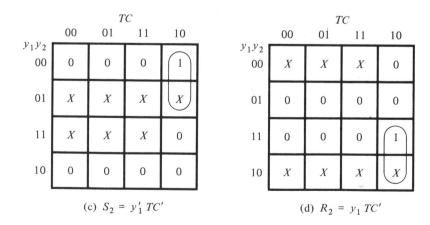

(c) $S_2 = y_1' TC'$

(d) $R_2 = y_1 TC'$

Figure 9-45 Maps for latch inputs

388

Logic Diagram

The circuit to be designed has two state variables, Y_1 and Y_2, and one output, Q. The output map in Fig. 9-44 shows that Q is equal to the state variable y_2. The implementation of the circuit requires two SR latches, one for each state variable. The maps for inputs S and R of the two latches are shown in Fig. 9-45. The maps are obtained from the information given in the transition table by using the conditions specified in the latch excitation table given in Fig. 9-14(b). The simplified Boolean functions are listed under each map.

The logic diagram of the circuit is shown in Fig. 9-46. Here we use two NAND latches with two or three inputs in each gate. This implementation is according to

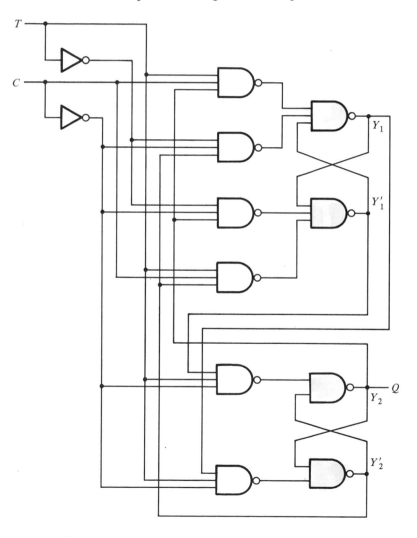

Figure 9-46 Logic diagram of negative-edge-triggered T flip-flop

the pattern established in Section 9-7 in conjunction with Fig. 9-38(b). The S and R input functions require six NAND gates for their implementation.

This example demonstrates the complexity involved in designing asynchronous sequential circuits. It was necessary to go through ten diagrams in order to obtain the final circuit diagram. Although most digital circuits are synchronous, there are occasions when one has to deal with asynchronous behavior. The basic properties presented in this chapter are essential to understand fully the internal behavior of digital circuits.

REFERENCES

1. Hill, F. J. and G. R. Peterson, *Introduction to Switching Theory and Logical Design*, 3rd ed. New York: John Wiley & Sons, 1981.

2. Kohavi, Z., *Switching and Finite Automata Theory*, 2nd ed. New York: McGraw-Hill Book Co., 1978.

3. Roth, C. H. Jr., *Fundamentals of Logic Design*, 2nd ed. St. Paul, Minn.: West Pub. Co., 1979.

4. Nagle, H. T. Jr., B. D. Carroll, and J. D. Irwin, *An Introduction to Computer Logic*. Englewood Cliffs, N.J.: Prentice-Hall, Inc., 1975.

5. Unger, S. H., *Asynchronous Sequential Switching Circuits*. New York: Wiley-Interscience, 1969.

6. McCluskey, E. J. Jr., *Introduction to the Theory of Switching Circuits*. New York: McGraw-Hill Book Co., 1965.

7. Givone, D. D., *Introduction to Switching Circuit Theory*. New York: McGraw-Hill Book Co., 1970.

PROBLEMS

9-1.   (a) Explain the difference between asynchronous and synchronous sequential circuits.
        (b) Define fundamental-mode operation.
        (c) Explain the difference between stable and unstable states.
        (d) What is the difference between an internal state and a total state?

9-2.   Derive the transition table for the asynchronous sequential circuit shown in Fig. P9-2. Determine the sequence of internal states Y_1Y_2 for the following sequence of inputs x_1x_2: 00, 10, 11, 01, 11, 10, 00.

9-3.   An asynchronous sequential circuit is described by the following excitation and output functions:

$$Y = x_1x_2' + (x_1 + x_2')y$$
$$z = y$$

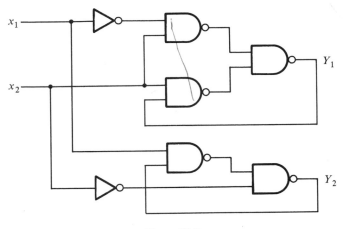

Figure P9-2

(a) Draw the logic diagram of the circuit.

(b) Derive the transition table and output map.

(c) Obtain a 2-state flow table.

(d) Describe in words the behavior of the circuit.

9-4. An asynchronous sequential circuit has two internal states and one output. The excitation and output functions describing the circuit are as follows:

$$Y_1 = x_1 x_2 + x_1 y_2' + x_2' y_1$$
$$Y_2 = x_2 + x_1 y_1' y_2 + x_1' y_1$$
$$z = x_2 + y_1$$

(a) Draw the logic diagram of the circuit.

(b) Derive the transition table and output map.

(c) Obtain a flow table for the circuit.

d draw state diagram

9-5. Convert the flow table of Fig. P9-5 into a transition table by assigning the following binary values to the states: $a = 00, b = 11, c = 01$.

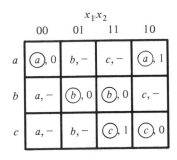

Figure P9-5

(a) Assign values to the extra fourth state to avoid critical races.

(b) Assign outputs to the don't-care states to avoid momentary false outputs.

(c) Derive the logic diagram of the circuit.

9-6.   Investigate the transition table of Fig. P9-6 and determine all race conditions and whether they are critical or noncritical. Also determine whether there are any cycles.

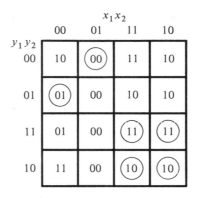

Figure P9-6

9-7.   Analyze the T flip-flop shown in Fig. 6-7(a), on page 209. Obtain the transition table and show that the circuit is unstable when both T and CP are equal to 1.

9-8.   Convert the circuit of Fig. 6-15, on page 218, into an asynchronous sequential circuit by removing the clock pulse (CP) signal and changing the flip-flops into SR latches. Derive the transition table and output map of the modified circuit and show that the result obtained is similar to the state table of Table 6-1.

9-9.   For the asynchronous sequential circuit shown in Fig. P9-9:

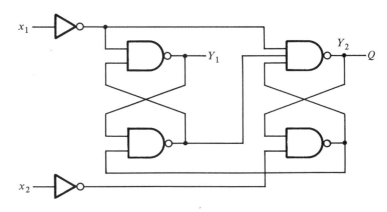

Figure P9-9

(a) Derive the Boolean functions for the outputs of the two SR latches Y_1 and Y_2. Note that the S input of the second latch is $x_1' y_1'$.

(b) Derive the transition table and output map of the circuit.

(c) Show that the circuit is a set-dominate flip-flop as defined in Problem 6-5 with x_1 being the S input and x_2 the R input.

9-10. Implement the circuit defined in Problem 9-3 with a NOR SR latch. Repeat with a NAND SR latch.

9-11. Implement the circuit defined in Problem 9-4 with NAND SR latches.

9-12. Obtain a primitive flow table for a circuit with two inputs, x_1 and x_2, and two outputs, z_1 and z_2, that satisfy the following four conditions:

(a) When $x_1 x_2 = 00$, the output is $z_1 z_2 = 00$.

(b) When $x_1 = 1$ and x_2 changes from 0 to 1, the output is $z_1 z_2 = 01$.

(c) When $x_2 = 1$ and x_1 changes from 0 to 1, the output is $z_1 z_2 = 10$.

(d) Otherwise, the output does not change.

9-13. A traffic light is installed at a junction of a railroad and a road. The traffic light is controlled by two switches in the rails placed one mile apart on either side of the junction. A switch is turned on when the train is over it and is turned off otherwise. The traffic light changes from green (logic 0) to red (logic 1) when the beginning of the train is one mile from the junction. The light changes back to green when the end of the train is one mile away from the junction. Assume that the length of the train is less than two miles.

(a) Obtain a primitive flow table for the circuit.

(b) Show that the flow table can be reduced to four rows.

9-14. It is necessary to design an asynchronous sequential circuit with two inputs, x_1 and x_2, and one output, z. Initially both inputs and output are equal to 0. When x_1 or x_2 becomes 1, z becomes 1. When the second input also becomes 1, the output changes to 0. The output stays at 0 until the circuit goes back to the initial state.

(a) Obtain a primitive flow table for the circuit and show that it can be reduced to the flow table shown in Fig. P9-14.

(b) Complete the design of the circuit.

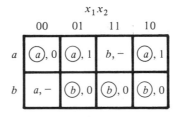

$$x_1 x_2$$

	00	01	11	10
a	$\textcircled{a}, 0$	$\textcircled{a}, 1$	$b, -$	$\textcircled{a}, 1$
b	$a, -$	$\textcircled{b}, 0$	$\textcircled{b}, 0$	$\textcircled{b}, 0$

Figure P9-14

9-15. Assign output values to the don't-care states in the flow tables of Fig. P9-15 in such a way as to avoid transient output pulses.

9-16. Using the implication table method, show that the state table listed in Table 6-4, on page 227, cannot be reduced any further.

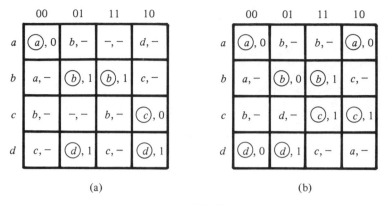

	00	01	11	10
a	(a), 0	b, −	−, −	d, −
b	a, −	(b), 1	(b), 1	c, −
c	b, −	−, −	b, −	(c), 0
d	c, −	(d), 1	c, −	(d), 1

(a)

	00	01	11	10
a	(a), 0	b, −	b, −	(a), 0
b	a, −	(b), 0	(b), 1	c, −
c	b, −	d, −	(c), 1	(c), 1
d	(d), 0	(d), 1	c, −	a, −

(b)

Figure P9-15

9-17. Reduce the number of states in the state table listed in Problem 6-14, on page 254. Use an implication table.

 Merge each of the primitive flow tables shown in Fig. P9-18.

	00	01	11	10
a	(a), 0	b, −	−, −	e, −
b	a, −	(b), 0	c, −	−, −
c	−, −	d, −	(c), 0	h, −
d	a, −	(d), 1	−, −	−, −
e	a, −	−, −	f, −	(e), 0
f	−, −	g, −	(f), 0	h, −
g	a, −	(g), 0	−, −	−, −
h	a, −	−, −	−, −	(h), 0

(a)

	00	01	11	10
a	(a), 1	f, −	−, −	e, −
b	c, −	−, −	j, −	(b), 0
c	(c), 0	d, −	−, −	b, −
d	c, −	(d), 0	g, −	−, −
e	a, −	−, −	g, −	(e), 1
f	a, −	(f), 1	g, −	−, −
g	−, −	d, −	(g), 0	k, −
h	(h), 0	d, −	−, −	k, −
j	−, −	f, −	(j), 1	b, −
k	a, −	−, −	j, 1	(k), 0

(b)

Figure P9-18

Proceed as follows:

(a) Find all compatible pairs by means of an implication table.

(b) Find the maximal compatibles by means of a merger diagram.

(c) Find a minimal set of compatibles that covers all the states and is closed.

9-19. (a) Obtain a binary state assignment for the reduced flow table shown in Fig. P9-19. Avoid critical race conditions.

$$x_1 x_2$$

	00	01	11	10
a	ⓐ, 0	ⓐ,1	b, −	d, −
b	a, −	ⓑ, 0	ⓑ, 0	c, −
c	a, −	−, −	d, −	ⓒ, 0
d	a, −	a, −	ⓓ, 1	ⓓ, 1

Figure P9-19

(b) Obtain the logic diagram of the circuit using NAND latches and gates.

9-20. Find a critical race-free state assignment for the reduced flow table shown in Fig. P9-20.

	00	01	11	10
a	ⓐ	d	ⓐ	c
b	a	ⓑ	ⓑ	d
c	d	ⓒ	b	ⓒ
d	ⓓ	ⓓ	e	ⓓ
e	f	c	ⓔ	c
f	ⓕ	b	a	ⓕ

Figure P9-20

9-21. Consider the reduced flow table shown in Fig. P9-21.

(a) Obtain the transition diagram and show that three state variables are needed for a race-free binary state assignment.

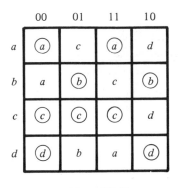

	00	01	11	10
a	(a)	c	(a)	d
b	a	(b)	c	(b)
c	(c)	(c)	(c)	d
d	(d)	b	a	(d)

Figure P9-21

(b) Obtain the expanded flow table using the multiple row method assignment as specified in Fig. 9-32(a).

9-22. Find a circuit that has no static hazards and implements the Boolean function:

$$F(A, B, C, D) = \sum(0,2,6,7,8,10,12)$$

9-23. Draw the logic diagram of the product of sums expression:

$$Y = (x_1 + x_2')(x_2 + x_3)$$

Show that there is a static 0-hazard when x_1 and x_3 are equal to 0 and x_2 goes from 0 to 1. Find a way to remove the hazard by adding one more OR gate.

9-24. The Boolean functions for the inputs of an SR latch are as follows. Obtain the circuit diagram using a minimum number of NAND gates.

$$S = x_1'x_2'x_3 + x_1x_2x_3$$
$$R = x_1x_2' + x_2x_3'$$

9-25. Complete the design of the circuit specified in Problem 9-13.

Digital Integrated Circuits

10

10-1 INTRODUCTION

The integrated circuit (IC) was introduced in Section 1-9, and the various IC digital logic families were discussed in Section 2-8. This chapter presents the basic electronic circuits in each IC digital logic family and analyzes their electrical operation. A basic knowledge of electronics is assumed.

The IC digital logic families to be considered here are:

RTL	Resistor-transistor logic
DTL	Diode-transistor logic
I^2L	Integrated-injection logic
TTL	Transistor-transistor logic
ECL	Emitter-coupled logic
MOS	Metal-oxide semiconductor
CMOS	Complementary metal-oxide semiconductor

The first two, RTL and DTL, have only historical significance since they are seldom used in new designs. RTL was the first commercial family to have been used extensively. It is included here because it represents a useful starting point for explaining the basic operation of digital gates. DTL circuits have been gradually replaced by TTL. In fact, TTL is a modification of the DTL gate. The operation of the TTL gate will be easier to understand after the DTL gate is discussed. The characteristics of TTL, ECL, and CMOS were presented in Section 2-8. These families have a large number of SSI circuits, as well as MSI and LSI circuits. I^2L and MOS are mostly used for constructing LSI functions.

The basic circuit in each IC digital logic family is either a NAND or a NOR gate. This basic circuit is the primary building block from which more complex

397

functions are obtained. An *RS* latch is constructed from two NAND or two NOR gates connected back to back. A master-slave flip-flop is obtained from the interconnection of about ten basic gates. A register is obtained from the interconnection of flip-flops and basic gates. Each IC logic family has available a catalog of integrated-circuit packages that provide various digital logic functions. The differences in the logic functions available from each logic family are not so much in the function that they achieve as in the specific characteristics of the basic gate from which the function has been constructed.

NAND and NOR gates are usually defined by the Boolean functions they implement in terms of binary variables. When analyzing them as electronic circuits, it is more convenient to investigate their input-output relationships in terms of two voltage levels: a *high* level (H) and a *low* level (L) (see Fig. 2-10). Binary variables take the values 1 and 0. When positive logic is adopted, the high voltage level is assigned the binary value of 1, and the low voltage level a binary 0. From the truth table of a positive-logic NAND gate, we deduce its behavior in terms of high and low levels as stated in Fig. 10-1. The corresponding behavior of the NOR gate is also stated in the same figure. These statements must be remembered because they will be used during the analysis of all the gates in this chapter.

The various digital logic families are usually evaluated by comparing the characteristics of the basic gate in each family. The most important characteristics were discussed in Section 2-8. They are listed here again for reference.

1. *Fan-out* specifies the number of standard loads that the output of the gate can drive without impairment of its normal operation. A standard load is defined as the current flowing in the input of a gate in the same IC family.

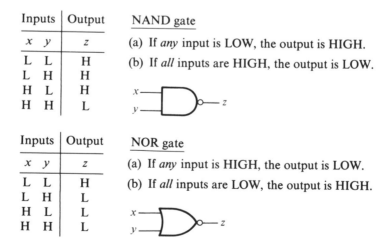

Inputs		Output
x	y	z
L	L	H
L	H	H
H	L	H
H	H	L

NAND gate

(a) If *any* input is LOW, the output is HIGH.

(b) If *all* inputs are HIGH, the output is LOW.

Inputs		Output
x	y	z
L	L	H
L	H	L
H	L	L
H	H	L

NOR gate

(a) If *any* input is HIGH, the output is LOW.

(b) If *all* inputs are LOW, the output is HIGH.

Figure 10-1   Input-output conditions for positive-logic NAND and NOR gates

2. *Power dissipation* is the power consumed by the gate, which must be available from the power supply.

3. *Propagation delay* is the average transition delay time for the signal to propagate from input to output when the signals change in value.

4. *Noise margin* is the limit of a noise voltage which may be present without impairing the proper operation of the circuit.

The *bipolar* junction transistor (BJT) is the familiar *npn* or *pnp* junction transistor. In contrast, the field-effect transistor (FET) is said to be *unipolar*. The operation of a bipolar transistor depends on the flow of two types of carriers: electrons and holes. A unipolar transistor depends on the flow of only one type of majority carrier which may be eletrons (n-channel) or holes (p-channel). The first five logic families listed previously, RTL, DTL, TTL, ECL, and I^2L, use bipolar transistors. The last two logic families, MOS and CMOS, employ a type of unipolar transistor called metal-oxide semiconductor field-effect transistor, abbreviated MOSFET, or MOS for short. We begin by describing the characteristics of the bipolar transistor and the basic gates used in the bipolar logic families. We then explain the operation of the MOS transistor in conjunction with its two logic families.

10-2 BIPOLAR TRANSISTOR CHARACTERISTICS

This section is devoted to a review of the bipolar transistor as applied to digital circuits. This information will be used for the analysis of the basic circuit in the five bipolar logic families. Bipolar transistors may be of the *npn* or *pnp* type. Moreover, they are constructed either with germanium or silicon semiconductor material. IC transistors, however, are made with silicon and are usually of the npn type.

The basic data needed for the analysis of digital circuits may be obtained from inspection of the typical characteristic curves of a common-emitter *npn* silicon transistor, shown in Fig. 10-2. The circuit in (a) is a simple inverter with two resistors and a transistor. The current marked I_C flows through resistor R_C and the collector of the transistor. Current I_B flows through resistor R_B and the base of the transistor. The emitter is connected to ground and its current $I_E = I_C + I_B$. The supply voltage is between V_{CC} and ground. The input is between V_i and ground, and the output is between V_o and ground.

We have assumed a positive direction for the currents as indicated. These are the directions in which the currents normally flow in an *npn* transistor. Collector and base currents I_C and I_B are positive when they flow into the transistor. Emitter current I_E is positive when it flows out of the transistor, as indicated by the arrow in the emitter terminal. The symbol V_{CE} stands for the voltage drop from collector

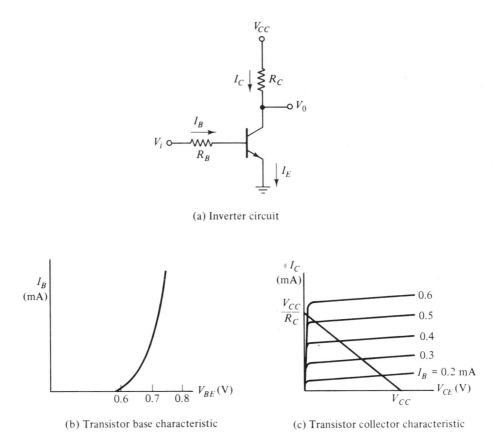

(a) Inverter circuit

(b) Transistor base characteristic

(c) Transistor collector characteristic

Figure 10-2 Silicon *npn* transistor characteristics

to emitter and is always positive. Correspondingly, V_{BE} is the voltage drop across the base-to-emitter junction. This junction is forward biased when V_{BE} is positive. It is reverse biased when V_{BE} is negative.

The base-emitter graphical characteristic is shown in Fig. 10-2(b). This is a plot of V_{BE} versus I_B. If the base-emitter voltage is less than 0.6 V, the transistor is said to be *cutoff* and no base current flows. When the base-emitter junction is forward biased with a voltage greater than 0.6 V, the transistor conducts and I_B starts rising very fast while V_{BE} changes very little. The voltage V_{BE} across a conducting transistor seldom exceeds 0.8 V.

The graphical collector-emitter characteristics, together with the load line, are shown in Fig. 10-2(c). When V_{BE} is less than 0.6 V, the transistor is cutoff with $I_B = 0$ and a negligible current flows in the collector. The collector-to-emitter circuit then behaves like an open circuit. In the *active* region, collector voltage V_{CE} may be anywhere from about 0.8 V up to V_{CC}. Collector current I_C in this region can be calculated to be approximately equal to $I_B h_{FE}$, where h_{FE} is a transistor parameter called the *dc current gain*. The maximum collector current depends not on I_B, but rather on the external circuit connected to the collector. This is because V_{CE} is always positive and its lowest possible value is 0 V. For example, in the inverter shown, the maximum I_C is obtained by making $V_{CE} = 0$ to obtain $I_C = V_{CC}/R_C$.

It was stated that $I_C = h_{FE}I_B$ in the active region. The parameter h_{FE} varies widely over the operating range of the transistor, but still it is useful to employ an average value for the purpose of analysis. In a typical operating range, h_{FE} is about 50, but under certain conditions it could go down to as low as 20. It must be realized that the base current I_B may be increased to any desirable value, but the collector current I_C is limited by external circuit parameters. As a consequence, a situation can be reached where $h_{FE}I_B$ is greater than I_C. If this condition exists, then the transistor is said to be in the *saturation* region. Thus, the condition for saturation is determined from the relationship:

$$I_B \geqslant \frac{I_{CS}}{h_{FE}}$$

where I_{CS} is the maximum collector current flowing during saturation. V_{CE} is not exactly zero in the saturation region but is normally about 0.2V.

The basic data needed for analyzing bipolar transistor digital circuits are listed in Table 10-1. In the cutoff region, V_{BE} is less than 0.6 V, V_{CE} is considered as an open circuit, and both currents are negligible. In the active region, V_{BE} is about 0.7 V, V_{CE} may vary over a wide range, and I_C can be calculated as a function of I_B. In the saturation region, V_{BE} hardly changes but V_{CE} drops to 0.2 V. The base current must be large enough to satisfy the inequality listed. To simplify the analysis, we will assume that $V_{BE} = 0.7$ V if the transistor is conducting, whether in the active or saturation region.

TABLE 10-1   Typical npn silicon transistor parameters

Region	$V_{BE}(V)$*	V_{CE} (V)	Current relationship
Cutoff	<0.6	Open circuit	$I_B = I_C = 0$
Active	0.6–0.7	>0.8	$I_C = h_{FE}I_B$
Saturation	0.7–0.8	0.2	$I_B \geqslant I_{CS}/h_{FE}$

*V_{BE} will be assumed to be 0.7 V if the transistor is conducting, whether in the active or saturation region.

The analysis of digital circuits may be undertaken using a prescribed procedure: For each transistor in the circuit determine if its V_{BE} is less than 0.6 V. If so, then the transistor is cutoff and the collector-to-emitter circuit is considered an open circuit. If V_{BE} is greater than 0.6 V, the transistor may be in the active or saturation region. Calculate the base current, assuming that $V_{BE} = 0.7$ V. Then calculate the maximum possible value of collector current I_{CS}, assuming $V_{CE} = 0.2$

V. These calculations will be in terms of voltages applied and resistor values. Then, if the base current is large enough that $I_B \geqslant I_{CS}/h_{FE}$, we deduce that the transistor is in the saturation region with $V_{CE} = 0.2$ V. However, if the base current is smaller and the above relationship is not satisfied, the transistor is in the active region and we recalculate collector current I_C using the equation $I_C = h_{FE}I_B$.

To demonstrate with an example, consider the inverter circuit of Fig. 10-2(a) with the following parameters:

$$R_C = 1 \text{ k}\Omega \qquad V_{CC} = 5 \text{ V (voltage supply)}$$
$$R_B = 22 \text{ k}\Omega \qquad H = 5 \text{ V (high-level voltage)}$$
$$h_{FE} = 50 \qquad L = 0.2 \text{ V (low-level voltage)}$$

With input voltage $V_i = L = 0.2$ V, we have that $V_{BE} < 0.6$ V and the transistor is cutoff. The collector-emitter circuit behaves like an open circuit; so output voltage $V_o = 5$ V $= H$.

With input voltage $V_i = H = 5$ V, we deduce that $V_{BE} > 0.6$ V. Assuming that $V_{BE} = 0.7$, we calculate the base current:

$$I_B = \frac{V_i - V_{BE}}{R_B} = \frac{5 - 0.7}{22 \text{ k}\Omega} = 0.195 \text{ mA}$$

The maximum collector current, assuming $V_{CE} = 0.2$ V, is:

$$I_{CS} = \frac{V_{CC} - V_{CE}}{R_C} = \frac{5 - 0.2}{1 \text{ k}\Omega} = 4.8 \text{ mA}$$

We then check for saturation:

$$0.195 = I_B \geqslant \frac{I_{CS}}{h_{FE}} = \frac{4.8}{50} = 0.096 \text{ mA}$$

and find that the inequality is satisfied since $0.195 > 0.096$. We conclude that the transistor is saturated and output voltage $V_o = V_{CE} = 0.2$ V $= L$. Thus the circuit behaves as an inverter.

The procedure just described will be used extensively during the analysis of the circuits in the following sections. This will be done by means of a qualitative analysis, i.e., without writing down the specific numerical equations. The quantitative analysis and specific calculations will be left as execises in the Problems section at the end of the chapter.

There are occasions where not only transistors but also diodes are used in digital circuits. An IC diode is usually constructed from a transistor with its collector connected to the base, as shown in Fig. 10-3(a). The graphic symbol employed for a diode is shown in Fig. 10-3(b). The diode behaves essentially like the base-emitter junction of a transistor. Its graphical characteristic, shown in Fig.

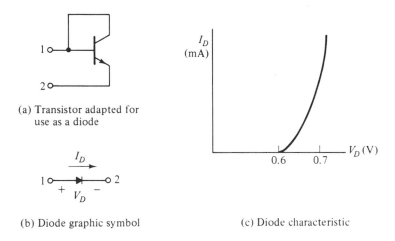

(a) Transistor adapted for
use as a diode

$$I_D$$

1 o————▶︎|——o 2
$+ \quad V_D \quad -$

(b) Diode graphic symbol

(c) Diode characteristic

Figure 10-3   Silicon diode symbol and characteristic

10-3(c), is similar to the base-emitter characteristic of a transistor. We can then conclude that a diode is off and nonconducting when its forward voltage, V_D, is less than 0.6 V. When the diode conducts, current I_D flows in the direction shown in Fig. 10-3(b), and V_D stays at about 0.7 V. One must always provide an external resistor to limit the current in a conducting diode, since its voltage remains fairly constant at a fraction of a volt.

10-3   RTL AND DTL CIRCUITS

RTL Basic Gate

The basic circuit of the RTL digital logic family is the NOR gate shown in Fig. 10-4. Each input is associated with one resistor and one transistor. The collectors of the transistors are tied together at the output. The voltage levels for the circuit are 0.2 V for the low-level and from 1 to 3.6 V for the high-level.

   The analysis of the RTL gate is very simple and follows the procedure outlined in the previous section. If any input of the RTL gate is high, the corresponding transistor is driven into saturation. This causes the output to be low, regardless of the states of the other transistors. If all inputs are low at 0.2 V, all transistors are cutoff because the $V_{BE} < 0.6$ V. This causes the output of the circuit to be high, approaching the value of supply voltage V_{CC}. This confirms the conditions stated in Fig. 10-1 for the NOR gate. Note that the noise margin for low signal input is $0.6 - 0.2 = 0.4$ V.

   The fan-out of the RTL gate is limited by the value of the output voltage when high. As the output is loaded with inputs of other gates, more current is consumed by the load. This current must flow through the 640-Ω resistor. A simple calculation (see Problem 10-1) will show that, if h_{FE} drops to 20, the output voltage drops to

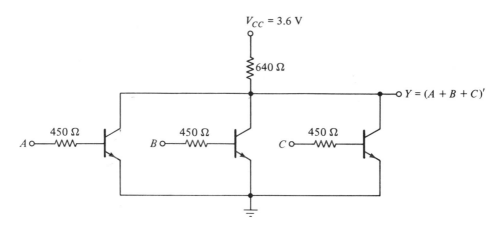

Figure 10-4 RTL basic NOR gate

about 1 V when the fan-out is 5. Any voltage below 1 V in the output may not drive the next transistor into saturation as required. The power dissipation of the RTL gate is about 12mW and the propagation delay averages 25 ns.

DTL Basic Gates

The basic circuit in the DTL digital logic family is the NAND gate shown in Fig. 10-5. Each input is associated with one diode. The diodes and the 5-kΩ resistor form an AND gate. The transistor serves as a current amplifier while inverting the digital signal. The two voltage levels are 0.2 V for the low-level and between 4 and 5 V for the high-level.

The analysis of the DTL gate should conform to the conditions listed in Fig. 10-1 for the NAND gate. If any input of the gate is low at 0.2 V, the corresponding

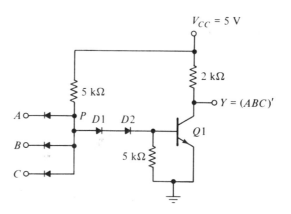

Figure 10-5 DTL basic NAND gate

input diode conducts current through V_{CC} and the 5-kΩ resistor into the input node. The voltage at point P is equal to the input voltage of 0.2 V plus a diode drop of 0.7 V, for a total of 0.9 V. In order for the transistor to start conducting, the voltage at point P must overcome a potential of one V_{BE} drop in $Q1$ plus two diode drops across $D1$ and $D2$, or $3 \times 0.6 = 1.8$ V. Since the voltage at P is maintained at 0.9 V by the input conducting diode, the transistor is cutoff and the output voltage is high at 5 V.

If all inputs of the gate are high, the transistor is driven into the saturation region. The voltage at P now is equal to V_{BE} plus the two diode drops across $D1$ and $D2$, or $0.7 \times 3 = 2.1$ V. Since all inputs are high at 5 V and $V_P = 2.1$ V, the input diodes are reverse biased and off. The base current is equal to the difference of currents flowing in the two 5-kΩ resistors and is sufficient to drive the transistor into saturation (see Problem 10-2). With the transistor saturated, the output drops to V_{CE} of 0.2 V, which is the low level for the gate.

The power dissipation of a DTL gate is about 12 mW and the propagation delay averages 30 ns. The noise margin is about 1 V and a fan-out as high as 8 is possible. The fan-out of the DTL gate is limited by the maximum current that can flow in the collector of the saturated transistor (see Problem 10-3).

The fan-out of a DTL gate may be increased by replacing one of the diodes in the base circuit with a transistor as shown in Fig. 10-6. Transistor $Q1$ is maintained in the active region when output transistor $Q2$ is saturated. As a consequence, the modified circuit can supply a larger amount of base current to the output transistor. The output transistor can now draw a larger amount of collector current before it goes out of saturation. Part of the collector current comes from the conducting diodes in the loading gates when $Q2$ is saturated. Thus, an increase in allowable collector saturated current allows more loads to be connected to the output, which increases the fan-out capability of the gate.

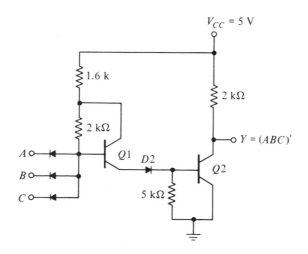

Figure 10-6   Modified DTL gate

High-Threshold Logic—HTL

There are occasions where digital circuits must operate in an environment which produces very high noise signals. For operation in such surroundings, there is available a type of DTL gate which possesses a high threshold to noise immunity. This type of gate is called a *high-threshold-logic* (HTL) gate.

The HTL gate is shown in Fig. 10-7. Comparing it with the modified DTL gate of Fig. 10-6, we note that the supply voltage has been raised to 15 V and a zener diode (Z) is used instead of a normal diode. The zener diode has the characteristic of maintaining a constant voltage of 6.9 V when reverse biased.

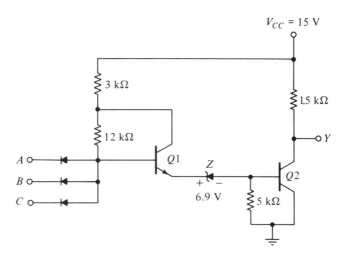

Figure 10-7 High-threshold-logic (HTL) gate

In order for output transistor $Q2$ to conduct, the emitter of $Q1$ must rise to a potential of one V_{BE} drop plus the fixed zener voltage of 6.9 V, for a total of about 7.5 V. The low level for the gate remains at 0.2 V, but the high level is about 15 V. With the input of 0.2 V, the base of $Q1$ is at 0.9 V and $Q2$ is off. The noise signal must be greater than 7.5 V to change the state of $Q2$. With all the inputs at 15 V, output transistor $Q2$ is saturated. The noise signal must be greater than 7.5 V (in the negative direction) to turn the transistor off. Thus, the noise margin of the HTL gate is about 7.5 V for both voltage levels.

10-4 INTEGRATED-INJECTION LOGIC (I²L)

Integrated-injection logic is the most recent digital logic family to be introduced commercially. Its main advantage is the high packing density of gates that can be achieved in a given area of semiconductor chip. This allows more circuits to be placed in the chip to form complex digital functions. As a consequence, this family is used mostly for LSI functions. It is not available in SSI packages containing individual gates.

The I²L basic gate is similar in operation to the RTL gate, with few major differences: (1) The base resistor used in the RTL gate is removed altogether in the I²L gate. (2) The collector resistor used in the RTL gate is replaced by a pnp transistor that acts as a load for the I²L gate. (3) I²L transistors use multiple collectors instead of the individual transistors employed in RTL.

The schematic diagram of the basic I²L gate is shown in Fig. 10-8. It has an npn transistor, $Q1$, with multiple collectors for the outputs. The base circuit has a pnp transistor, $T1$, connected to supply voltage V_{BB}. Unlike other logic families, the I²L basic gate operation cannot be analyzed when standing alone. One must show its interconnection to other gates to make any sense.

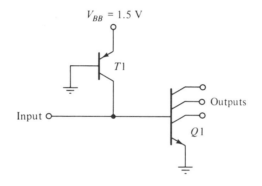

Figure 10-8   I²L basic gate

Figure 10-9 shows the interaction of the basic gate formed by $Q1$ and $T1$ with other gates in its input and output. Here we see that one collector of $Q2$ supplies the input to the basic gate. Transistor $T1$ in the basic gate acts as a load that injects current to the collector of $Q2$. One of the collectors of $Q1$ acts as an output of the basic gate and is connected to the base of $Q3$. Transistor $T3$, connected to the base of $Q3$, acts as a load to inject current to the collector of $Q1$ in the basic gate. The basic gate here acts as an inverter and its equivalent circuit is shown in Fig. 10-9(b). Using multiple collectors and a pnp transistor instead of a load resistor turns out to be a more efficient method of construction, since they reduce the chip area required and allow the packing of more circuits. The pnp transistor, although shown to be connected to the base of a given gate, acts as a collector load for all the other gates that are connected to this base.

The basic I²L gate, when connected to other gates, performs the NOR logic function. This is demonstrated in the circuit diagram shown in Fig. 10-10. The logic function that the circuit implements is drawn with graphic gate symbols in Fig. 10-10(a), which shows the interconnection of two NOR gates and an inverter. This is implemented with three I²L gates, $Q1$, $Q2$, and $Q3$, as shown in Fig. 10-10(b). The output transistors are also shown for completeness. The collectors of $Q1$ and

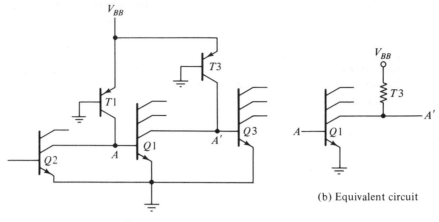

(b) Equivalent circuit

(a) Inverter gate $Q1$

Figure 10-9 Connection of other gates to the inputs and outputs of a basic I^2L gate

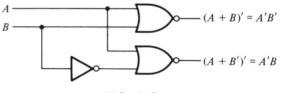

(a) Logic diagram

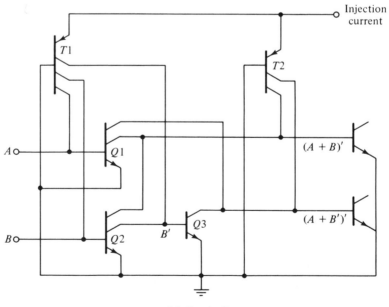

(b) Circuit diagram

Figure 10-10 Typical connections among I^2L gates

$Q2$ are tied together to form one NOR function. Input B is complemented by transistor $Q2$. The collectors of $Q3$ and $Q1$ are tied together to form the second NOR function. The base of each npn transistor receives the injection current from the multiple-collector pnp transistors $T1$ and $T2$. The emitters of the npn transistors are connected to the base of the pnp transistor to facilitate the construction.

10-5   TRANSISTOR-TRANSISTOR LOGIC (TTL)

The original basic TTL gate was a slight improvement over the DTL gate. As the TTL technology progressed, additional improvements were added to the point where this logic family became the most widely used type in the design of digital systems. There are many versions (or "series") of the TTL basic gate. The names and characteristics of five versions appear in Table 10-2, together with their propagation delay and power dissipation values. The speed-power product is an important parameter for comparing the basic gates. This is a product of the propagation delay and the power dissipation measured in picojoules (pJ). A low value for this parameter is a desirable figure, because it indicates that a given propagation delay can be achieved without excessive power dissipation, or vice versa.

TABLE 10-2   TTL versions and their characteristics

Name	Abbreviation	Propagation delay (ns)	Power dissipation (mW)	Speed-power product (pJ)
Standard TTL	TTL	10	10	100
Low-power TTL	LTTL	33	1	33
High-speed TTL	HTTL	6	22	132
Schottky TTL	STTL	3	19	57
Low-power Schottky TTL	LSTTL	9.5	2	19

The standard TTL gate was the first version in the TTL family. This basic gate was then constructed with different resistor values to produce gates with lower dissipation or higher speed. The propagation delay of a saturated logic family depends largely on two factors: storage time and RC time constants. Reducing the storage time decreases the propagation delay. Reducing resistor values in the circuit reduces the RC time constants and decreases the propagation delay. Of course, the trade-off is a higher power dissipation because lower resistances draw more current from the power supply. The speed of the gate is inversely proportional to the propagation delay.

In the low-power TTL gate the resistor values are higher than in the standard gate to reduce the power dissipation, but the propagation delay is increased. In the high-speed TTL gate, resistor values are lowered to reduce the propagation delay, but the power dissipation is increased. The Schottky TTL is a later improvement in the technology that removes the storage time of transistors by preventing them from going into saturation. This version increases the speed of operation without an excessive increase in power dissipation. The low-power Schottky TTL version sacrifices some speed for reduced power dissipation. It is about equal to standard TTL in propagation delay but has only one-fifth the power dissipation. It has the best speed-power product and, as a consequence, it became the most popular version in new designs.

All TTL versions are available in SSI packages and in more complex forms as MSI and LSI functions. The differences in the TTL versions are not in the digital functions that they perform, but rather in the values of resistors and type of transistor that their basic gate uses. In any case, TTL gates in all versions come in three different types of output configurations.

1. Open-collector output.

2. Totem-pole output.

3. Three-state (or tri-state) output.

These three types of outputs will be considered in conjunction with the circuit description of the basic TTL gate.

Open-collector Output Gate

The basic TTL gate shown in Fig. 10-11 is a modified circuit of the DTL gate. The multiple emitters in transistor $Q1$ are connected to the inputs. These emitters behave most of the time like the input diodes in the DTL gate since they form a *pn* junction

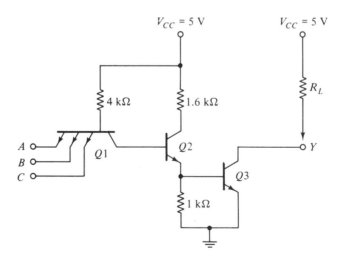

Figure 10-11 Open-collector TTL gate

with their common base. The base-collector junction of $Q1$ acts as another *pn* junction diode corresponding to $D1$ in the DTL gate (see Fig. 10-5). Transistor $Q2$ replaces the second diode, $D2$, in the DTL gate. The output of the TTL gate is taken from the open collector of $Q3$. A resistor connected to V_{CC} must be inserted external to the IC package for the output to "pull up" to the high voltage level when $Q3$ is off; otherwise, the output acts as an open circuit. The reason for not providing the resistor internally will be discussed later.

The two voltage levels of the TTL gate are 0.2 V for the low level and from 2.4 to 5 V for the high level. The basic circuit is a NAND gate. If any input is low, the corresponding base-emitter junction in $Q1$ is forward biased. The voltage at the base of $Q1$ is equal to the input voltage of 0.2 V plus a V_{BE} drop of 0.7 V or 0.9 V. In order for $Q3$ to start conducting, the path from $Q1$ to $Q3$ must overcome a potential of one diode drop in the base-collector *pn* junction of $Q1$ and two V_{BE} drops in $Q2$ and $Q3$, or $3 \times 0.6 = 1.8$ V. Since the base of $Q1$ is maintained at 0.9 V by the input signal, the output transistor cannot conduct and is cutoff. The output level will be high if an external resistor is connected between the output and V_{CC} (or an open circuit if a resistor is not used).

If all inputs are high, both $Q2$ and $Q3$ conduct and saturate. The base voltage of $Q1$ is equal to the voltage across its base-collector *pn* junction plus two V_{BE} drops in $Q2$ and $Q3$, or about $0.7 \times 3 = 2.1$ V. Since all inputs are high and greater than 2.4 V, the base-emitter junctions of $Q1$ are all reverse biased. When output transistor $Q3$ saturates (provided it has a current path), the output voltage goes low to 0.2 V. This confirms the conditions of a NAND operation.

In the above analysis, we said that the base-collector junction of $Q1$ acts like a *pn* diode junction. This is true in the steady-state condition. However, during the turn-off transition, $Q1$ does exhibit transistor action resulting in a reduction in propagation delay. When all inputs are high and then one of the inputs is brought to a low level, both $Q2$ and $Q3$ start turning off. At this time, the collector junction of $Q1$ is reverse biased and the emitter is forward biased; so transistor $Q1$ goes momentarily into the active region. The collector current of $Q1$ comes from the base of $Q2$ and quickly removes the excess charge stored in $Q2$ during its previous saturation state. This causes a reduction in the storage time of the circuit as compared to the DTL type of input. The result is a reduction of the turn-off time of the gate.

The open-collector TTL gate will operate without the external resistor when connected to inputs of other TTL gates, although this is not recommended because of the low noise immunity encountered. Without an external resistor, the output of the gate will be an open circuit when $Q3$ is off. An open circuit to an input of a TTL gate behaves as if it has a high-level input (but a small amount of noise can change this to a low level). When $Q3$ conducts, its collector will have a current path supplied by the input of the loading gate through V_{CC}, the 4-kΩ resistor, and the forward-biased base-emitter junction.

Open-collector gates are used in three major applications: driving a lamp or relay, performing wired logic, and for the construction of a common-bus system.

An open-collector output can drive a lamp placed in its output through a limiting resistor. When the output is low, the saturated transistor $Q3$ forms a path for the current that turns the lamp on. When the output transistor is off, the lamp turns off because there is no path for the current.

If the outputs of several open-collector TTL gates are tied together with a single external resistor, a wired-AND logic is performed. Remember that a positive-logic AND function gives a high level only if all variables are high; otherwise, the function is low. With outputs of open-collector gates connected together, the common output is high only when all output transistors are off (or high). If an output transistor conducts, it forces the output to the low state.

The wired logic performed with open-collector TTL gates is depicted in Fig. 10-12. The physical wiring in (a) shows how the outputs must be connected to a common resistor. The graphic symbol for such a connection is demonstrated in (b). The AND function formed by connecting together the two outputs is called a wired-AND function. The AND gate is drawn with the lines going through the center of the gate to distinguish it from a conventional gate. The wired-AND gate is not a physical gate but only a symbol to designate the function obtained from the indicated connection. The Boolean function obtained from the circuit of Fig. 10-12 is the AND operation between the outputs of the two NAND gates:

$$Y = (AB)' \cdot (CD)' = (AB + CD)'$$

The second expression is preferred since it shows an operation commonly referred to as an AND-OR-INVERT function (see Section 3-7).

Open-collector gates can be tied together to form a common bus. At any time, all gate outputs tied to the bus, except one, must be maintained in their high state. The selected gate may be either in the high or low state, depending on whether we want to transmit a 1 or 0 on the bus. Control circuits must be used to select the particular gate that drives the bus at any given time.

Figure 10-13 demonstrates the connection of four sources tied to a common bus line. Each of the four inputs drives an open-collector inverter, and the outputs of the inverters are tied together to form a single bus line. The figure shows that

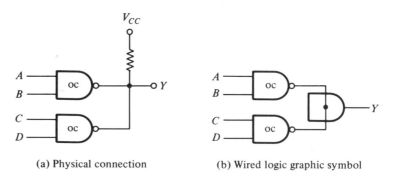

(a) Physical connection   (b) Wired logic graphic symbol

Figure 10-12   Wired-AND of two open-collector (oc) gates, $Y = (AB + CD)'$

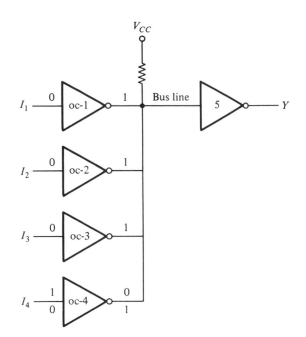

V_{CC}

I_1 — 0 | oc-1 | 1 — Bus line — 5 — Y

I_2 — 0 | oc-2 | 1

I_3 — 0 | oc-3 | 1

I_4 — 1 / 0 | oc-4 | 0 / 1

Figure 10-13 Open-collector gates forming a common bus line

three of the inputs are 0, which produces a 1 or high level on the bus. The fourth input, I_4, can now transmit information through the common bus line into inverter 5. Remember that an AND operation is performed in the wired logic. If $I_4 = 1$, the output of gate 4 is 0 and the wired-AND operation produces a 0. If $I_4 = 0$, the output of gate 4 is 1 and the wired-AND operation produces a 1. Thus, if all other outputs are maintained at 1, the selected gate can transmit its value through the bus. The value transmitted is the complement of I_4, but inverter 5 in the receiving end can easily invert this signal again to make $Y = I_4$.

Totem-pole Output

The output impedance of a gate is normally a resistive plus a capacitive load. The capacitive load consists of the capacitance of the output transistor, the capacitance of the fan-out gates, and any stray wiring capacitance. When the output changes from the low to the high state, the output transistor of the gate goes from saturation to cutoff and the total load capacitance, C, charges exponentially from the low to the high voltage level with a time constant equal to RC. For the open-collector gate, R is the external resistor marked R_L. For a typical operating value of $C = 15$ pF and $R_L = 4$ kΩ, the propagation delay of a TTL open-collector gate during the turn-off time is 35 ns. With an *active pull-up* circuit replacing the passive pull-up resistor R_L, the propagation delay is reduced to 10 ns. This

413

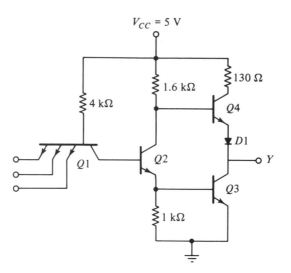

Figure 10-14   TTL gate with totem-pole output

configuration, shown in Fig. 10-14, is called a *totem-pole* output because transistor $Q4$ "sits" upon $Q3$.

The TTL gate with the totem-pole output is the same as the open-collector gate, except for the output transistor $Q4$ and the diode $D1$. When the output Y is in the low state, $Q2$ and $Q3$ are driven into saturation as in the open-collector gate. The voltage in the collector of $Q2$ is $V_{BE}(Q3) + V_{CE}(Q2)$ or $0.7 + 0.2 = 0.9$ V. The output $Y = V_{CE}(Q3) = 0.2$ V. Transistor $Q4$ is cutoff because its base must be one V_{BE} drop plus one diode drop, or $2 \times 0.6 = 1.2$ V, to start conducting. Since the collector of $Q2$ is connected to the base of $Q4$, the latter's voltage is only 0.9 V instead of the required 1.2 V, and so $Q4$ is cutoff. The reason for placing the diode in the circuit is to provide a diode drop in the output path and thus ensure that $Q4$ is cutoff when $Q3$ is saturated.

When the output changes to the high state because one of the inputs drops to the low state, transistors $Q2$ and $Q3$ go into cutoff. However, the output remains momentarily low because the voltages across the load capacitance cannot change instantaneously. As soon as $Q2$ turns off, $Q4$ conducts because its base is connected to V_{CC} through the 1.6-kΩ resistor. The current needed to charge the load capacitance causes $Q4$ to momentarily saturate, and the output voltage rises with a time constant RC. But R in this case is equal to 130 Ω, plus the saturation resistance of $Q4$, plus the resistance of the diode, for a total of approximately 150 Ω. This value of R is much smaller than the passive pull-up resistance used in the open-collector circuit. As a consequence, the transition from the low to high level is much faster.

As the capacitive load charges, the output voltage rises and the current in $Q4$ decreases, bringing the transistor into the active region. Thus, in contrast to the other transistors, $Q4$ is in the *active* region when in a steady-state condition. The final value of the output voltage is then 5 V, minus a V_{BE} drop in $Q4$, minus a diode drop in $D1$ to about 3.6 V. Transistor $Q3$ goes into cutoff very fast, but during the initial transition time both $Q3$ and $Q4$ are on and a peak current is drawn from the power supply. This current spike generates noise in the power supply distribution system. When the change of state is frequent, the transient current spikes increase the power supply current requirement and the average power dissipation of the circuit increases.

The wired-logic connection is not allowed with totem-pole output circuits. When two totem-poles are wired together with the output of one gate high and the output of the second gate low, the excessive amount of current drawn can produce enough heat to damage the transistors in the circuit (see Problem 10-7). Some TTL gates are constructed to withstand the amount of current that flows under this condition. In any case, the collector current in the low gate may be high enough to move the transistor into the active region and produce an output voltage in the wired connection greater than 0.8 V, which is not a valid binary signal for TTL gates.

Schottky TTL Gate

As mentioned before, a reduction in storage time results in a reduction of propagation delay. This is because the time needed for a transistor to come out of saturation delays the switching of the transistor from the on condition to the off condition. Saturation can be eliminated by placing a Schottky diode between the base and collector of each saturated transistor in the circuit. The Schottky diode is formed by the junction of a metal and semiconductor, in contrast to a conventional diode which is formed by the junction of p-type and n-type semiconductor material. The voltage across a conducting Schottky diode is only 0.4 V, as compared to 0.7 V in a conventional diode. The presence of a Schottky diode between the base and collector prevents the transistor from going into saturation. The resulting transistor is called a *Schottky transistor*. The use of Schottky transistors in a TTL decreases the propagation delay without a sacrifice of power dissipation.

The Schottky TTL gate is shown in Fig. 10-15. Note the special symbol used for the Schottky transistors and diodes. The diagram shows all transistors to be of the Schottky type except $Q4$. An exception is made of $Q4$ since it does not saturate but stays in the active region. Note also that resistor values have been reduced to further decrease the propagation delay.

In addition to using Schottky transistors and lower resistor values, the circuit of Fig. 10-15 includes other modifications not available in the standard gate of Fig. 10-14. Two new transistors, $Q5$ and $Q6$ have been added, and Schottky diodes are inserted between each input terminal and ground. There is no diode in the totem-pole circuit. However, the new combination of $Q5$ and $Q4$ still gives the two

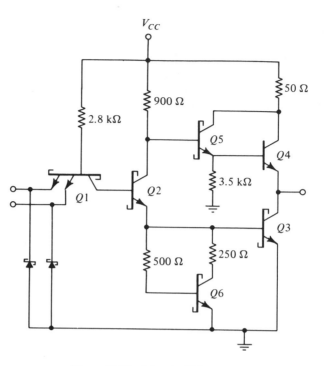

Figure 10-15   Schottky TTL gate

V_{BE} drops necessary to prevent $Q4$ from conducting when the output is low. This combination comprises a double emitter-follower called a *Darlington pair*. The Darlington pair provides a very high current gain and extremely low resistance. This is exactly what is needed during the low-to-high swing of the output, resulting in a decrease of propagation delay.

The diodes in each input shown in the circuit help clamp any ringing that may occur in the input lines. Under transient switching conditions, signal lines appear inductive; this, along with stray capacitance, cause signals to oscillate or "ring." When the output of a gate switches from the high to the low state, the ringing waveform at the input may have excursions below ground as great as 2–3 V, depending on line length. The diodes connected to ground help clamp this ringing since they conduct as soon as the negative voltage exceeds 0.4 V. When the negative excursion is limited, the positive swing is also reduced. The success of the clamp diodes in limiting line effects has been so successful that all versions of TTL gates use them.

The emitter resistor of $Q2$ in Fig. 10-14 has been replaced in Fig. 10-15 by a circuit consisting of transistor $Q6$ and two resistors. The effect of this circuit is to reduce the turn-off current spikes discussed previously. The analysis of this circuit, which helps to reduce the propagation time of the gate, is too involved to present in this brief discussion.

Three-state Gate

As mentioned earlier, the outputs of two TTL gates with totem-pole structures cannot be connected together as in open-collector outputs. There is, however, a special type of totem-pole gate that allows the wired connection of outputs for the purpose of forming a common-bus system. When a totem-pole output TTL gate has this property, it is called a *three-state* (or tri-state) gate.

A three-state gate exhibits three output states: (1) a low-level state when the lower transistor in the totem-pole is on and the upper transistor is off; (2) a high-level state when the upper transistor in the totem-pole is on and the lower transistor is off: and (3) a third state when both transistors in the totem-pole are off. The third state provides an open circuit or high-impedance state which allows a direct wire connection of many outputs to a common line. Three-state gates eliminate the need for open-collector gates in bus configurations.

Figure 10-16(a) shows the graphic symbol of a three-state buffer gate. When the control input C is high, the gate is enabled and behaves like a normal buffer with the output equal to the input binary value. When the control input is low, the output is an open circuit which gives a high impedance (the third state) regardless of the value of input A. Some three-state gates produce a high-impedance state when the control input is high. This is shown symbolically in Fig. 10-16(b). Here we have two small circles, one for the inverter output and the other to indicate that the gate is enabled when C is low.

The circuit diagram of the three-state inverter is shown in Fig. 10-16(c). Transistors $Q6$, $Q7$, and $Q8$ associated with the control input form a circuit similar to the open-collector gate. Transistors $Q1$–$Q5$, associated with the data input, form a totem-pole TTL circuit. The two circuits are connected together through diode $D1$. As in an open-collector circuit, transistor $Q8$ turns off when the control input at C is in the low-level state. This prevents diode $D1$ from conducting, and also, the emitter in $Q1$ connected to $Q8$ has no conduction path. Under this condition, transistor $Q8$ has no effect on the operation of the gate and the output in Y depends only on the data input at A.

When the control input is high, transistor $Q8$ turns on, and the current flowing from V_{CC} through diode $D1$ causes transistor $Q8$ to saturate. The voltage at the base of $Q5$ is now equal to the voltage across the saturated transistor, $Q8$, plus one diode drop, or 0.9 V. This voltage turns off $Q5$ and $Q4$ since it is less than two V_{BE} drops. At the same time, the low input to one of the emitters of $Q1$ forces transistor $Q3$ (and $Q2$) to turn off. Thus both $Q3$ and $Q4$ in the totem-pole are turned off and the output of the circuit behaves like an open circuit with a very high output impedance.

A three-state bus is created by wiring several three-state outputs together. At any given time, only one control input is enabled while all other outputs are in the high-impedance state. The single gate not in a high-impedance state can transmit binary information through the common bus. Extreme care must be taken that all except one of the outputs are in the third state; otherwise, we have the undesirable

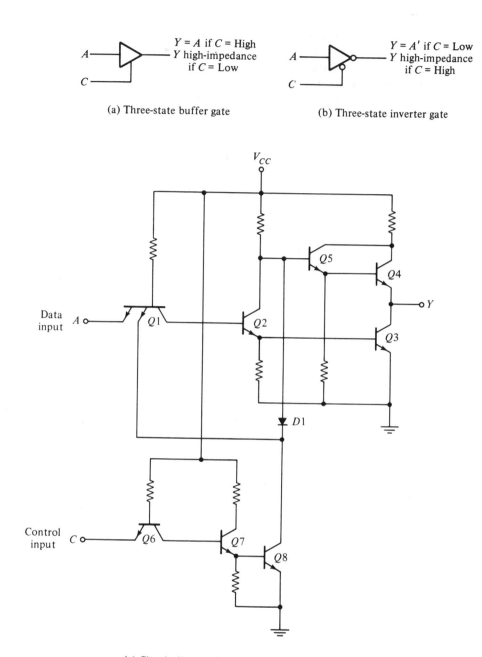

$Y = A$ if C = High
Y high-impedance
if C = Low

(a) Three-state buffer gate

$Y = A'$ if C = Low
Y high-impedance
if C = High

(b) Three-state inverter gate

(c) Circuit diagram for the three-state inverter of (b)

Figure 10-16 Three-state TTL gate

418

condition of having two active totem-pole outputs connected together.

An important feature of most three-state gates is that the output enable delay is longer than the output disable delay. If a control circuit enables one gate and disables another at the same time, the disabled gate enters the high-impedance state before the other gate is enabled. This eliminates the situation of both gates being active at the same time.

There is a very small leakage current associated with the high-impedance condition in a three-state gate. Nevertheless, this current is so small that as many as 100 three-state outputs can be connected together to form a common bus line.

10-6 EMITTER-COUPLED LOGIC (ECL)

Emitter-coupled logic (ECL) is a nonsaturated digital logic family. Since transistors do not saturate, it is possible to achieve propagation delays of 2 ns and even below 1 ns. This logic family has the lowest propagation delay of any family and is used mostly in systems requiring very-high-speed operation. Its noise immunity and power dissipation, however, are the worst of all the logic families available.

A typical basic circuit of the ECL family is shown in Fig. 10-17. The outputs provide both the OR and NOR functions. Each input is connected to the base of a transistor. The two voltage levels are about -0.8 V for the high state and about -1.8 V for the low state. The circuit consists of a differential amplifier, a temperature- and voltage-compensated bias network, and an emitter-follower output. The emitter outputs require a pull-down resistor for current to flow. This is obtained from the input resistor, R_P, of another similar gate or from an external resistor connected to a negative voltage supply.

The internal temperature- and voltage-compensated bias circuit supplies a reference voltage to the differential amplifier. Bias voltage V_{BB} is set at -1.3 V, which is the midpoint of the signal logic swing. The diodes in the voltage divider, together with $Q6$, provide a circuit that maintains a constant V_{BB} value despite changes in temperature or supply voltage. Any one of the power supply inputs could be used as ground. However, the use of the V_{CC} node as ground and V_{EE} at -5.2 V results in best noise immunity.

If any input in the ECL gate is high, the corresponding transistor is turned on and $Q5$ is turned off. An input of -0.8 V causes the transistor to conduct and places -1.6 V on the emitters of all transistors (V_{BE} drop in ECL transistors is 0.8 V). Since $V_{BB} = -1.3$ V, the base voltage of $Q5$ is only 0.3 V more positive than its emitter. $Q5$ is cutoff because its V_{BE} voltage needs at least 0.6 V to start conducting. The current in resistor R_{C2} flows into the base of $Q8$ (provided there is a load resistor). This current is so small that only a negligible voltage drop occurs across R_{C2}. The OR output of the gate is one V_{BE} drop below ground, or -0.8 V, which is the high state. The current flowing through R_{C1} and the conducting transistor causes a drop of about 1 V below ground (see Problem 10-9). The NOR output is one V_{BE} drop below this level, or at -1.8 V, which is the low state.

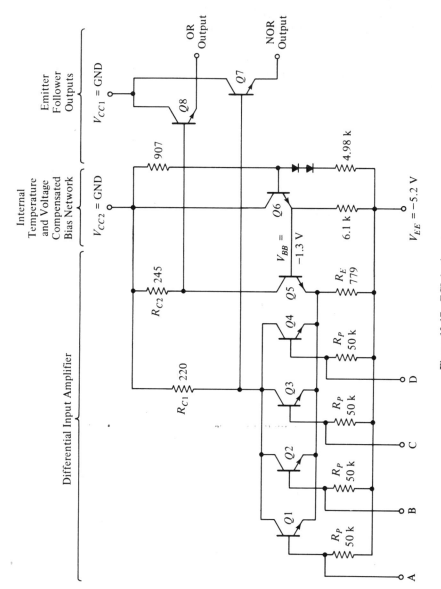

Figure 10-17 ECL basic gate

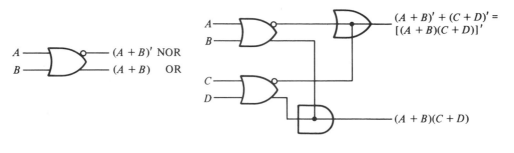

(a) Single gate   (b) Wired combination of two gates

Figure 10-18   Graphic symbols of ECL gates

If all inputs are at the low level, all input transistors turn off and $Q5$ conducts. The voltage in the common-emitter node is one V_{BE} drop below V_{BB} or -2.1 V. Since the base of each input is at a low level of -1.8 V, each base-emitter junction has only 0.3 V and all input transistors are cutoff. R_{C2} draws current through $Q5$ that results in a voltage drop of about 1 V, making the OR output one V_{BE} drop below this, at -1.8 V or the low level. The current in R_{C1} is negligible and the NOR output is one V_{BE} drop below ground, at -0.8 V or the high level. This verifies the OR and NOR operations of the circuit.

The propagation delay of the ECL gate is 2 ns, and the power dissipation is 25 mW. This gives a speed-power product of 50, which is about the same as for Schottky TTL. The noise margin is about 0.3 V and not as good as in the TTL gate. High fan-out is possible in the ECL gate because of the high input impedance of the differential amplifier and the low output impedance of the emitter-follower. Because of the extreme high speed of the signals, external wires act like transmission lines. Except for very short wires of a few centimeters, ECL outputs must use coaxial cables with a resistor termination to reduce line reflections.

The graphic symbol for the ECL gate is shown in Fig. 10-18(a). Two outputs are available: one for the NOR function and the other for the OR function. The outputs of two or more ECL gates can be connected together to form wired logic. As shown in Fig. 10-18(b), an *external* wired connection of two NOR outputs produces a wired-OR function. An *internal* wired connection of two OR outputs is employed in some ECL ICs to produce a wired-AND (sometimes called dot-AND) logic. This property may be utilized when ECL gates are used to form the OR-AND-INVERT and the OR-AND functions.

10-7 METAL-OXIDE SEMICONDUCTOR (MOS)

The field-effect transistor (FET) is a unipolar transistor, since its operation depends on the flow of only one type of carrier. There are two types of field-effect transistors: the junction field-effect transistor (JFET) and the metal-oxide semiconductor (MOS). The former is used in linear circuits and the latter in digital circuits. MOS transistors can be fabricated in less area than bipolar transistors.

The basic structure of the MOS transistor is shown in Fig. 10-19. The p-channel MOS consists of a lightly doped substrate of n-type silicon material. Two regions are heavily doped by diffusion with p-type impurities to form the *source* and *drain*. The region between the two p-type sections serves as the *channel*. The *gate* is a metal plate separated from the channel by an insulated dielectric of silicon dioxide. A negative voltage (with respect to the substrate) at the gate terminal causes an induced electric field in the channel which attracts p-type carriers from the substrate. As the magnitude of the negative voltage on the gate increases, the region below the gate accumulates more positive carriers, the conductivity increases, and current can flow from source to drain provided a voltage difference is maintained between these two terminals.

There are four basic types of MOS structures. The channel can be a p- or n-type, depending on whether the majority carriers are holes or electrons. The mode of operation can be enhancement or depletion, depending on the state of the channel region at zero gate voltage. If the channel is initially doped lightly with p-type impurity (diffused channel), a conducting channel exists at zero gate voltage and the device is said to operate in the *depletion* mode. In this mode, current flows unless the channel is depleted by an applied gate field. If the region beneath the gate is left initially uncharged, a channel must be induced by the gate field before current can flow. Thus, the channel current is enhanced by the gate voltage and such a device is said to operate in the *enhancement* mode.

The source is the terminal through which the majority carriers enter the bar. The drain is the terminal through which the majority carriers leave the bar. In a p-channel MOS, the source terminal is connected to the substrate and a negative voltage is applied to the drain terminal. When the gate voltage is above a threshold voltage V_T (about -2 V), no current flows in the channel and the drain-to-source path is like an open circuit. When the gate voltage is sufficiently negative below V_T, a channel is formed and p-type carriers flow from source to drain. P-type carriers are positive and correspond to a positive current flow from source to drain.

In the n-channel MOS, the source terminal is connected to the substrate and a positive voltage is applied to the drain terminal. When the gate voltage is below

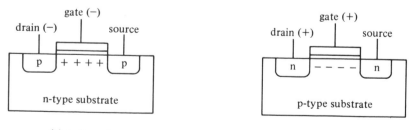

(a) p-channel

(b) n-channel

Figure 10-19 Basic structure of MOS transistor

the threshold voltage V_T (about 2 V) no current flows in the channel. When the gate voltage is sufficiently positive above V_T to form the channel, n-type carriers flow from source to drain. N-type carriers are negative, which corresponds to a positive current flow from drain to source. The threshold voltage may vary from 1 to 4 V depending on the particular process used.

The graphic symbols for the MOS transistors are shown in Fig. 10-20. The accepted symbol for the enhancement type is the one with the broken-line connection between source and drain. In this symbol, the substrate can be identified and is shown connected to the source. We will use an alternative symbol that omits the substrate; in this symbol, the arrow is placed in the source terminal to show the direction of *positive* current flow (from source to drain in the p-channel and from drain to source in the n-channel).

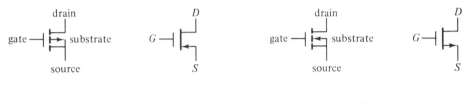

(a) p-channel   (b) n-channel

Figure 10-20   Symbols for MOS transistors

Because of the symmetrical construction of source and drain, the MOS transistor can be operated as a bilateral device. Although normally operated so that carriers flow from source to drain, there are circumstances when it is convenient to allow carrier flow from drain to source (see Problem 10-12).

One advantage of the MOS device is that it can be used not only as a transistor, but as a resistor as well. A resistor is obtained from the MOS by permanently biasing the gate terminal for conduction. The ratio of the source-drain voltage to the channel current then determines the value of the resistance. Different resistor values may be constructed during manufacturing by fixing the channel length and width of the MOS device.

Three logic circuits using MOS devices are shown in Fig. 10-21. For an n-channel MOS, supply voltage V_{DD} is positive (about 5 V) to allow positive current flow from drain to source. The two voltage levels are a function of the threshold voltage V_T. The low level is anywhere from zero to V_T, and the high level ranges from V_T to V_{DD}. The n-channel gates usually employ positive logic. The p-channel MOS circuits use a negative voltage for V_{DD} to allow positive current flow from source to drain. The two voltage levels are both negative above and below the negative threshold voltage V_T. P-channel gates usually employ negative logic.

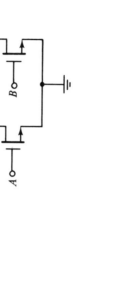

V_{DD} o

$$Y = (A + B)'$$

B o

(c) NOR gate

Figure 10-21 n-channel MOS logic circuits

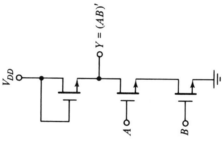

V_{DD} o

$$Y = (AB)'$$

A o

B o

(b) NAND gate

V_{DD} o

$Q1$

$$Y = A'$$

$Q2$

A o

(a) Inverter

input voltage is low (below V_T), $Q2$ turns off. Since $Q1$ is always on, the output voltage is at about V_{DD}. When the input voltage is high (above V_T), $Q2$ turns on. Current flows from V_{DD} through the load resistor $Q1$ and into $Q2$. The geometry of the two MOS devices must be such that the resistance of $Q2$, when conducting, is much less than the resistance of $Q1$ to maintain the output Y at a voltage below V_T.

The NAND gate shown in Fig. 10-21(b) uses transistors in series. Inputs A and B must both be high for all transistors to conduct and cause the output to go low. If either input is low, the corresponding transistor is turned off and the output is high. Again, the series resistance formed by the two active MOS devices must be much less than the resistance of the load resistor MOS. The NOR gate shown in Fig. 10-21(c) uses transistors in parallel. If either input is high, the corresponding transistor conducts and the output is low. If all inputs are low, all active transistors are off and the output is high.

10-8   COMPLEMENTARY MOS (CMOS)

Complementary MOS circuits take advantage of the fact that both n-channel and p-channel devices can be fabricated on the same substrate. CMOS circuits consist of both types of MOS devices interconnected to form logic functions. The basic circuit is the inverter, which consists of one p-channel transistor and one n-channel transistor as shown in Fig. 10-22(a). The source terminal of the p-channel device is at V_{DD}, and the source terminal of the n-channel device is at ground. The value of V_{DD} may be anywhere from $+3$ to $+18$ V. The two voltage levels are 0 V for the low level and V_{DD} for the high level.

To understand the operation of the inverter, we must review the behavior of the MOS transistor from the previous section:

1. The n-channel MOS conducts when its gate-to-source voltage is positive.

2. The p-channel MOS conducts when its gate-to-source voltage is negative.

3. Either type of device is turned off if its gate-to-source voltage is zero.

Now consider the operation of the inverter. When the input is low, both gates are at zero potential. The input is at $-V_{DD}$ relative to the source of the p-channel device and at 0 V relative to the source of the n-channel device. The result is that the p-channel device is turned on and the n-channel device is turned off. Under these conditions, there is a low-impedance path from V_{DD} to the output and a very-high-impedance path from output to ground. Therefore, the output voltage approaches the high level V_{DD} under normal loading conditions. When the input is high, both gates are at V_{DD} and the situation is reversed: The p-channel device is off and the n-channel device is on. The result is that the output approaches the low level of 0 V.

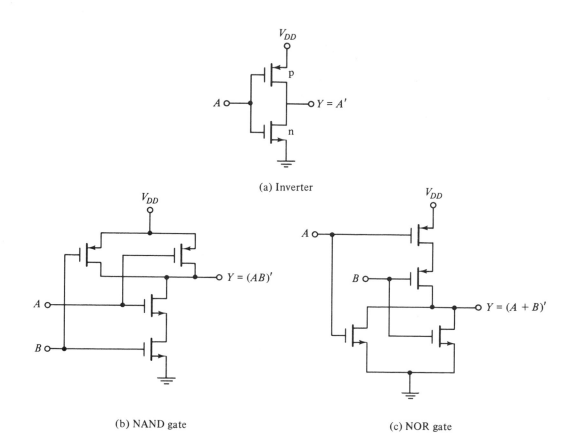

(a) Inverter

(b) NAND gate

(c) NOR gate

Figure 10-22 CMOS logic circuits

In either logic state, one MOS transistor is on while the other is off. Because one transistor is always turned off, the dc power dissipation of the CMOS circuit is extremely low, usually on the order of 10 nW. The major power drain occurs when the CMOS circuit changes state.

CMOS logic is usually specified for single-supply operation over the 5–15-V range, but some circuits may be operated at 3 V or 18 V. Operating CMOS at large values of supply voltage produces a greater power dissipation. The propagation delay time decreases and the noise margin improves with increased power supply voltage. The propagation delay of the inverter is about 25 ns. The noise margin is usually about 40% of the V_{DD} supply voltage value. The advantages of CMOS, i.e., low power dissipation, excellent noise immunity, high packing density, and a wide range of supply voltages, make it a strong contender for a popular standard as a digital circuit family.

Two other CMOS basic gates are shown in Fig. 10-22. A two-input NAND gate consists of two p-type units in parallel and two n-type units in series, as shown in Fig. 10-22(b). If all inputs are high, both p-channel transistors turn off and both

426

n-channel transistors turn on. The output has a low impedance to ground and produces a low state. If any input is low, the associated n-channel transistor is turned off and the associated p-channel transistor is turned on. The output is coupled to V_{DD} and goes to the high state. Multiple-input NAND gates may be formed by placing equal numbers of p-type and n-type transistors in parallel and series, respectively, in an arrangement similar to that shown in Fig. 10-22(b).

A two-input NOR gate consists of two n-type units in parallel and two p-type units in series, as shown in Fig. 10-22(c). When all inputs are low, both p-channel units are on and both n-channel units are off. The output is coupled to V_{DD} and goes to the high state. If any input is high, the associated p-channel transistor is turned off and the associated n-channel transistor turns on. This connects the output to ground, causing a low-level output.

REFERENCES

1. Taub, H., and D. Schilling, *Digital Integrated Electronics*. New York: McGraw-Hill Book Co., 1977.

2. Grinich, V. H., and H. G. Jackson, *Introduction to Integrated Circuits*. New York: McGraw-Hill BookCo., 1975.

3. Morris, R. L., and J. R. Miller, Eds., *Designing with TTL Integrated Circuits*. New York: McGraw-Hill Book Co., 1971.

4. Garret, L. S., "Integrated-Circuit Digital Logic Families." *IEEE Spectrum* (October, November, December, 1970).

5. De Falco, J. A., "Comparison and Uses of TTL Circuits." *Computer Design* (February, 1972).

6. Blood, W. R. Jr., *MECL System Design Handbook*. Phoenix, Ariz.: Motorola Semiconductor Products Inc., 1972.

7. *Data Book Series SSD-203B: COS/MOS Digital Integrated Circuits*, Somerville, N.J.: RCA Solid State Division, 1974.

PROBLEMS

10-1.   (a) Determine the high-level output voltage of the RTL gate for a fan-out of 5. (b) Determine the minimum input voltage required to drive an RTL transistor to saturation when $h_{FE} = 20$. (c) From the results in (a) and (b), determine the noise margin of the RTL gate when the input is high and the fan-out is 5.

10-2.   Show that the output transistor of the DTL gate of Fig. 10-5 goes into saturation when all inputs are high. Assume that $h_{FE} = 20$.

10-3.   Connect the output Y of the DTL gate shown in Fig. 10-5 to N inputs of other similar gates. Assume that the output transistor is saturated and its base current is 0.44 mA. Let $h_{FE} = 20$.

(a) Calculate the current in the 2-kΩ resistor.

(b) Calculate the current coming from each input connected to the gate.

(c) Calculate the total collector current in the output transistor as a function of N.

(d) Find the value of N that will keep the transistor in saturation.

(e) What is the fan-out of the gate?

10-4.   Draw the interconnection of I^2L gates to form a 2 $\times$ 4 decoder.

10-5.   Let all inputs in the open-collector TTL gate of Fig. 10-11 be in the high state of 3 V.

(a) Determine the voltages in the base, collector, and emitter of all transistors.

(b) Determine the minimum h_{FE} of $Q2$ that ensures that this transistor saturates.

(c) Calculate the base current of $Q3$.

(d) Assume that the minimum h_{FE} of $Q3$ is 6.18. What is the maximum current that can be tolerated in the collector to ensure saturation of $Q3$?

(e) What is the minimum value of R_L that can be tolerated to ensure saturation of $Q3$?

10-6.   (a) Using the actual output transistors of two open-collector TTL gates, show (by means of a truth table) that when connected together to an external resistor and V_{CC}, the wired connection produces an AND function. (b) Prove that two open-collector TTL inverters when connected together produce the NOR function.

10-7.   It was stated in Section 10-5 that totem-pole outputs should not be tied together to form wired logic. To see why this is prohibitive, connect two such circuits together and let the output of one gate be in the high state and the output of the other gate be in the low state. Show that the load current (which is the sum of the base and collector currents of the saturated transistor $Q4$ in Fig. 10-14) is about 32 mA. Compare this value with the recommended load current in the high state of 0.4 mA.

10-8.   For the following conditions, list the transistors that are off and those that are conducting in the three-state TTL gate of Fig. 10-16(c). (For $Q1$ and $Q6$, it would be necessary to list the states in the base-emitter and base-collector junctions separately.)

(a) When C is low and A is low.

(b) When C is low and A is high.

(c) When C is high.

What is the state of the output in each case?

10-9.   Calculate the emitter current I_E across R_E in the ECL gate of Fig. 10-17 when:

(a) At least one input is high at -0.8 V.

(b) All inputs are low at -1.8 V.

Now assume that $I_C = I_E$. Calculate the voltage drop across the collector resistor in each case and show that it is about 1 V as required.

10-10. Calculate the noise margin of the ECL gate.

10-11. Using the NOR outputs of two ECL gates, show that when connected together to an external resistor and negative supply voltage, the wired connection produces an OR function.

10-12. The MOS transistor is bilateral, i.e., current may flow from source to drain or from drain to source. Using this property, derive a circuit that implements the Boolean function:

$$Y = (AB + CD + AED + CEB)'$$

using six MOS transistors.

10-13. (a) Show the circuit of a four-input NAND gate using CMOS transistors. (b) Repeat for a four-input NOR gate.

Laboratory
Experiments

11

11-0 INTRODUCTION TO EXPERIMENTS

This chapter presents 15 laboratory experiments in digital circuits and logic design. They provide hands-on experience for the student using this book. The digital circuits can be constructed by using standard integrated circuits (ICs) mounted on breadboards that are easily assembled in the laboratory. The experiments are ordered according to the material presented in the book.

A logic breadboard suitable for performing the experiments must have the following equipment:

1. LED (light-emitting diode) indicator lamps.

2. Toggle switches to provide logic 1 and 0 signals.

3. Pulsers with pushbuttons and debounce circuits to generate single pulses.

4. A clock pulse generator with at least two frequencies, a low frequency of about one pulse per second to observe slow changes in digital signals and a higher frequency of about 10 KHz or higher for observing waveforms in an oscilloscope.

5. A power supply of 5 V for TTL ICs.

6. Socket strips for mounting the ICs.

7. Solid hookup wire and a pair of wire strippers for cutting the wires.

Logic breadboards that include the required equipment are available from several manufacturers; two of them are the Digi-Designer from E & L Instruments and the Digital Trainer ET-3200 from Heathkit. Each of these breadboards contains four LED lamps, four toggle switches, two pulsers, a variable clock pulse generator, power supply, and an IC socket strip. Some of the experiments will require additional switches, lamps, or IC sockets. Extended breadboards with more sockets and plug-in switches and lamps are available from the same vendors.

Additional equipment required are a dual-trace oscilloscope (for experiments 1, 2, 8, and 15), a logic probe to be used for debugging, and a number of ICs. The ICs required for the experiments are of the transistor–transistor logic (TTL) type, series 7400.

The integrated circuits to be used in the experiments can be classified as small-scale integration (SSI) or medium-scale integration (MSI) circuits. SSI circuits contain individual gates or flip-flops, and MSI circuits perform specific digital functions. The eight SSI gate ICs needed for the experiments are shown in Fig. 11-1. They include 2-input NAND, NOR, AND, OR, and XOR gates, inverters, and 3-input and 4-input NAND gates. The pin assignment for the gates is indicated in the diagram. The pins are numbered from 1 to 14. Pin number 14 is marked V_{CC}, and pin number 7 is marked GND (ground). These are the supply terminals, which must be connected to a power supply of 5 V for proper operation. Each IC is recognized by its identification number; for example, the 2-input NAND gates are found inside the IC whose number is 7400.

Detailed descriptions of the MSI circuits can be found in data books published by the manufacturers. The best way to acquire experience with commercial MSI circuits is to study their description in a data book that provides complete information on the internal, external, and electrical characteristics of the integrated circuits. Various semiconductor companies publish data books for the TTL 7400 series. Examples are: *The TTL Data Book for Design Engineers*, published by Texas Instruments, and the *Logic Databook*, published by National Semiconductor Corp.

The MSI circuits that are needed for the experiments are introduced and explained when they are used for the first time. The operation of the circuit is explained by referring to similar circuits in previous chapters. The information given in this chapter about the MSI circuits should be sufficient for performing the experiments adequately. Nevertheless, a reference to a data book will always be preferable, as it gives more detailed description of the circuits.

We will now demonstrate the method of presentation of MSI circuits adopted here. This will be done by means of a specific example that introduces the ripple counter IC, type 7493. This IC is used in experiment 1 and in subsequent experiments to generate a sequence of binary numbers for verifying the operation of combinational circuits.

The information about the 7493 IC that is found in a data book is shown in Fig. 11-2(a) and (b). Part (a) shows a diagram of the internal logic circuit and its connection to external pins. All inputs and outputs are given symbolic letters and assigned to pin numbers. Part (b) shows the physical layout of the IC with its 14-pin assignment to signal names. Some of the pins are not used by the circuit and are marked as NC (no connection). The IC is inserted into a socket, and wires are connected to the various pins through the socket terminals. When drawing schematic diagrams in this chapter we will show the IC in a block diagram form as in Fig. 11-2(c). The IC number 7493 is written inside the block. All input terminals are placed on the left of the block and all output terminals on the right. The letter symbols of the signals, such as A, $R1$, and QA, are written inside the block, and the

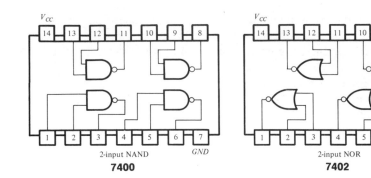

7400
2-input NAND

7402
2-input NOR

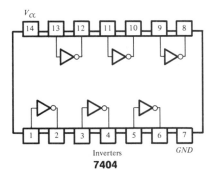

7404
Inverters

7408
2-input AND

7410
3-input NAND

7420
4-input NAND

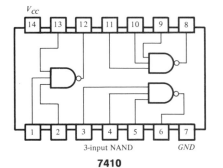

7432
2-input OR

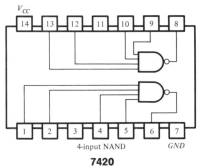

7486
2-input XOR

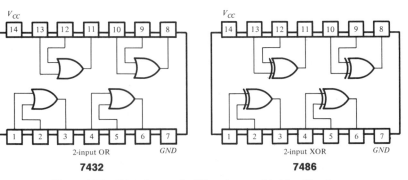

Figure 11-1 Digital gates in IC packages with identification number and pin assignment

432

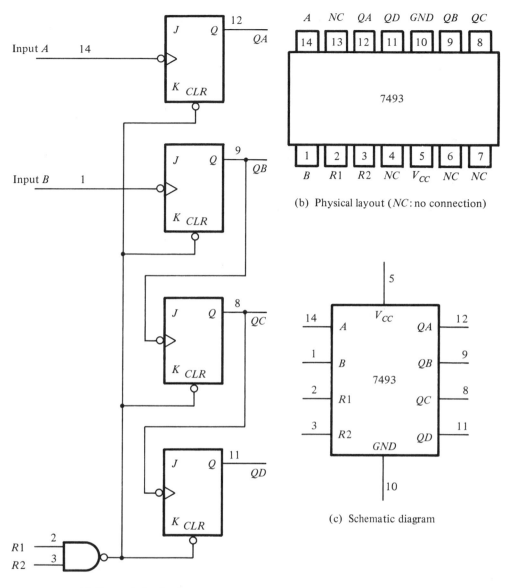

(b) Physical layout (*NC*: no connection)

(c) Schematic diagram

(a) Internal circuit diagram

Figure 11-2 IC type 7493 ripple counter

corresponding pin numbers, such as 14, 2, and 12, are written along the external lines. V_{CC} and GND are the power terminals connected to pins 5 and 10. The size of the block may vary to accommodate all input and output terminals. Inputs or outputs may sometimes be placed on the top or the bottom of the block for convenience.

The operation of the circuit is similar to the ripple counter shown in Fig. 7-12 with an asynchronous clear to each flip-flop as shown in Fig. 6-14. When inputs $R1$ or $R2$ or both are equal to logic 0 (ground for TTL circuits), all asynchronous clears are equal to 1 and are disabled. To clear all four flip-flops to 0, the output of the NAND gate must be equal to 0. This is accomplished by having both inputs $R1$ and $R2$ at logic 1 (about 3 to 5 V in TTL circuits). Note that the J and K inputs show no connections. It is characteristic of TTL circuits that an input terminal with no external connections has the effect of producing a signal equivalent to logic 1. Also note that output QA is not connected to input B internally.

To operate the circuit as a binary counter, output QA at pin 12 must be connected to input B at pin 1. Reset inputs $R1$ and $R2$ at pins 2 and 3 must be grounded. Pins 5 and 10 must be connected to a 5-V power supply. The input pulses must be applied to input A at pin 14, and the four flip-flop outputs are taken from QA, QB, QC, and QD, at pins 12, 9, 8, and 11, respectively, with QA being the least significant.

The preceding demonstrates the way we will present the MSI circuits to be used for the experiments. Invariably, only the block diagram, as shown in Fig. 11-2(c), will be presented, and the explanation of the circuit will be given with reference to logic diagrams from previous chapters. The letter symbols to be shown for the inputs and outputs in the IC block will be according to the symbols used in the data book.

TABLE 11-1 Integrated circuits required for the experiments

IC number	Description	Refer to
	Various gates	Fig. 11-1
7447	BCD-to-seven-segment decoder	Fig. 11-8
7474	Dual D flip-flops	Fig. 11-13
7476	Dual JK flip-flops	Fig. 11-12
7483	4-bit binary adder	Fig. 11-10
7489	16 × 4 random-access memory	Fig. 11-18
7493	4-bit ripple counter	Fig. 11-2
74151	8 × 1 multiplexer	Fig. 11-9
74155	3 × 8 decoder	Fig. 11-7
74157	Quad 2 × 1 multiplexers	Fig. 11-17
74161	4-bit synchronous counter	Fig. 11-15
74179	4-bit shift register	Fig. 11-16
74194	4-bit bidirectional shift register	Fig. 11-19
7730	Seven-segment LED display	Fig. 11-8
72555	Precision timer	Fig. 11-21

Table 11-1 lists all the ICs that will be needed for the experiments together with the figure in which they are presented. This is in addition to the eight gate ICs shown in Fig. 11-1.

The chapter is divided into 15 sections with each section covering one experiment. The section number designates the experiment number. Each experiment should take about 2 to 3 hours of laboratory time, equivalent to one laboratory period.

11-1 BINARY AND DECIMAL NUMBERS

This experiment demonstrates the count sequence of binary numbers and the binary-coded decimal (BCD) representation. It serves as an introduction to the breadboard used in the laboratory and acquaints the student with the cathode ray oscilloscope. Reference material from the text that may be useful to know while performing the experiment can be found in Section 1-2, on binary numbers, and Section 1-6, on BCD numbers.

Binary Count: IC type 7493 consists of four cells called flip-flops, as shown in Fig. 11-2. The cells can be connected to count in binary or in BCD. Connect the IC to operate as a 4-bit binary counter by wiring the external terminals as shown in Fig. 11-3. This is done by connecting a wire from pin 12 (output QA) to pin 1 (input B). Input A at pin 14 is connected to a pulser that provides single pulses. The two reset inputs $R1$ and $R2$ are connected to ground. The four outputs go to four indicator lamps with the low-order bit of the counter from QA connected to the rightmost indicator lamp. Do not forget to supply 5 V and ground to the IC. All connections should be made with the power supply in the off position.

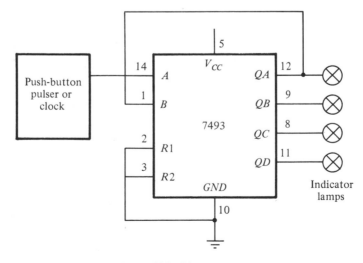

Figure 11-3 Binary counter

Turn the power on and observe the four indicator lamps. The 4-bit number in the output is incremented by one for every pulse generated in the pushbutton pulser. The count goes to binary 15 and then back to 0. Disconnect the input of the counter at pin 14 from the pulser and connect it to a clock generator that produces a train of pulses at a low frequency of about one pulse per second. This will provide an automatic binary count. Note that the binary counter will be used in subsequent experiments to provide the input binary signals for testing combinational circuits.

Oscilloscope Display: Increase the frequency of the clock to 10 KHz or higher and connect its output to an oscilloscope. Observe the clock output on the oscilloscope and sketch its waveform. If a dual-trace oscilloscope is available, connect the output of QA to one channel and the output of the clock to the second channel. Note that the output of QA is complemented everytime the clock pulse goes through a negative transition from 1 to 0. (The two waveforms should look similar to the timing diagram shown in Fig. 7-15 for the count pulses and Q_1.)

When the count pulses into the counter occur at constant frequency, the frequency at the output of the first cell, QA, is one half that of the input clock frequency. Each cell in turn divides its incoming frequency by two. The 4-bit counter divides the incoming frequency by 16 at output QD. Obtain a timing diagram showing the time relationship of the clock and the four outputs of the counter. Make sure that you include at least 16 clock pulses. The way to proceed with a dual-trace oscilloscope is as follows. First observe the clock pulses and QA and record their timing waveforms. Then repeat by observing and recording the waveforms of QA together with QB, followed by the waveforms of QB with QC and then QC with QD. Your final result should be a diagram showing the time relationship of the clock and the four outputs in one composite diagram having at least 16 clock pulses.

BCD Count: The BCD representation uses the binary numbers from 0000 to 1001 to represent the coded decimal digits from 0 to 9. IC type 7493 can be operated as a BCD counter by making the external connections shown in Fig. 11-4. Outputs QB and QD are connected to the two reset inputs, $R1$ and $R2$. When both $R1$ and $R2$ are equal to 1, all four cells in the counter clear to 0 irrespective of the input pulse. The counter starts from 0, and every input pulse increments it by 1 until it reaches the count of 1001. The next pulse changes the output to 1010, making QB and QD equal to 1. This momentary output cannot be sustained, because the four cells immediately clear to 0, with the result that the output goes to 0000. Thus, the pulse after the count of 1001 changes the output to 0000, producing a BCD count.

Connect the IC to operate as a BCD counter. Connect the input to a pulser and the four outputs to indicator lamps. Verify that the count goes from 0000 to 1001.

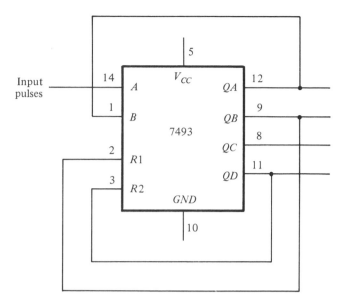

Figure 11-4 BCD counter

Disconnect the input from the pulser and connect it to a clock generator with a frequency of 10 KHz or higher. Observe the clock waveform and the four outputs on the oscilloscope. Obtain an accurate timing diagram showing the time relationship between the clock and the four outputs. Make sure to include at least 10 clock pulses in the oscilloscope display and in the composite timing diagram.

Output Pattern: When the count pulses into the BCD counter are continuous, the counter keeps repeating the sequence from 0000 to 1001 and back to 0000 over and over. This means that each bit in the four outputs produces a fixed pattern of 1's and 0's, which is repeated every ten pulses. These patterns can be predicted from the list of the binary numbers from 0000 to 1001. The list will show that output QA, being the least significant bit, produces a pattern of alternate 1's and 0's. Output QD, being the most significant bit, produces a pattern of eight 0's followed by two 1's. Obtain the pattern for the other two outputs and then check all four patterns on the oscilloscope. This is done with a dual-trace oscilloscope by displaying the clock pulses in one channel and one of the output waveforms in the other channel. The pattern of 1's and 0's for the corresponding output is obtained by observing the output levels at the vertical positions where the pulses change from 1 to 0.

Other Counts: IC type 7493 can be connected to count from 0 to a variety of final counts. This is done by connecting one or two outputs to the reset inputs, $R1$ and $R2$. Thus, if $R1$ is connected to QA instead of QB in Fig. 11-4, the resulting count will be from 0000 to 1000, which is 1 less than 1001 ($QD = 1$ and $QA = 1$).

Utilizing your knowledge of how $R1$ and $R2$ affect the final count, connect the 7493 IC to count from 0000 to the following final counts.

(a) 0101

(b) 0111

(c) 1011

Connect each circuit and verify its count sequence by applying pulses from the pulser and observing the output count in the indicator lamps. If the initial count starts with a value greater than the final count, keep applying input pulses until the output clears to 0.

11-2   DIGITAL LOGIC GATES

In this experiment you will investigate the logic behavior of various IC gates:

7400 Quadruple 2-input NAND gates

7402 Quadruple 2-input NOR gates

7404 Hex inverters

7408 Quadruple 2-input AND gates

7432 Quadruple 2-input OR gates

7486 Quadruple 2-input XOR gates

The pin assignments to the various gates are shown in Fig. 11-1. "Quadruple" means that there are four gates within the package. The TTL digital-logic gates and their characteristics are discussed in Section 2-8. NAND implementation is discussed in Sections 3-6 and 4-7.

Truth Tables: Use one gate from each IC listed above and obtain the truth table of the gate. The truth table is obtained by connecting the inputs of the gate to switches and the output to an indicator lamp. Compare your results with the truth tables listed in Fig. 2-5.

Waveforms: For each gate listed above, obtain the input–output waveform relationship of the gate. The waveforms are to be observed in the oscilloscope. Use the two low-order outputs of a binary counter (Fig. 11-3) to provide the inputs to the gate. As an example, the circuit and waveforms for the NAND gate are illustrated in Fig. 11-5. The oscilloscope display will repeat this waveform, but you should record only the nonrepetitive portion.

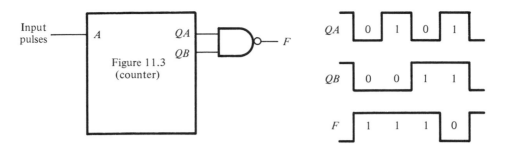

Figure 11-5 Waveforms for NAND gate

Propagation Delay: Connect all six inverters inside the 7404 IC in cascade. The output will be the same as the input except that it will be delayed by the time it takes the signal to propagate through all six inverters. Apply clock pulses to the input of the first inverter. Using the oscilloscope, determine the delay from the input to the output of the sixth inverter during the upswing and again during the downswing of the pulse. This is done with a dual-trace oscilloscope by applying the input clock pulses to one of the channels and the output of the sixth inverter to the second channel. Set the time base knob to the lowest time-per-division setting. The rise or fall time of the two pulses should appear on the screen. Divide the total delay by six to obtain an average propagation delay per inverter.

Universal NAND Gate: Using a single 7400 IC, connect a circuit that produces:

(a) an inverter.

(b) a 2-input AND.

(c) a 2-input OR.

(d) a 2-input NOR.

(e) a 2-input XOR (see Fig. 4-21).

In each case, verify your circuit by checking its truth table.

NAND Circuit: Using a single 7400 IC, construct a circuit with NAND gates that implements the Boolean function:

$$F = AB + CD$$

1. Draw the circuit diagram.

2. Obtain the truth table for F as a function of the four inputs.

3. Connect the circuit and verify the truth table.

4. Record the patterns of 1's and 0's for F as inputs A, B, C, and D go from binary 0 to binary 15.

5. Connect the four outputs of the binary counter shown in Fig. 11-3 to the four inputs of the NAND circuit. Connect the input clock pulses from the counter to one channel and output F to the other channel of a dual-trace oscilloscope. Observe and record the 1's and 0's pattern of F after each clock pulse and compare it to the pattern recorded in Step 4.

11-3 SIMPLIFICATION OF BOOLEAN FUNCTIONS

This experiment demonstrates the relationship between a Boolean function and the corresponding logic diagram. The Boolean functions are simplified by using the map method as discussed in Chapter 3. The logic diagrams are to be drawn using NAND gates as explained in Section 3-6.

The gate ICs to be used for the logic diagrams must be those from Fig. 11-1 that contain NAND gates.

7400 2-input NAND.

7404 Inverter (1-input NAND).

7410 3-input NAND.

7420 4-input NAND.

If an input to a NAND gate is not used, it should not be left open but instead should be connected to another input that is used. For example, if the circuit needs an inverter and there is an extra 2-input gate available in a 7400 IC, then both inputs of the gate are to be connected together to form a single input for an inverter.

Logic Diagram: This part of the experiment starts with a given logic diagram from which we proceed to apply simplification procedures to reduce the number of gates and possibly the number of ICs. The logic diagram shown in Fig. 11-6 requires two ICs, a 7400 and a 7410. Note that the inverters for inputs x, y, and z are obtained from the remaining three gates in the 7400 IC. If the inverters were taken from a 7404 IC, the circuit would have required three ICs. Also note that in drawing SSI circuits, the gates are not enclosed in blocks as is done with MSI circuits.

Assign pin numbers to all inputs and outputs of the gates and connect the circuit with the x, y, z inputs going to three switches and the output F to an indicator lamp. Test the circuit by obtaining its truth table.

Obtain the Boolean function of the circuit and simplify it using the map method. Construct the simplified circuit without disconnecting the original circuit. Test both circuits by applying identical inputs to both and observing the separate outputs. Show that for each of the eight possible input combinations, the two

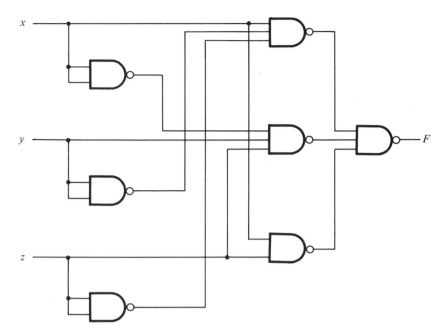

Figure 11-6 Logic diagram for experiment 3

circuits have identical outputs. This will prove that the simplified circuit behaves exactly as the original circuit.

Boolean Functions: Given the two Boolean functions in sum of minterms:

$$F_1(A, B, C, D) = (0, 1, 4, 5, 8, 9, 10, 12, 13)$$
$$F_2(A, B, C, D) = (3, 5, 7, 8, 10, 11, 13, 15)$$

Simplify the two functions by means of maps. Obtain a composite logic diagram with four inputs, A, B, C, D, and two outputs, F_1 and F_2. Implement the two functions together using a minimum number of NAND ICs. Do not duplicate the same gate if the corresponding term is needed for both functions. Use any extra gates in existing ICs for inverters when possible. Connect the circuit and check its operation. The truth table for F_1 and F_2 obtained from the circuit should conform with the minterms listed above.

Complement: Plot the following Boolean function in a map:

$$F = A'D + BD + B'C + AB'D$$

Combine the 1's in the map to obtain the simplified function for F in sum of products. Then combine the 0's in the map to obtain the simplified function for F' also in sum of products. Implement both F and F' using NAND gates and connect the two circuits to the same input switches but to separate output indicator lamps. Obtain the truth table of each circuit in the laboratory and show that they are the complements of each other.

11-4 COMBINATIONAL CIRCUITS

In this experiment you will design, construct, and test four combinational logic circuits. The first two circuits are to be constructed with NAND gates, the third with XOR gates, and the fourth with a decoder and NAND gates. Reference to parity generator can be found in Section 4-9. Implementation with a decoder is discussed in Section 5-5.

Design Example: Design a combinational circuit with four inputs, A, B, C, D, and one output F. F is to be equal to 1 when $A = 1$ provided that $B = 0$, or when $B = 1$ provided that either C or D is also equal to 1. Otherwise, the output is to be equal to 0.

1. Obtain the truth table of the circuit.
2. Simplify the output function.
3. Draw the logic diagram of the circuit using NAND gates with a minimum number of ICs.
4. Construct the circuit and test it for proper operation by verifying the conditions stated above.

Majority Logic: A majority logic is a digital circuit whose output is equal to 1 if the majority of the inputs are 1's. The output is 0 otherwise. Design and test a 3-input majority circuit using NAND gates with a minimum number of ICs.

Parity Generator: Design, construct, and test a circuit that generates an even-parity bit from four message bits. Use XOR gates. Adding one more XOR gate, expand the circuit so it generates an odd parity bit also.

Decoder Implementation: A combinational circuit has three inputs, x, y, z, and three outputs, F_1, F_2, F_3. The simplified Boolean functions for the circuit are as follows:

$$F_1 = xz + x'y'z'$$
$$F_2 = x'y + xy'z'$$
$$F_3 = xy + x'y'z$$

Implement and test the combinational circuit using a 74155 decoder IC and external NAND gates.

The block diagram of the decoder and its truth table are shown in Fig. 11-7. The 74155 can be connected as a dual 2 × 4 decoder or as a single 3 × 8 decoder. When a 3 × 8 decoder is desired, inputs C1 and C2 must be connected together as well as inputs G1 and G2, as shown in the block diagram. The function of the circuit is similar to the one shown in Fig. 5-12. G is the enable input and must be equal to 0 for proper operation. The eight outputs are labeled with symbols given in the data book. As in Fig. 5-12, the 74155 uses NAND gates, with the result that the selected output goes to 0 while all other outputs remain at 1. The implementation with the decoder is as shown in Fig. 5-11 except that the OR gates must be replaced with external NAND gates when the 74155 is used.

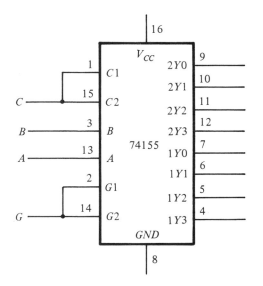

Truth table

Input				Outputs							
G	C	B	A	$2Y0$	$2Y1$	$2Y2$	$2Y3$	$1Y0$	$1Y1$	$1Y2$	$1Y3$
1	X	X	X	1	1	1	1	1	1	1	1
0	0	0	0	0	1	1	1	1	1	1	1
0	0	0	1	1	0	1	1	1	1	1	1
0	0	1	0	1	1	0	1	1	1	1	1
0	0	1	1	1	1	1	0	1	1	1	1
0	1	0	0	1	1	1	1	0	1	1	1
0	1	0	1	1	1	1	1	1	0	1	1
0	1	1	0	1	1	1	1	1	1	0	1
0	1	1	1	1	1	1	1	1	1	1	0

Figure 11-7   IC type 74155 connected as a 3 × 8 decoder

11-5 CODE CONVERTERS

The conversion from one binary code to another is common in digital systems. In this experiment you will design and construct three combinational circuit converters. Code conversion is discussed in Section 4-5.

Reflected Code to Binary: Design a combinational circuit with four inputs and four outputs that converts a four-bit reflected code number (Table 1-4) into the equivalent four-bit binary number. Implement the circuit with exclusive-OR gates. (This can be done with one 7486 IC.) Connect the circuit to four switches and four indicator lamps and check for proper operation.

9's Complementer: Design a combinational circuit with four input lines that represent a decimal digit in BCD and four output lines that generate the 9's complement of the input digit. Provide a fifth output that detects an error in the input BCD number. This output should be equal to logic 1 when the four inputs have one of the unused combinations of the BCD code. Use any of the gates listed in Fig. 11-1, but minimize the total number of ICs used.

Seven-Segment Display: A seven-segment indicator is used for displaying any one of the decimal digits 0 through 9. Usually, the decimal digit is available in BCD.

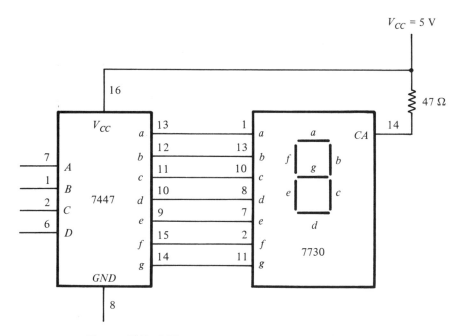

Figure 11-8 BCD-to-seven-segment decoder (7447) and seven-segment display (7730)

A BCD-to-seven-segment decoder accepts a decimal digit in BCD and generates the corresponding seven-segment code. This is shown pictorially in Problem 4-14.

Figure 11-8 shows the connections necessary between the decoder and the display. The 7447 IC is a BCD-to-seven-segment decoder/driver. It has four inputs for the BCD digit. Input D is the most significant and input A the least significant. The 4-bit BCD digit is converted to a seven-segment code with outputs a through g. The outputs of the 7447 are applied to the inputs of the 7730 (or equivalent) seven-segment display. This IC contains the seven LED (light-emitting diode) segments on top of the package. The input at pin 14 is the common anode (CA) for all the LEDs. A 47 Ω resistor to V_{CC} is needed in order to supply the proper current to the selected LED segments. Other equivalent seven-segment display IC's may have additional anode terminals and may require different resistor values.

Construct the circuit shown in Fig. 11-8. Apply the 4-bit BCD digits through four switches and observe the decimal display from 0 to 9. Inputs 1010 through 1111 have no meaning in BCD. Depending on the decoder, these values may cause either a blank or a meaningless pattern to be displayed. Observe and record the output displayed patterns of the six unused input combinations.

11-6 DESIGN WITH MULTIPLEXERS

In this experiment you will design a combinational circuit and implement it with multiplexers as explained in Section 5-6. The multiplexer to be used is IC type 74151, shown in Fig. 11-9. The internal construction of the 74151 is similar to the diagram shown in Fig. 5-16 except that there are eight inputs instead of four. The eight inputs are designated $D0$ through $D7$. The three selection lines, C, B, and A, select the particular input to be multiplexed and applied to the output. A strobe control, S, acts as an enable signal. The function table specifies the value of output Y as a function of the selection lines. Output W is the complement of Y. For proper operation, the strobe input S must be connected to ground.

Design Specifications: A small corporation has 10 shares of stock, and each share entitles its owner to one vote at a stockholder's meeting. The 10 shares of stock are owned by four people as follows:

Mr. W: 1 share

Mr. X: 2 shares

Mr. Y: 3 shares

Mrs. Z: 4 shares

Each of these persons has a switch to close when voting yes and to open when voting no for his or her shares.

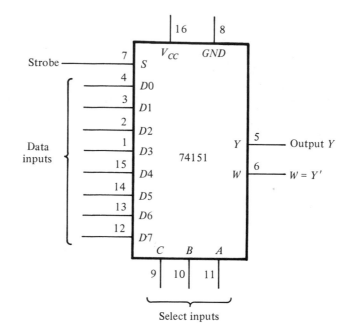

Function table

Strobe S	Select			Output Y
	C	B	A	
1	X	X	X	0
0	0	0	0	D0
0	0	0	1	D1
0	0	1	0	D2
0	0	1	1	D3
0	1	0	0	D4
0	1	0	1	D5
0	1	1	0	D6
0	1	1	1	D7

Figure 11-9 IC type 74151 8×1 Multiplexer

It is necessary to design a circuit that displays the total number of shares that vote yes for each measure. Use a seven-segment display and a decoder as shown in Fig. 11-8 to display the required number. If all shares vote no for a measure, the display should be blank. (Note that binary input 15 into the 7447 blanks all seven segments.) If 10 shares vote yes for a measure, the display should show 0. Otherwise, the display shows a decimal number equal to the number of shares that vote yes. Use four 74151 multiplexers to design the combinational circuit that converts the inputs from the stock owners' switches into the BCD digit for the 7447. Do not use 5 V for logic-1. Use the output of an inverter whose input is grounded.

11-7 ADDERS AND SUBTRACTORS

In this experiment you will construct and test various adders and subtractor circuits. The subtractor circuit is then used for comparing the relative magnitude of two numbers. Adders are discussed in Section 4-3. Subtraction with 2's complement is explained in Section 1-5. A 4-bit parallel adder is introduced in Section 5-2, and the comparison of two numbers is explained in Section 5-4.

Half-Adder: Design, construct, and test a half-adder circuit using one XOR gate and two NAND gates.

Full-Adder: Design, construct, and test a full-adder circuit using two ICs, 7486 and 7400.

Parallel Adder: IC type 7483 is a 4-bit binary parallel adder. Its internal construction is similar to Fig. 5-5. The pin assignment is shown in Fig. 11-10. The two 4-bit input binary numbers are $A1$ through $A4$ and $B1$ through $B4$. The 4-bit sum is obtained from $S1$ through $S4$. $C0$ is the input carry and $C4$ the output carry.

Test the 4-bit binary adder 7483 by connecting the power supply and ground terminals. Then connect the four A inputs to a fixed binary number such as 1001 and the B inputs and the input carry to five toggle switches. The five outputs are applied to indicator lamps. Perform the addition of a few binary numbers and check that the output sum and output carry give the proper values. Show that when the input carry is equal to 1, it adds 1 to the output sum.

Adder-Subtractor: The subtraction of two binary numbers can be done by taking the 2's complement of the subtrahend and adding it to the minuend. The 2's complement can be obtained by taking the 1's complement and adding 1. To perform $A - B$, we complement the four bits of B, add them to the four bits of A, and add 1 through the input carry. This is done as shown in Fig. 11-11. The four XOR gates complement the bits of B when the mode select $M = 1$ (because $x \oplus 1 = x'$) and leave the bits of B unchanged when $M = 0$ (because $x \oplus 0 = x$). Thus, when the mode select M is equal to 1, the input carry $C0$ is equal to 1 and the

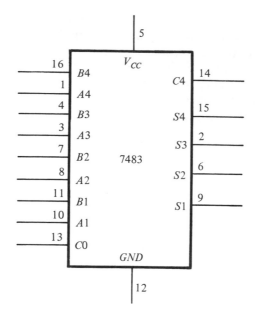

Figure 11-10   IC type 7483 4-bit binary adder

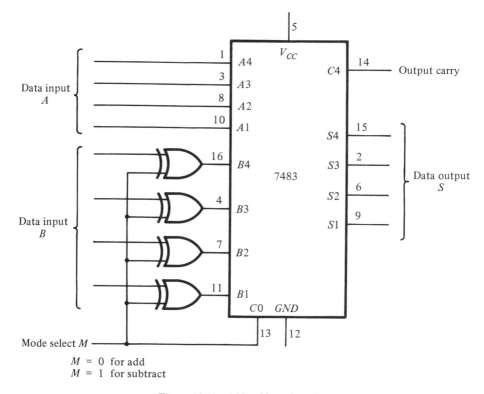

$M = 0$ for add
$M = 1$ for subtract

Figure 11-11   4-bit adder-subtractor

sum output is A plus the 2's complement of B. When M is equal to 0, the input carry is equal to 0 and the sum generates $A + B$.

Connect the adder-subtractor circuit and test it for proper operation. Connect the four A inputs to a fixed binary number 1001 and the B inputs to switches. Perform the following operations and record the values of the output sum and the output carry $C4$.

$$9 + 5 \qquad 9 - 5$$
$$9 + 9 \qquad 9 - 9$$
$$9 + 15 \qquad 9 - 15$$

Show that during addition the output carry is equal to 1 when the sum exceeds 15. Also show that when $A \geqslant B$, the subtraction operation gives the correct answer, $A - B$, and the output carry $C4$ is equal to 1. But when $A < B$, the subtraction gives the 2's complement of $B - A$ and the output carry is equal to 0.

Magnitude Comparator: The comparison of two numbers is an operation that determines whether one number is greater than, equal to, or less than the other number. Two numbers A and B can be compared by first subtracting $A - B$ as done in Fig. 11-11. If the output in S is equal to zero, we know that $A = B$. The output carry from $C4$ determines the relative magnitude: when $C4 = 1$, we have $A \geqslant B$; when $C4 = 0$, we have $A < B$; and when $C4 = 1$ and $S \neq 0$, we have $A > B$.

It is necessary to supplement the subtractor circuit of Fig. 11-11 to provide the comparison logic. This is done with a combinational circuit that has five inputs, $S1$ through $S4$ and $C4$, and three outputs designated by x, y, and z, so that:

$$x = 1 \quad \text{if} \quad A = B \quad (S = 0000)$$
$$y = 1 \quad \text{if} \quad A < B \quad (C4 = 0)$$
$$z = 1 \quad \text{if} \quad A > B \quad (C4 = 1 \text{ and } S \neq 0000)$$

The combinational circuit can be implemented with the two ICs 7404 and 7408.

Construct the comparator circuit and test its operation. Use at least two sets of numbers for A and B to check each of the outputs x, y, and z.

11-8   FLIP-FLOPS

In this experiment you will construct, test, and investigate the operation of various flip-flop circuits. The internal construction of the flip-flops can be found in Sections 6-2 and 6-3.

SR **Latch:** The *SR* latch is a basic flip-flop made with two cross-coupled NAND gates. Construct a basic flip-flop circuit and connect the two inputs to switches and the two outputs to indicator lamps. Set the two switches to logic 1, then momentarily turn each switch separately to the logic 0 position and back to 1. Obtain the truth table of the circuit.

RS **Flip-Flop:** Construct a clocked *RS* flip-flop with four NAND gates. Connect the *S* and *R* inputs to two switches and the clock input to a pulser. Verify the characteristic table of the flip-flop.

D **Flip-Flop:** Construct a clocked *D* flip-flop with four NAND gates. This can be done by modifying the circuit shown in Fig. 6-5 as follows. Remove gate number 5. Connect the output of gate 3 to the input of gate 4, where gate 5 was originally connected. Show that the modified circuit is identical to the original circuit by deriving the Boolean function for the output of gate 4 in each case. Connect the modified *D* flip-flop circuit and verify its characteristic table.

Master-Slave Flip-Flop: Construct a clocked master-slave *JK* flip-flop with one 7410 and two 7400 ICs. Connect the *J* and *K* inputs to logic 1 and the clock input to a pulser. Connect the normal output of the master flip-flop to one indicator lamp and the normal output of the slave flip-flop to another indicator lamp. Press the pushbutton in the pulser and then release it to produce a single positive pulse. Observe that the master flip-flop changes when the pulse goes positive and the slave flip-flop follows the change when the pulse goes negative. Repeat a few times while observing the two indicator lamps. Explain the transfer sequence from input to master and from master to slave.

Disconnect the clock input from the pulser and connect it to a clock generator with a frequency of 10 KHz or higher. Using a dual-trace oscilloscope, observe the waveforms of the clock and the master and slave outputs. Verify that the delay between the master and slave outputs is equal to the pulse width. Obtain a timing diagram showing the relationship between the clock waveform and the master and slave flip-flop outputs.

Edge-triggered *D* flip-flop: Construct a *D*-type positive-edge-triggered flip-flop using six NAND gates. Connect the clock input to a pulser, the *D* input to a toggle switch, and the output *Q* to an indicator lamp. Set the value of *D* to the complement value of *Q*. Show that the flip-flop output changes only in response to a positive transition of the clock pulse. Verify that the output does not change when the clock input is logic 1, or when the clock goes through a negative transition, or when it is logic 0. Continue changing the *D* input to correspond to the complement of the *Q* output at all times.

Disconnect the input from the pulser and connect it to the clock generator. Connect the complement output *Q'* to the *D* input. This causes the output to complement with each positive transition of the clock pulse. Using a dual-trace oscilloscope, observe and record the timing relationship between the input clock and output Q. Show that the output changes in response to a positive edge transition.

IC Flip-Flops: IC type 7476 consists of two JK master-slave flip-flops with preset and clear. The pin assignment for each flip-flop is shown in Fig. 11-12. The function table specifies the circuit operation. The first three entries in the table specify the operation of the asynchronous preset and clear inputs. These inputs behave like a NAND SR latch and are independent of the clock or the J and K inputs (the X's indicate don't-care conditions). The last four entries in the function table specify the clock operation with both the preset and clear inputs maintained at logic 1. The clock value is shown as a single pulse. The positive transition of the pulse changes the master flip-flop, and the negative transition changes the slave flip-flop as well as the output of the circuit. With $J = K = 0$, the output does not change. The flip-flop toggles or complements when $J = K = 1$. Investigate the operation of one 7476 flip-flop and verify its function table.

IC type 7474 consists of two D positive-edge-triggered flip-flops with preset and clear. The pin assignment is shown in Fig. 11-13. The function table specifies

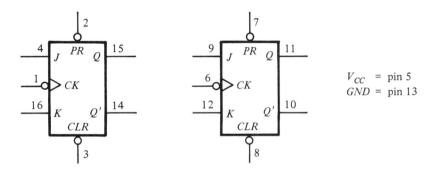

V_{CC} = pin 5
GND = pin 13

Function table

Inputs					Outputs	
Preset	Clear	Clock	J	K	Q	Q'
0	1	X	X	X	1	0
1	0	X	X	X	0	1
0	0	X	X	X	1	1
1	1	⊓	0	0	No change	
1	1	⊓	0	1	0	1
1	1	⊓	1	0	1	0
1	1	⊓	1	1	Toggle	

Figure 11-12 IC type 7476 dual JK master-slave flip-flops.

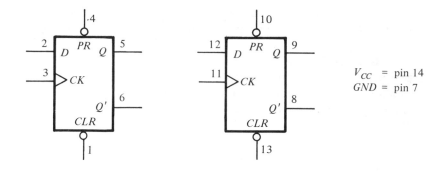

V_{CC} = pin 14
GND = pin 7

Function table

Inputs				Outputs	
Preset	Clear	Clock	D	Q	Q'
0	1	X	X	1	0
1	0	X	X	0	1
0	0	X	X	1	1
1	1	↑	0	0	1
1	1	↑	1	1	0
1	1	0	X	No change	

Figure 11-13 IC type 7474 dual D positive-edge-triggered flip-flop

the preset and clear operations and the clock operation. The clock is shown with an upward arrow to indicate that it is a positive-edge-triggered flip-flop. Investigate the operation of one of the flip-flops and verify its function table.

11-9 SEQUENTIAL CIRCUITS

In this experiment you will design, construct, and test three synchronous sequential circuits. Use IC type 7476 JK flip-flops (Fig. 11-12) in all three designs. Choose any gate type that will minimize the total number of ICs. The design of synchronous sequential circuits is covered in Sections 6-6, 6-7, and 6-8.

Up–Down Counter with Enable: Design, construct, and test a 2-bit counter that counts up or down. An enable input E determines whether the counter is on or off. If $E = 0$, the counter is disabled and remains at its present count even though clock pulses are applied to the flip-flops. If $E = 1$, the counter is enabled and a second input, x, determines the count direction. If $x = 1$, the circuit counts up with

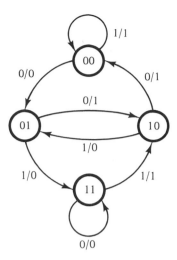

Figure 11-14 State diagram for experiment 9

the sequence 00, 01, 10, 11 and the count repeats. If $x = 0$, the circuit counts down with the sequence 11, 10, 01, 00 and the count repeats. Do not use E to disable the clock. Design the sequential circuit with E and x as inputs.

State Diagram: Design, construct and test a sequential circuit whose state diagram is shown in Fig. 11-14. Designate the two flip-flops as A and B, the input as x, and the output as y.

Connect the output of the least significant flip-flop B to the input x and predict the sequence of states and output that will occur with the application of clock pulses. Verify the state transition and output by testing the circuit.

Design of Counter: Design, construct, and test a counter that goes through the following sequence of binary states: 0, 1, 2, 3, 6, 7, 10, 11, 12, 13, 14, 15, and back to 0 to repeat. Note that binary states 4, 5, 8, and 9 are not used. The counter must be self-starting; that is, if the circuit starts from any one of the four invalid states, the count pulses must transfer the circuit to one of the valid states to continue the count correctly.

Check the circuit operation for the required count sequence. Verify that the counter is self-starting. This is done by initializing the circuit to each unused state by means of the preset and clear inputs and then applying pulses to see whether the counter reaches one of the valid states.

11-10 COUNTERS

In this experiment you will construct and test various ripple and synchronous counter circuits. Ripple counters are discussed in Section 7-4, and synchronous counters are covered in Section 7-5.

Ripple Counter: Construct a 4-bit binary ripple counter using two 7476 ICs (Fig. 11-12). Connect all asynchronous clear and preset inputs to logic 1. Connect the count pulse input to a pulser and check the counter for proper operation.

Modify the counter so it will count down instead of up. Check that each input pulse decrements the counter by 1.

Synchronous Counter: Construct a synchronous 4-bit binary counter and check its operation. Use two 7476 ICs and one 7408 IC.

Decimal Counter: Design a synchronous BCD counter that counts from 0000 to 1001. Use two 7476 ICs and one 7408 IC. Test the counter for the proper sequence. Determine whether it is self-starting. This is done by initializing the counter to each of the six unused states by means of the preset and clear inputs. The application of pulses must transfer the counter to one of the valid states if the counter is self-starting.

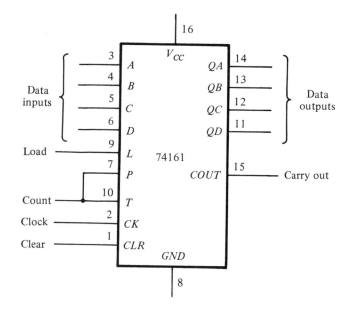

Function table

Clear	Clock	Load	Count	Function
0	X	X	X	Clear outputs to 0
1	↑	0	X	Load input data
1	↑	1	1	Count to next binary value
1	↑	1	0	No change in output

Figure 11-15   IC type 74161 binary counter with parallel load

Binary Counter with Parallel Load: IC type 74161 is a 4-bit synchronous binary counter with parallel load and asynchronous clear. The internal logic is similar to the circuit shown in Fig. 7-19. The pin assignment to the inputs and outputs is shown in Fig. 11-15. When the load signal is enabled, the four data inputs are transferred into four internal flip-flops QA through QD, with QD being the most significant bit. There are two count-enable inputs called P and T. Both must be equal to 1 for the counter to operate. The function table is similar to Table 7-6 with one exception: the load input in the 74161 is enabled when equal to 0. To load the input data, the clear input must be equal to 1 and the load input must be equal to 0. The two count inputs have don't-care conditions and may be equal to either 1 or 0. The internal flip-flops trigger on the positive transition of the clock pulse. The circuit functions as a counter when the load input is equal to 1 and both count inputs P and T are equal to 1. If either P or T goes to 0, the output does not change. The carry-out output is equal to 1 when all four data outputs are equal to 1. Perform an experiment to verify the operation of the 74161 IC according to the function table.

Show how the 74161 IC together with a 2-input NAND gate can be made to operate as a synchronous BCD counter that counts from 0000 to 1001. Do not use the clear input. Use the NAND gate to detect the count of 1001, which then causes all 0s to be loaded into the counter.

Connect each of the four circuits shown in Fig. 7-20 to achieve a mod-6 counter. Remember that the load input is enabled when equal to 0 and therefore a NAND gate will be needed in each case.

11-11   SHIFT REGISTERS

In this experiment you will investigate the operation of shift registers. The IC to be used is the 74179 shift register with parallel load. Shift registers are explained in Section 7-3. Some applications are introduced in Section 7-6.

IC Shift Register: IC type 74179 is a 4-bit shift register with parallel load and asynchronous clear. The internal logic is similar to Fig. 7-9 except that the 74179 is unidirectional, that is, it can shift in one direction only. The pin assignment to the inputs and outputs is shown in Fig. 11-16. When the load input is enabled, the four data inputs are transferred into four internal flip-flops, QA through QD. When the shift input is enabled, the information in the register is shifted from QA towards QD and the value from the serial input is transferred into QA. The function table shows that all flip-flop changes occur on the negative transitions of the clock pulse. To load the input data, the load input must be equal to 1 and the shift input must be equal to 0. To shift the data, the shift input must be equal to 1 but the load input may be equal to 1 or 0 as indicated by the don't-care condition. If both the load and shift are equal to 0, the clock pulses do not change the output.

Perform an experiment that will verify the operation of the 74179 IC according to the given function table.

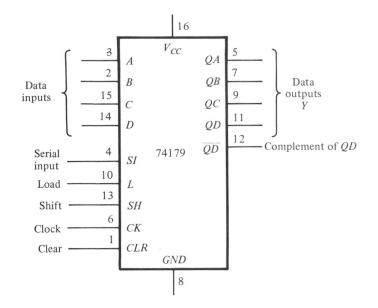

Function table

Clear	Clock	Load	Shift	Function
0	X	X	X	Clear outputs to 0
1	↓	1	0	Load input data
1	↓	X	1	Shift in the direction from QA to QD
1	↓	0	0	No change in output

Figure 11-16 IC type 74179 shift register with parallel load

Ring Counter: A ring counter is a circular shift register with the signal from the serial output in QD going into the serial input. Use the load input to preset the ring counter to an initial value of 1000. Rotate the single bit and check the state of the register after each clock pulse.

A switch-tail ring counter uses the complement output of QD for the serial input. Preset the switch-tail ring counter to 0000 and predict the sequence of states that will result from shifting. Verify your prediction by observing the state sequence after each shift.

Feedback Shift Register: A feedback shift register is a shift register whose serial input is connected to some function of selected register output bits. Connect a feedback shift register whose serial input is the exclusive-OR of outputs QC and QD. Predict the sequence of states of the register starting with $ABCD = 1000$. Verify your prediction by observing the state sequence after each clock pulse.

Bidirectional Shift Register: The 74179 IC can only shift right from *QA* towards *QD*. It is possible to utilize the parallel load circuit to obtain a shift left from *QD* towards *QA*. This is accomplished by connecting the output of each flip-flop to the input of the flip-flop on its left and using the load input as a shift-left control. Input *D* becomes the serial input for the shift-left operation.

Connect the 74179 as a bidirectional shift register (without parallel load). Connect the serial input for shift right to a toggle switch. Construct the shift left as a ring counter by connecting the serial output from *QA* to the serial input at *D*. Clear the register and then check its operation by shifting a single 1 from the serial input switch. Shift right three more times and then rotate left with the shift left (load) control. A single 1 should remain visible while shifting.

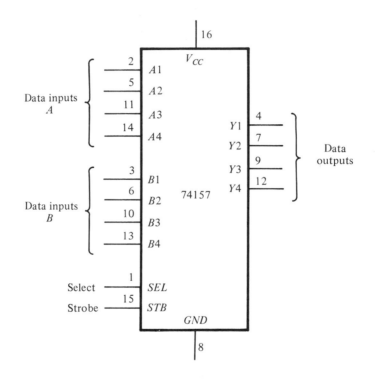

Function table

Strobe	Select	Data outpus *Y*
1	*X*	All 0's
0	0	Select data inputs *A*
0	1	Select data inputs *B*

Figure 11-17   IC type 74157 quadruple 2 × 1 multiplexers

Bidirectional Shift Register with Parallel Load: The 74179 IC can be converted to a bidirectional shift register with parallel load in conjunction with a multiplexer circuit. We will use IC type 74157 multiplexers for this purpose. This is a quadruple 2-to-1 multiplexer whose internal logic is as shown in Fig. 5-17. The pin assignment to the inputs and outputs of the IC is shown in Fig. 11-17. Note that the enable input is called a strobe in the 74157 IC.

Design a bidirectional shift register with parallel load using the 74179 and 74157 ICs. The circuit should have the following capabilities:

1. Asynchronous clear.

2. Shift right.

3. Shift left.

4. Parallel load.

5. Synchronous clear.

6. No change of output.

Derive a table for these six operations as a function of the clear, clock, shift, and load inputs of the 74179 and the strobe and select inputs of the 74157. Connect the circuit and verify your function table. Use the load input to provide an initial value into the register and connect the serial outputs to the corresponding serial inputs in order not to lose the information while shifting.

11-12   SERIAL ADDITION

In this experiment you will construct and test a serial adder-subtractor circuit. Serial addition of two binary numbers can be done by means of shift registers and a full adder as explained in Section 7-3. Example 7-3 (page 270) shows that the number of gates for the full-adder can be reduced if a *JK* flip-flop is used for storing the carry.

Serial Adder: Starting from the diagram of Fig. 7-11, design and construct a 4-bit serial adder using the following ICs: 74179 (two), 7408, 7486, and 7476. Note that 74179 has a complement output for QD which is equivalent to the variables x' and y' in Fig. 7-11. Provide a facility for register B to accept parallel data from four toggle switches and connect its serial input to ground so that 0's are shifted into register B during the addition. Provide a toggle switch to clear the registers and the flip-flop. Another switch will be needed to specify whether register B is to accept parallel data or is to be shifted during the addition.

Testing the Adder: To test your serial adder, perform the binary addition $5 + 6 + 15 = 26$. This is done by first clearing the registers and the carry flip-flop.

Parallel-load into register B the binary value 0101. Apply four pulses to add B to A serially and check that the result in A is 0101. (Note that clock pulses for the 7476 must be as shown in Fig. 11-12.) Parallel-load into B 0110 and add it to A serially. Check that A has the proper sum. Parallel-load into B 1111 and add to A. Check that the value in A is 1010 and that the carry flip-flop is set.

Clear the registers and flip-flop and try a few other numbers to verify that your serial adder is functioning properly.

Serial Adder-Subtractor: If we follow the procedure used in Example 7-3 to design a serial subtractor that subtracts $A - B$, we will find that the output difference is the same as the output sum but that the input to the J and K of the borrow flip-flop needs the complement of x (see Problem 7-10 and its answer in the Appendix). Using the other two XOR gates from the 7486, convert the serial adder to a serial adder-subtractor with a mode control M. When $M = 0$, the circuit adds $A + B$. When $M = 1$, the circuit subtracts $A - B$ and the flip-flop holds the borrow instead of the carry.

Test the adder part of the circuit by repeating the operations recommended above to ensure that the modification did not change the operation. Test the serial subtractor part by performing the operations $15 - 4 - 5 - 13 = -7$. Binary 15 can be transferred to register A by first clearing it to 0 and adding 15 from B. Check the intermediate results during the subtraction. Note that -7 will appear as the 2's complement of 7 with a borrow of 1 in the flip-flop.

11-13   MEMORY UNIT

In this experiment you will investigate the behavior of a random-access memory (RAM) unit and its storage capability. The RAM will be used to simulate a read-only memory (ROM). The ROM simulator will then be used to implement combinational circuits as explained in Section 5-7. The memory unit is discussed in Section 7-8.

IC RAM: IC type 7489 is a 16×4 random access memory. The internal logic is similar to the circuit shown in Fig. 7-30 for a 4×3 RAM. The pin assignment to the inputs and outputs is shown in Fig. 11-18. The four address inputs select one of 16 words in the memory. The least significant bit of the address is A, and the most significant is D. The memory enable (ME) input must be equal to 0 to enable the memory. If ME is equal to 1, the memory is disabled and all four outputs are at a logic 1 level. The write enable (WE) input determines the type of operation as indicated in the function table. The write operation is performed when $WE = 0$. This is a transfer of the binary number from the data inputs into the selected word in memory. The read operation is performed when $WE = 1$. This transfers the complement value stored in the selected word into the output data lines. The outputs are open-collector to allow external wired logic for memory expansion.

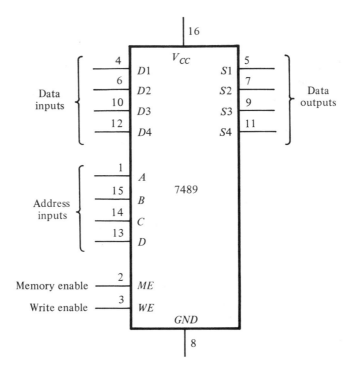

Function table

ME	WE	Operation	Data outputs
0	0	Write	Complement of data inputs
0	1	Read	Complement of selected word
1	X	Disable	All 1's

Figure 11-18 IC type 7489 16 × 4 RAM

Testing the RAM: An open-collector gate requires an external resistor for proper operation. However, an open-collector gate can be operated without an external resistor if its output is connected to the input of another gate. Since the outputs of the 7489 produce the complement values, we might as well insert four inverters to change the outputs to their normal value and, at the same time, avoid the need for external resistors. The RAM can be tested after making the following connections. Connect the address inputs to a binary counter using the 7493 IC, as shown in Fig. 11-3. Connect the four data inputs to toggle switches and the data outputs to four 7404 inverters. Provide four indicator lamps for the address and four more for the outputs of the inverters. Connect input *ME* to ground and *WE* to a toggle switch (or a pulser that provides a negative pulse). Store a few words into the memory and then read them to verify that the write and read operations are functioning properly. You must be careful when using the *WE* switch. Always leave the *WE* input in the read mode, unless you want to write into memory. The proper way to write is first to set the address in the counter and the inputs in the four toggle switches. To store the word in memory, flip the *WE* switch to the write position and then return it to the read position. Be careful not to change the address or the inputs when *WE* is in the write mode.

ROM Simulator: A ROM simulator is obtained from a RAM when operated in the read mode only. The pattern of 1's and 0's is first entered into the simulating RAM by placing the unit momentarily in the write mode. Simulation is achieved by placing the unit in the read mode and taking the address lines as inputs for the ROM. The ROM can then be used to implement any combinational circuit.

Implement a combinational circuit using the ROM simulator that converts a 4-bit binary number to its equivalent reflected (Gray) code as defined in Table 1-4. This is done as follows. Obtain the truth table of the code converter. Store the truth table into the 7489 memory by setting the address inputs to the binary value and the data inputs to the corresponding reflected code value. After all 16 entries of the table are written in memory, the ROM simulator is set by connecting the *WE* line to logic 1 permanently. Check the code converter by applying the inputs to the address lines and verifying the correct outputs in the data-output lines.

Memory Expansion: Expand the memory unit to a 32×4 RAM using two 7489 ICs. Use the *ME* inputs to select between the two ICs. Note that since the data outputs are open-collector, you can tie pairs of terminals together to obtain a logic wired-OR operation in conjunction with the output inverter. Test your circuit by using it as a ROM simulator that adds a 3-bit number to a 2-bit number to produce a 4-bit sum. For example, if the input of the ROM is 10110, then the output is calculated to be $101 + 10 = 0111$. (The first three bits of the input represent 5, the last two bits represent 2, and the output sum is binary 7.) Use the counter to provide four bits of the address and a switch for the fifth bit of the address.

11-14   LAMP HANDBALL

In this experiment you will construct an electronic game of handball using a single light to simulate the moving ball. This project demonstrates the application of a bidirectional shift register with parallel load. It also shows the operation of the asynchronous inputs of flip-flops. We will first introduce an IC that is needed for this experiment and then present the logic diagram of the simulated lamp handball game.

IC Type 74194: This is a 4-bit bidirectional shift register with parallel load. The internal logic is similar to Fig. 7-9. The pin assignment to the inputs and outputs is shown in Fig. 11-19. The two mode-control inputs determine the type of operation as specified in the function table. The operation of the circuit is described in detail in Section 7-3 in conjunction with Fig. 7-9.

Logic Diagram: The logic diagram of the electronic lamp handball is shown in Fig. 11-20. It consists of two 74194 ICs, a dual D flip-flop 7474 IC, and three gate ICs: 7400, 7404, and 7408. The ball is simulated by a moving light that is shifted left or right through the bidirectional shift register. The rate at which the light moves is

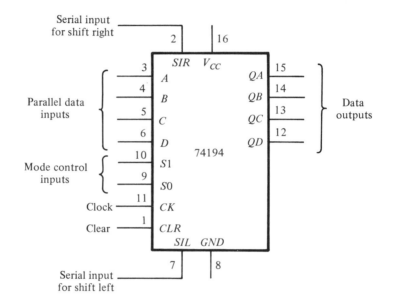

Function table

Clear	Clock	Mode S1	Mode S0	Function
0	X	X	X	Clear outputs to 0
1	↑	0	0	No change in output
1	↑	0	1	Shift right in the direction from QA to QD. SIR to QA
1	↑	1	0	Shift left in the direction from QD to QA. SIL to QD
1	↑	1	1	Parallel load input data

Figure 11-19 IC type 74194 bidirectional shift register with parallel load

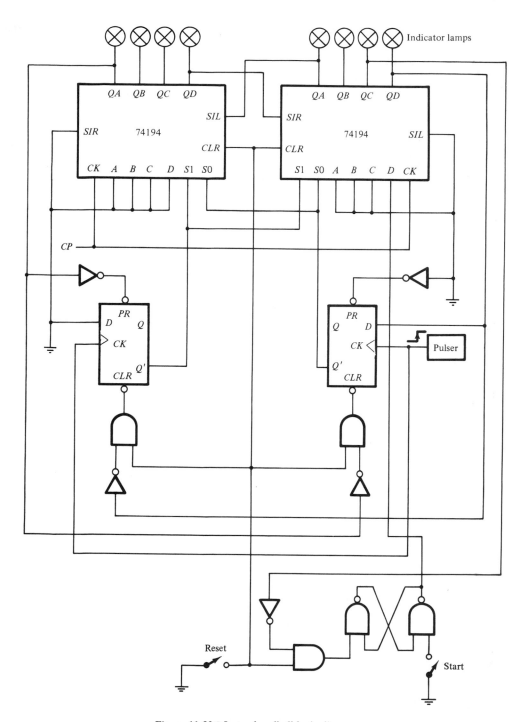

Figure 11-20 Lamp handball logic diagram

determined by the frequency of the clock. The circuit is first initialized with the *reset* switch. The *start* switch starts the game by placing the ball (an indicator lamp) at the extreme right. The player must press the pulser pushbutton to start the ball moving to the left. The single light shifts to the left until it reaches the leftmost position (the wall), at which time the ball returns to the player by reversing the direction of shift of the moving light. When the light is again at the rightmost position, the player must press the pulser again to reverse the direction of shift. If the player presses the pulser too soon or too late, the ball disappears and the light goes off. The game can be restarted by turning the start switch on and then off. The start switch must be open (logic 1) during the game.

Circuit Analysis: Prior to connecting the circuit, analyze the logic diagram to ensure that you understand how the circuit operates. In particular try to answer the following questions:

1. What is the function of the reset switch?

2. Explain how the light in the rightmost position comes on when the start switch is grounded. Why is it necessary to place the start switch in the logic 1 position before the game starts?

3. What happens to the two mode-control inputs $S1$ and $S0$ once the ball is set in motion?

4. What happens to the mode-control inputs and to the ball if the pulser is pressed while the ball is moving to the left? What happens if it is moving to the right but has not reached the rightmost position yet?

5. Suppose that the ball returned to the rightmost position but the pulser has not been pressed yet; what is the state of the mode control inputs if the pulser is pressed? What happens if it is not pressed?

Playing the Game: Wire the circuit of Fig. 11-20. Test the circuit for proper operation by playing the game. Note that the pulser must provide a positive edge transition and that both the reset and start switches must be open (be in the logic 1 state) during the game. Start with a low clock rate and increase the clock frequency to make the handball game more challenging.

Lamp Ping-Pong: Modify the circuit of Fig. 11-20 so as to obtain a lamp ping-pong game. Two players can participate in this game with each player having his own pulser. The player with the right pulser returns the ball when in the extreme right position, and the player with the left pulser returns the ball when in the extreme left position. The only modification required for the ping-pong game is a second pulser and a change of few wires.

With a second start circuit, the game can be made to start (serve) by either one of the two players. This addition is optional.

11-15 CLOCK PULSE GENERATOR

In this experiment you will use an IC timer unit and connect it to produce clock pulses at a given frequency. The circuit requires the connection of two external resistors and two external capacitors. The cathode ray oscilloscope is used to observe the waveforms and measure the frequency.

IC Timer: IC type 72555 (or 555) is a precision timer circuit whose internal logic is shown in Fig. 11-21. (The resistors R_A and R_B and the two capacitors are not part of the IC.) It consists of two voltage comparators, a flip-flop, and an internal transistor. The voltage division from $V_{CC} = 5$ V through the three internal

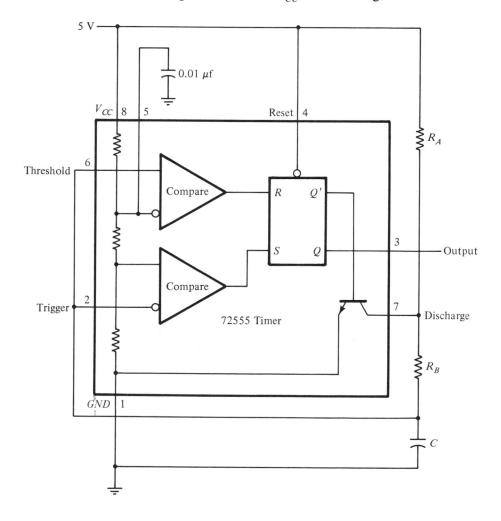

Figure 11-21 IC type 72555 timer connected as a clock pulse generator

465

resistors to ground produce $\frac{2}{3}$ and $\frac{1}{3}$ of V_{CC} (3.3 V and 1.7 V) into the fixed inputs of the comparators. When the threshold input at pin 6 goes above 3.3 V, the upper comparator resets the flip-flop and the output goes low to about 0 V. When the trigger input at pin 2 goes below 1.7 V, the lower comparator sets the flip-flop and the output goes high to about 5 V. When the output is low, Q' is high and the base-emitter junction of the transistor is forward-biased. When the output is high, Q' is low and the transistor is cut off (see Section 10-2). The timer circuit is capable of producing accurate time delays controlled by an external RC circuit. In this experiment the IC timer will be operated in the astable mode to produce clock pulses.

Circuit Operation: Fig. 11-21 shows the external connections for the astable operation. The capacitor C charges through resistors R_A and R_B when the transistor is cut off and discharges through R_B when the transistor is forward-biased and conducting. When the charging voltage across capacitor C reaches 3.3 V, the threshold input at pin 6 causes the flip-flop to reset and the transistor turns on. When the discharging voltage reaches 1.7 V, the trigger input at pin 2 causes the flip-flop to set and the transistor turns off. Thus the output continually alternates between two voltage levels at the output of the flip-flop. The output remains high for a duration equal to the charge time. This duration is determined from the equation:

$$t_H = 0.693(R_A + R_B)C$$

The output remains low for a duration equal to the discharge time. This duration is determined from the equation:

$$t_L = 0.693R_BC$$

Clock Pulse Generator: Starting with a capacitor C of 0.001 μf, calculate values for R_A and R_B to produce clock pulses as shown in Fig. 11-22. The pulse width is 1 μs in the low level, and it is repeating at a frequency rate of 100 KHz (every 10 μs). Connect the circuit and check the output in the oscilloscope.

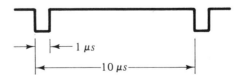

Figure 11-22   Output waveform for clock generator

Observe the output across the capacitor C and record its two levels to verify that they are between the trigger and threshold values.

Observe the waveform in the collector of the transistor at pin 7 and record all pertinent information. Explain the waveform by analyzing the circuit action.

Connect a variable resistor (potentiometer) in series with R_A to produce a variable-frequency pulse generator. The low-level duration remains at 1 μs. The frequency should range from 20 KHz to 100 KHz.

Change the low-level pulses to high-level pulses with a 7404 inverter. This will produce positive pulses of 1 μs with a variable frequency range.

Appendix

Chapter 1

1-1.   0, 1, 2, 10, 11, 12, 20, 21, 22, 100, 101, 102, 110, 111, 112, 120, 121, 122, 200, 201.

1-2.   (a) 1313, 102210
       (b) 223, 11314.52
       (c) 1304, 336313
       (d) 331, 13706

1-3. $(100021.1111 \ldots)_3$; $(3322.2)_4$; $(505.333 \ldots)_7$; $(372.4)_8$; $(FA.8)_{16}$.

1-4.   1100.0001; 10011100010000; 1010100001.00111; 11111001110.

1-5.   2.53125; 46.3125; 117.75; 109.875.

1-6.
decimal	binary	octal	hexadecimal
225.225	11100001.001110011	341.16314	E1.399
215.75	11010111.110	327.6	D7.C
403.9843	110010011.111111	623.77	193.FC
10949.8125	10101011000101.1101	25305.64	2AC5.D

1-7.   (a) 73.375
       (b) 151
       (c) 78.5
       (d) 580
       (e) 0.62037
       (f) 35
       (g) 8.333
       (h) 260

468

1-8.   1's complement: 0101010; 1000111; 1111110; 01111; 11111.
       2's complement: 0101011; 1001000; 1111111; 10000; 00000.

1-9.   9's complement: 86420; 90099; 09909; 89999; 99999.
       10's complement: 86421; 90100; 09910; 90000; 00000.

1-10. $(175)_{11}$.

1-14. (a) Six possible tables.
       (b) Four possible tables.

1-15. (a) 1000 0110 0010 0000
       (b) 1011 1001 0101 0011
       (c) 1110 1100 0010 0000
       (d) 1000011 0101100

1-17. 0000, 0001, 0010, 0011, 0100, 0101, 0110, 0111, 1011, 1100, 1101, 1110.

1-18. 00001, 01110, 01101, 01011, 01000, 10110, 10101, 10011, 10000, 11111.

1-20   000, 001, 010, 101, 110, 111, representing 0, 1, 2, 3, 4, 5, respectively.

1-21. Two bits for suit, four bits for number, J = 1011, Q = 1100, K = 1101.

1-23. (a) 0000 0000 0000 0001 0010 0111
       (b) 0000 0000 0000 0010 1001 0101
       (c) 1110 0111 1110 1000 1111 0101

1-24. (a) 597 in BCD
       (b) 264 in excess-3
       (c) Not valid for 2421 code of Table 1-2
       (d) FG in alphanumeric

1-25. 0010000001 + 10000011010 = 10100011011.

1-26. $L = (A + B) \cdot C$.

Chapter 2

2-1.   Closure, associative, commutative, distributive; identity for + is 2; identity for · is 0; no inverses.

2-2.   All postulates are satisfied except for postulate 5; there is no complement.

2-5.   (a) x
       (b) x
       (c) y
       (d) $z(x + y)$
       (e) 0
       (f) $y(x + w)$

2-6. (a) $A'B' + B(A + C)$
      (b) $BC + AC'$
      (c) $A + CD$
      (d) $A + B'CD$

2-7. (a) 1
      (b) $B'D' + A(D' + BC')$
      (c) 1
      (d) $(A' + B)(C + D)$

2-11. (b) $F = (x' + y')' + (x + y)' + (y + z')'$ has only OR and NOT operators.
       (c) $F = [(xy)' \cdot (x'y')' \cdot (y'z)']'$ has only AND and NOT operators.

2-12. (a) $T_1 = A'(B' + C')$
       (b) $T_2 = A + BC = T_1'$

2-13. (a) $\Sigma(1, 3, 5, 7, 9, 11, 13, 15) = \Pi(0, 2, 4, 6, 8, 10, 12, 14)$
       (b) $\Sigma(1, 3, 5, 9, 12, 13, 14) = \Pi(0, 2, 4, 6, 7, 8, 10, 11, 15)$
       (c) $\Sigma(0, 1, 2, 8, 10, 12, 13, 14, 15) = \Pi(3, 4, 5, 6, 7, 9, 11)$
       (d) $\Sigma(0, 1, 3, 7) = \Pi(2, 4, 5, 6)$
       (e) $\Sigma(0, 1, 2, 3, 4, 5, 6, 7)$, no maxterms
       (f) $\Sigma(3, 5, 6, 7) = \Pi(0, 1, 2, 4)$

2-14. (a) $\Pi(0, 2, 4, 5, 6)$
       (b) $\Pi(1, 3, 4, 5, 7, 8, 9, 10, 12, 15)$
       (c) $\Sigma(1, 2, 4, 5)$
       (d) $\Sigma(5, 7, 8, 9, 10, 11, 13, 14, 15)$

2-18. $F = x \oplus y = x'y + xy'$; (dual of F) $= (x' + y)(x + y') = xy + x'y' = F'$.

2-20. $F = xy + xz + yz$.

Chapter 3

3-1. (a) y
      (b) $ABD + ABC + BCD$
      (c) $BCD + A'BD'$
      (d) $wx + w'x'y$

3-2. (a) $xy + x'z'$
      (b) $C' + A'B$
      (c) $a' + bc$
      (d) $xy + xz + yz$

3-3. (a) $D + B'C$
      (b) $BD + B'D' + A'B$ or $BD + B'D' + A'D'$

(c) $ln' + k'm'n$

(d) $B'D' + A'BD + ABC'$

(e) $xy' + x'z + wx'y$

3-4. (a) $A'B'D' + B'C'D' + AD'E$

(b) $DE + A'B'C + B'C'E'$

(c) $BDE' + B'CD' + B'D'E' + A'B'D' + CDE'$

3-5. (a) $F_1 = \Pi(0, 3, 5, 6); F_2 = \Pi(0, 1, 2, 4)$

(b) $F_1 = x'y'z + x'yz' + xy'z' + xyz; F_2 = xy + xz + yz$

(c) $F_1 = (x + y + z)(x + y' + z')(x' + y + z')(x' + y' + z);$
$F_2 = (x + y)(x + z)(y + z)$

3-6. (a) y

(b) $(B + C')(A + B)(A + C + D)$

(c) $(w + z')(x' + z')$

3-7. (a) $z' + xy = (x + z')(y + z')$

(b) $C'D + A'B'CD' + ABCD' = (A + B' + D)(A' + B + D)(C + D)$
$(C' + D')$

(c) $A'C' + AD' + B'D' = (A' + D')(C' + D')(A + B' + C')$

(d) $B'D' + A'CD' + A'BD = (A' + B')(B + D')(B' + C + D)$

(e) $w'z' + vw'x + v'wz = (v' + w')(w' + z)(w + x + z')(v + w + z')$

3-8. (a)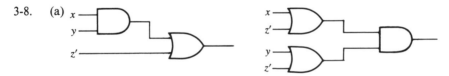

3-9. (a) $F_1 = A + D'E' + CD' = (A'D + A'C'E)'$

(b) $F_2 = A'B' + C'D' + B'C' = (BD + BC + AC)'$

3-11. (a) $F = BD + D'(AB'C' + A'B'C)$

3-12. (a) $(A' + B' + C')(A + B' + C + D')(A + B + C' + D')$

(b) $(C + D)(C' + D')(A + B)(A' + B')$

3-13. AND-AND $\rightarrow$ AND, AND-NAND $\rightarrow$ NAND, NOR-NAND $\rightarrow$ OR,
NOR-AND $\rightarrow$ NOR, OR-OR $\rightarrow$ OR, OR-NOR $\rightarrow$ NOR, NAND-NOR
$\rightarrow$ AND, NAND-OR $\rightarrow$ NAND.

3-15. (a) $F = 1$

(b) $F = CD' + B'D' + ABC'D$

3-16. (a) $F = A'C + B'D'; A'(C + D')(B' + C)$

(b) $x'z' + w'z; (w' + z')(x' + z)$

(c) $AC + CE' + A'C'D; (A' + C)(C + D)(A + C' + D')$
    or $AC + CD' + A'C'E; (A' + C)(C + E)(A + C' + E')$

(d) $A'B + B'E'; (A' + B')(B + E')$

3-17. (a) $B'(A + C' + D')$

  (b) $A'D + ABC'$

  (c) $B'D + B'C + CD$

3-18. $F = x'y + xz$ (needs four NAND); $F = (x' + z)(x + y)$(needs four NOR).

3-19. $d = ABC'DE + AB'CDE' + ABCD'E$.

3-20. $B'D'(A' + C) + BD(A' + C)$; $[B' + D(A' + C')] [B + D'(A' + C)]$;

  $[D' + B(A' + C')] [D + B'(A' + C)]$.

3-21. $f \cdot g = x'yz' + w'y'z + wxy'z'$.

3-24. (a) $F = A'CEF'G'$

  (b) $F = ABCDEFG + A'CEF'G' + BC'D'EF$

  (c) $F = A'B'C'DEF' + A'BC'D'E + CE'F + A'BD'EF$

Chapter 4

4-1. Inputs: a, b, c, d.

  Outputs: $F = abc + abd + bcd + acd + a'b'c' + a'c'd' + a'b'd'$

  $+ b'c'd'; F = \Pi(3, 5, 6, 9, 10, 12)$(cannot be simplified further).

4-2. Inputs: A_3, A_2, A_1.

  Outputs: B_6 to B_1; $B_1 = A_1$; $B_2 = 0$; $B_3 = A_1'A_2$; $B_4 = A_1(A_2A_3'$

  $+ A_2'A_3)$; $B_5 = A_3(A_1 + A_2')$; $B_6 = A_2A_3$.

4-3. Outputs: w, x, y, z; $w = a_0a_1b_0b_1$; $x = a_1a_0'b_1 + a_1b_1b_0'$

  $y = a_1b_0b_1' + a_0a_1'b_1 + a_0b_0'b_1 + a_0'a_1b_0$; $z = a_0b_0$.

4-4. Outputs: x, y, z; $x = a_1b_1 + a_1a_0b_0 + b_1b_0a_0$;

  $y = a_1'a_0'b_1 + a_1'b_1b_0' + a_1'a_0b_1'b_0 + a_1b_1'b_0' + a_1a_0'b_1' + a_1a_0b_1b_0$.

  $z = a_0b_0' + a_0'b_0$.

4-5. Inputs: A, B, C, D.

  Outputs: w, x, y, z; $w = A'B'C'$; $x = BC' + B'C$; $y = C$; $z = D'$.

4-6. Inputs: A, B, C, D.

  Outputs: $F_4F_3F_2F_1$; $F_1 = D$; $F_2 = CD' + C'D$; $F_3 = (C + D)$

  $B' + BC'D'$; $F_4 = (B + C + D)A' + AB'C'D'$.

4-7. Inputs: $F_8F_4F_2F_1$.

  Outputs: $\underset{10^1}{S_8S_4S_2S_1} \quad \underset{10^0}{L_8L_4L_2L_1}$;

  $L_2 = L_8 = S_8 = 0$; $L_1 = L_4 = F_1$; $S_1 = F_2$; $S_2 = F_4$;

  $S_4 = F_8$.

4-8. Inputs: A, B, C, D.

  Output: $F = AB + AC$.

4-11. Inputs: A, B, C, D.
Outputs: $w, x, y, z; w = AB + AC'D'; x = B'C + B'D + BC'D';$
$y = CD' + C'D; z = D.$

4-12. Inputs: A, B, C, D.
Outputs: $w, x, y, z; w = A; x = A'C + BCD + A'B + A'D$
$y = AC'D' + A'C'D + ACD + A'CD'$ or $y = AC'D'$
$+ B'C'D + ACD + B'CD'; z = D.$

4-13. Inputs: w, x, y, z.
Outputs: $E \underline{\quad ABCD \quad}; E = wx + wy; A = wx'y';$
$10^1 \quad 10^0$
$B = w'x + xy; C = w'y + wxy'; D = z.$

4-14. Inputs: A, B, C, D (Blank display for invalid input bit combinations)
Outputs: $a = A'C + A'BD + B'C'D' + AB'C'$
$b = A'B' + A'C'D' + A'CD + AB'C'$
$c = A'B + A'D + B'C'D' + AB'C'$
$d = A'CD' + A'B'C + B'C'D' + AB'C' + A'BC'D$
$e = A'CD' + B'C'D'$
$f = A'BC' + A'C'D' + A'BD' + AB'C'$
$g = A'CD' + A'B'C + A'BC' + AB'C'$

(Total of 21 NAND gates)

4-15. Full-adder circuit.

4-16. Full-adder circuit.

4-19.

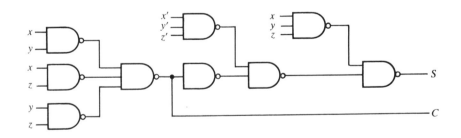

4-20. $F = ABC' + A'B + B' = A' + B' + C'$ (two NOR gates).

4-21. (a) Full-adder, F_1 is the sum, F_2 is the carry
(b) $F = A'B'C' + A'BC + AB'C + ABC'$

4-28. Input variables: A, B, C, D; output variables: w, x, y, z.
$w = A, x = A \oplus B, y = x \oplus C, z = y \oplus D.$

4-29. $C = x \oplus y \oplus z \oplus P$ (three exclusive-OR gates).

4-30.

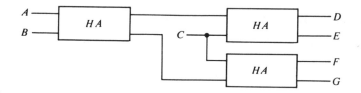

4-31. $F = (A \oplus B)(C \oplus D)$.

Chapter 5

5-1. Same as Fig. 5-2 except that $B = 1101$.

5-3. The exclusive-OR gate is used to form the 1's complement of B when $V = 1$. The 2's complement is obtained by adding $1 = V$ to the input carry.

5-4. $C_5 = G_4 + P_4G_3 + P_4P_3G_2 + P_4P_3P_2G_1 + P_4P_3P_2P_1C_1$.

5-5. (b) $C_4 = (G_3'P_3' + G_3'G_2'P_2' + G_3'G_2'G_1'P_1' + G_3'G_2'G_1'C_1')'$

5-6. (c) $C_4 = (P_3' + G_3'P_2' + G_3'G_2'P_1' + G_3'G_2'G_1'C_1')'$

5-7. (a) 60 ns
       (b) 120 ns

5-9. 312.

5-10. Inputs: x_8, x_4, x_2, x_1; outputs: y_8, y_4, y_2, y_1.
       $y_1 = x_1', y_2 = x_2, y_4 = x_2 \oplus x_4, y_8 = (x_2 + x_4 + x_8)'$.

5-15. All ten AND gates require four inputs equivalent to the minterms m_0 through m_9.

5-17. $F_1(x, y, z) = \Sigma(0, 1, 6)$.
       $F_2'(x, y, z) = \Sigma(4, 5)$ (use NOR gate).
       $F_3(x, y, z) = \Sigma(0, 1, 6, 7) = F_1 + m_7$.

5-22. Inputs: $D_0D_1D_2D_3$; outputs: x, y, E. Priority given to input with highest subscript number.

$x = D_2 + D_3, \quad y = D_3 + D_1D_2', \quad E = D_0 + D_1 + D_2 + D_3$.

5-23. I_0 through $I_7 = C', 1, C', 0, C', C', 0, C$.

5-29. (a) 1024×5
       (b) 256×8
       (c) 1024×2

Chapter 6

6-4.

Q	J	K'	Q(t + 1) = JQ' + K'Q
0	0	0	0
0	0	1	0
0	1	0	1
0	1	1	1
1	0	0	0
1	0	1	1
1	1	0	0
1	1	1	1

6-5.

Q	SD	R	Q(t + 1) = S + R'Q
0	0	0	0
0	0	1	0
0	1	0	1
0	1	1	1
1	0	0	1
1	0	1	0
1	1	0	1
1	1	1	1

6-7. Output of gate:

	1	2	3	4	5	6	7	8	9	
(a)	1	1	0	1	1	0	0	1	1	
(b)	0	1	1	0	1	1	0	1	0	
(c)	1	1	1	0	0	1	1	0	1	
(d)	1	0	0	1	1	1	1	0	0	
(e)	1	1	0	1	1	0	0	1	1	
(f)	1	1	0	1	1	1	0	1	0	$CP = 1$
	1	1	0	1	1	0	0	1	1	$CP = 0$

6-10.

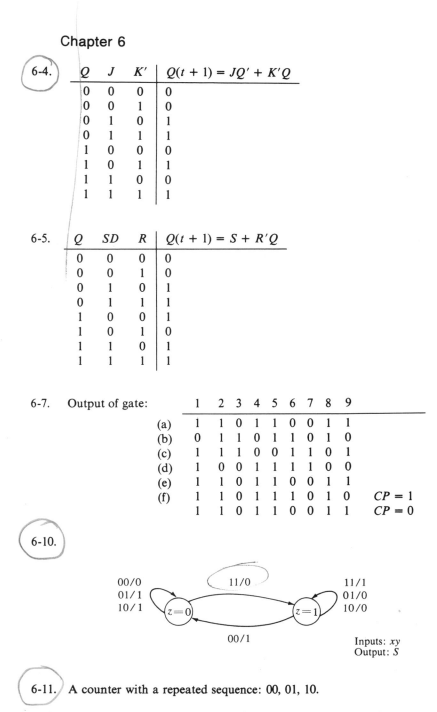

00/0
01/1
10/1
$z=0$
11/0
$z=1$
00/1
11/1
01/0
10/0

Inputs: xy
Output: S

6-11. A counter with a repeated sequence: 00, 01, 10.

6-12. $x = 1$; binary sequence is: 1, 8, 4, 2, 9, 12, 6, 11, 5, 10, 13, 14, 15, 7, 3.
$x = 0$; binary sequence is: 0, 8, 12, 14, 7, 11, 13, 6, 3, 9, 4, 10, 5, 2, 1.

6-13.

P.S.	Next state								Output z			
	$xy = 00$		$xy = 01$		$xy = 10$		$xy = 11$		$xy = 00$	$xy = 01$	$xy = 10$	$xy = 11$
A B	A	B	A	B	A	B	A	B				
0 0	1	0	0	0	1	1	0	1	0	0	0	0
0 1	0	1	0	1	1	0	1	1	1	0	0	0
1 0	1	0	1	0	0	0	1	0	0	0	0	1
1 1	1	0	1	0	1	0	1	0	1	0	0	1

$$A(t + 1) = xB + y'B'A' + yA + x'A; \quad B(t + 1) = xA'B' + x'A'B + yA'B$$

6-14.

Present State	Next State 0 1	Output 0 1
a	f b	0 0
b	d a	0 0
d	g a	1 0
f	f b	1 1
g	g d	0 1

6-15. State: a f b c e d g h g g h a
       Input: 0 1 1 1 0 0 1 0 0 1 1
       Output: 0 1 0 0 0 1 1 1 0 1 0

6-16. State: a f b a b d g d g g d a
       Input: 0 1 1 1 0 0 1 0 0 1 1
       Output: 0 1 0 0 0 1 1 1 0 1 0

6-18.

J K'	Q(t + 1)
0 0	0
0 1	Q(t)
1 0	Q'(t)
1 1	1

Q(t)	Q(t + 1)	J K'
0	0	0 X
0	1	1 X
1	0	X 0
1	1	X 1

6-19.

SD R	Q(t + 1)
0 0	Q(t)
0 1	0
1 0	1
1 1	1

Q(t)	Q(t + 1)	SD R
0	0	0 X
0	1	1 X
1	0	0 1
1	1	X 0 } either
		1 X }

6-20. (a) $TA = A + B'x$; $TB = A + BC'x + BCx' + B'C'x'$;
$$TC = Ax + Cx + A'B'C'x'$$

(b) $SA = A'B'x$; $RA = A$; $SB = A + C'x'$; $RB = BC'x + Cx'$;
$$SC = A'B'x' + Ax; RC = A'x$$

(c) $JA = B'x$, $KA = 1$; $JB = A + C'x'$, $KB = C'x + Cx'$;
$$JC = A'B'x' + Ax, KC = x; y = A'x$$

6-21. $(A = 2^3, B = 2^2, C = 2^1, D = 2^0)$; $TA = (D + C + B)x$;
$TB = (D + C)x$; $TC = Dx$; $TD = 0$.

6-22. $JA = x$, $KA = x'$; $JB = Ax'$, $KB = 1$; $JC = Bx + Ax$, $KC = Bx'$.

6-23. $JQ_8 = Q_1Q_2Q_4$ $JQ_4 = Q_1Q_2$ $JQ_2 = Q_8'Q_1$ $JQ_1 = 1$
$KQ_8 = Q_1$ $KQ_4 = Q_1Q_2$ $KQ_2 = Q_1$ $KQ_1 = 1$

6-24. $\begin{bmatrix} 2 & 4 & 2 & 1 \\ A & B & C & D \end{bmatrix}$; $TA = BCD + A'B$; $TB = CD + A'B$; $TC = D + A'B$;
$$TD = 1.$$

6-25. (a) $JA = B$, $KA = 1$; $JB = A'$, $KB = 1$

(b) $JA = BC$, $JB = C$, $JC = A'$
$$KA = 1, KB = C, KC = 1$$

(c) $JA = BC$, $JB = C$, $JC = B' + A'$
$$KA = B, KB = A + C, KC = 1$$

6-26. $SA = BC'$ $SB = B'C$ $SC = B'$

$RA = BC$ $RB = AB$ $RC = B$

6-27. $TA = A \oplus B$; $TB = B \oplus C$; $TC = AC + A'B'C'$

6-28. $JA = B'$ $JB = A + C$ $JC = A'B$
$KA = 1$ $KB = 1$ $KC = 1$

6-29. $DA = A'B'C + ACD + AC'D'$ $DC = B$
$DB = A'C + CD' + A'B$ $DD = D'$

6-31. $JA = yC + xy$ $JB = xAC$ $JC = x'B + yAB'$
$KA = x' + y'B'$ $KB = A'C + x'C + yC'$ $KC = A'B' + xB + y'B'$

6-32. (a) $A(t + 1) = AB'C'x' + A'BC'x + A'BCx + AB'C'x + AB'Cx$.
$B(t + 1) = A'BC'x' + A'B'Cx$.
$C(t + 1) = A'B'Cx' + A'BC'x' + A'BCx' + AB'C'x' + AB'Cx'$.
$d(A, B, C, x) = \Sigma(0, 1, 12, 13, 14, 15)$ (don't-care terms).

Chapter 7

7-1.   Use an external NAND gate.

7-2.   (a) Change inverter associated with CP into a buffer gate, or (b) use flip-flops that trigger on the negative edge.

7-4. $A(t + 1) = AB' + Bx'$; $B(t + 1) = x$.

7-9. $A = 0010, 0001, 1000, 1100$; $Q = 1, 1, 1, 0$.

7-10. $D = x \oplus y \oplus Q$; $JQ = x'y$; $KQ = (x' + y)'$

7-13. 200 ns; 5 MHz.

7-14. Ten flip-flops will be complemented.

7-17. $1010 \rightarrow 1011 \rightarrow 0100$ $1110 \rightarrow 1111 \rightarrow 0000$
       $1100 \rightarrow 1101 \longrightarrow$ Self-starting.

7-18. $000 \rightarrow 001 \rightarrow 010 \rightarrow 011 \rightarrow 100 \longrightarrow$
       $101 \rightarrow 110 \quad 111$ Not self-starting.

7-21. $JQ_1 = KQ_1 = 1$.
       $JQ_2 = KQ_2 = Q_1Q_8$.
       $JQ_4 = KQ_4 = Q_1Q_2$.
       $JQ_8 = Q_1Q_2Q_4$; $KQ_8 = Q_1$.

7-30. (a) Unused states (in decimal): 2   4   5   6 9 10 11 13
           Next state (in decimal):   9 10   2 11 4 13   5   6
       (b) $2 \rightarrow 9 \rightarrow 4 \rightarrow 8$ 8 is a valid state
           $10 \rightarrow 13 \rightarrow 6 \rightarrow 11 \rightarrow 5 \rightarrow 0$ 0 is a valid state

7-32. (a) 13, 32
       (b) 32, 768

7-35. (a) 16
       (b) 8, 16
       (c) 16
       (d) $16 + 255k$ where k is the number of 1's in the word to be stored

Chapter 8

8-8.   MUX1: 0, A_3A_4, 0, 0
       MUX2: S, 1, 0, 0

8-9. $DT_0 = S'T_0 + ZT_1$
       $DT_1 = ST_0 + ET_3$
       $DT_2 = Z'T_1 + E'T_3$
       $DT_3 = T_2$

8-13.

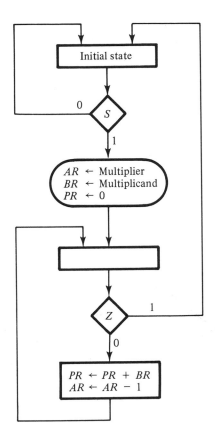

8-14. $(2^n - 1)(2^n - 1) < (2^{2n} - 1)$ for $n \geqslant 1$

8-16.   Product = 1010001011

8-17. $2t(n + 1)$

8-18.   (a) $JG_1 = G_2$
        $KG_1 = ZG_2$
        $JG_2 = G_1 + S$
        $KG_2 = 1$

        (b) $DG_1 = T_1 + T_2 + Z'T_3$
        $DG_2 = ST_0 + T_2$

        (c) MUX1: $0, 1, 1, Z'$
        MUX2: $S, 0, 1, 0$

        (d) $DT_0 = S'T_0 + ZT_3$
        $DT_1 = ST_0$
        $DT_2 = T_1 + Z'T_3$
        $DT_3 = T_2$

Chapter 9

9-2. Sequence of Y_1Y_2: 00, 00, 01, 11, 11, 01, 00.

9-3. (d) When the input is 01, the output is 0. When the input is 10, the output is 1. Whenever the input assumes one of the other two combinations, the output retains its previous value.

9-4. (c)

	00	01	11	10
a	ⓐ,0	b,1	c,1	d,0
b	a,0	ⓑ,1	c,1	ⓑ,0
c	ⓒ,1	b,1	ⓒ,1	d,1
d	c,1	b,1	c,1	ⓓ,1

9-5. (c) $Y_1 = x_1'x_2 + x_2y_2$
$Y_2 = x_2 + x_1y_2$
$z = x_1x_2y_1' + x_1y_2'$

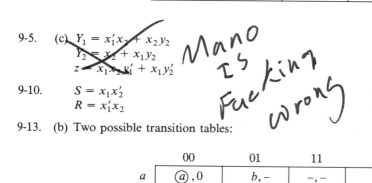

9-10. $S = x_1x_2'$
$R = x_1'x_2$

9-13. (b) Two possible transition tables:

	00	01	11	10
a	ⓐ,0	b,–	–,–	e,–
b	ⓑ,1	ⓑ,1	–,–	d,–
d	a,–	ⓓ,1	–,–	ⓓ,1
e	ⓔ,1	d,–	–,–	ⓔ,1

	00	01	11	10
a	ⓐ,0	b,–	–,–	b,–
b	c,–	ⓑ,1	–,–	ⓑ,1
c	ⓒ,1	d,–	–,–	d,–
d	a,–	ⓓ,1	–,–	ⓓ,1

9-18. 3a: $(a, b) (c, d) (e, f, g, h)$
       3b: $(a, e, f) (b, j) (c, d) (g, h) (k)$

9-20. Add states g and h to binary assignment.

	00	01	11	10
0	a	g	b	f
1	c	h	d	e

9-22. $F = A'D' + AC'D' + A'BC + A'CD'$

9-23. $Y = (x_1 + x_2')(x_2 + x_3)(x_1 + x_3)$

Chapter 10

10-1. (a) 1.05 V
       (b) 0.82 V
       (c) 0.23 V

10-2. $I_B = 0.44$ mA, $I_{CS} = 2.4$ mA

10-3. (a) 2.4 mA
       (b) 0.82 mA
       (c) $2.4 + 0.82 N$
       (d) 7.8
       (e) 7

10-5. (b) 3.53
       (c) 2.585 mA
       (d) 16 mA
       (e) 300 Ω

10-9. (a) 4.62 mA
       (b) 4 mA

10-10. 0.3 V

Index